D0650259

KATHARINE DREXEL

A BIOGRAPHY

*Katharine Drexel - Age 18*

# Katharine Drexel
## A BIOGRAPHY

*by*

Sister Consuela Marie Duffy, S.B.S.

*with an Introduction by*

HIS EMINENCE

RICHARD CARDINAL CUSHING

MOTHER KATHARINE DREXEL GUILD
Sisters of the Blessed Sacrament
Bensalem, PA 19020

*Fifth Printing December 2012*
*Mizzou Media - University of Missouri Bookstore*
*Page layout and design by Paul Garrison*

Nihil Obstat

JAMES MCGRATH, J.C.D.

*Censor Librorum*

Imprimatur

JOHN CARDINAL KROL

*Archbishop of Philadelphia*

*Cover design, cover photo and all other photos are used with permission from the Sisters of the Blessed Sacrament Archives*
Library of Congress Catalog Card Number 66-29382
COPYRIGHT © 1966 THE SISTERS OF THE BLESSED SACRAMENT
MANUFACTURED IN THE UNITED STATES OF AMERICA

*To the Memory of*
*My Father and Mother, James J. and Mary Duffy*

# Table of Contents


*Foreword*........................................XV
*Introduction*....................................XVII
*Preface*.........................................XIX

1. Pioneer Backgrounds..........................23
2. Childhood And Youth..........................30
3. Training For Life..............................40
4. A Study In Contrasts..........................46
5. Shadows Fall..................................56
6. A Cry For Justice..............................64
7. Travel Luxurious And Otherwise.......... 75
8. Evolution Of A Vocation....................85
9. Schooling For The Apostolate............107
10. Birth Of A Congregation....................126
11 To The Pueblos...............................135
12. On The River James..........................146
13. Navajo Frontiers..............................154
14. A Mission To Fulfill..........................174
15. To The South..................................180
16. The Poorest Nun In The World...........188
17. A Rule To Live By.............................195
18. Loss And Gain.................................206
19. Deep River Gateway..........................218
20. Into The Deep South.........................224
21. The Willing Spirit............................237
22. Jubilee Interlude..............................248
23. Apostolic Contemplative.....................255
24. The Bridegroom Comes.......................262
25. A Daughter Of The Church..................269

*Appendix I*......................................279
*Appendix II*.....................................281
*Footnotes*.......................................287
*Index*............................................303

# *Foreword*

On March 4th, 1955 the Philadelphia Archdiocese newspaper, the *Catholic Standard and Times*, in an editorial, wrote, "Rev. Mother Katharine Drexel belonged to Philadelphia and to America, but one cannot help seeing in the story of her life that she belonged to God...." Since the original printing of this book in the mid 1960's the depth of truth revealed in these words has become startlingly evident. In Rome on November 20, 1988 Pope John Paul II beatified Katharine Drexel and gave her the title Blessed. On October 1, 2000 he canonized her and gave her the title Saint. Mother Katharine Drexel now belongs to the Universal Church in the official Communion of Saints.

In each step of the process her holiness and zeal were affirmed. She belonged to God alone. Her passionate love of God, and God's love of her opened the eyes of her heart wide to see the face of God in all, but very especially in the poor among the Black and Native American peoples. She was God's instrument for evangelization and social justice!

Her Beatification and Canonization were the result of faith filled prayers that led to healings, which upon intense scrutiny by the medical profession in the United States and in Europe stated there were no known medical reasons for the healings. These two physical healings/cures are officially called miracles.

Each miracle dealt with the restoration of hearing. The first miracle for her beatification concerned a teen-age boy who suffered hearing loss. The second miracle which resulted in her canonization focused on a baby girl born deaf. In both of these situations it was the family members who prayed through the intercession of St. Katharine Drexel that their child would be healed. The response in each instance was positive with the restoration of full hearing for both children. These children now grown, give witness in their daily lives of the powerful workings of God.

As we read the story of her life and reflect on the miracles we might ask ourselves is there a message for us regarding "hearing ... listening"? A possible response can be found in the writings of Katharine Drexel:

> "I looked up in wonder at God's wonderful ways and thought how little we imagine what may be the result of listening and acting on a desire He puts into the heart. If He puts it into the heart, He will bless it, if we try to act upon it, great will be the effect before God – for it will be a success before God, even if it be not so to our weak understanding."

It seems St. Katharine is drawing our attention through these miracles to the importance of daily listening and acting on the desires God places in our heart.

As Sisters of the Blessed Sacrament, daughters of Katharine Drexel, we would like to express our deepest gratitude to the parish community of St. Katharine Drexel in Sugar Grove, Illinois for listening and acting on the desire that God placed in their hearts to make possible an updated version of this powerful story of faith of a woman passionate for God and for God's poor. We are also grateful for the skilled efforts of Mizzou Media in this endeavor.

May the story of St. Katharine's life challenge each of us today to hear the cry of the poor as she did ... to listen and to act daily on the desires God places in our hearts to make our world ... a better and holier place. St. Katharine Drexel pray for us!

Gratefully in the Eucharist,
*The Sisters of the Blessed Sacrament*

# Introduction:

No one with any acquaintance of Mother Katharine Drexel and her heroic pioneer work among the Indians and Negroes of the United States can fail to rejoice at the publication of a scholarly, definitive life of that great religious leader. We of Boston think of her as one of our own for we have watched for nearly half a century the work of her order, the Sisters of the Blessed Sacrament for Indians and Colored People, in their social center in Roxbury, where in that predominantly Negro section of the city, they have drawn into an understanding of the Faith and of the love of neighbor which the Faith enjoins the people, adults as well as children, into the third generation.

My personal acquaintance with Mother Katharine and my knowledge of her work obtained through over forty-five years of priestly services in behalf of the missionary life of the Church prompt me to salute her even at this late date as the greatest personal benefactor of the Home Missions of the Catholic Church in the United States of America. She gave to this cause not only the wealth she inherited as a member of a family known throughout the world, but she gave herself adorned by prayer and sacrifices with virtues found only in those whose memory has been perpetuated in the calendars and on the altars of the Catholic Church as saints.

Katharine Drexel's impulse for charity which resulted in the consecration of her own life and the dedication and founding of her order was originally anxiety for the Indians whom governmental inertia or bad faith was depriving of their opportunity to hear the Gospel preached to them. Soon, however, in the decade which followed the founding of her order in 1891, it became clear to those who had the prescience to interpret socioeconomic currents, that the treatment of the Negro was unjust and the continuance of such policy was sure to work harm not only for the Negro but for the totality of American citizens, both those whose education and power to reason made them culpable and those who, for lack of both, were drifting or being led into error. Moreover, it was becoming clear that the Negroes could not furnish their own leadership until they had further opportunities of education. This Katharine Drexel undertook to offer through the schools and the university her religious community would establish.

The story of the great undertaking of Katharine Drexel has a place in the annals of her order, in the history of the Catholic Church in the United States, in the secular history of the United States, and in the history of the development of ideas. Sister Consuela Marie, S.B.S., one of the faculty of Xavier University in New Orleans, La., has undertaken this work of love and patriotism for which she is eminently qualified. She has had free access to all the documents, and in this scholarly work which she offers, we all have an intense interest. I take this opportunity of thanking her in the name of all who will read this biography of a truly great American, a totally dedicated follower of Christ. Katharine Drexel devoted her wealth and her life to help right injustice. She leads all people to embrace one another in the love of God. May her life be an inspiration to us in this hour of national need.

RICHARD CARDINAL CUSHING
Archbishop of Boston

# *Preface*

This book is about a person who made a distinctive contribution to American history, but who went about it noiselessly, avoiding fanfare, and shrinking from fame. She saw a cause to be supported, a way of life to be established in the highways as well as the ghetto byways of America. The cause was God's; the way of life was America's. She served them both.

The life story of Katharine Drexel, foundress of the Sisters of the Blessed Sacrament for Indians and Colored People, spans a long period of time and covers eventful and far reaching developments in the history of the United States. She was born in 1858; she died in 1955. Within those intervening ninety-six years, she engaged in an activity phenomenal in its extent and breathtaking in its inspiration. The facts of her life story have been put together in this book from abundant original source material in the Archives of the Sisters of the Blessed Sacrament at their Motherhouse in Cornwells Heights, Pennsylvania.

These Archives hold some 3,000 letters of Katharine Drexel from her childhood (preserved by her family), through her young womanhood, and her life as a religious. Hundreds of letters of this last period have been kindly sent by Chancery Offices and Motherhouses throughout the United States. The chronology files include some 18,000 letters received by Mother Katharine from bishops, priests, and lay people in connection with her vast and widely spread mission programs. Locked in these letters is an authentic record of some of the struggles, the agony of pioneers who lived, suffered and died for the extension of the Mystical Body of Christ in America. In addition to these and travel diaries, some fifty volumes of Community Annals and innumerable small notebooks in which Katharine Drexel wrote her meditations and retreat notes interspersed with her reflections and resolutions, present an array of historical records that should be a biographer's paradise. This book has been built from these definitive sources.

We present the evidence of her life drawn from original and authentic records. The task of selection, the obligation of choice is the biographer's. It would take many volumes to include all the details, all the intricacies of this life story. Libraries might welcome the tomes, but the writer has interpreted her task and viewed her privilege as one of presenting Katharine Drexel to the general public in the progressive encounters of her amazing life, tracing through its various stages the working of rich efficacious graces that marked her out even in her earliest years as one on whom God had special designs, and who cooperated completely with those designs.

Undoubtedly, many will feel that other details should have been included, all missions traced in their development. They all follow a more or less definite pattern; as many as seemed feasible for a single volume have been included. Katharine Drexel is the subject of this book, her virtue its inspiration, her correspondence with grace its incentive, her understanding of the American Race Problem its contribution to our national development. May her example and her life help to erase the blot of race prejudice and race hatred too long staining the pages of our nation's history.

It goes without saying that this book could never have been put together without much help. Those who have helped are too numerous to mention. Many Sisters alive today knew Katharine Drexel well and intimately. Their memoirs written and oral have been basic material. Librarians both at the Motherhouse and Xavier University, New Orleans, have given valuable assistance. The writer hopes she may include here a general sincere expression and of gratitude to every Mother and Sister in the Congregation, and a specific one to Rev. Harry J. Sievers, S.J., and Rev. Michael J. Curley, C.Ss.R. She acknowledges her indebtedness to Rev. Francis J. Litz, C.Ss.R. , Vice Postulator of Mother Katharine's Cause, who requested that this book be written and who gave valuable suggestions as it progressed. She is finally grateful to His Eminence, Cardinal Cushing, who in the midst of his multiple activities graciously wrote the Introduction to this book.

SISTER CONSUELA MARIE DUFFY, S.B.S.
Xavier University, New Orleans, La.
February 12, 1966

# Chapter 1
# Pioneer Backgrounds

Back in 1874, the three Drexel sisters were doing the Grand Tour of Europe with their mother and father. Letters describing their escalating joy at the sights and experiences were sent back regularly to their governess, Miss Cassidy, in Philadelphia. Noticing their use of superlatives, the governess wrote to Katharine Drexel, the second eldest, that she hoped they would return the loyal hearted Americans they had started out. Katharine sent an immediate and enthusiastic reply: "Don't be worried on that score, Miss Cassidy, for I am *now* and will be more of an American than ever on my return. I love my country with all of my heart, the people, the habits, the cities, everything!"[1] Her life was to prove how much she loved America and all its people. This is her story, the story of a loyal American whose roots go back to the earliest days of American history and whose life and deeds may continue to affect generations of Americans yet unborn.

She was born into a wealthy Philadelphia family November 26, 1858, three years before the struggle over slavery precipitated our young and prosperous nation into a bloody civil war. In the course of time, she would dedicate her life and her fortune to the education and guidance of America's two underprivileged races, the Indians and the Colored, citizens by right of birth in the "Land of the free and the home of the brave." Her parents, Francis Anthony Drexel, nationally and internationally well known banker, and her mother, Hannah Langstroth Drexel, had been married at Assumption Church in Philadelphia, September 28, 1854. The Certificate of Marriage shows the Reverend C. S. Carter, Vicar General of the Diocese officiated, and that Joseph Drexel and Caroline Drexel were witnesses.[2] Katharine, baptized in the Church of the Assumption December 29, 1858,[3] was the second child of this marriage. Her mother, gravely ill from the time of her birth, breathed her last five weeks later to the intense grief of her husband. His daughter, Elizabeth aged three, and five weeks old Katharine could not be aware of their loss. For two years these two children were to be cared for by their aunt, Mrs. Anthony J. Drexel, who took them into her home and poured out on them the love and tender solicitude of a mother.

In addition to the grace of God, heredity and environment play a large part in the personality development and character integration of all human beings. Katharine Drexel came into the world with a heritage rich not only in monetary values, but also rich in ancestral talent, patriotism, and moral stamina. Her paternal grandfather, Francis Martin Drexel, first saw the light of day in the town of Dornbirn in the Austrian Tyrol. His earliest years were spent in a substantial home set in a magnificent background of Alpine splendor. The glory of his natural surroundings must have stirred at an early age the sensitivity to beauty that resulted in his emergence as an artist of note and international distinction. In the course of his extensive travels in search of a market for his art, he developed a business acumen that skyrocketed him to the top of the financial world.

Fortunately for his posterity, Francis Martin Drexel kept a diary and wrote a short autobiography.[4] In his introduction he told his purpose in writing it. "Having conversed with children born in America from German parents, who were not able to say where their mother or father was from, except from Germany, an ignorance which could not do honor to them or to their parents, I am anxious to leave this to my children that at least if they wish to peruse it, they may find who my parents were and when I was born.

"My father's name was Franz Joseph Drexel, and my mother's, Magdalin Wilhelm both from Dornbirn in Vorarlberg, Tirol, near Lake Constanz, five miles from the point where the Rhine River and the Lake meet. My birthplace lies in a beautiful valley, divided by the Rhine. From the mountains close by, there are beautiful views of the Lake and the Rhine. In that place I was born April 1, 1792, said to have been Easter Sunday morning. My father was extensively engaged in commercial pursuits."

Franz Joseph Drexel had great plans for his son and intended he should follow him in business. After giving him a fundamental education, the best that day could provide, he sent him at the age of eleven to Italy. He spent eleven months there, became fluent in the Italian tongue and did well in his studies. When war broke out again with France, and the sovereignty of his country was handed over to Bavaria, his father finding himself almost impoverished, called him home. "Finally," his diary continues, "instead of sending me for further education to France, he permitted me to follow my natural inclination for painting which I had from infancy. I never had any inclination for mercantile affairs."

January 1806, young Francis Martin was apprenticed to a painter in a nearby village. Following the Tyrolese Revolution against Bavaria, the rumor spread that France was planning to conscript into the French regiments all young men above 16 years of age. His father then decided he should leave his country and try his fortune in the wide world. The diary account of his escape sounds like many a freedom crash through a Berlin Wall made in our day. "Accordingly in 1809, August 6, about 6:00 o'clock my father who had in the forenoon engaged some Swiss to conduct us at night over the Rhine, a young man named Caspar Thurnher and myself started for Lustena, a village on the Rhine. We met the ferryman there by appointment, and at 10:00 o'clock that night crossed the Rhine at a most dangerous point. This precaution was necessary as the stream on the side was guarded by the French and on the other by the Swiss. We parted from my father at the boat on a night as dark as any night had ever been, and after great toil we reached the opposite shore. The ferryman directed us how and where to proceed to avoid the guard posts.

"After wading through the ditches, morass, and bushes for about three quarters of an hour, we spied a light in the distance and resolved to head for it. It took another half an hour to get there. This was the village of Diebelsa and it was Saturday night. The place was Catholic and the light was left for the good of the souls departed. Though it was midnight, we knocked at a door and had to knock long and loud before we were heard. We begged to be directed to a public house but they got up and let us in. Thurnher, my companion, told them a long invented yarn about how we missed the way, and from what city in Switzerland we had come. But they were not deceived by his ingenious story. They knew my father and recognized my resemblance to him. They wished us well and showed us to a public house."

Francis Drexel's father must have been well known, for throughout his son's diary there are many references to different friends of his father in many places. From this point on, the diary records his wanderings through Switzerland, Italy, Bavaria, and France. The characters he met, the places he stayed, the vain attempts for permanent painting employment make a thrilling account. His home training must have been of high order for he steered clear of the many moral snares along the way of his wanderings. Gradually he acquired a little security, sufficient clothes, and a reputation as a portrait artist. In 1812 he returned and made a visit by night to his home where in the dark, his mother embraced him warmly. He attended a masquerade ball but otherwise, he wrote, he did not leave his home as another conscription of young men was announced. His escape the second time still with the help of his father, was as dangerous and adventurous as the first. Once more he was on his own in the world — a wanderer doing portraits when and where he could.

The Congress of Vienna in 1815 re-aligned the map of Europe and shattered the fragile empire the unbridled ambition of Napoleon had attempted to erect. Once again the Tyrol was part of Austria, free from Bavarian rule, and the young Francis Martin returned, but not for long. He was soon on the open road again seeking a fortune.

This time his travels carried him through many countries and many cities where his portraits were well received, if not munificently paid for. And then came a sudden decision. "Hearing that there were many passenger boats going down the Rhine to Amsterdam for America, I resolved to go too, and see the other half of the world or at least some of it. I reasoned this way to myself: 'Since my native land had but five thousand inhabitants it could never afford me professional employment. I would thus be obliged to be away from home and it would matter little whether I was one hundred or ten thousand miles away.' If I did not do well, I resolved to return after six months, but if I did well, after six years. By no means, however, would I stay there indefinitely."

Thus it was that Katharine's grandfather by this time a professional artist, joined three hundred and fifty passengers and sailed on a ship called *John of Baltimore* on a voyage across the deep that took exactly seventy-two days. They left Amsterdam May 18, 1817, and disembarked in Philadelphia opposite Callowhill Street, July 28. His diary testifies that ocean voyaging in 1817 was a long drawn out, torturous experience. He was not long, however, in the new world before he was employed again, and painting for an ever growing clientele.

The years passed with ever widening opportunities for his art. Francis Martin Drexel came to look on the young United States as a new home. In 1821 he married Katharine Hookey. Though the Hookey family had been prominent in St. Augustine's Church almost from the time the church was built, Francis Martin Drexel and Katharine Hookey were married by Bishop Conwell in St. Mary's Church.[5] Francis Martin Drexel was a member of Holy Trinity parish and also one of its trustees.[6] Three sons and three daughters were to bless this marriage. Katharine's father, Francis Anthony, the eldest son, was born January 20, 1824, and baptized in St. Joseph's Church, Philadelphia, March 4, 1824.[7] All the other children received the sacrament of Baptism in Holy Trinity Church.[8]

Meeting some difficulty in providing for this growing family, despite the fact that for five years his paintings were displayed in the annual exhibition of the Academy of Fine Arts, the elder Drexel decided to try his fortune in South America. In two different journeys in the next nine years he was to paint portraits of great leaders in several Spanish American lands and in Mexico.

In 1826 he left for a stay lengthened into five years in Peru, Chile, Ecuador, and Bolivia. He recorded that he made a grand total of $22,600, of which he sent $12,500 home to his wife, paid $3,300 for expenses and left $6,800 still owed to him in South America. He was back again in Philadelphia in 1830 but five years later was trying his fortune in Mexico and Central America.[9]

The financial panic of 1837 broke upon the American scene with devastating results. Jackson's deadly opposition to the United States Bank, his order to Taney, his Secretary of the Treasury, to deposit government funds in designated state banks instead, the issuance of 'wild cat' currency, and the Jackson Specie Circular ordering government officials to accept only gold or silver in payment for public lands, the violent drop in the London Stock Exchange, ended in the complete collapse of American financial security and the disastrous panic of 1837.

In the midst of the financial chaos, Francis Martin returned to the United States and opened a small broker's office in Louisville, Kentucky. Here he manipulated and managed a business of the various currencies in hectic circulation. But realizing that the whole situation was veering toward a financial leadership of Philadelphia as a result of Mr. Biddle's skillful operation of his state bank, Mr. Drexel moved his office to 34 South Third Street. He was soon established as a broker in a sea of constantly ebbing and flowing currencies. When the crash came to Biddle's successor, Mr. Drexel's international experience and keen ability to sift through a situation, made him aware of the burgeoning financial opportunity. In his projection into the future he envisioned a specific involvement for each of his sons, Francis Anthony then 14, Anthony J. 12, and Joseph W. only 5 years of age. He would train his own sons and their apprenticeship would be from the ground up. Reunited with his family again for whose welfare he had sought economic security, he set about his latest and what was to be his final venture with all the resourcefulness of his person.[10]

Francis Anthony, Katharine's father, had a rugged introduction to the banking world where he would one day walk as one of its peers. The young lad ate a cold dinner from a basket kept under the counter. He frequently served as night watchman sleeping under the same counter. As part of his early education, his mother had included a classic training in music. With the father the passion was for painting; with his eldest son, it was to be for music. Several years after his introduction into his father's limited banking business via this counter service, he added to his meager salary by playing the organ in St. John's Church at Manayunk. Each Sunday he walked six miles out and six miles back to Philadelphia. His income on this project amounted to one hundred fifty dollars a year.

By 1847 Mr. Drexel was able to help the nation financially in the war with Mexico and he took his two eldest sons into a partnership which he called Drexel & Co. When Francis A. was only 23 and Anthony J. 21, the father left them in full charge and headed for California where in 1849 he joined the Gold Rush. In San Francisco he formed a new allied house. Drexel, Sather & Church established itself in the mid-stream of the gold flow of that era. The panic of 1857 brought him back to Philadelphia where he liked what he saw of his sons' efficiency and expert management. Death came to him suddenly in the midst of this financial organization and growth. Stepping to a platform on his return from a business trip, he reached for a portfolio a boy had held for him and he alighted. As the train began to move, he fell and was thrown under the wheels. He died shortly after, on June 6, 1863.

Immediately, his youngest son, Joseph W., joined the company and within five years he was sent to Paris to create the new allied firm of Drexel, Harjes, & Co. In another four years he was the senior partner in the newly organized New York House of Drexel, Morgan and Co., which in a few years was joined by the Morgan House of London.

Katharine's father had come a long way. The man, who in addition to munificent benefactions during his life, would distribute $1,500,000 at his death and leave $14,000,000 to charity, had started from very humble beginnings. He learned the hard way but he learned well from his father whose ability paved the way and whose integrity laid the foundations of the Drexel Banking houses with their world wide reputation for reliability. Francis Martin Drexel had entered the banking world a man of wisdom and experience. He had been thrown on his own at a very early age, he had traveled and he knew the worlds, he had a willingness to work and the ability to work strenuously, he knew men, he understood his times, he had faith in God and in America.

Through her father, the heritage that came to Katharine Drexel was to mingle a deep sensitivity to the beautiful, an appreciation of art and music, a willingness to spend and be spent in the service of others, a keen business instinct, and an ever deepening appreciation of the gift of Faith. From her mother she was also to inherit a legacy of note. Her mother, Hannah Langstroth, was born at Greenwood Farm near Philadelphia, January 14, 1826, the daughter and fourth youngest of Piscator Langstroth and Eliza Lehman Langstroth. Through the Levering-Keyser-Lehman-Langstroth families, Katharine was to inherit a sense of thrift, personal responsibility, moral stamina, filial fear of God, and a love of her neighbor. On her mother's side. Katharine could trace her descendents back to the shores of America before the new nation of the United States was formed. Rosier Levering of Gemen, Germany, is the first authentically established ancestor of the American branch of the Levering family.[11] Her grandson, William Levering, at the age of six was brought by his parents to the New World in 1685.[12] There are not too many families in America today whose origins go back to the very roots of American history. Four years after William Penn founded the colony of Pennsylvania as a haven for Quakers, Katharine Drexel's maternal forebears hewed a home from its timber and cast the seeds for their food into its good rich earth.

Katharine was never to know her mother who died five weeks after giving her birth. When she was old enough to realize, she often expressed feelings of deep gratitude and love for the mother who had given her life for her. Sixty-five years after her mother's death, a small box was brought to Mother M. Katharine in the Motherhouse of her Congregation in Cornwells Heights,

Pennsylvania, by an employee of Drexel & Co. For all those years the box had been locked away in a safe of the Drexel brothers. After their death the combination was lost. Because of its unusual construction all efforts to open it were fruitless. Experts were powerless before it. Finally at that late date nitroglycerine was used to blow it open. Among the items found within was this box containing Hannah Drexel's gold thimble, gold lorgnette, several jewelled barrettes, a brooch, and a number of visiting cards printed in Spencerian script:

MRS. FRANCIS A. DREXEL<br>433 RACE STREET

Though the house had long been demolished, the cards indicated the birthplace of Katharine Drexel. Mother Katharine handled the objects lovingly and decided they would be used for sacred vessels in the service of the altar.

Years later, after her retirement from the active apostolate as the result of a heart condition, and in the midst of her life of prayer at the Motherhouse, her thought turned in gratitude and love to her mother. Her sister, Louise Drexel Morrell, had built a beautiful shrine Church of the True Cross on the family grounds at Torresdale, Pennsylvania. In the basement crypt she provided burial vaults and had the bodies of her mother, father, and husband moved there. Mother M. Katharine thought of her own mother, Mrs. Hannah Langstroth Drexel, a Baptist Quaker, and Cardinal Dougherty was petitioned to have her remains moved from the cemetery in the little churchyard of the "Brethren" (German Baptists known as Dunkards) in Germantown, Pennsylvania, and placed in a vault with the rest of the family. As a result of her loving concern and a careful investigation by the Chancery Office of an evidence of Mrs. Drexel's desire which indicated she was a catechumen, Cardinal Dougherty granted the permission for the reburial. In the warmth of a tender affectionate nature that was hers, Katharine loved this mother she had never known. In her old age she loved her still.

# Chapter 2
# Childhood And Youth

Katharine's childhood was a radiant springtime. Everything that could have been fitted into a human existence to permeate it with joy and happiness was a constituent part of her earliest days. The gift of faith, the deep affection of devoted parents, the love and attention of numerous relatives, a thorough and complete education under competent tutors, travel in this country and abroad, material wealth, a home and family life of peace, tenderness, and joy — all these were part of her privileged childhood. April 10, 1860, a year and four months after her mother's death, Katharine's father married Emma Bouvier, daughter of Michael Bouvier of Philadelphia and Louise C. Vernou Bouvier. Newspapers at the time recorded that the wedding party left the mansion of the bride's father on Broad Street near Thompson and proceeded in a long line of carriages to Old St. Joseph's Church in Willing's Alley which was soon filled. A specially selected orchestra and choir supplied the music.[1] The newspapers also announced that after the wedding the newlyweds left on a short European tour. But it was much more than a short tour, extending from the date of the wedding, April 10, 1860, to early October of the same year. Spring changed into summer, and summer to autumn before they came back. They left New York on the *Arabia*, and toured France, Germany, Switzerland, Italy (including a private interview with Pope Pius IX), England and Ireland before their return on the steamer *Africa*.[2]

Then a new life began for the two Drexel daughters, Elizabeth and Katharine. Mr. and Mrs. Francis Anthony Drexel made their winter home at 1503 Walnut Street in what was then a very fashionable neighborhood. Everything that could add to its nineteenth century comfort and décor was lavished on it. The religious element was not overlooked. Mrs. Drexel, a woman of deep faith and love of God, fitted out an oratory as a place of prayer for her family. The appointments of this cherished place – altar, pictures, crucifix, bust of Our Lady, pedestals, and candelabra – were later to be prized as precious heirlooms in the family. Both Mr. and Mrs. Drexel integrated prayer into the daily life of the family. Their personal example was to leave permanent impress on their children.

In addition to this winter home, for the first ten years of their married life they rented a comfortable home set in three acres of farm land in Nicetown, Pennsylvania. Summer life here was a pastoral joy for the children and parents. A highlight of the day was the morning walk with their mother accompanying Mr. Drexel to the Reading Railroad station where he boarded a train for Philadelphia and his bank. During the day on the farm, there was a hayloft to explore and a large play yard to enjoy. Best of all, there was a donkey cart which Elizabeth and Katharine drove to the store several times a week to purchase kerosene, a very vital item in this summer place which knew neither electricity nor gas.[3]

The second Mrs. Drexel drew the two Drexel children to her heart and poured out on them all the tenderness that a mother could. October 2, 1863, her own child, Louise, was born. Coming as she did on the feast of the Guardian Angels, she was called "Angels' Gift." Katharine was particularly thrilled with this gift from the angels. Even in her old age she would refer to her as "My little sister." Emma Bouvier Drexel never made any distinction between the children. They were as much her children as if she had borne them all. She showered on each of them the fullness of her mother's love and the warmth of her affectionate nature. She set an example herself of noble Christian womanhood which was to make a deep and lasting impression on her daughters.

Mrs. Drexel's erudition, her vision, her understanding of human nature, and her capacity for giving and attracting love were all illuminated by a deep reverence for God and a lifelong fulfillment of the greatest commandment – the love of God above all else and the love of a neighbor as self. If by the grace of God, the Drexel daughters were later to evidence munificent charity in their lives, they were following a pattern set by this woman and seconded by her devoted husband. A person of wealth and erudition as she was, with all avenues of pleasure and cultural enjoyments opened to her, she sacrificed her leisure and freely gave a large portion of her time to the education of her children and the service and assistance of the poor.

Three afternoons weekly the doors of her Walnut Street home were thrown open to the poor in need of help. Clothing, medicine, rent money, amounting to some twenty thousand dollars a year were generously distributed by her as well as her time and her sympathy.[4] Being an efficient business woman as well as a philanthropist, she employed a well qualified person to investigate and ascertain the need where assistance was given. As her daughters grew older they helped in this tri-weekly encounter with Philadelphia's poor and they learned well from her example and that of their father that wealth was entrusted to them by God as a means of helping those in need. Each of the Drexel daughters was to remember that lesson and put it into practice as long as she lived. In addition to her wealth, Katharine would one day give herself to God, and for love of Him, to her neighbor. But no one could have dreamed of this in the early years of her life.

To all appearances, young Katharine was a normal child of a wealthy family with a love for the simple pleasures of life, a tender affection for her family, a delightful sense of humor, a charming simplicity, a keen and eager mind, and an unaffected devotion to God. The seed of faith that would later fructify in an apostolate of faith, hope, and charity spread throughout the United States, was planted deep in her soul. Family prayers at night time, the rosary during the day were a natural (and supernatural) part of her young life. In the tutorial education of the children, great stress was placed upon writing letters and compositions as a means of developing correctness of speech and a certain elegance of style. Letters to Mama, Papa, to sister Louise were the common order of assignment. Katharine's letters, particularly to her mother, demonstrate the deep affection and the tender love she had for her. The letters were evidently cherished by Emma Drexel for she kept them all carefully tied with white ribbon in her writing desk. Due to that act of appreciation on her part, the letters have come down to us. There are many more than could be recorded in a book of this kind but some excerpts will tell us much about the loving relationship between the two, and the happy family life. This one in her own handwriting at the age of six is still preserved:

> Dear Mama,
>
> Happy Birthday. I hope you will be pleased with Grandpa's likeness and present. May the Blessed Mother send you a kiss from Heaven.
>
> *Your affectionate little daughter,*
>
> KATIE[5]

When she was nine years old she wrote the following letters to cherished baby sister Louise, on her birthday:

> Dear Louise:
>
> Happy birthday and many happy returns of birthdays as happy as these you have passed up to your seventh in our snug little nest. That the holy angels whose feast it is may ever bless and protect you and keep you as pure and as innocent as they are themselves in Heaven is the prayer of your lovingest.
>
> SISTER KATIE[6]

Though her century did not have the scientific knowledge or know-how of our Space Age, young Kate was so impressed with her lesson on the moon that she tried to pass on her new found information to her beloved little sister:

> Dear Louise:
>
> I suppose you have often seen the moon shining in the heavens on a bright night and have wished that you could live in it, but I can tell you, you would not like it as much as you think. If some kind fairy took you up there, you would be very glad to get back to the earth again. In the first place you would see no pretty white clouds or blue sky. You would see nothing but a great black sky, through which the sun would pour down its burning rays without even so much as a cloud to shield you from them. Just think how warm it must be up there. The sun does not go down in the evening, it stays up for two long weeks without even setting. Consequently, there are two weeks of daylight and two weeks of darkness. But in the dark times it would be illuminated on one of its sides by our Earth, which to the people of the moon (if there are any inhabitants) would look the same as the moon does to us, only thirteen times larger. Think how

beautiful our Earth must look to the lunarists. That, we must confess, is one of the advantages they enjoy over us....[7]

Her love for her sister Louise is evidenced in another letter written in French to her mother. We give the English translation here:

Dear Mama:

Tomorrow will be Christmas. Oh! what fun I shall have enjoying bonbons and receiving so many lovely things. Mama dear, before going any further with this letter, I must ask you to let Louise have some bonbons, too. You were saying that she does not know the taste of bonbons. I assure you she knows the taste of them very well. Now that she knows almost the whole alphabet, you will let her have some bonbons? She is just a little girl, so intelligent and sweet, you really cannot refuse her some sweets.

Now I want to tell you something else. I think our playhouse is the loveliest in the whole world with its carpet and furniture. Its kitchen will be like the one in this book. You know what I mean, do you not?

I am going to make the Stations for you, my darling Mama and for Papa and Louise, too. I am trying to study hard so that I may make my First Communion this year. Mama dear, my letter is nearly finished. A thousand thanks, my dear Mama, for all the Christmas presents you will give me. Nothing in the world could please me more than if you like this letter. I am hoping it will please you as much as your presents will please me.

In closing my letter I wish you, Papa, and my dear sisters a joyous, merry Christmas. Accept, dear Mama, my wishes which are so sincere and grant me what I am asking of you.

From your little daughter who loves you.
KATIE DREXEL[8]
December 23, 1867

A word of explanation is due here about the bonbons. Mrs. Drexel did not approve of candy for children. As a matter of fact, Mother Katharine frequently told her sisters as they were enjoying candy at recreation that as a child she was allowed only to have candy once a year at Christmas. The longing expressed in the above letter to make her First Holy Communion was to be repeated in the other letters. This little girl for all the joys and happiness of her young life had a strong desire to receive the Holy Eucharist. In another French letter written earlier this year, the same request appeared:

Dear Mama,

It is a week since I wrote you. I am so sorry that you have a headache on the first day of Lent. I hope there will be no more headaches. I am so happy it is cold today for I can go skating this afternoon with Papa. Every time we go skating he says it is the last time.

Mama dear, I have $3.19 but I really need $11.81. This letter is not a bit like Lizzie's. I composed this one myself. You must not laugh, dear

Mama, at my English letter to Saint Joseph; I really know how to spell now. Please keep all my French letters so you can see what progress I am making. Mama, I wrote this one all by myself. I am hoping St. Joseph will make me speak French. Dear Mama, I am going to make my First Communion and you will see how I shall try to be good. Let me make it in May, the most beautiful of all the months.

Good-bye now, I shall write you soon again.
KATIE DREXEL WHO LOVES YOU.[9]

Katharine lived before the time of Pope Pius X whose magnificent charity and understanding of children and the tender love of the Savior for them, would make it possible for them to receive their Eucharistic God into their young hearts as soon as they reached the age of reason. Three years would elapse before Katharine's desire for the Blessed Sacrament would be fulfilled. June 3, 1870, at the age of eleven she received her First Holy Communion. She was prepared for the great event as Elizabeth had been and later, Louise would be, by the Religious of the Sacred Heart in the nearby convent. Bishop Wood said the Mass for the group of children prepared by the religious, and immediately after it administered the Sacrament of Confirmation.[10]

Katharine said little about her first meeting with her Eucharistic God. In a letter to her aunt, Madame Bouvier, she had much to say about the breakfast but little about her First Communion. But that was Kate's way. Her secret was her own. Years later, in the privacy of her retreat notes as a religious, in the year 1920, she makes reference to it. The meeting was more intimate than anyone suspected: "I remember my First Communion and my letter on that day," she wrote. "Jesus made me shed my tears because of his Greatness in stooping to me. *Truth* made me feel the mite I was...."[11] The attraction of the child for the Blessed Sacrament was quite evident and it was a great joy to her to be taken out to visit a church. The oratory in her home, though, of course, the Blessed Sacrament was not there, was a place to which she often retreated for short periods of prayer.

It seemed to have come naturally for the Drexels to pray. In Katharine's childhood it was part of their daily lives to pray together and separately. All her life she would recall the example of prayer given by her father. Daily after his return from a busy day at the bank, after greeting his family and before doing anything else, he would retire to his room for a half hour intimate converse with God. This busy banker found a source of peace and union with God in daily prayer. After his period of prayer he frequently poured out his soul in his favorite classics on the organ.

There was nothing stilted, however, about the piety of the Drexels. Certainly there was no trace of anything stilted in Katharine. She loved God but she loved nice things too, and was by no means a repressed religious child. It was Mrs. Drexel's practice to give the sewing of the children's wardrobe to the Magdalens at the Convent of the Good Shepherd. Incidentally, she had garments made here also for distribution to the poor thus helping the sisters as well as the poor. At the various seasons she would take the three girls with her and make arrangements with the Magdelans for their clothes as well as clothes for herself. The dresses for the children were to be made plainly which seemed to make little difference to Elizabeth and little Louise. Katharine, however, had different ideas. On one occasion when all arrangements had been completed and they had started for the door, Katharine hurried back to the sister who had measured her. Clasping her hand she said, "Please do put lots of lace and ruffles on my dress, just like Mama's!"[12]

The family life of the Drexel children was extended to cover the close relatives in the city and there were many. A glance at the Drexel-Langstroth-Bouvier Who's Who in the Appendix to this book will illuminate this fact. When the family was in town, Mrs. Drexel and the children spent one afternoon with Grandma Bouvier. The children romped and played with many first cousins as Mother and Grandmother talked. Mr. Drexel took the two older children each Sunday after ten o'clock Mass for a short visit with Grandmother and Grandfather Bouvier. Grandma Drexel was visited Sunday afternoons. Emma Bouvier Drexel made a special point of seeing that Elizabeth and Katharine had intimate contact with their maternal grandmother, Grandmother Langstroth. Each Saturday a maid took the children to her home to spend the day there with other little cousins. These were days of special delight for Lizzie and Katie. Grandmother Langstroth had a very special room in her home which she named the "Children's Playground." In it was just about everything a child could desire for playtime. There were toys of every make, but best of all there was a collection of dolls of every size and wardrobe. It was the dolls the children loved most. They could select the ones they wanted to play with – always with the injunction that everything was to be put back in order when the day of fun was over.

An interesting item about these play days is recorded in the Annals of the Sisters of the Blessed Sacrament. It was entered there by Mother M. Mercedes, second superior general of the Sisters of the Blessed Sacrament, who was told it by "Cousin Bessie." Mother Mercedes was Mother M. Katharine's companion on her second visit to Rome for the final approbation of the Rule. Their vessel had a twenty-four hour stop at Funchal, Madeira. Mother M. Katharine took advantage of the stop to see her cousin who had married Mr. A. Jardin and taken up residence there.

It was forty years since these first cousins had met. In the course of this reunion, Madame Jardin had a short talk alone with Mother Mercedes. She remarked out of Mother Katharine's hearing that as a child, Katharine was one of the most generous, loving, unselfish creatures she had ever met. She loved to wait on others and help them by doing little things for them. She was a special favorite of Grandmother Langstroth of whom she related this incident. "In grandmother's room there were dolls of all descriptions and innumerable toys. One of the dolls was a Negro coachman who sat in state driving a very sumptuous carriage. He used to get a new velvet suit every year. As no one appeared particularly to want him, Katharine adopted him as her own and was quite satisfied with her selection until one day Bessie had six dolls and Lizzie Drexel had commandeered the remaining seventeen and would not allow little Katie to play with any. Katie went quietly to Grandma Langstroth and said with tears in her eyes, "Grandma, can't I have just one teeny weeny little doll for my very own?" Then it was that Grandma, rightly indignant, made an investigation and saw that then and thereafter Katie had her share of dolls and toys."[13]

Once, the ideal relations between the Drexels and the Langstroths were almost dissolved. It all happened one day at dinner with Grandma and Grandpa Langstroth. Lizzie looked at her grandmother sadly and with great sympathy in her voice said, "Oh Grandma, I am so very sorry for you because you can never go to Heaven!" Grandma as well as everyone else was stunned.

"And why cannot Grandmother go to Heaven?" she asked.

"You are a Protestant and Protestants never go to Heaven."[14]

Had she shot her, Lizzie could not have hurt her more. For several days there was anguish in the heart of this sincere and deeply religious Christian woman in the thought that her cherished grandchildren were being raised in bigotry. Finally the remark was traced to something Johanna had said. Johanna was a trusted servant of the family. Coming straight from Ireland, she had entered the Religious of the Sacred Heart, but her health did not permit her to continue there. Madame Bouvier (Mrs. Emma Drexel's sister) had asked her mother to take the young girl into her service which she did. At the birth of Louise, she had sent her to her daughter to help care for the new baby and the other children. Thus began a service that was to last her whole life long. When in later years her health failed, Mrs. Louise Drexel Morrell had a special room fixed for her in the country home at Torresdale and a special attendant to take care of her. She visited her daily when she was home and wrote to her when she was traveling. She is buried in the Sisters' cemetery in Cornwells Heights. On her tombstone Mrs. Morrell had inscribed: "Well done, thou good and faithful servant!"[15]

Johanna had come from Irish stock with a deep and rugged faith. She knew her ancestors had suffered and died for the faith. Neither hunger nor the sword could take it from them. It was THE FAITH. Anything else was anathema. An ecumenical day had not dawned in her life and she evidently knew nothing of an ecumenical spirit. Some of her remarks were evidently interpreted too literally by Elizabeth. Grandmother Langstroth was greatly relieved when the matter was straightened out.

There was another incident told by Mother Katharine later herself. On several occasions when the Dunkard Elder was there for dinner and supper, naturally Grandma requested him to ask the blessing. Lizzie and Katie were in a quandary as to what they should do about assisting at a prayer conducted by a Protestant minister. Lizzie settled the matter by deciding that both of them would hold up their rosary beads in full view during the prayer, just to show they were Catholics! That over zealous eccentricity must have been straightened out too, but it probably amused Grandmother Langstroth as it amused Mother Katharine when she recalled it.

There was a deep affection in all these families. It was not to dawn on Katharine until her thirteenth year that Mrs. Emma Drexel was not her real mother. Elizabeth may have known it but evidently nothing was said to Katharine. It was this grandmother situation that revealed the truth to her. It began with her wonderment about the fact that she and Lizzie had three Grandmothers while all the rest of their cousins had two. Many, many years later she confided to a Sister of the Blessed Sacrament that the revelation was quite a shock to her. It may well have been the first sorrow in a life that would be given to God and lived in imitation of the Incarnate Word who "for the joy set before Him endured a Cross" (Heb. 12, 2). But she knew the deep affection Emma Drexel had always lavished on her and was soon consoled. Never in her life would she let anyone refer to Mrs. Emma Drexel as her stepmother. At the same time she had cherished an ever deepening emotion of love and gratitude for the woman who had given her life for her, as already indicated.

Scripture tells us that "God is a consuming Fire" (Heb. 12,29). The Incarnate Son of God epitomized His mission to the spreading of that Fire. "I have come to cast fire upon the earth and what will I but that it kindled" (Luke 12, 49). The kindling of this fire, the burning love of God poured in the hearts of men is first accomplished in the Sacrament of Baptism. Every sacramental grace thereafter intensifies it. But this fire is an all embracing one including a love of self (rightly ordered) and a love of neighbor. The inception and first growth of this theological virtue of charity takes place in the home. It must flourish between husband and wife, between parents and children. There is ample evidence that such was the case with the family of Katharine. We record here two New Year's Day letters sent by Francis A. Drexel to his beloved wife. They speak for themselves.

Jan'y 1st, 1863

My dearly beloved and affectionate Wife:

It is well in the beginning of another year, to give expression to the thoughts that have been active in the one just gone by, as well as to form resolutions which may govern us in that which is to come.

Many various blessings have been conferred upon us the time we have been united. A special Providence it has been that has brought us together, and if we operate according to its designs, it will be the means of amending much in us that needs correction. A similarity in feeling and disposition, unless regulated by mutual love and forbearance, does not in general produce perfect concord. What each of us offends in, we are less liable to forgive in the other. Mutual forbearance is necessary for us both and for my part I feel that you have shown it toward me in a greater degree than I have returned it. Had I performed my religious duties with more seriousness and attention I should probably not now stand self convicted. We have received many and various blessings. Let us not be forgetful of them but in time to come may we show by our punctuality in approaching the Blessed Sacrament and the attention and devotion that we manifest in preparing for it, that we appreciate the means of salvation which have been designed to sustain our spiritual life. May our hearts be continually directed towards Him who suffered and died for us and gave his flesh for our life. When tempted let us instantly call on Our Blessed Mother. She is our friend and will help us.

God has also bestowed on us abundance. Continue your charities in His name. Be the dispenser of his gifts and let us also extend the charity of thought towards those who offend us.

In conclusion, my dear, dear one, let me wish you a happy New Year indeed, a strength to bear all the little trials that may befall you. May your warm, tender, and loving heart beat yet more tenderly toward your own loving and affectionate husband pardoning him for his faults and sustaining him in his trials and thus make home a heaven here below.

*Affectionately your own,*
Frank[16]

Jan'y 1st, 1864

My Own Darling,

Another circle has been added to those gone by, and during it God has been very bountiful to us, giving us an abundance of both spiritual and temporal blessings, not the least of which is that sweet pledge of our affections – Louise. Having followed His divine order may she be preserved to us, be a means of strengthening and increasing our affections.

The tender cares of a mother have kept us much apart and thrown additional responsibilities on you; but may we not expect increased blessings on both mother and father and also as the child increases in age, our alleviation?

The past year has separated me from my dearly beloved father. He has gone before me and needs all our prayers for his soul. Remember him as you would me.

I have to thank you for your kind forbearance and gentle love which you have bestowed upon me. You have overcome yourself; I have retrograded. I will try to do better and will pray for help to Him from whom only help can come.

*With the most tender affection,*
*Your husband* F. A. Drexel[17]

In connection with the mutual love in the family there was one remembrance of her early life that was very dear to Mother Katharine. It went back very far in her life. As a matter of fact, it was the first remembrance she had of the ocean. Her father, mother and sister waded out in the water but she was petrified, thoroughly frightened by the waves breaking on the beach and the vast expanse of water before her. Her father called to her to follow but noticing her fright, he came back, sat her on his shoulders and together they went out to sea. In her own words: "There I was piggyback with my little arms hugged tight around his neck. The salt spray splashed into my face, Papa ducked and I was under the water; he met a great wave which dashed against and then over us. Frightened beyond words, I held on like grim death, feeling my only safety was in my father's arms. But when he brought me back to shore, my fear was gone. Many times in life after, that incident has given me courage, for I felt my Heavenly Father's Arms were as protectingly around me as had been dear Papa's. "[18]

# Chapter 3
# Training For Life

Mrs. Drexel was determined to provide her daughters with the best education obtainable in that period. An outstanding Philadelphia music teacher, Mr. Michael Cross, was engaged to give piano lessons. Professor Allen, co-author of the Allen Greenough *Latin Grammar*, and his daughter Bessie became their Latin instructors. Miss Justine Clave was given the direction of their French. Other studies were in the capable hands of Miss Cassidy who was to play a major part in the intellectual formation and philosophic training of the three daughters. Mrs. Bouvier Drexel had consulted her sister, Madame Bouvier of the Religious of the Sacred Heart in nearby Eden Hall, when she was looking for someone to help her in the moral and scholastic training of her daughters. On her recommendation, Miss Cassidy was introduced to the family where she was to wield so tremendous an influence in the young lives.

Shortly after Miss Cassidy had come to America from Ireland with her mother, father, and sister, in search of a new life in a new world, her father died and she became the support of the family. Her education had been broad and deep with special emphasis on philosophy and literature. It was through her guidance and under her tutelage that the Drexel girls would read deeply into literature and make the acquaintance of the masters, as fountains of knowledge, and models for their individual styles. Composition and letter writing were to play a large part in her intellectual direction of the young thirsting minds of these select pupils. Mrs. Drexel fitted up an attractive classroom with desks, maps, pictures, plants, everything that could provide a pleasant atmosphere for the educational development of her cherished children.

Under this general tutelage the Drexel daughters were trained not only in correct habits of orderly thinking and purposeful concentration but they were to acquire a penetration of the liberal arts and a corresponding mental poise and dignity. There is a calmness and composure of the mind well stored with facts, integrated and made part of the whole vision of life. Inner wells of wisdom were dug in the hearts of the Drexel daughters deep enough to flow quietly through the whole course of their lives.

Compositions, letters, textbooks of this educational period were well preserved in the Drexel family and there are files of them still in the archives of the Sisters of the Blessed Sacrament. Darras, *Church History;* Balmes, *European Civilization*; Lingard, *History of England;* Guizot, *History of France* are among many texts used and still preserved. All copies of the classic Latin authors, Horace, Cicero, Livy, Tacitus still have well marked notations of their translators of long ago. The same is true of the copies of French classics and English especially Chaucer, Shakespeare and Pope. Logic, moral philosophy, the masterpieces of fiction in English literature, comparative history, and a prominent place for the History of the United States and its Constitution were all fitted into the educational schema. On Sunday evenings Mrs. Drexel arranged little literary seminars on the saints where they read, narrated and discussed the lives of various saints including their patron saints and the family favorite, St. Francis of Assisi. The devotion to the poor man of Assisi was fostered in Katharine as a child. It was to remain with her all her life. The knowledge of these saints, the family discussion of their lives with explanations of teachings of the Church were part of Mrs. Drexel's provision for the growth of her children in religious knowledge as well as secular.

Mr. Drexel made his own distinctive contribution to the education of his children by carefully arranged summer travel to points of historic and geographical interest in the United States. He was a firm believer in the "See America First" policy. The vacations he took in the fall each year were spent in trips to the White Mountains, to Maine, to California, Colorado, the Great Lakes region, and New Orleans. Years later Louise writing from the White Mountains were she was spending a few weeks vacation, would recall one of these vacations in a letter to Mother M. Katharine:

> ... From Jefferson, Mt. Washington is plainly visible. When looking at it I often think of that Sunday afternoon we all, with Louise and Lillie Dixon besides, went for a walk in quest of Tuckerman's Ravine. We got off the path and dear Papa refused to go a step further. Dear Mama thought this ridiculous and said so strongly. During the altercation, dear Lise knelt by a boulder and finished some prayers. I presume the rest of us were onlookers. Surely you recall the scene and how we laughed at the battle of words.... These White Mountains hold many tender memories for us....[1]

Shortly after Miss Cassidy came to the Drexel family and the voluminous letter writing began, we find this introduction in a letter written by Kate to her mother away on a short trip:

> Dear Mamma:
>
> Although you are far away from home you will like to know what is passing in our little nest. Last Sunday, as you already know was Louise's birthday. We began the day by going to Holy Communion all around

> then came home to enjoy an elegant breakfast with the perfume of roses and geranium leaves. Louise received twenty seven gifts....[2]

The letter goes on to describe the rest of the day but this opening is significant – the beginning of the birthday celebration was the reception of their Eucharistic God by all.

Interspersed throughout the many letters of her childhood, in which she is generally known as Kate, with their chatty and childlike account of little happenings of every-day life, runs a thread of expression about God and the saints that show spiritual depths developing in Katharine. But letters were not the only order of the day. There were compositions on multitudinous topics, religious, literary, historic and general: *Fifty Years Hence, Comments on the First Three Christian Centuries, Anne of Warwick*, etc. The last topic indicates the cosmopolitan reach of Katharine's interest, for this composition began with a letter:

> My dear Mamma:
>
> I know that a frown will come over an ordinarily bright face and exclamations of certain kind will come from a pretty mouth when you hear that I have taken for the subject of this week's composition, *Anne of Warwick, Consort of Wicked Richard III of England.* I know that for the sake of your daughter (whose special favorite this queen was and is) you will have the patience to listen to the history of an unfortunate woman whose sad and romantic life might well render her the interesting heroine of a novel.[3]

Back in 1870 when Katharine was nearing her twelfth birthday, Mr. Drexel purchased a ninety acre farm in Torresdale, Pennsylvania, as a country place for his family. Mrs. Drexel was delighted with the historical background of the location and entered this note in her journal, "John Hart" came to this country in 1682 with Penn, received by purchase 500 acres of land lying in the southern part of the township on the western side of the Poquessing Creek. Part of this, our own land now...."[4]

The spacious nineteenth century farm house was remodeled, cottages built for the servants and a substantial stable, carriage house, and barn erected. To the delight of all the family, the new home was ready for occupancy June, 1871. A statue of St. Michael carved in Caen stone above the entrance and a stained glass window fitted in an alcove window at the head of the first flight of stairs established the great Archangel as the special patron of this home which the family was to call "the nest." The surrounding farm lands were changed into verdant sloping lawns. In addition to stately trees already on the property, new ones were planted and flower beds of many varieties were laid out. The final effect one of breathtaking beauty. "My picture gallery" was the way Mr. Drexel referred to it. This ideal home in an ideal setting was to play an important part in the life of the Drexels and in the life, too, of the Congregation of the Sisters of the Blessed Sacrament which Katharine would later found.

From the very beginning it was to have a religious life also. Louise has left this brief history of a Sunday School:

> St. Michael's was first occupied in 1870. Shortly therafter our own dear mother proposed to her two eldest daughters one being about 14 and the other 11 years of age, to establish a Sunday School for the children of the men who worked on the place. The Sunday School was held with the greatest regularity. The older children were taught by Elizabeth, the youngest by Katharine. After the lessons were recited, the children were assembled around the piano in the parlor and hymns were sung. After a very few years the number of children increased, so that fifty or more came every Sunday. Just before St. Michael's was closed for the winter, prizes were given out for the best lessons and best attendance, and on Christmas Day the children assembled for a celebration when they received useful gifts (such as dresses, knitted jackets, etc.) also cake, candy, etc. This Sunday School was held until 1888.[5]

Each of the three daughters was in the course of the years ahead, trained to assume part of the upkeep of this new home. The responsibility of the kitchen and the stable was assigned to Elizabeth, Kate was housekeeper and that included supervision of the butler, seamstress, laundress, coach-man, etc. The farm, the garden, and the dogs were assigned to Louise.

Besides private tutors, letter writing, composition assignments, travel in America there were other ways of learning enjoyed in the family. Foreshadowing the European study programs arranged today for the twentieth century college student and the widely operating student exchange programs, the grand tour of Europe was considered a requisite part of the education of the well-to-do in the nineteenth century. Mr. and Mrs. Drexel took their three daughters abroad for an extensive tour of cultural and religious places of interest in Europe. They sailed on the *Scotia* of the Cunard Line, September 1874, and did not return to the United States till May 1875. England, France, Germany, Switzerland, Austria, Italy were all visited in a well planned and thoroughly enjoyed itinerary with the best accommodations that day could provide. Christmas was spent in Naples with the waters of the Bay gleaming in the warm sunlight before them while the Isle of Capri lay a thing of beauty across the distant horizon. From all the places visited, from the cathedrals, the monasteries, the museums, and the art galleries, letters were dutifully sent back to Miss Cassidy. These letters still preserved in the archives of the Sisters of the Blessed Sacrament could fill an interesting volume in themselves. Someday they will.

Sometime after the family returned home Katharine was to write one of her weekly compositions on one incident of her travels which we share with the reader here. Despite the note of humor and playful narration, there is an evidence of deep faith here in the determination of both Katharine and her sister Elizabeth to receive the sacrament of Penance. In all their letters, underneath the sparkling incidents is this steady flow of the undercurrent of faith:

AN AFTERMATH

One day in Vienna, Lise and I took a notion of going to confession. I shall not attempt to deny that our ardor for this disagreeable duty was somewhat stimulated by the next to impossibility of procuring an English confessor. Anyhow we felt virtuous in making the attempt and tried to delude ourselves into the idea that we were extremely desirous of carrying it out. Early in the morning we made our first essay by hammering rather violently at a sacristy door in the little church, not far from our hotel, until before us there appeared a young "gent" with a very amiable and astonished countenance. I'll acknowledge our situation was rather awkward, for speaking no German the great question was how to communicate our wants to the sacristan above mentioned. Lise being a young lady of resources, however, advanced towards a confessional not far distant and then coolly pointing to it with one hand repeated with true German *pronunciation*, the following sentence which she learned from Papa: "Ist der prater sprikesie Englisher?" The young man's countenance evidently underwent a violent struggle between a smiling and a serious expression, but saying something in German his amiable visage disappeared behind the sacristy door, leaving two unfortunate females in a complete quandary as to how to proceed. Was his speech intended to indicate that he was going to make inquiries for us? Did it mean an unsatisfactory "I don't know what you are saying"? Or was the "Prater Englisher" to be brought forward?

Whilst thus soliloquizing the sacristan again made his appearance, whispering to us a lot of un-understandable German with provoking rapidity. Fortunately we managed to catch in the course of his monologue the names of several churches in which we concluded that the desired linguistic clergyman was to be found, so saying "Tanken" many times by way of expressing our unfelt gratitude, we returned to the hotel to institute a most vigorous search in Murray and Baedeker for the Church of St. Anne and St. Catherine. It was not long before Mlle, Lise, Joe and I armed with a conspicuous red Murray proceeded towards St. Catherine's, but unfortunately a cross looking sexton who was shutting up the church only shrugged his shoulders at our question and seemed to reply, "I don't understand what you are saying, nor don't want to either."

I will not tire you by telling you how we finally were directed to the other end of the city towards on Italian hospital (some idiot I suppose taking us for Italians) and how we got into a nunnery, stupefying the countenances of the good religious, the Monas-

> tery of St. Anne, and being misunderstood by the brother; how we were conducted to view the vault of Marie Antoinette, etc. Suffice it to say that we returned to the hotel that afternoon unsuccessful and feeling like two very injured and virtuous girls. I hated to be defeated in my purpose so again out sallied Joe and I towards St. Anne's feeling convinced that the Englisher prater must reside in that abbey as we had been twice directed to it. I often wonder how I summoned up the courage to ring for the second time that day at the door but it seemed as if reverses on this occasion only made me more persevering. The same brother that had opened the door for me in the afternoon now came forward. He evidently recognized me and this time told us to wait, then disappeared.
>
> In a minute the brother's brown robe of St. Francis was visible in the dim light of the hall, beckoning for us to follow him. Accordingly going where he led, we traversed the whole extent of the long hall and turned down another equally lengthy. Then, behold, we found ourselves face to face with a tall, elegant looking monk, whose handsome features and long grey beard came out in strange relief, from the surrounding dimness, by the light of the candle which he was holding. His piercing, black eyes looked curiously toward me and then he asked in very broken English what I desired. I felt unable to answer for a moment as the strange situation in which I found myself rushed forcibly to my mind; but soon summoning up courage, I explained to him my business. He replied that he hardly understood English well enough to hear confessions, but asked if I could speak French. I immediately held forth in that language, but expressed my fear of not being able to confess in a foreign tongue. "Voyons, mon enfant, il ne faut pas avoir peur" he replied in the kindest and most fatherly tone. "Je vous aiderais. Demain matin a sept heures vous me rencontrerez ici, n'est ce pas?" I could not resist his kind voice, so thanking him many times we departed to communicate the conclusion of our little adventure to Mamma.[6]
>
> K. M. D.

Such were the backgrounds, the homes, the devout and devoted parents, the teachers, the relatives, the travels, all contributing to the formation of a young woman on whom God would set His seal and who was to hear and follow His call to spend herself and her fortune wherever she could reach Indians and Colored People in the broad expanse of the United States of America.

# Chapter 4
# A Study In Contrasts

1876, the Centennial Year of the Declaration of Independence, was a momentous one in the Drexel family. Miss Cassidy had suggested to Kate that she keep a hebdomadal, a weekly diary of interesting happenings. This she did faithfully.[1] Great preparations were on foot for celebrations in the historic city of Philadelphia. Patriotism for some can be a matter of flag waving, parade marching and banner displaying. It may have been these things for Katharine Drexel but it was much more. It was an instinctive reverence for the ideals of the men who fought to be free, and an ever growing enthusiasm for the nation they founded and the government they formed.

This diary is a mine of interest. She began it a few days before her big sister Elizabeth's debut in January 1876. "Louise and I amused ourselves," she wrote, "in looking at the men who were draping chandeliers with green smilax vines and pinks. Then after taking one proud look at the table elegantly set with large India dishes and a handsome gift candelabra at each end, we departed to dress ourselves for an afternoon ride. On our return all were edified by the spectacle of two swallow-tailed waiters flying around in search of tumblers and plates. The India dishes were now filled with fancy cakes, meringues, jellied chickens, chicken salad and various other dainties. How I should have liked to take a sly nibble at some of these *friandises*, but the swallow-tails were always sure to appear just as I was taking an innocent walk around the table, intending at their departure from the room to make a grab at some of the goodies."[2]

The hebdomadal account of the opening of the Centennial Year is a classic in its own right, giving us an intimate view of Philadelphia of long ago:

> I am happy to say that our New Year's Eve was commenced in the most patriotic manner or if not in the most patriotic manner, at least with most patriotic feelings. Louise was wild with excitement. She decorated herself with five penny flags and danced violently before the dining room door. Lise and I rushed around the house lighting the gas for our illumination, whilst Hans was conducted to the balcony to drape our enormous "stars and stripes" over the balustrade. This outward manifestation of inward love for country was no sooner made than a natural curiosity to see ourselves as others would see us took possession of us. Mama kindly enabled us to satisfy this youthful desire by proposing that she and Papa should accompany us in a little promenade on Chestnut

and Walnut Streets. Poor Mr. D. was far from relishing the prospects of a nocturnal walk for he was very tired, having worked hard at the office during the entire day and besides, "il n'y a rien qui reprodit comme l'enthousiasm des autres." Never-the-less, the whole family stalked out on their tour.

I never felt more indignation than when I saw about three fourths of the houses on Walnut Street in total darkness, notwithstanding the express orders of the Mayor that every citizen should illuminate and drape his house on the evening of the 31st of December. Chestnut Street, however, presented a more lively appearance. Nearly every building was brilliantly lit up; flags were waving in all directions; the store windows were draped in red, white and blue goods; the street was thronged with people; a calcium light poured down its effulgence on the Chestnut Street theatre covered with flags of all nations; and Chinese lanterns gleamed from the walls of many of the houses. How we should have loved to walk down to the old State House, but Mr. D. was beginning to hum and we know that this was a sure sign of his ennui, so reluctantly we retraced our steps.

The joyful ringing of many church bells, the solemn boom of the cannons, the melancholy sound of penny trumpets awakened Lise and me from a sound sleep and admonished us that the Old Year had come to a close and that 1876 our Centennial Year at last arrived. We sat up in our beds till the last peal of the bells died away, wished that we were by Independence Hall to see the hoisting of the United States Flag, and then I blush to say that we spontaneously sunk on our pillows not even to dream of the old patriots whose heroic love of country caused liberty to be rung throughout the land, nearly one hundred years ago.[3]

From a glowing pen of this young writer we extract this scintillating account of the opening day of the great Centennial. There are asides here one would not find in a history book, but for all that they were part of history too:

THE MEMORABLE DAY

The tenth of May – our great Centennial opening day, had at last arrived! Behold our family assembled on the balcony in front of the house and like every other on the square, we too gaze up our ordinarily modest-looking Walnut Street through the many colored flags which wave to and fro from each domicile, and through the fresh verdure of the trees which line the sidewalks, we try to gain the first glimpse of our Centennial procession. Hark! the music comes nearer and nearer. In a minute more the Mayor and the really aristocratic looking members of the City Council, tall, handsome and broad shouldered men, ride past on prancing horses. These are followed by companies of infantry, some dressed in grey, some in red and blue, others in blue and white; sunburnt marines in their solid blue suits with white hats; and regiments wearing short yellow knee breeches, black, cut-a-ways and three cornered hats a la Washington. Then there are war horses drawing bulky field-pieces;

drums beating, aide-de-camps galloping here and there with messages from their generals. Such is the brilliant pageant which meets our gaze. Almost one hour has elapsed since the first band passed us and now that the last company of musicians marches by, the crowd that fills the street demonstrates its appreciation by clapping hands, etc. Had these people felt as I did, there would have been three hearty cheers.

Good gracious! What a scramble there was to get me dressed before nine o'clock that I might join Uncle John Lankenau's party going to the Centennial Opening. I was in full time, however, and on arriving saw our punctual and fussy Uncle descending the stairs just preparing for a regular onslaught, for Mamma had lent him our carriage for this occasion and I dare say he was unaware of its arrival. He was accompanied by the German Ambassador, a middle-sized bilious looking man with light mustachios who was dressed on this occasion in an appallingly grand uniform of dark blue cloth trimmed with gold lace. Uncle John immediately introduced him as Baron Shibilibiloi, or some such unpronounceable name and simultaneously off went the three cornered hat and a most reverential bow ensued. This kind of treatment went rather hard at first, being always considered a mere child at home but I believe I acted my part of young lady admirably until we arrived at the front door.

This was a trying moment. The ceremonious old Baron stood expectantly at one side of the door, Uncle John at the other, I somewhere in the middle, two or three feet from the door. What was a poor fellow expected to do? I looked towards Uncle John, he looked towards the street. At last I made a dart in the direction of the door and slipped nicely through to the other side followed by the Baron and Mr. L. Unfortunately my misery was not over. There was the carriage in front of the house and the whole ceremonious maneuver had to be gone over. I whispered in agony to ask him what in the name of— I was expected to do. No response, so I took two steps and found myself half in the carriage in a fearful state of uncertainty. No sooner done than Uncle John gave a loud hem saying: "Hold on, Kate, you go in our carriage." I darted out again and was just making some apologies in the coolest and easiest manner possible, when a furious blush suffused my face and spoilt in my eyes everything. As soon as possible, I retreated to the house, bound to unburden my uncomfortable feelings to a sympathizing cousin.

Soon the carriage came to the door and we, too, were en route for the Centennial Buildings. It is unnecessary for me to say how we floundered in the muddy walks outside of the grounds to find the entrance and on getting in we went around at a distracting pace to find Mr. Bartle who was to lend us his apartments in the main building, and how that tall young gentleman turned up, hot and flurried, just in the very moment we least expected to find him and courteously led us to his rooms. Here were assembled about twenty other people whom he had invited on this occasion, all talking and looking out from a long line of windows into the large square between Memorial Hall and the main building.

It was not long before we were comfortably seated amongst them and following the example of all present we too looked eagerly into the animated square which lay before us. To our left, from a platform which extended from the main building, were seated a medley of nine hundred individuals, both male and female, who were to sing the Centennial Choruses. Mr. Thomas, in the meantime, was leading the orchestra, whilst it played the National airs of all the countries represented by an ambassador. Still on the left hand side as far as the eye could reach, filling every square inch of the ground, crowding the roof and the Centennial cars, representing to the vision a mass of hats, appeared the populace who had come to see the exhibition. In the alley retained as a passage for the invited guests, between the main building and Memorial Hall, a line of soldiers continually pressed forcibly against the crowd to keep the people in proper bounds, and in one corner we witnessed a regular fight which was taking place between some insubordinate man and one of the military. But the most singular sight of all was presented by the two large prancing bronze horses in front of Memorial Hall. About twenty individuals who had taken refuge from the crush of the people had managed to climb with great agility on the pedestal which supported the horses and were now comfortably seated with open umbrellas on the back, necks, and raised legs and tail of the noble animals. Soon we heard the air resound with clapping hands and loud hurrahs and turning our eyes from the crowd we saw advancing up the main alley no less important personages than the Emperor and Empress of Brazil.

I don't know how it was but I occupied myself entirely with the Empress, altogether forgetful of her loving spouse and satisfied myself with seeing that she was stout, a little above middle height and middle age. I suppose that I may add, with a kind, benevolent face that was not anything like as ugly as I expected. She appeared to be very lame, taking two men to assist her to mount the platform which she was to occupy in front of Memorial Hall. She was dressed in lilac silk and wore something which looked like a white wreath upon her head.

In a little while there was some more clapping and in marched the President, some regiments of soldiers and the whole Diplomatic Corps. We now felt as if we had fully commenced the business of the day. A silence ensued and something evidently was going on. On looking at the program it appeared that Bishop Sidney was repeating or mumbling the Centennial prayer. Not a sound reached our ear; but as I afterward heard, "It was no small loss."[4]

Katharine Drexel had a facile pen, a delightful sense of humor, a captivating enthusiasm for living and a great love of her native land. Judging from the journals she wrote and those written by her sisters, she appears a woman of her times, a good Christian woman but one whose life was set in wealth and surrounded by pleasure, whose every desire was fulfilled and every need satisfied. On the surface it looked as if she was finding everything she wanted in life, that she was accepting life as it came to her and was fully satisfied with all it offered. But the intimate desires of Katharine were not ordinary, nor could they be satisfied in an ordinary way. There were other gifts she possessed, other insights she had into the meaning of life that are not recorded in her chatty letters or sprightly compositions.

In addition to the voluminous writings that were preserved in her family and are thus available to the present writer, other writings, brief and terse, secretly recorded in very small notebooks marked "Private" in her own hand writing, have come down to us. "Little" here is meant to be taken literally. No notebook could be smaller than these, three, measuring 2 x 2 ½ and three, 2 x 3 ½. It was as if in a book that could be easily hidden away she would entrust a few records of her spiritual accounts. Katharine was a Banker's Daughter. She believed in account keeping even in spiritual matters. These notes show us another side of this young woman of wealth; they record another type of desires and ambitions that all the wealth of this world could not satisfy. Hers was a desire for God, a desire to please Him, a desire to live a life of sacrifice and prayer for His greater honor and glory. Underneath her carefree existence, the pleasures rippling on the outer stream of her life, there were swiftly moving currents, deep rivers of spiritual insight flowing quietly, known only to God, to herself, and her spiritual director.

Katharine was particularly blessed in matters of spiritual direction. In 1872 – she was then fourteen – there came into her life a holy priest who was to exert a lasting influence in her spiritual life. Father James O'Connor had come to the United States from Ireland at the age of fifteen. In his preparation for the priesthood he had studied at St. Charles Seminary, Philadelphia, and later at the Propaganda in Rome. He was ordained in Rome in 1848, and the following year, he was appointed rector of St. Michael's Seminary in the diocese of Pittsburgh. In 1862 he was named rector of St. Charles Seminary in Overbrook, Philadelphia. In the course of the years, strained relations developed between him and Archbishop Wood. He was relieved of the rectorship of the Seminary in 1872, and appointed pastor of St. Dominic's in Holmesburg. As far as Philadelphia of that day was concerned, Holmesburg was out in the country. But the hand of God was in all this. The Drexel country home was within his parish and he became a very intimate friend of the Drexel family and the spiritual advisor of young Katharine. Even after his appointment and consecration as Bishop of Omaha four years later, he would continue in a long line of letters to direct and guide her.[5]

This summer home, St. Michael at Torresdale, was no ordinary summer home. The very first year it was opened as the Drexel's summer home, Archbishop Wood of Philadelphia came out in the autumn of 1870 and celebrated Mass in the parlor. An altar and requirements for Mass were supplied by the Religious of the Sacred Heart at nearby Eden Hall. For the next twelve years he would say Mass there once a year and he extended the permission for Mass to be said several times a year. In 1883 he authorized the pastor of St. Dominic's to say Mass at this home four times a year. Eventually after Archbishop Wood's death, Archbishop Ryan would give the permission for Mass to be said whenever a priest visited.[6]

As the pastor and a visitor at their home, Father O'Connor came to know the family very well and young Katharine particularly well. It is evident from her brief notes that she turned to him for special guidance even in her early years. Neither this concern for her spiritual progress nor the depths of her spiritual aspirations at this time could be discerned nor even surmised if it were not for her own sparse private notes and a volume of correspondence she carried on with him after he was made Bishop of Omaha.

Safe in the archives of the Sisters of the Blessed Sacrament are these small notebooks in which Katharine recorded in pencil her thoughts, resolutions and the directions she had been given.[7] Some are dated, others not. Their earliest date is a list of New Year's resolutions for 1874 together with a set of notes before that, evidently 1873, when she was fifteen years old. To illustrate the poise and counterpoise in her life and character, some of these notes are recorded here:

> *July 8, 1873* --- Vacations have commenced and I now take the resolution to say prayers etc. for ¾ of an hour every day. First I will say the beads for Grandma Langstroth, then my Scapular prayers, Sacred Heart and cord of St. Joseph prayers for a happy death and that I will make a good confession. Then a meditation on Father Faber and 5 prayers. I will try to be patient and kind. My meditation for today is on death. Every single thing we do is making death easier or harder.
>
> *November, 1873* --- What a long time it has been since I have made my "accounts," so long in fact that it has been nearly four months and I almost forgot how I advanced in virtue. However, I will put down my "accounts" as far as I am able. I am getting quite scrupulous, and really every scruple as Father Faber says, is mixed up with sin and vanity.
>
> *January 1, 1874* --- Another year has come around and I will renew my resolutions again for I am but little better. I was much better in May than I am now because I suppose I have relied too much on myself. In

impatience, with God's help, I am a little better although I have not the same occasion for sinning against it. During the year 1874, I am resolved:

1. To overcome Pride and Vanity
2. To speak French
3. Attention to Prayers
4. Attention to Studies

*March, 1874* --- Next Wednesday will be Lent and so to please God and mortify my flesh, I resolve:

1. Not to eat between meals
2. Not to take water between meals
3. Dinner, everything but once
4. No butter, no fruit
5. To speak French
6. To give money to the poor

It is interesting throughout these brief notes to find several resolutions about speaking French. Evidently this part of her scholastic training was a little irksome to her. Hence she makes it one of her resolutions in her striving for holiness of life.

> *May 1, 1874* --- A wreath of flowers collected by me, K.D. most unworthy sinner, to be presented to Mary at the hour of my death, commenced the year 1874 on the first day of May.

Following the above entrance is a list of the days of the month with crosses after each which evidently marked a fulfillment of some resolution. There is no indication what the resolution was. The markings go as far as May 7; the other dates in the month are blank. At least, she started out well!

> *Undated, 1876* --- How many things in looking over my book I have commenced to do and then have not completed! If God will help me however, I intend and must do what Father O'Connor has told me to do which are the following rules:
>
> 1. Never to omit my morning prayers but to devote from 5 to 8 minutes in the morning devotions in a prayerbook.
> 2. During the day or if I prefer when the clock strikes offer all my actions to God.
> 3. Make meditation in Following of Christ or other books for about 10 or 15 minutes or perhaps less times.
> 4. Read a life of a saint or some good book such as "The Monks of the West" every three months. Novels of the day every once in a while.
> 5. Examine conscience thoroughly every day and see if the duties proposed have been fulfilled.
>
> *September, 1876* --- My spiritual father has told me that my predominant passion is scrupulosity. His parting advice to me was always to pray fervently to God each day that He might aid me to know my vocation in life. He dwelt at length on the importance of this prayer. I am to write

to him in any difficulty whatsoever. I wish all the days of my life to say some prayer for this S.F. At present I repeat 9 Ave's, the Veni Sanctus, Fly to the Patronage of St. Joseph, and 3 Hail Holy Queens to the Blessed Virgin.

*October, 1876* --- I wish very much at present to receive dear Jesus for it is a long time since I have been to Holy Communion. But I'm awfully unworthy of this greatest of favors, sinning every second. I intend from today to please Him more. Therefore I will endeavor to be less selfish and to be kind.

*Undated, 1878* --- I am resolved during this year to try to overcome impatience and give attention to lessons. I, Katie, put these resolutions at the feet of Jesus, Mary and Joseph hoping that they will find acceptance there. May Jesus, Mary and Joseph help me to bear much fruit in the year 1878.

January...about the same
April...a little better
May...little better with God's help
June...slight relaxation from the last
July, August, September...I think relaxed
November...relaxed

Thus it goes with the holy ones of God. They keep on climbing, failure after failure. We are so tempted to think that saints get that way with little effort. Here in intimate notes is a record of resolutions made again and again, and broken. The ordinary person gives up trying. The one really aiming at sanctity keeps on going. So it seems to have been with Katharine. She resolved, failed, admitted her failure, and then took a fresh start.

There follows in this notebook, a month by month record of her resolutions on Pride and Vanity, Impatience, and Attention to Study. They follow the same pattern with the same apparently bleak results. A glance at one will suffice for all.

*Pride and Vanity*
I am worse
April...The same. Did not try to overcome
May...Bad, not trying to overcome
June...I never tried
July, August, September ...Bad
November...

There is an anatomy of holiness partly demonstrated in these frank recordings of a young woman who found her human nature a great block to sanctity. This is not the story of a person so faithful to every inspiration, so swept on by grace, so wrapt in prayer, that she scaled the heights quickly. Hers was an ordinary down to earth confrontation with her instability and her weakness. But she kept on going and she kept on trying. She admitted her defeats, but was not vanquished by them. Rather she rose up and, relying on the grace of God, tried again for victory.

> *February 2, 1878* --- I will try to offer up my work for the intention of the Sacred Heart. There is a pretty example of this in the Messenger about how a poor Chinese child could be saved by these means and pray for us afterwards in Heaven. Lent has commenced and still I am as bad as ever and perhaps worse. How is it possible I could treat Him so badly after all He has done for me? I hope I will make a good confession next Saturday and the Bread of Life will strengthen me against all evil. Is it not wonderful to think what Infinite Love is shown by him to us miserable sinners?
>
> *April, 1878* --- We go to Holy Communion every week. Mamma says she thinks we ought to make more improvement. So do I. I mean to try to speak French this month and study very hard and overcome pride and vanity which it seems to me I really never try to correct. I intend to try and end this Lent as well as last year. I intend to try and overcome myself and get the approbation of others. "Choose a secret place to thyself, love to dwell with thyself alone, seek not to be talking with anyone but rather say prayers to God that you may keep your conscience clear."
>
> *May, 1878* --- I am now reading Father Faber's Spiritual Conferences. May is not yet finished. I have put down the account and find that I have done scarcely anything to correct pride and vanity. I will try to be kind as that seems to be the virtue which makes us humble. I asked Jesus to give me the grace of kindness and maybe He will give it to me. May the Blessed Virgin help me to do so. I read today that Jesus in giving Himself to us is our kind protector and deliverer from sin. I am a little better but like a vain wretch I am proud of it. Should I not thank Jesus for helping me? Yes, dear Jesus, I have asked you for this so often and you have done as you say: "Ask ... etc." I hope I will not relapse. May J.M.J. help me not to. "I will sing Thy strength and will extol Thy mercy in the morning. For Thou art my support and my refuge in the day of trouble." Ps.
>
> *December 31, 1881* --- Oh Dear Little Infant Jesus, by your humble crib, I will make my resolutions for the coming year. In the presence of the Blessed Virgin, St. Joseph, my Guardian Angel, and St. Catherine, and in your presence, Infant Jesus, I here protest that of myself I can do nothing.
>
> No cake for 1882
> No preserves until June 1882
> No grapes, no honey until July 1st

There was nothing half hearted or ephemeral about her resolutions. They were very much down to earth, very practical and all embracing. In one fell swoop, cake, preserves, grapes and honey checked out for six months!

In a booklet dated 1882-1883, Katharine wrote out a list of her intentions for the Novena to the Holy Spirit. It is an amazing list, demonstrating the universality of her interest and concern. She had a way of including the whole world and forgetting no one:

> Grace to bear all crosses patiently, acceptably to God and meritoriously for M ... and family.
>
> That the Consolator Optimus may enlighten and comfort Uncle John Lankenau.
>
> That Papa, if it be well pleasing to God, may be inspired to add to his donations to St. Dominic's.
>
> The Sanctification of our (the families') souls. Veni, Veni. That we may never commit a mortal sin.
>
> For Thibault that he may make a good First Communion and Confirmation.
>
> For Uncle John and Uncle Stacke, Joe Patterson, George Dixon, Uncle Micke, Aunt Heloise, Bishop O'Connor, Father Ardea, Father Wall, Archbishop Wood, Leo XIII, Father Taylor, Miss Bessie, Miss Julia, Aunt Lydia, Lydie, Aunt Lou, Aunt Zen, Aunt Al, Aunt Nole, The Prince, Father Pila Matthews, Pattersons, Dixons, Miss Bulger's family and self, Servants, All the intentions of the Servants of the Holy Ghost, The Allen children—their Baptism, Elize, Grandparents Langstroth, Drexel, Bouvier, Frank L., Aunt Mary, Mrs. Dick.
>
> Conversion: (Twelve names including some of her relatives are listed here.)

All her life Katharine was to keep notes on retreats, on spiritual advice, on her resolutions. Running through all these is an ever deepening thirst for God and an impelling desire to please Him. The exquisite balance and counterbalance of her character and personality are evident in the two types of writing in which she engaged: a restrained, enthusiastic but controlled love of the world about her, and a deep longing for the perfection of a rich spiritual life within her. Underneath the light, gay, and sometimes humorous vein of her letter writing was a keen awareness of the sacredness and holiness of life which she discussed in her intercourse with God, and which she recorded briefly in these private notes. Evidently material wealth and the kingdoms of this world did not satisfy her; she sought the Kingdom of God and the wealth of another order.

# Chapter 5
# Shadows Fall

Formal school life ended for Katharine July 2, 1878. Well disciplined erudition, cultural contacts with old and current civilizations had been blended together to give her a background of knowledge and power of penetration that would equip her well for whatever the years ahead might bring. She had indeed been well prepared to take a leading place in the society in which her family moved. In a letter to Bishop O'Connor, May 28 of that last year of her formal schooling, Katharine made this reference to it:

> This will be a perpetual vacation for me, and yet strange to say, I do not feel particularly hilarious at the prospect. One looks forward so many years to finishing school, and when at last the time comes, a kind of sadness steals over one whose cause is hard to analyze. Perhaps it comes from this — there was a definite future to look to, up to the time of leaving school. Then the future suddenly looks all vague and uncertain....[1]

What should have been a big day in Katharine's life took place in January 1879. She was introduced to society in a debut attended with all the elegance and splendor a millionaire's daughter could have. By this time Katharine's composition writing had ended, though her letter writing was to continue. It is significantly astounding that one looks in vain for an account of this debut. Here we come to a high point, or what would seem in the natural course of events to have been a high point of her story, and all we find about it is one lone sentence in a rather long letter she sent to Bishop O'Connor January 4, three days after the big event. After a paragraph in which she tells of visits to the theater in December with her father and Elizabeth to enjoy several Shakespearean plays, she starts a second paragraph with this statement: "to this list of dissipations can be added dutiful evening calls on aunts and cousins, besides attending a little party the other night where I made my debut."[2] Not even a whole sentence about her debut! This may well be THE understatement of the nineteenth century. Probably no one else said so little about so much. To those who were privileged to know Katharine Drexel intimately as a religious, this is significant of one who never wanted to be the center of the limelight, who always brushed aside or ignored any reference to her, individually. She may have perfected this self forgetfulness as a religious. She was certainly well on the way long before.

Following her debut, the family summers at St. Michael's were interspersed with visits to the seashore and the country estates of relatives and friends. One delightful gathering after another was arranged in honor of Elizabeth and Katharine and a great deal of matchmaking progressed for the young society belles. Kate and Elizabeth wrote long letters to their mother, so long that the thoughtful mother advised them not to take so much time out, but to get all the enjoyment they could, "Mind, do not in a short visit as the present, consume any of your delightful moments in unnecessary writing. No news is good news and I should regard as a sinful waste of time any effort on your part to open a regular correspondence with those at home."[3] But from Long Branch, New Jersey, and from Cape May, letters continued to come. In the middle of one of Kate's letters we find this:

> ... Who do you suppose greeted us on the Dixon's porch on our arrival here with Aunt Lizzie, Uncle Joe, etc. – Prince Michael by Jove! In order to make us feel overwhelmed with honor, Aunt Lizzie immediately whisked us into a corner and imparted to us confidentially that His Royal Highness intended passing the week with her and then added one of those sweet little lies which the Recording Angel blotted out on the spot with a tear, "Children, he stayed on your account, so do make a fuss over him. Won't you?" And so we did in the ocean particularly where we were soon jumping, swimming — don't think us accomplished — I mean trying to swim, floating, prancing, and dashing spray into the face of this same lordly prince.... I proceed to tell you about this morning. It was piously commenced on our parts by assisting at an 8 o'clock Mass....[4]

Mr. Drexel too entered into the correspondence and came down on weekends when he could arrange it. August 18, 1880, he wrote as follows:

> DREXEL AND COMPANY
> AMERICAN AND FOREIGN BANKERS
> 34 SOUTH THIRD ST.
> PHILADELPHIA
>
> My Dear Children:
>
> Having both time and inclination I take advantage of them to drop you a few lines. Express again to Mrs. Childs and Miss Stanley my appreciation of their kindness to me on my visit.
>
> I hope you are careful not to get into deep water either with the beaux or the surf. Auster is doing well as can be expected. Our Indian coachman is to be commended for his driving which is far superior to Henry's.
>
> Mr. Childs can probably arrange to have the train you leave on stopped at Torresdale and your luggage checked. It seems very lonely at St. Michael's without you, but life is made up of sacrifices and we

> willingly bear your absence when we know you are enjoying yourselves. Please remember me to Rev. Dr. Morton, and with all sorts of love and kisses, I am children,
>
> *Your affectionate father,*
> F. A. DREXEL[5]

It is evident that Mr. Drexel had a keen eye for any proposals for his daughters' hands. We find this advice in another letter dated August 4, 1881, a year later, "don't let that blue shirted Englishman steal away your hearts and above all be careful not to go into danger in bathing...."[6]

In the midst of this warm affectionate letter writing between parents and daughters, one letter had an unusual opening. It was written by Mrs. Drexel August 17, 1880:

> My Own Darlings:
>
> Last night I had a dream in which I saw a painting of a door, such as we have often remarked in the walls of church sanctuaries abroad, the opening of reliquaries and tabernacles all bedecked and be-jewelled, and it was locked. I inquired for the key and Kate informed me that the meaning of the painting was that Jesus held the key, as this was the door of His Heart, which He opened only to those who knocked and asked. You, Lizzie, smiled at Kate's pious interpretation, which you denounced as gammon and spinach, and I became alarmed at the thought of your incredulity. At this juncture, I awakened with the entire scene impressed upon my mind, but its meaning and origin I have not yet been able to solve except it is that you both are much in my thoughts either sleeping or waking....[7]

It was a strange dream and one that Mrs. Drexel must have pondered over. What it meant to Kate or what impression it made on her we cannot know. Four days later she opened another letter to her mother:

> Dearest One,
>
> Bless your heart for that heart to heart communication of yours, I mean the nice long one telling us of your Blessed Margaret—like dream, your trip to Cape May, etc....[8]

Late in the year of 1879 a long shadow reached the periphery of the happiness of the Drexel family. More and more Mrs. Drexel felt exhausted, felt her strength going. She was careful to hide her weakening health from her family. As a matter of fact, in an attempt to do that, she had submitted to what was supposed to be a minor operation in her home in Philadelphia. A doctor had told her she should go to a hospital but she did not want to arouse concern or worry in the family. Calmly giving an excuse at St. Michael's that there was some furniture to be arranged and some repair work to be laid out, she left with a maid for her city home, instead of a hospital. There, as impossible as it seems to imagine, she submitted to an operation that she was told would be minor and would remove and cut out the cause of the ever recurring pain. The seat of the trouble proved to be cancer.[9]

When Mr. Drexel came to her too late to stop this ill-arranged and ill-provided-for operation, he was almost overcome with grief at her condition. Mother Katharine years later told the writer he said, "Emma, Emma, oh why did you let anyone do this?" She tried to explain, heroic soul as she was, that she thought she would have been able to save the whole family distress and worry. Nothing could spare them that now. The best doctors were employed. A trip to Colorado in 1880 especially planned for her did not help. In 1882 they went to Sharon Springs, New York, to avoid travel to a more distant place. That year the family stayed at St. Michael's till December 20. January 29, 1883, Mrs. Drexel died. She had suffered tortures and suffered bravely. She often said to her husband after paroxysms of intense pain, "Oh Frank, how I pray that when your time comes, you will be spared all this, and now I offer this pain I suffer, for you."[10]

Katharine was her mother's special nurse during all this agonizing, long drawn-out preamble to death. She was at her side constantly ready for any service, anguished at the sight of her cherished mother's sufferings. Many years later she would tell some of her religious sisters, she realized at this period the enormity of original sin through which suffering and death entered the world.[11] All her life she was to remember her mother's resignation to the Will of God and her heroic acceptance of suffering in her last months on earth. It was at the bedside of her mother, she confided further, that the thought of the religious life came to her constantly and forcibly.[12] She had always wanted to serve God but she had never envisaged a day when their happy family circle would be broken. The possibility of her mother's death had never entered her mind till it came with heart-rending finality.

The grief of the family was deep. Newspapers carried glowing tributes and laudatory editorials, and the whole city mourned this woman. The rich who knew her and the countless poor she had befriended rose up to praise her and bless her memory. The editor of *The Public Ledger* in this editorial of February 2, 1883, said among other things: "The poor, the sick, the unemployed, the dying were the constant objects of her cheering visits. Few women ever secured so many situations for needy but industrious and worthy persons — men, women, boys and girls. The families she has aided can be numbered by the hundreds, some of them supported entirely by her in time of need. And one of the most touching scenes of her funeral was that the hundreds who passed through her late home for two hours yesterday morning for a mournful farewell were largely composed of those to whom she had been a benefactress in every way in which distress can be alleviated or relieved. Their sorrow was unmistakable." After the funeral, Mr. Drexel retired to his room and for hours played the organ as if he would pour out in music the grief of his soul that was almost too heavy to bear.

The three daughters assumed responsibilities for the various phases of the family existence as their mother had so well trained them to do. In drawing closer to one another they tried to resume the well-knit family life. Later in the year Mr. Drexel arranged to take the three daughters again on a European tour. His aim was definitely to take their minds away from their loss, to distract them in their sorrow. Early in October 1883 they sailed, and traveled in Holland, Germany, Italy, France and England, while Miss Cassidy was installed as the general manager of the home. Again there was the chain of letters, and from their enthusiastic accounts it was evident the trip fulfilled its purpose. All of these letters make delightful reading but it will require another and a later volume to share them all with the reader. They were back in the United States early in May 1884.

In September of that same year, Mr. Drexel and his three daughters made an exciting trip to the great Northwest. The Northern Pacific R.R. gave them a private car, The Yellowstone. The object of the trip was a business one to investigate and decide if the bonds of the Northern Pacific would be a good investment for Drexel & Co. Two members of the Drexel Company, Mr. Joseph Shoemaker and Mr. George S. Thomas, were in the party and Mr. Drexel also include his niece, Mary Dixon, to accompany his daughters.[13] (Mary's mother, Elizabeth Bouvier Dixon, had died that year.) Altogether this trip from Torresdale to Portland, Oregon, with a detour to Yellowstone National Park, according to Katharine's diary, covered going and coming, 6,838 miles. (The Banker's Daughter was always conscious of figures!)[14] It was on this trip that the Drexel girls had their first brush with the law. Innocently, they had picked up some pieces of stone and minerals. Later on entering a hotel, the gentlemen of the party were put under arrest for violating a law, the Wyoming Act, which under the local interpretation there, made it an offense to carry away any object from its natural position. They had a real court trial too, in a country store, on the violation of a law they never knew existed. But all ended well. When it was over they could appreciate the humor of the whole experience.[15]

It was shortly after their return form abroad that Mr. Drexel came home one evening and made a strange announcement to his family. He told the daughters he had accomplished something that day that he was sure would please them, both in the way he had arranged it, and the way he had assured that his treasured daughters would be protected from fortune hunters. He seemed quite happy about his plan and said he had considered it a good day's work. When he was questioned about the nature of this good work, he simply replied, "I have made my will."[16]

Something like a cold chill went through his three attentive daughters. Was this an intimation they would lose him too? Less than a year later Francis

Anthony Drexel died suddenly in his city residence. Very early in February 1885 he caught a cold which developed into pleurisy. His two doctors were not alarmed and prescribed treatments and medicines which were administered by Elizabeth. In those days trained nurses were not necessarily part of a sick room and his daughters became his devoted nurses. All seemed to be going well and the patient seemed to be far on the road to recovery. February 12, 1885, he spent an hour at his beloved organ. Sunday, February 15, he had made an hour's meditation in the morning which he usually made in the afternoon. Later he took up a copy of *The Newcomes* and read quietly. Kate, the nurse on duty at the moment, was in the next room when she heard a noise and rushed in to find her father slumped in his chair. She called to her sisters to come quickly, grabbed a wrap and ran as fast as she could to St. Patrick's Church. There she burst upon a small group of priests who seemed to be in conference. "Come quick," she screamed, "my father is dying." When the startled priests did not move immediately, she cried out, "My God, he won't come and my father is dying." One of the priests arose and said, "My child, I will come." Just as they came out of the door, one of the servants was there with a cab waiting for them. This servant had taken a cab to St. John's and a priest had gone from there. But Mr. Drexel had given up his soul to God when the priests arrived.

Once again a Drexel was buried with all the solemn requiem of the Church. Archbishop Ryan celebrated the Pontifical Mass at St. Mary's. Two thousand people filled the church and countless others stood outside. Every class of society was represented including all members of the banking houses of the Drexels in Philadelphia and New York, a Stock Exchange Committee, representatives of the Corporation of the German Hospital, and countless others, rich and poor. Resolutions of sympathy, glowing tributes of newspapers, letters of condolence paid reverent tribute to this outstanding citizen. Possibly the greatest tribute to Francis Anthony Drexel was in his own will.[17]

The will of Mr. Drexel caused nation-wide comment then, as it did again in 1955 on the death of Mother M. Katharine. His instinct for charity was well known, his business acumen highly respected. Both were evidenced in his will. It had one of the tightest spendthrift clauses, which forbade any husband having anything to do with the administration of his wife's property and which also provided for every contingency in case his daughters died without issue. Mr. Drexel appointed his brother, Anthony J. Drexel, and his intimate friend, Mr. George Childs, and his brother-in-law, Mr. John D. Lankenau, as the executors of his will. Mr. George Childs was owner and editor of the *Philadelphia Ledger.* The friendship between him, his wife, and the Drexel family was very intimate, so intimate that the Drexel girls always called him uncle and he in turn looked on them as his nieces.

Article V of the will provided first that the executors should make an inventory and valuation of all his residuary estate, both real and personal, deducting collateral, inheritance tax, debts, charges, and necessary expenses for the administration of the estate. Then out of the net residuary estate they were to distribute one-tenth immediately, in the proportions he had arranged, to a long list of institutions and communities named in the will: 5/100 — Cathedral of St. Peter and St. Paul, Conferences of St. Vincent de Paul of the Archdiocese of Philadelphia, St. Joseph's Church (Willings Alley), St. John's Orphan Asylum, St. Joseph's Hospital, St. Mary's Hospital, Sisters of St. Francis, the Philadelphia Theological Seminary of St. Charles Borromeo, St. Joseph's College, House of the Good Shepherd, The West Philadelphia Industrial School; 3/100 — St. Bonifacius Church, St. Joseph's Hospital (Reading, Pa.), St. James Parochial School, St. Peter's Church, Roman Catholic Society of St. Joseph for educating and maintaining poor orphan children, St. Vincent's Home, Catholic Home for Destitute Children, Little Sisters of the Poor, Sisters of Mercy, St. Vincent's Orphan Asylum, LaSalle College, Sharon Hill Academy, Lankenau Hospital; 2/100 — Institute of Ladies of the Sacred Heart of Eden Hall; 1/100 — St. Catherine's Female Orphan Asylum, St. Mary Magdalene de Pazzi's Asylum for Italian Orphan Girls, St. Anne's Widows' Asylum, Institute of Ladies of the Sacred Heart of Philadelphia. This net residuary estate was about $15,500,000. One tenth of that was distributed immediately.

Article VII stated that the remaining nine-tenths of the net residuary estate ($14,000,000) should be called the Trust Estate. The annual net income of the Trust was to be divided one-third part to each of his three daughters. This will specifically stated: "… and if any one of my said three daughters should die without issue living at her death, but leaving her two sisters surviving, then to pay the share of the income of the daughter so dying to her two surviving sisters equally between them during their lives respectively; or should one of my said daughters only survive and no issue of the other, then to pay the whole share of the income of the daughter so dying to her that survived during her life … but should all of my said daughters die leaving none of their issue living at the death of the last survivor of them . . this trust shall terminate, and at this termination the whole of the corpus of said Trust Estate shall go … to the same institutions or such of them as may then exist, to whom I have hereinbefore bequeathed among them, the one-tenth part in cash of the net value of my said residuary estate."

Thus it was that at Mother M. Katharine's death in 1955, the same institutions which had received at his death in 1885 pro rata shares of the one-tenth of Mr. Drexel's Estate, then received the same share of the fourteen million dollars. Mr. Drexel could never have dreamed that his Kate would one day not only become a religious but would found a community for the Indians and Colored of America. His one thought after providing for his daughters munificently was to guard them from those who seek to marry them for their fortune. Had he known of the later foundation of his cherished daughter, this will would have been very different.

In the Providence of God, Katharine was to live till her ninety-seventh year, and for the last ten years of her life after the death of her sister, Louise Drexel Morrell, to be the lone income beneficiary of the will. She never planned to break her father's will nor did she ever have any desire to do so. She was to disburse its benefactions to the Indian and Colored races while she lived, and to instruct the sisters of her Community to trust in the Providence of God for His care. She undoubtedly realized that many of her own foundations, particularly Xavier University of New Orleans, her Indian Schools at St. Catherine's, Santa Fe, and St. Michael's, Arizona, and Holy Providence School at the Motherhouse needed this money more than many of the institutions profiting by the will. But she also felt that Catholic Americans could and should rally to the upkeep of the various works supported for so long a period by her father's wealth. She gave it all while she lived. She counted on the generosity of Americans to give after her death. Above all, she counted on Divine Providence.

# Chapter 6
# A Cry For Justice

Immediately after the death of Mr. Drexel, his sister-in-law, Mrs. Anthony J. Drexel, opened up her summer home, installed a few servants and begged the three grief stricken daughters to go there directly after the funeral. This they did, but not for long as they wanted to make the necessary adjustments and take up their family life again within bonds that now were closer than ever.

The Drexel daughters had been reared in an atmosphere of charity, an ardent and grateful love of God that sought to express its gratitude to Him by sharing the good things entrusted to them. Each of Mr. Drexel's children inherited a keen business instinct and a power of meticulous order in procedure. These women of wealth like their parents before them, would give endlessly of their wealth and their time to serve God and benefit their neighbor, but the giving would be carefully planned and prudently administered. They were resolved to continue the many charitable works of both their mother and father and to institute their own. The eldest daughter, Elizabeth, led the way.

As a member of the boards of St. John, St. Joseph, and St. Vincent Orphan Asylums, Mr. Drexel had made liberal donations to these institutions. Elizabeth was to add a continuing note to this phase of his charity. It was evident to her that the children who had lived and received a rudimentary education at these asylums were far too young to be thrown on their own resources as happened in those days. She determined to erect a trade school for them where they could be prepared for useful occupations and a good means of livelihood.[1] No such schools were in operation any place in the area at that time and she set out to form plans and to gather as much information as she could. She purchased 200 acres at Eddington, Pennsylvania, and determined the school would be called St. Francis de Sales Industrial School as a living memorial to her father. The completed building was blessed by Archbishop Ryan July 28, 1888. From that day to this, thousands of young men have been trained there to honorable and profitable living.

In the course of the years, each of the daughters would give freely to an area of her choice. Louise was to give aid to the Josephite Fathers who established in Baltimore a foundation independent of the Mill Hill Foundation in England. In 1888 she purchased a $29,000 piece of property for them in Baltimore. She gave an additional $30,000 for renovations and improvements for the establishment of Epiphany College. Her interest was largely centered in works that would help the Colored. In 1889 after her marriage to Colonel

Edward Morrell, she and her husband donated $30,000 for another piece of land for the Josephites and for years took care of their insurance, repairs, etc. The high point of Louise Drexel Morrell's zeal for the betterment of the Negro population would come in 1894 when she and Colonel Morrell bought one of the plantations of General Philip St. George Cocke, forty miles northwest of Richmond. They established there St. Emma's Industrial and Agricultural Institute, a military school for the higher education of young Negro men. Proficiency in a trade was to be part of its educational formation.[2] It is a thriving military academy today with the picturesque setting of sixteen hundred acres overlooking the historic James River.

The three sisters answered an appeal for help from the Catholic University at Washington, D. C., by a donation of $50,000 for the establishment of the Francis A. Drexel Chair of Moral Theology. The same year they gave $30,000 in answer to an urgent request from the Sisters of St. Francis for the purchase of a piece of property in connection with St. Agnes Hospital.[3] And thus it went on and on. As long as each of the daughters lived she studied needs, helped causes and spread the charity of Christ in every direction. Truly was this a remarkable family.

Katharine's initial special charity was to be expended on the Indians. It seems she always had an interest in them. In the only interview she ever gave a reporter — at the dedication of the new Xavier University buildings in New Orleans, October 12, 1932 — she said that as a child she loved to read about the Indians in the early days of American history and that even then she had come to her own conclusion: The real reason Christopher Columbus had discovered America was to save the souls of the Indians! This had been her reaction to a picture of Christopher Columbus landing on the shores of the New World while Indians watched in the background. In her young womanhood, this latent interest was to become actual in a very interesting way.

Shortly after the death of Francis Anthony Drexel, whose will with its munificent bequests had been published throughout the land, a butler announced to the three Drexel daughters in their Philadelphia home, "Two gentlemen, priests, downstairs to see the Misses Drexel." The three looked at each other and finally Louise said, "Kate, you go down." All unconcerned, down went Kate to an interview that was indeed to be a turning point in her life. The visitors were two Indian missioners, Bishop Martin Marty, O.S.B., at the time Vicar Apostolic of Northern Minnesota, and Reverend Joseph Stephan, Director of the Bureau of Catholic Indian Missions. Both these men were zealous missionaries to the Indians, full of plans for the preservation of their faith and painfully aware of the loss of faith of many. They were seeking financial aid to further Catholic effort among them. Specifically, they asked for help to erect schools for their Catholic education.[4] They were no mere theorists. Both had spent consecrated years in the service of the Indians and shared with them the physical hardships and the frustrations of their existence. They had fought and fought hard for a just proportionment under Grant's Peace Policy.

Now that it had failed utterly they were determined to ground mission security in the erection of Catholic schools. Katharine would know later, she could not have guessed then, the tortuous windings of Catholic Indians and missionaries in the dead end avenues of Grant's Peace Policy.

At its first proclamation in 1870, Grant's Peace Policy for the American Indian flashed like a torch in the midst of what Helen Hunt Jackson has so well called "A Century of Dishonor." In a gesture of justice and equity the American Government had adopted the Indian as its ward and ostensibly held itself responsible for his education and his welfare. But the Indian, the only real American on these shores, had other ideas. He would not forcibly be driven from the land of his ancestors. He resented government interference into his affairs; he more than resented forced exodus from the lands of his fathers. For the white men in America he could trust and did trust, he found many who exploited and cheated him. He rose up and in desperation used the only method he knew in retaliation. Uprisings, massacres, bloodshed were the marks of his anger. And every time he thus exerted himself, the United States Army crushed his uprising or took him captive and marched him, his wife, and his children to other land areas assigned him by the government.

President Grant may not have been the first national leader to realize the inhumanity and the futility of this procedure; he was at least the first to formulate another national procedure. In his 1870 message to Congress, he enunciated his new policy: "Indian agencies being civil offices, I determined to give all the agencies to such religious denominations as had hitherto established missioners among the Indians and perhaps to some other denominations who would undertake the work on the same terms — i.e. missionary work."[5] The agency thus was to be assigned to a particular religious group and the government agent in each case, that is in each agency, was to be named by that group.

It was a laudable, sensible plan, whose execution was possible and whose end, honorable. The plan was all right but its method of execution violated distributive justice and fundamental honesty. In addition to financial assistance that was to be given for the education of the Indians and their welfare, the plan specifically stated the agencies would be given to "such religious denominations as had hitherto established missionaries among the Indians." This clause was outrageously violated and lamentably contradicted. At the announcement of this plan in 1870, there were seventy-two Indian agencies; in thirty-eight of these, Catholic missionaries were the first to establish themselves. In flagrant disregard of this fact as well as the Indian's right to choose his own religion, only eight agencies, Colville and Tulalip in Washington Territory, Umatilla and Grand Ronde in Oregon, Flathead in Montana, Standing Rock and Devil's Lake in Dakota, Papago in Arizona, were assigned to the Catholic Church. Some eighty thousand Catholic baptized Indians were put under Protestant control.[6]

The initial letter dividing the Indian Agencies among the Christian Societies speaks for itself. Using a system of railroads as dividing lines, whole tribes of Indians, some possibly included in the etc's., were rapidly parceled out to various denominations with no attempt to ascertain their desires in this fundamental right of worshiping God.

INITIAL LETTER DIVIDING THE INDIAN

AGENCIES AMONG THE CHRISTIAN SOCIETIES

Washington, D. C., August 11, 1870

Honorable J. D. Cox, Secretary of Interior

Sir: Agreeably to your suggestion of yesterday I have made a rapid sketch of localities where the various Christian denominations of our country may most naturally follow up their work, in most instances already commenced, on behalf of the Indians.

First in order come the Quakers, the Orthodox branches of which society are already established in Kansas and the Western Indian Territory.

Going South, next in order come the Baptists in Cherokee country, side by side with the Presbyterians, or rather the American Board of Commissioners for Foreign Missions, of which Reverend Mr. Treat, of Boston, is secretary. These two societies have had the larger part of the mission work to do in the eastern side of the Indian Territory among the Cherokees, Creeks, Choctaws, Chickasaws, and others, and although other societies are working efficiently there, the prominence of these two societies ought to give them the choice of agent or general superintendent.

Crossing the northern plains of Texas you meet the Wichitas, Kiowas, Comanches, Cheyennes, Arapahoes, and the Apaches. These are now in the care of the orthodox Quakers.

Next across in New Mexico, which is more directly reached by way of Kansas Pacific Railroad, you have first the Utes near Maxwell's at the base of Rattoon Mountains. These you can assign to the American Missionary Society, Reverend Mr. Whipple, secretary; and you can continue their mission field down into Southern New Mexico and Arizona, giving them a portion of the Pueblo villages, on the Rio Grande, and the Apaches of New Mexico and Southeastern Arizona. Other Pueblo villages on the Rio Grande are claimed by the Roman Catholics, and as they have missions there these can be assigned to them. Passing westward you come to the Navajos, Moquis, Pimas and these, together with the Utes on the San Juan River, ought to be assigned to the Presbyterian Board, which already has missions there, and they are alone in the field. The secretary is Reverend Mr. Lowrie, 20 Centre Street, New York.

At present the basis of supplies in that direction ceases with the Moquis, and the tribes and people in Western Arizona are supplied via San Francisco. The tribes in Western Arizona are assigned to the Reformed Church, of which Reverend Mr. Ferris is secretary, office corner of Vesey and Church Streets, New York; this society, formerly known as the "Dutch" Reformed Church.

As these tribes will hereafter be supplied via Union Pacific Railroad and Salt Lake, I have continued (on the map) their mission work up among the tribes in Salt Lake Valley to the railroad.

As the Roman Catholics already have missions among the Indians on and near Puget Sound, and General Parker says also among the Nez Perces and at the head of the Missouri River, and the Powder River Sioux, I have marked these reservations down to that Church.

Coming down the Missouri, the great reservation of the Blackfeet, Assinaboines, Piegans, etc., has been placed at the disposal of the Methodists of which Reverend Dr. J. S. Durbin and Dr. Harris are Secretaries, 805 Broadway.

Continuing down the Missouri, you next come to the Episcopal and American Board of Commissioners for Foreign Missions Societies' missions in Dakota, and these reservations, I think, might without jarring be placed in the care of these two societies. The Episcopal Society is what is known as the evangelical branch of that Church, and differs only in church discipline from the Presbyterian. The Reverend Mr. Anthon is secretary, 13 Bible House, New York, "American Church Missionary Society," and Dr. Treat of Boston, secretary of the other.

Along the line of the Union Pacific Railroad the Baptists have established, or are commissioned to establish, mission stations, and as there are numbers of stray bands of Indians along that railroad I have marked these, together with the tribes in Southern Idaho, to the Baptists. Honorable Nathan Bishop, 11 East Twenty-fourth Street, New York, will respond to the letters addressed to that society.

This brings us back to Omaha and Nebraska, and there the Hicksite Society of Friends are already successfully operating.

In Minnesota the Yankton Sioux are under the hospitable care of the Episcopalians, of which the Honorable William Welsh, of Philadelphia, is the efficient patron.

In northern Minnesota, the Chippewas, if not already provided for, might be recommended to the able supervision of the Unitarians, of which society Dr. Henry W. Bellows, of New York, is President.

These are simply suggestions made in response to your kind request.[7]

*Faithfully, your obedient servant,*

VINCENT COLYER

SECRETARY OF BOARD

Neither the Catholic Indians nor Catholic leaders took this biased appointment lying down, but appeals went unanswered and the forced arrangements went on. As an example of the type of appeals from Catholic Indians, we quote in part from a memorandum of the Catholic Commissioner, Charles Ewing, to the Secretary of the Interior:

OFFICE OF CATHOLIC COMMISSIONER

FOR INDIAN AFFAIRS

Washington, D. C., October 19, 1874

To the Honorable
COLUMBUS DELANO, Secretary of the Interior

Sir: I must urge upon your immediate attention the consideration of certain questions in the administration of the affairs of the Great and Little Osages, that have repeatedly been presented to your department by this people through their National Counsel, by delegations and by petitions numerously signed, but which have so far elicited no response. If these men have any rights that the Government official must respect, then their petitions must be considered and answered.

The facts are of record in your department and are as follows:

On the 31st of March last, an Osage Indian Delegation, with the Governor of the Nation at their head, came to this city and without suggestions or assistance drew up and addressed to Honorable Assistant Secretary Cowan, the following Communization, viz:

Sir: The undersigned, Governor, Chiefs, and Councilors of the Great and Little Osage Nation of Indians, and all duly constituted delegates of said Nation, would respectfully beg leave to call your attention to the fact that last June, they together with all the Chiefs, Councilors and Head — men of their Nation signed a petition or a memorial addressed to his Excellency, our great father and friend, the President, asking that their former Catholic Missionaries and school teachers be restored to them and allowed to locate again in the Osage Nation and resume their Christian labors among the Osage people, in which they had been engaged for many years previous to the late war of rebellion.

Catholic missionaries have been among our people for several generations. Our people are familiar with their religion. The great majority of them are of the Catholic Faith, and believe it is right. Our children have grown up in this Faith. Many of our people have been educated by the Catholic Missionaries, and our people are indebted to them for all the blessings of Christianity and civilization that they now enjoy, and have for them a grateful remembrance. Since the missionaries have been taken away from us, we have done but little good and have made poor advancement in civilization and education. Our whole nation has grieved ever since these missionaries have been taken away from us, and we have prayed continuously that the Great Spirit might move upon the heart of our great father, the President, and cause him to return these missionaries to us. We trust that he will do so, because in 1865, when we signed the treaty of that date, the Commissioners who made it promised us that if we signed it we should again have our missionaries; and we have sought every opportunity to remind our great father of his promise, and we hope that he will have it carried out in good faith.

Religion among the whites is a matter of *conscience and voluntary choice.* It is so among our neighboring tribes and Nations in the Indian territory; it is so throughout all Christendom; and why should it not be so among the Osages? Give us, we beseech you, our own choice in this matter. The same God that made the white man also made the red one, and we pray you to remember that He has made us all alike, with the same natural aspirations and desires for happiness in this world as well as in the world to come.

*We have the honor to be, very respectfully,*
*Your obedient servants and friends,*
JOSEPH PAW-NE-NO-POSH,
GOVERNOR, OSAGES

BIG CHIEF, BIG CHIEF BAND: WHITE HAIR, BLACK DOG, STRIKE AX, CHE-TO-PAS, HARD ROPE, WAH-TE-IN-KAH, ALEXANDER BEYETT, SAMUEL, AUGUSTUS CAPTAIN, PAUL AKEN, (INTERPRETER).

Commissioner Charles Ewing concludes his memorandum:

The petition of a defenseless people for simple justice at the hands of a great Government, is the strongest appeal that my head or heart can conceive; and it is of course unnecessary for me to urge it upon you. It is as plain and open as the day and if you decline (which I cannot believe) to comply with the repeated petitions of this people, it is useless for me to urge you to do it.

You must give this agency to the Catholic Church, or you publish the announcement that President Grant has changed his policy, and that he now intends to force that form of Christianity on each Indian tribe that he may think is best for each.

*I am, very respectfully,*
*Your obedient servant,*
CHARLES EWING,
COMMISSIONER.[8]

The struggles, the appeals to Washington both by the missionaries and the Indians themselves are too many to be recorded here. Appeals of Catholic Bishops were ignored, appeals of Catholic Indians for Catholic agencies were denied, missionaries' hands in many instances were tied. All of this had led Catholic authorities to realize the necessity of having a Catholic Indian commissioner in Washington to protect Catholic interests. Thus it was that Charles Ewing, January 2, 1874, was appointed Catholic Commissioner of Indian Affairs by Archbishop Bayley of Baltimore, who had made the appointment at the request of those Bishops who had Indians in their diocese. Outstanding Catholic, brilliant lawyer and Army man that he was, he fulfilled that office well. Later the same year, Reverend J. Brouillet, Vicar General of the Diocese of Nesqually, Washington Territory, was named to assist him. In 1879 the Bureau of Catholic Indian Missions was established. Two years later it was officially incorporated under the U.S. Incorporation Laws.[9]

At the time of this interview with Katharine Drexel, Father Stephan was the Director of the Bureau. The Contract School System was in effect whereby assistance for support and tuition of Indian students was supplied by the Government to organizations furnishing schools and teachers. The hope and dream of these two visiting missionaries was to have schools built in which young Catholic Indians could be strengthened in their faith. At the long end of the failure of the Peace Policy, these intrepid missionaries would forge ahead to save the countless souls caught in the shambles of the shattered program. Some historians give the year of this interview with Katharine Drexel, 1885, as the end of the Policy, but its death knell had really been rung in 1882.[10] Battered by bitter recrimination, sectarianism, favoritism, denial of basic rights to the Indians, it had dragged on till 1881, the end of Hayes' administration.[11] The whole policy was shot through with holes of unfulfilled promises, and rents of contradictory pledges even during Grant's administration, but it struggled on as the discussions and disagreements deepened.

In 1879 the Society of the Friends, who it would seem had been the most generously treated in the whole arrangement, announced their resignation although they did not relinquish control for several years later. At the annual joint meeting of the Indian Commissioners and the missionary representatives in January 1881, it was quite evident that a general collapse of Protestant participation was about to take place.[12] They were offered fresh promises. The Catholic missionaries and the American Bishops, though never resigned to the arbitrary distribution of agencies, had never spoken of withdrawal. Nor did they then. Catholic effort for the Indian began with the earliest discoverers and explorers of this land. It flourished before the birth of the United States of America. It was deep seated; it was vitally part of the Church. It would go on for all souls as long as America existed. But not the Peace Policy.

On his election in 1881 Garfield had announced he was adverse to the Policy. An assassin's bullet terminated his brief tenure in office, but his Vice President, Arthur, was of the same mind. When he assumed the Presidency, among his first cabinet appointments was that of Henry M. Teller, the senator from Colorado, as Secretary of the Interior. Teller was an open advocate of congressional control over the Indian rather than the practice flowing from Grant's policy of having agents selected by religious societies. In 1882 the Methodists had sent in a name for the agency at Yakima, Washington. The new Secretary of the Interior paid no attention to the request and appointed a man of his own choosing. When objections were sent to him with reference to a violation of the Government's Peace Policy, Teller replied, "I do not know what you mean by the Peace Policy of the Government."[13] The 1882 official Governmental list of Indian Agency assignments had a new conclusive word in its title: "List of Indian Agencies *Formerly* Assigned to the Several Religious Denominations."[14] Grant's Peace Policy was dead and buried.

All the disappointments and frustrations of the lingering death of the Policy were in back of the two who had crossed the country to appeal to the Drexels for help. Nothing could dampen the zeal or weaken their enthusiasm for the Indian cause. They described the plight of the Indian, the dire poverty of many areas, the tremendous missionary opportunities for the salvation of thousands of souls if means for building and equipping schools were available. They told their tale to a more than interested listener. She gave them plenty of time and asked many questions. Katharine was appalled at the extreme poverty they described. She who had every wish fulfilled was amazed that in her native land such crying need should be the portion of its original settlers. This young woman of strong faith came to a firm determination to do what she could and all she could to hold the line of Catholic Faith among the American Indians, a line that had first been drawn by the blood of martyrs, before America was a nation.

From this point on, her benefactions and those of her sisters, too, began to flow into the Office of the Bureau of Catholic Indian Missions. In addition they began to flow in separate checks to a long stream of appeals, which in the course of all the years of her life was to find its way to her desk. By 1907 Katharine's donations and those of her sisters to Indian Missions totaled not less than $1,500,000.[15] This amount was given quietly for the erection, equipment, and salaries of Catholic Indian schools and chapels. It was the explanation of the Contract System made by Bishop Marty and Father Stephan, whereby the Government would help with the support and board of students in existing buildings staffed with teachers, that had especially appealed to Katharine's zeal and her keen business instinct which was also part of her heritage. The Contract System providing this support died in 1900, but Katharine Drexel's benefactions to the Indians would continue as long as she lived.

In a pastoral letter addressed to the clergy and laity of the Diocese of Cleveland, December 9, 1901, Bishop F. Horstmann made a stirring appeal for a diocesan, parish to parish, enrollment in a Society for the Preservation of the Faith among the Indians. In the course of the stirring pastoral, these significant facts on the Indian situation were recorded:

> "... You are all aware how the so-called contract schools for the education of Indian children came into existence; how the General Government contributed yearly a per capita sum for the support of the Indian children who were receiving their education in schools erected by the various religious denominations on Indian reservations; how in time, all these schools, except those of the Catholic Church, proved practically failures; how then an agitation began against any Government appropriations for these Catholic schools; and how all such appropriation ceased

> last year. Shall the grand work of so many years be allowed to die for want of support?
>
> All who have investigated the Catholic schools admit that the Catholic plan for the civilization of the Indians is the only practical one. It depends on us whether it shall continue. United States Commissioner Jones, in his last report, confesses that the Government schools are a failure, and that the $45,000,000 which have been thus expended have been wasted. Since 1822 the various societies of Europe, but especially the Propagation of the Faith of Lyons, have contributed to the Church here the enormous sum of over $7,000,000. And what have we Catholics done in return? What are we doing now for our dependent Indians? We number over ten millions. We should surely take care of our own, even if we do little or nothing for the conversion of the pagans of Asia, Africa, South America, and the Islands of the Pacific. As has been well said, "The work of converting the Indians is incumbent upon the whole Church in America. It should not be left to the charity of the few, but every individual should feel it a duty to bear his part in this great obligation. It would be sad, indeed, to think for a moment that the Catholics of America would fail to supply such a material help to their struggling missionaries as would enable them successfully to contend against the giant efforts which enemies of the faith are making to sow the seeds of heresy and unbelief among the Indian Catholics." We must keep up the Catholic schools. Mother Katharine Drexel, superioress of the Sisters of the Blessed Sacrament, most generously contributes $70,000 each year for the support of the Indian schools. At least $70,000 more is necessary to save the schools from destruction....[16]

By the benefactions of her life and by her personal dedication, Katharine would write a vital chapter in the preservation of the Faith of the American Indians. Surely her name must be included among those valorous Jesuits, Benedictines, and Franciscan missionaries many of whom gave their all — their martyred lives — to lead the Indian to Christ. In the course of time Katharine would give her all too. She would keep a rendezvous with the American Indians and Colored till her death. Then she would leave a long line of schools, religious centers all over the country to serve, educate, and inspire the people she loved so well. All of this was done quietly and without fanfare. Even to this day it is difficult to list all her donations. The archives of the Sisters of the Blessed Sacrament are filled with letters of appeal that came to her from many parts of this country and from places abroad. She had a quiet way of answering these. She had a keen eye for the future of mission works and the great part they would play in the preservation of the Faith of the Indians and Colored. She knew her wealth, though she gladly gave it, would never take care of all that needed to be done. She did not want it thought that her fortune was a bottomless source of income. Note her concern in this letter which she wrote in answer to Father Stephan's request for a list of money she had donated to missions in addition to that given through the Bureau of Catholic Indian Missions which he had disbursed:

> March 27, 1909
>
> Enclosed please find a list of moneys donated to Indian Missions during the year 1908. All amounts paid to the Bureau such as salary of priests at Government schools and sisters salaries which are paid through the Bureau, or any money that has been sent to you or placed to the credit of Dr. Dyer, has not been entered on this memorandum. This only shows the amounts sent directly by us to the Missions. Will you please in giving an account of the salary of priests at Government schools enter them as paid by the Bureau? I really feel that this schedule showing what we do for the Missions does harm to the work in so far that the people are less ready to help the cause. So many of the priests engaged in Colored work have this experience and they fear having it known that aid is received from us simply because the faithful think if Mother Katharine assists the Mission it is not in very great need. It is because of this that I fear having what I give published. With regard to the Government schools I think it best if you publish this assistance as coming from the Bureau....[17]

Three years later in answering a letter from Monsignor Ketcham, then director of the Bureau of Catholic Indian Missions, she makes a similar request:

> March 30, 1912
>
> I beg to enclose statement showing the assistance given by us to the Indian Missions during the year 1911. Some of the items under the heading of "Catholic Indian Bureau" are not meant for publication; the "Insurance on Indian Missions" I beg you to omit, as the publication of it might cause an avalanche of appeals for similar assistance to descend upon you.
>
> I beg, too, that the assistance we have given may appear in the name of "A friend of the Missions," and the same when sending reports to the Bishops, please do not use my name....[18]

A great desire to be hidden in God and to have Him alone know her efforts inspired her deep-seated inclination to cover up her benefactions. But she was a very practical person. Practical concern for the future upkeep of many missionary projects entered, too, into her calculations. Hers was to be an intensive apostolate for the American Indian. Her donations were sent to the Bureau of Catholic Indian Missions in large amounts. She requested that careful record be sent her of how they were spent and thus she made sure it was used for the purpose given.

This giving on her part would continue as long as she lived. She would give her fortune, she would give herself. She would give all. She would give because she loved God with a flaming love, and she loved her neighbor, particularly her Colored and Indian neighbor, as herself for the love of God.

# CHAPTER 7

# Travel Luxurious and Otherwise

The shock of her father's death just two years after the intense sufferings and painful death of her mother had a serious effect on Katharine's health. First an attack of jaundice and then severe internal trouble caused a loss of weight and a general weakening of her whole system, so much so that her sisters and others were greatly alarmed. Different doctors were consulted[1] but even a year later, and by this time her benefactions were flowing in large amounts to the Indian Missions, Katharine was far from well. The shattered health of Katharine was evidently the reason for the decision of the three sisters to make another tour of Europe. During it they planned to investigate school methods and building construction as a help to their plan for disbursing educational aid. They sailed July 31, 1861, on the *S.S. Ambria.*[2]

After some sightseeing they headed for Schwalbach with its famous baths. Lizzie wrote, "Immediately on arrival here we showed Dr. DaCosta's note of recommendation to Dr. Funkensteine, one of the resident physicians, who proved to be able to understand all Kate's symptoms in the English language and to speak the same tolerably well." They were told that the "kur" (cure) would take five weeks. While Katharine submitted to mud baths and half glasses of the Weinbrunner Spring water twice a day, the sisters had exciting excursions through the surrounding areas always followed by a faithful valet, Martin, and the faithful Johanna or Joe, as Kate called her.[3] The valet, according to her letter, annoyed Lizzie very much by always keeping a distance of twelve yards from them and never speaking unless spoken to. After all, he had been appointed to guard them and he did that well. The treatment seems to have done Katharine much good, and at the end of five weeks the three sisters with Johanna and Martin left for the various points in the European tour.

There is a very good record of this tour in a diary kept by Katharine, still intact in the Motherhouse Archives. Once the baths were taken care of, she did the tour in regal fashion stopping at the best hotels. In this diary Katharine's notes are brief and to the point. But always her scintillating style shines through, and now and then the inner reflections of her soul are poured out.

> *August 11, 1886* — Via Bonn and Konigswinter where excursions are made to Drachenfels and the Abbey of Heisterback to which we drove

three years ago with our dear Papa. (Day by day brief summary of places visited, follows.)

*September 25* — Hotel des Alpes. Bold view of Monch, Eiger Monch, Schwarz Monch. Expedition to summit. Clouds scudding through the narrow valley. It surrounds us. Desolation, absolutely nothing to be seen. We wait for ten minutes; still no view. Then for one minute the clouds are blown over the peaks, the sun shines upon the white snow on their tops. Clouds again spread around them. All is obscured. Again five minutes and again a peep of the valley. Simile of faith and hope!

*September 28* — Mass. Ascent of the Scheinege Platte. From the Alpenrose we look down on the Lutchine Valley. Falls of Staubbach and Schmadri. Houses look so small and man an atom in the great creation. Immutable mountains, man's life, the whole span like the passing of a cloud over the unchanging mountains. Human affairs immeasurably small, a field like a patch in a garment, daily comforts are beneath notice. I felt as if standing at the Day of Judgment. How have you passed *your life*? How tiny the years of man appear in face of the mountains. Man so small! Behold the Handmaid of the Lord! The Blessed Virgin realized her smallness. Why did a Creator require a handmaid? It is such an honor to serve Him! We do so by obeying Him Whom all nature tremblingly obeys forever. Him, the Creator of Nature's Great Laws. Singing of the yodel as we descend.

*September 29* — Dine in Merringen at Hotel Sauvage. Conversation after dinner at the rear of the hotel. The Falls of Reichenback dashing over the rocks, foaming white in the dark forest of pines on the mountain wall ¼ mile from us. We acknowledged that God had given us this time of repose in order to form our plans in some measure in the future so that the A.M.D.G. might not be lost sight of in the distractions of life. Thus the Aare passes through the lonely valleys of Switzerland, walled out by the Alps from all the world, previous to broadening out and becoming a blessing to the numerous villages and noisy cities through which it passes.

*September 30* — Stern realities, no beauty save the red leaf of the low huckleberry bushes. Vegetation almost disappears. Bleak rocks confusion, broken boulders, sheer mountain walls, all give evidence to some mighty Power. *Grimsel* Hospice. Lake in a desolate basin. Jagged mountains over the ravine, the Agassiz Horn. Finsternathorn seen from rocks to the right of the hospice. Aare formed to the West of hospice by the discharge of two vast glaciers. Agassiz, Desor, and Vogt spent considerable time here making their observations. Aare glacier like an apostolic man. He is melted by God's love, the Sun, which causes him to dash down the mountain side to fertilize the valleys. His novitiate is the passing through the wild, obscure mountain pass, observed by none but God's love, the Sun. Even this is often shut out from the torrent by the dreary mountain walls. The torrent dashes over the stones which oppose its downward course, directed by God's great law of gravity. It is opposed by the boulders, knocked by them into foam; but still it dashes on, on to the valleys which it fertilizes, and into the thronged cities whose population receives its life from its broad calm waters. Thus the will must be opposed, broken; but man must follow out his sublime vocation. Hotel du Rhone.

*October 1* — Four in hand we start over the Furka. Leaders break away from harness. View of the contortions of the glacier. Then the fantastic ice masses seen as we ascend the long zigzags. We descend at the Belvue and walk on the rocks at the side of the upper glacier. Superb view of the Bernese Alps in hazy glorified distant light, high in closed land, and immediately below us a desolate stoney barren valley. *Behold He cometh leaping upon the mountains, etc.* The condescension of the Incarnation never appeared to me more admirable. The contrast between the Creator of the Mighty forces of nature, and the laws which restrain them and the Verbum Caro Factum est. We saw men climbing the glacier. They seemed as small as flies.[4]

Only a few of these notes are recorded here. They are brief, just a sentence or two about the travels and scenic splendors of each day as they met them. Interspersed here and there, are definite remarks about schools they visited and arrangements they found in various places. These were included in the travel notes for future reference for the schools each of the sisters would erect.

Katharine in whose veins ran an artist's love for the beautiful, and whose soul was sensitive to the presence and power of God in the world about her, drank in the beauty of the places visited. It would seem that at each new manifestation of the power and beauty of God, she was drawn to a greater consecration of herself and her life to her Creator. She who knew the best hotels in Europe, who spoke familiarly and comprehensively of its art treasures, basilicas, monasteries, cathedrals, and concert halls, she who all her life was attended by servants, would find her desire for God so strong that she would relinquish everything else. She who had millions would give away her last cent, she would turn away from wealth, from the cultural contacts of Europe and the luxuriant ease of American society into which she had a brilliant debut. She would brave American frontiers, she would cross the frontier line and spend her life on the other side of that line, working all the time for the eradication of the line that segregated American citizens. She would walk with God in territories where missionaries to the Indians had labored and been martyred, and through fields, bayous, crowded ghettos where millions of Americans had not yet come to a full share of the American way of life. She loved God, she loved America. She wanted the American Indian and Colored to be drawn to God and to share all the privileges of life in this land of the free.

She who had everything life could offer wanted to give it all away and to give herself to God and to the service of the under-privileged of America.

Letters came regularly across the miles of the ocean from Father Stephan and priests she was helping in the Indian missions. They were long, detailed business letters. Katharine had bravely stepped into the Indian mission problem from her first contact with the two missionaries who had visited her home the year before. All during this trip while she traveled from one beauty spot to another, studied educational structures and methods, and submitted to the famous bath treatments, she kept in touch with her missionaries or rather they kept in touch with her. Father Stephan's letters were long, several times a month, reporting on the various schools she was helping, giving itemized accounts of expenses. It would seem that she was in the Indian business as something that was a natural part of her life. These amazing Drexel women with everything at their command that money could buy, set about first and seriously to disburse help and share their wealth with those in need.

In addition to this Indian mission direction and help, moving along with her prolific sightseeing, there is another element in this tour that touches the religious vocation of Katharine. The main problem with the Indian missions was the great need of priests to staff them. Some sisters were available but a sufficient number of priests to take charge could not be found. In a talk which Mother M. Katharine gave to a Catholic Students Mission Crusade Convention held in Dayton, Ohio, August 18-21, 1921, she explained how this need played an important part in one of her interviews with Pope Leo XIII. She said in part: "When I was still in my youth, God's Providence brought me in touch with three magnificent missionaries, Bishop Marty, Monsignor Stephan, and Bishop O'Connor. Bishop Marty and Monsignor Stephan told me of their personal experiences with the Indians of Dakota, and with joy I gave them the means to erect a boarding school for the Indians. Bishop O'Connor tried in vain to obtain priests to open a mission for his Arapahoe and Shoshone Indians in Wyoming. He could find sisters but no order of men. But what could sisters do without a priest? I was willing to give the means to put up the mission buildings, but without a priest to minister to the sisters and the heathens — what use?

"At this time my two then unmarried sisters and I were going on a trip to Europe. Bishop O'Connor asked me whether I would not try to find in Europe an order of priests willing to work for this Indian mission of his. I remember summoning up my courage and asking in several European monasteries, but always in vain.

'Then we went to Rome and had a private audience with Pope Leo XIII. Kneeling at his feet, my girlish fancy thought that surely God's Vicar would not refuse me. So I pleaded missionary priests for Bishop O'Connor's Indians. To my astonishment His Holiness responded, 'Why not, my child, yourself become a missionary?' In reply I said, 'Because, Holy Father, sisters can be had for missions, but no priests."[5]

This was all that Mother M. Katharine had to say about the interview in this address, but years later she explained to this writer that after this conversation she was suddenly sick all over, so sick that she could not get out of the Vatican quickly enough. Once outside, she sobbed and sobbed much to her sisters' dismay. She did not know, she said, what Pope Leo meant and she was very frightened and sick.

When was this interview? There is a record of a private interview with Pope Leo XIII granted to the three sisters January 27, 1887.[6] A letter from Katharine to Miss Cassidy dated January 30th, three days later, mentions another brief audience they had that day. The letter gave no details but simply said:

> January 30, 1887
>
> All accounts of our sweet audience (27th instant) in the Throne Room at the feet of Our Holy Father, and also today's great privilege of assisting at His Holiness' own Mass followed by a little audience, all this, I say, must be crowded out by the business to be answered in your last two letters.[7]

The effects of this interview were too deep in Katharine's soul for recording in a letter.

That same year, November 20, 1887, a child from Lisieux would kneel at the feet of the Pope Leo XIII and beg the permission to enter Carmel the following year when she would be fifteen. This fourteen year old girl, Therese Martin, whom the world would later know and honor as the Little Flower, had come to Rome specifically to get help in fulfilling her vocation. There were no doubts in her mind about what God wanted her to do. She knew her vocation was to Carmel. A desire to give herself to God was so strong that she wanted to make it a reality as soon as she reached the minimum canonical age. It is not difficult to understand the opposition to her plans that arose in many quarters.

She was only a child; the Carmelite way of life is severe, especially exacting in the case of a child growing physically. Mr. Martin loving this child as he did, and dreading to lose her, though he was willing to make the sacrifice, had arranged to take Therese and Celine on a pilgrimage to Rome. The itinerary included a general public audience with Pope Leo XIII. Each visitor knelt briefly before the Sovereign Pontiff to receive his blessing. Two Noble Guards were on hand to give each pilgrim a sign to rise and pass on promptly. No one spoke. The Vicar-General of Bayeux, Father Reverony, as Therese drew near the throne, announced that he forbade anyone to address the Holy Father. Therese was stunned for that was exactly what she had intended to do. As Katharine Drexel often turned to her elder sister, Elizabeth, when she was in a quandary, and the directive and assuring answer was always forthcoming, Therese turned to her elder sister, Celine, "What shall I do?'

The answer was swift and terse, "Speak."

Speak Therese did. "Holy Father, I have a great favor to ask you." As Pope Leo bent toward her she continued, "Holy Father, in honor of your jubilee, allow me to enter the Carmel at the age of fifteen."

The Vicar-General was slightly annoyed, "Holy Father, this is a child who desires to become a Carmelite, and the superiors of the Carmel are looking into the matter."

"Well, my child," said Pope Leo, "do whatever the superiors may decide."

But Therese tried again. "Holy Father, if only you were to say 'yes', everyone else would be willing."

"Well, Child! Well, you will enter if it be God's Will!"[8]

At this point the guards literally lifted Therese from her knees. She left the audience weeping.

These two interviews are an interesting study in similarity and contrast. Both came out of the interview weeping. Both wanted to give God everything. But there the similarity ceases. Katharine was twice as old as Therese. Both her interviews in 1887 were private, and this second one following the Mass which she mentions in her letter to Miss Cassidy may have been a personal one. Katharine had no intention of speaking to the Pope about her vocation. It would never have even occurred to her to project her personal problem into such a sacred atmosphere. There was nothing personal in her question about the possible availability of priests for the Indian missions except her willingness to support them. Her own struggle about her vocation was locked in her heart in an anguish only God could penetrate.

Accordingly, when Pope Leo XIII seemed to look through her and ask smilingly: "Why not, my child, yourself become a missionary?" despite her quick almost defensive answer, her whole nature trembled and she was suddenly very sick. This was a new angle; this was not a contemplative life to which at this period she seemed inclined. What did Pope Leo mean? She did not know and the tears flowed. It was as if all the fonts of sorrow, death, loss, uncertainty opened up at once to overwhelm her.

From her chatty letters with their expressed love of the beauties of nature and her strong desire to steer clear of the vanities of life, the reader might conclude that all was calm and peaceful interiorly in her life. But held beneath the surface for a long time, was this question of how she was to consecrate her life to God. Should she follow the advice or what seems to have been the advice of Bishop O'Connor and prepare to take her place in the society and social life into which she was born? Her mother's death, as already indicated, had given her a view of life she never had before. All that money could buy was available to her mother but no earthly support could help her. It was her faith that carried Mrs. Drexel through the agony of a cancerous death, that gave her in the last moments of her life, the courage and the hope to bear her suffering at the foot of the Cross. Strong, valiant woman that she was, her only help outside the tender love and affection of her family was the grace of God crowning a life which had served Him so well.

Katharine had been her nurse; she stood by silently and in agony, unable to lessen her mother's pain. Truly she saw, as she said, the effects of original sin; she saw as she had never seen before, the vanity of all that was not God. She had always tried to give God the first place in her life; now she felt a call to give Him everything, to consecrate her life entirely to Him. But at the same time Bishop O'Connor had spoken about her taking a place in society and serving God there. Which should she do? She was confused.

This trip to Europe had more than fulfilled its purpose. Katharine's health was restored, much useful information about schools had been gathered, the high spots of Europe had been visited with a delightful two months in Spain. The Iberian Peninsula held no particular attraction for Mr. Drexel and he had not included it in their last European tour of 1883, but the Drexel girls were eager to tour Spain and spent two months visiting its leading points of attraction. From there they made their way to Rome where the two interviews with Pope Leo XIII took place. Eventually on April 19, 1887, they sailed from Queenstown on the S.S. *Etruria* for home.[9]

By this time, more and more appeals for help were coming from the desperate Indian missions, and there were repeated suggestions and repeated invitations to the Drexel sisters from Father Stephan to come out and see the condition for themselves. Finally, the three sisters decided to make the tour. This type of touring would be the exact antithesis of their travel abroad. There were no first class hotels to accommodate them, no railroads to bear them on, in many places no decent roads to follow. Leaving Philadelphia September 19, 1887, they went by train to Omaha, spent a day there buying trinkets and gifts to distribute to the Indians. September 23, they left with Bishop O'Connor by rail. Later that day the railroad travel ended and the party formed a strange caravan to cross the trackless and remote Indian reservations. Elizabeth and Louise, ardent horsewomen as they were, had brought their saddles and they raced across the prairies as if they were discovering the territory. Kate, never eager for horseback riding, drove in a carriage with Bishop O'Connor and Father Stephan. The riding was hard and rough. There were no hotels or motels along the way. In this primitive fashion, accepting rough accommodations and what food they could get, they traveled on.

It was a long, tedious, and penitential trip but it was made for the good of others and neither Kate nor her sisters counted the cost. The first mission visited was St. Francis, Rosebud Agency, South Dakota. Father Stephan had not notified the mission these distinguished visitors were coming. The mission was new, the building or part of it still under construction, and the children coming in. On top of this, the startled Sisters of St. Francis from Stella Niagara found themselves hostesses to a bishop, a priest, three society leaders and a man servant. Within a short time, however, the Sisters had everything under control with improvised beds. Here the Drexel sisters had their first live contact with real Indians and they wrote in their diaries glowing descriptions of all they saw.[10]

Their next stop was Holy Rosary Mission, Pine Bluff Agency. This, too, was a new mission still in construction stages. It was ration day when they arrived and the Sioux were coming in from all directions for supplies. It was here they were introduced to Chief Red Cloud, and presented him with a bridle and his wife with a black fringed shawl. They honored him especially by visiting his simple home and leaving a supply of sugar there. Father Stephan had explained to Red Cloud that these were his friends and they were going to supply means for the development of the mission and especially a school for the education of the children of the tribe. This made a deep impression on Red Cloud and he never forgot the debt of gratitude due, as later events would show. Here, Bishop O'Connor left them to return to Omaha. The rest of the party, like hardy pioneers of old, pressed on for more inspection of Indian settlements.[11] Where trains were available they used them, but for a great part of these unique excursions, they used horses and a carriage. The carriages used were really wagons given a better sounding name.

At their next stop, Immaculate Conception Mission, Stephan, South Dakota, they saw their first Indian dance, at least they saw a part of it. When the Indians appeared attired in war paint, bells, and a few feathers, the sisters were very uncomfortable.

"What shall we do?" Kate whispered to Elizabeth. "Shall we stay or go? This is awful."

"I am watching the sisters," replied Elizabeth. "If they stick it out, we had better stay."

But fortunately, Father Stephan had a very sore foot and he limped off. The Drexel sisters followed him.[12]

Turtle Mountain, Belcourt, North Dakota, was one of their last inspections. Here they found Mercy Sisters teaching in a school comprising eleven log cabins, rough hewn wood interior as well as exterior. From there they went on to Bethlehem Church at St. John's, three miles from the Canadian border. Truly it was a Bethlehem built of logs, mud, and hay. Despite the bitter cold weather, the sisters visited other poor chapels in a forty mile drive eastward to Rugby where they boarded a train for St. Paul.[13] After attending a Mass said for them by Father Stephan, they made a dash for an honest to goodness hotel. That evening, October 10, they left for Chicago and finally on October 12, boarded the Limited for New York. October 16 they were back at St. Michael's. Louise wrote briefly in her diary, "Pennsylvania's beauties doubly appreciated after a course of Prairie!"[14]

Katharine lost no time in engaging a firm of architects to draw up plans for the construction of boarding schools which she determined to erect for the Indians whose poverty she had witnessed and whose needs she realized. Within five years, as a result of her zeal for souls and her love of God and her neighbor, her benefactions stretched in a long line of mission schools from the great Northwest to the Mexican border. They were built among the Puyallups in Washington, the Cheyennes and Arapahoes in Wyoming, the Sioux in Dakota, the Coeur d'Alene, and Nez Perce in Idaho, the Mission Indians in California, the Chippewas in Wisconsin, the Crows and Blackfeet in Montana, the Cherokees, Comanches, and the Osages in Indian Territory and Oklahoma, and the Pueblo Indians in New Mexico.[15] Kate with her keen, orderly business instinct followed a definite procedure in all this. She paid for the land and the erection of plain, serviceable buildings. Then the grounds and the buildings were deeded to the Catholic Indian Bureau. Father Stephan obtained a contract from the Government which paid about $100.00 a year for each Indian pupil.[16]

But with the erection of schools, another need came painfully to the fore. Who would teach in the schools? Where were the additional priests to staff them? Father Stephan had even suggested the foundation of an educational center just to train teachers for the Indians. Trained teachers for the Indian missions were difficult to find as both Bishop O'Connor and Father Stephan knew from their unsuccessful efforts to meet the distressing need. Katharine knew it too, as she stormed Heaven and contacted heads of religious orders.

In the fall of 1888 Father Stephan prevailed on the three sisters to undertake another rough riding visit to a different section of the Indian Northwest; the Chippewa at Odanah, and the White Earth and Red Lake Reservations. They left St. Michael's September 17, with an existential knowledge of the hardships of the travel ahead. Bishop O'Connor and Father Stephan met them in Detroit the following day. Again Katharine rode by carriage with Bishop O'Connor and Father Stephan while her two sisters galloped ahead on horses. They took in all the details of the missions visited and made it a point to visit Indian homes and speak to the Indians.[17] The transition from the society receptions of the world in which they moved, to the bleak, stark poverty of the Indian missions was made easy for them by the charity that burned in their hearts. Where others might have selfishly turned away from this down to earth contact with raw poverty, they saw in the Indians their brothers and sisters whose souls were bought with the Blood of Christ. They wanted to help better their condition. They wanted to share their faith with them and to give the means that would make their Christian education possible. And all the while as Katharine poured money into the Indian missions, her soul was torn by her vocation dilemma.

There was no sign, however, of her worry or confusion as she was one of the four bridesmaids, and a dazzling one, at her sister Louise's wedding. January 17, 1889, Louise married Colonel Edward Morrell, a brilliant young lawyer also from a socially prominent family. Archbishop Ryan presided and Bishop O'Connor celebrated the Nuptial Mass. Shortly after the wedding breakfast at the Drexel city home, the happy pair left for a honeymoon in the South.

From the time Colonel Morrell first began to call on Louise, Katharine heard the faint peal of wedding bells and sensed another separation in the family. One day coming in from the summer house on the spacious Torresdale grounds where the two lovers had talked long together, Louise confided to Katharine that Ned and she both had the same idea; they both wanted to use their wealth to help those in need. Katharine knew then she would lose Louise, but she rejoiced at her sister's happiness in one worthy of her affection.[18] She was glad, too, that her sister knew and could follow the vocation God had given her without the torment of soul she herself was experiencing.

# CHAPTER 8
# EVOLUTION OF A VOCATION

Religious vocations never follow a set pattern. There are no two alike. Some have known all their lives, or have heard all their lives, the quiet voice of God claiming them for His own. Others late in life, have been blinded like Paul and directed to an end they had never considered before. To the Apostles the incarnate Son of God spoke quietly a simple sentence, "Come, follow Me," and these ordinary men who had not known Him, who had no intimation of the tremendous apostolate on which they would embark in following Him, rose, left their nets, and followed Him. Katharine Drexel's religious vocation, like every other religious vocation, was unique. In its origin, it bore the same stamp as all such calls — the invitation from God and the grace to respond to it. But its development was long drawn out, uncertain for years of its direction, and deep in prolonged anguish of soul for this young woman.

Everything in her actions and notes give evidence of the fact that her main desire was to be pleasing to God and to use her wealth to help others. Once she became interested in the Indians, she sought a way to help them, and also the American Colored, while still enjoying the warm companionship of her sisters and the delights of her home. Then the idea began to grow that she should dispose of her wealth, put it in the hands of those who would disburse it to the Indians and Colored, while she herself became a contemplative nun. It was Bishop O'Connor who blocked definitely and purposefully, any early decision about her vocation. If we can judge by his letters, he was first inclined to believe that her place was in the world where by her example and her charity, she could advance God's cause and be an inspiration to others.

The best way to study the evolution of this vocation is to trace its developments, its falterings, its various phases as revealed in the many letters that passed between young Katharine and Bishop O'Connor. When in 1876, he left Holmesburg to become Vicar Apostolic of Nebraska with his episcopal residence in Omaha, she was eighteen years of age, and he was her spiritual director. His direction was to continue for years through letters. Practically all Bishop O'Connor's letters to Katharine, as well as most of hers to him, are still preserved in the Generalate Archives at the Motherhouse of the Sisters of the Blessed Sacrament in Cornwells Heights, Pennsylvania. Some of Katharine's letters with intimate conscience matter were evidently destroyed by Bishop O'Connor; the rest were sent back by the Chancery Office after Bishop O'Connor's death. Because so much of this correspondence has been kept, it is possible for this generation to trace therein the development of her vocation and the directing hand of God in its fulfillment.

As already noted, it was especially after her mother's death in 1883 that this desire for religious life began to grow in her soul. And yet she was not sure. She loved God indeed, but she loved life too and all it was offering her. She was a very attractive young woman. Suitors are plentiful for millionaires' daughters. She was in a quandary. Her confessor in Philadelphia, Father McGoldrick, had suggested that she try a plan proposed by St. Ignatius when a course of action is to be determined: write out on paper all the reasons for and against the course of action. Four months after her mother's death, she sat down and very carefully in two parallel columns, wrote out her reasons for and against the religious life. The long foolscap on which she wrote it out is still preserved in the Archives of the Sisters of the Blessed Sacrament.

**MY REASONS FOR ENTERING RELIGION**

1. Jesus Christ has given His life for me. It is but just that I should give Him mine. Now in religion we offer ourselves to God in a direct manner, whereas in the married state natural motives prompt us to sacrifice self.
2. We were created to love God. In religious life we return Our Lord, love for love, by a constant voluntary sacrifice of our feelings, our inclinations, our appetites. Against all of which nature powerfully rebels but it is by conquering the flesh that the soul lives.
3. I know in truth that the love of the most perfect creature is vain in comparison with Divine Love.
4. When all shadows shall have passed away I shall rejoice if I have given in life an entire heart to God.
5. In the religious life our Last End is kept continually before the mind.
6. A higher place in Heaven is received for all eternity.
7. The attainment of perfection should be our chief employment in life. Our Lord has laid a price upon its acquirement when he says, "If thou *wilt* be perfect go sell what thou hast and give to the poor and thou shalt have treasure in Heaven and come follow Me....He that followeth Me *walketh not in darkness.*" How can I doubt that these words are true wisdom, and if true wisdom why not act upon them?

## MY OBJECTIONS TO ENTERING RELIGION

1. How could I bear separation from my family? I who have never been away from home for more than two weeks. At the end of one week I have invariably felt "homesick."
2. I hate community life. I should think it maddening to come in constant contact with many different *old maidish* dispositions. I hate never to be alone.
3. I fear that I should murmur at the commands of my Superior and return a proud spirit to her reproofs.
4. Superiors are frequently selected on account of their holiness, not for ability. I should hate to owe submission to a woman whom I felt to be stupid, and whose orders showed her thorough want of judgment.
5. In the religious life how can spiritual dryness be endured?
6. I do not know how I could bear the privations and poverty of the religious life. I have never been deprived of luxuries. When with very slight variety the same things are exacted of me day in and day out, year in and year out, I fear weariness, disgust and a want of *final* perseverance which might lead me to leave the convent. And what then!!

This analysis she sent in a letter to Bishop O'Connor.

St. Michel, May 21, 1883

As you can readily see by the bulk of this letter I have availed myself of your extremely kind permission. In presenting "my papers" for your perusal I feel that I am imposing upon time that can ill be spared from important business. And yet, I would not confide these papers to anyone else. I confess, I have come to no conclusion about my vocation in writing them; but I know that I cannot do better than submit everything to you whom God in His mercy has given me to lead me to Him and Heaven. I hope the matter of my "papers" may prove intelligible; I fear it may not.

I have made a novena to the Holy Ghost and have received the prayers of several very holy souls. After that, I have tried to lay open my heart to you. But it is a difficult matter to know ourselves, and I trust I have not been self-deceived. If my papers are all wrong, please tell me, and in what way, and I shall make as many attempts as you may require of me. If you were to tell me you thought that God called me to the married state, I should feel that a great weight were off of my mind and yet I should not in the least feel satisfied with the consequence of such a decision, namely, a low place in Heaven.... The religious life seems to me like a great, risky speculation. If it succeeds, I gain immense treasures, but if I fail I am ruined.

Please do not feel obliged, dear Father, to answer me for months, if it is not convenient for you to do so soon. I am in no hurry about the response. I think it is clearly my vocation at present, to remain an old maid. My reasons for desiring a speedy decision as to my vocation have now been removed. The gentleman who was paying me attention has proposed, and I have refused the offered heart. I have every reason to believe that it was not a very ardent one. *No one* (not even my sisters) knows of this little affair except Papa, who gave me my free choice, saying that he desired but my happiness.

If Lise and Louise knew that I was writing to you, they would certainly ask me to send their warm remembrances. I hope we shall never forget what you were and are to us in our first great sorrow. I close with a big apology for boring you with such a mass of egotistical matter....[1]

As far as her religious vocation was concerned, Bishop O'Connor did not seem to have been impressed. If she were a woman of weak desires, she might well have desisted from any further efforts. The Bishop's letter, however, sifted not only her desires but the nature of a religious vocation itself. Anyone battling with the problem: *To Be or Not To Be a Religious,* might well weigh Bishop O'Connor's words.

Omaha, Nebraska, May 26, 1883

Yours of the 21 inst., with accompanying paper is received....

Most of the reasons you give, in your paper, for and against entering the states considered, are impersonal, that is abstract and general. These are very well as far as they go, in settling one's vocation, but additional and personal reasons are necessary to decide it. The relative merits of the two states cannot be in question. It is of faith that the religious state is, beyond measure, the more perfect. It must be admitted, too, that in both, dangers and difficulties are to be encountered and overcome. One of these states is for the few, the other, for the many.

In the religious state, a young lady becomes the mystic "sponsa Christi." She gives her heart to Him, and to Him alone. If she loves others it is in Him, and for Him she does so. And loving Him with this undivided and exceptional love, she seeks to liken herself to Him as perfectly as possible, by the practice of the three virtues that were peculiarly manifested by Him, during His mortal life — poverty, chastity and obedience. If she *desires* this union with Our Lord, and is not daunted by the difficulties to be overcome in acquiring the perfection it implies, and calls for, and there is nothing in her natural disposition, and no such want of virtuous habits, as would make it imprudent in her to aspire to it, she has what is called a religious vocation....

You give positive personal reasons for not embracing the religious state. The first — the difficulty you would find in separation from your family, does not merit much consideration, as that would have to be overcome, in any case. The second — your dislike for Community life is a very serious one, and if it continues to weigh with you, you should give up all thought of religion. You would meet many perfect souls there, but some, even among superiors, who would be far from perfect. To be in constant communion with these, to be obliged to obey them, is the greatest cross of the religious life. Yet to this, all who "would be perfect," must be prepared to submit. Indeed, toleration of their faults and shortcomings, is in the Divine economy, one of the indispensable means of acquiring perfection. The same must be said of "the privations and

> poverty," and the monotony of the religious life, to which you allude. If you do not feel within you the courage, with God's help, to bear them, for the sake of Him to whom they lead, go no further in your examination. Thousands have borne such things, and have been sanctified by them, but only such as had foreseen them, and resolved, not rashly, to endure them for Our Lord.
>
> Think over what I have here said, at your leisure, and let me know what further conclusions you may come to....

Her next letter we do not have, but the Bishop's answer to it did not point out a way to the solution of her problem. By this time Kate was twenty-five years of age. She felt the decision of her life's work was long overdue, and yet Bishop O'Connor advised delay. He insisted there was no need to hurry. "Think, pray, wait," were really not much incentive to Kate who wanted the matter settled, but she gratefully received his letter. His answer shows his deep concern for this spiritual child and his sincere desire that she make no mistake in choosing, nor he in guiding her.

> Omaha, August 5, 1883
>
> God I trust, will reward the simplicity with which you have opened your heart to me, His unworthy minister, by enabling me to help you to a choice of the state of life He would have you enter. I know He must love you with a special love, and I am full of confidence that He will not allow me to mislead you....
>
> What most makes me hesitate to say that you have a vocation to religion, is the fear that you might not have the strength to endure the sacrifices it calls for. From *your* home, from *your* table, to the cell and the refectory of a nun, would be a very great change, indeed. And what makes me hesitate, in this matter, should cause you to do the same. How then, may the doubt be removed? By your continuing in the course you have already begun. One or two days in the week, come down to convent rations, and, on other days, for a time, abstain from the one dish you most relish. Dress occasionally, and especially when you see company, in the colors that least become you. These acts of self-denial, in addition to what you already do, will, I think, soon enable you to measure your strength.
>
> You are in doubt in regard to a matter of the very gravest importance to yourself individually. It is a doubt that, usually, takes time to solve. Don't be in a hurry. Think, pray, wait, and all will turn out for your peace and happiness....
>
> Give my love to all the family....

The attitude of Bishop O'Connor to Katharine's choice of a state of life does not appear to be one of severe testing of her strength and character. He, evidently, was not sure where God was calling her. He did want to help her. He himself turned to God for direction.

> Omaha, August 28, 1883
>
> Every day since the receipt of your last letter, I have made special commemoration for you at Mass. I shall continue to do so, till God's Will in your regard is made clear to you, that is, as clear as can be expected in such matters. Whatever may be the issue of your investigations, it will be no slight consolation to you, in the future, to have taken so much pains to learn the Will of your Divine Master in regard to the state of life you should embrace....

The exquisite sensitivity to Divine inspiration and the ready docility of her soul are evidenced in her answer. Incidentally, too, it is evident that both she and Bishop O'Connor had a very dim view of "convent rations."

> September 8, 1883
>
> You cannot imagine what a consolation it is for me each morning to know that Our Lord will be reminded of my soul at the Holy Sacrifice. At the same time I very much fear that I may fail to correspond with the inspirations of the Holy Ghost, with the graces bestowed upon me, and for which I shall have to render an account. God is to lead my soul on the road He wills and I wish to follow Him and obey His call. It seems to me that He calls me to "come down to the convent rations" not only on "one or two days in the week," but every day unless my doing so should attract attention.
>
> Now whether this is really the desire of the Holy Spirit, or whether it proceeds from my scrupulosity, or *a wish to show you that I have courage*, I am at loss to determine....
>
> I fear to undertake anything, no matter how small it may be unless it is in conformity with the Divine Will, because God gives me the strength necessary to perform what He prompts; but if I follow the inspirations of pride He will not support me and I shall fail. I have not yet told you that I have been receiving Holy Communion three times a week since the first of July.
>
> If you should approve of my coming down to convent rations every day, would you think it *en regle* five times a week to take soup for supper in place of tea or coffee (nun's rations) which is not procurable in anything but a wee after dinner cup at our late dinners (nun's supper time). This soup, in addition to bread (2 rolls), fruit and cheese? For more than a month I have not been able to stay at home of an afternoon oftener than two or three times a week. Lise and Louise wish to take turns with me in carriage driving and I could not, without being unamiable, refuse their desire. Would you wish me to go openly contrary to family opinions? I suppose I should not bore you about such matters, but should decide them for myself as I think best.
>
> In your last letter, dear Father, you say nothing about your own health. Is it to be inferred that Manitou air and springs have made you

> feel entirely well? When we were in Colorado we must have taken the same route as you did, by the Grand Canyon of the Arkansas to Leadville.
>
> On the third of October we sail for Europe. The cholera has destroyed the prospect of a tour in the Holy Land. Papa and sisters are all well and would send you their affectionate remembrances did they know I was writing to you....

Even on board the ocean liner, Katharine's thoughts were far removed from the luxuriant ease of an ocean crossing or the glamorous sightseeing ahead. It was an encounter with God she sought; it was life's travel to the Kingdom of Heaven in which she yearned to be more and more involved. Her keen penetrating vision saw life as a passage to eternity and everything else valuable in so far as it furthered that passage and attained its end.

> On Board the *Scythia*
>
> I have been entertaining myself on the passage, by reading of the heroines, part of whose lives are sketched in the "Annals of the Sisters of Mercy." I shall finish both volumes before we land at Liverpool, and then, are there any other procurable books which you would think beneficial to my soul? Since dear Mamma's rest in God I have felt no inclination to read novels. Perhaps I am wrong in indulging in my feelings; but when dear Mamma went to our true home, I felt life to be too serious a passage into eternity to wish to spend my odd minutes in reading of the joys of this world. I believe I am partially afraid of becoming again interested in what I have learned from experience to be so transitory. I ardently hope I shall never through all life forget the truths which struck me so forcibly by Momma's death-bed. There, I could clearly solve the problems of life. Teach me, dear Father, to make it a way to Heaven. Any one but you would think that I were morbid or sad in indulging such thoughts, and that I should not tell them to any one else.
>
> Papa, Lise and Lou wish to be remembered affectionately to you. If the good weather continues we expect to land at Liverpool on Friday evening, from there we are bound immediately to Brussels. It has been the greatest consolation to me while "on board" to think of your daily memento at Mass. If you answer me according to your accustomed kindness, please direct to Drexel Harjes & Co., 31 Boulevard Haussmann, Paris.

In his response, Bishop O'Connor extended a restraining hand on what might well terminate in over-emphasis and lack of balance. He follows this with his first definite direction on her vocation, the first conclusion at which he arrives. Evidently, he was straining for the light to guide her. God was biding His time to reveal His will.

> Omaha, October 25, 1883
>
> The lights you received at your dear Mother's deathbed, were precious graces, merited by your heroic charity to her during her long and painful illness. You will not lose sight of them. They will illumine and

cheer your path through life, and lead you to her who, most probably, obtained them for you. But, like other graces, they must be used under direction, lest they lead you too far from the path of prudence. To read a good novel occasionally will not hurt you, and may help you, so you must not consider an indulgence of this kind opposed to the high purposes you formed on the occasion referred to above.

And now, let me acquaint you with the conclusion I have reached in regard to your vocation. It is this, that you remain in the world, but make a vow of virginity for one year, to be renewed every year, with the permission of your director, till you or he thinks it well for you to omit or make it perpetual. This, I think, is what is best for you to do now, and as far as I can see, in the immediate future.

Your vocation to *religion* is not pronounced, and without a very decided vocation, one in your position should not enter it. On the other hand, your vocation to celibacy, and perhaps, to a life of celibacy, is sufficiently evident to warrant or even require you to give it a trial. Should the future make known to you that God asks of you the practice of this virtue only for a time, nothing will prevent your entering another state of life. Should you, on the other hand, feel called to remain the Sponsa Christi, to the end, you can do so, and make use of the liberty you will enjoy in the world to be of immense service to others, by deed, and by example.

Give the matter a few days consideration and fervent prayer, and if you conclude to adopt the course I have recommended, you would do well to make your first vow at the next sanctuary of the Blessed Virgin you visit after the receipt of this note. At all events, let me know what you think of my view of the matter. Should you conclude to make the vow, all that is necessary for you to do is to promise Our Lord, in any form of words, or even mentally, to practice for love of Him, till that day of the year, the holy virtue of chastity. You *need* not mention the matter even to your confessor....

Katharine's whole being rose up against this advice. But even though it contradicted her desires, she was ready to obey if this really was the will of God. Was Bishop O'Connor aware of the torture of soul of this young woman who by this time had a very definite attraction for religious life and a great desire to turn away from the world and all its pomps? She trusted Bishop O'Connor implicitly but his advice clashed with the impelling desires of her soul. She was torn apart.

Hotel Danieli, Venice, November 20, 1883

For two days after receipt of your letter I thought over all your advice and then on Sunday, November 18th, after receiving Holy Communion, I made my first vow before the Madonna of St. Mark's, a picture supposed to have been painted by St. Luke and which seems to be much venerated in Venice.

The outlook in the future to a life of perpetual celibacy *is contrary to my present inclinations to the religious life.* If, however, God calls me to remain in the world, to be exposed to its temptations, to be obliged to serve it, to remain in the world and yet not be of the world, to know how great is the beauty of God's House, and yet to have duties which constantly withdraw from it, to feel that God has given graces, which to quote your own words "*must* be used under direction lest they lead from the path of prudence" and yet to be deprived of daily direction such as those in religion receive, to be looked down upon as an old maid — if all this is for God's greater glory — I must drown inclination and say *Fiat.* Most likely I can, *with God's Grace,* do more for Him in the world.

I shall reduce myself to an hour and a half prayers each day since you think it "quite enough whilst travelling," but at the same time I am going to ask you whether there is to be *no exception* to the rule; for instance on a day on which I have to prepare for Holy Communion or confession, or at a place where there is every opportunity of having a "religious spree" such as on especial festivals and stations at Rome, or at Loretta, or Lourdes etc., etc. You are going to deprive me of a glorious contemplated "spree" at Padua and Assissium where we are going to make pilgrimages on leaving here. For of course I shall have to reduce myself to an hour and half devotion at these places as elsewhere until I hear from you....

Katharine's next letter is a classic. She lays bare her soul, her whole concept of life, her ultimate reactions to the cultural pursuits, the travel, the joys, the privileges of wealth with which she is surrounded. They were all sawdust. There was only one Reality — God and a way of life pleasing to Him.

Hotel Belle Vue, San Remo, January 27, 1884

... Do please be patient with all the egos it will be necessary to use in opening my whole heart to you. It is a very sorrowful heart because like the little girl who wept when she found that her doll was stuffed with sawdust and her drum was hollow, I, too, have made a horrifying discovery and my discovery like hers is true. I have ripped both the doll and the drum open and the fact lies *plainly* and *in all its* glaring reality before me: *All, all, all* (there is no exception) is passing away and *will* pass away. European travel brings vividly before the mind how cities have risen and fallen, and risen and fallen; and the same of empires and kingdoms and nations. And the billions and billions who lived their common every day life in these nations and kingdoms and empires and cities, where are they? The ashes of the kings and mighty of this earth are mingled with the dust of the meanest slave. The handsome sculptured sepulchers, the exquisitely finished Etruscan vases, the tombs of Egyptian mummies are *exposed in museums,* the dust of the great which these sepulchers and vases were intended to preserve is scattered to the winds unless perhaps with the exception of the mummy whose face grins from without his winding-sheet upon every idle eye who chooses to gaze within the gilded case once so reverently respected. Day succeeds day and, as Byron so beautifully expresses it, when the heavens grow red in the western sky, "The day joins *the past eternity.*" How long will the sun and moon, the stars continue to give forth light? Who can tell? Of one thing alone we are *sure.*

In God's own time – then shall come the Son of Man in great power and majesty to render to each according to his works.

The reward and punishment for these will not pass away, nor does *the* Day, Eternity, then opening before us. An *eternity* of happiness infinite, or an *eternity* of misery infinite!

The question *alone* important, the solution of which depends upon how I have spent my life, is *the state of my soul at the moment of death.* Infinite misery or infinite happiness! There is no half and half, either one or the other. And this question for me is to be decided at most in seventy years, seventy short years compared with Eternity, seventy long years of time. God grant that the time or trial and probation and exile may not last for seventy years longer. And 95 years after my death my body will be a bony, grinning skeleton like that of the deceased who lay on the bones and skulls of the Capuchin convent in Rome. On this bony arm was tied a tag with "Died 1774."

This is ripping open the doll and discovering it to be made of sawdust! A melancholy, grim, frightfully grim, disillusionizer! All is stuffed with sawdust. Nothing more so than the ballrooms of the palaces with their bright frescoed ceilings and marble floors, those who formerly danced within them now represented on the walls in laces and velvets and ermines.

And now to return to the little girl. What was the consequence of her finding out that her doll was stuffed with sawdust? She says she does not wish to play with dolls any more. Once being fully convinced that dolls are not flesh and blood she asks herself seriously what is the good fondling that which is in reality but a bag of ugly sawdust. Now, dear Father, that is my case. I am disgusted with the world. God in His mercy has opened my eyes to the fact of the *vanitas vanitatis*, and as He has made me see the vile emptiness of this earth I look to Him, the God of Love, in hope. He will not leave me to despair because of the dreariness of all the joys which cannot satisfy my heart. He is the God of Love and pitying me He will open my eyes still more and discover to me the joyful, true depths of all the things invisible. "Show Thy face and we shall be saved; let Thy voice sound in my ears. For Thy voice is sweet, and Show Thy face exceedingly beautiful."

I hope that God may place me in a state of life where I can best know Him, love Him and serve Him for Whom alone I am created. I am ambitious. I desire to become the disciple of Our Lord Jesus Christ. What am I to do *now,* what am I to do in the future? In today's meditation my text chanced to be, "Why askest thou Me, (concerning the doctrine of Jesus and His disciples) ask them who have heard what I have spoken unto them; behold they know what things I have said." And therefore, what course should I now adopt to become a disciple, please instruct me, dear Father....

One thing more in answer to your letter. I have not had "everything to tempt me to take a very different course from what I have taken." It has been altogether "the result of surrounding, controlling circumstances," viz., the mother whom God gave us. *She* plainly saw the *vanitas vanitatis*, and did not hide the fact from us. She never prevented our entering into society, in fact, encouraged it, provided us with the means of going into the world abundantly, so that our friends marvelled at the variety and elegance of our toilets. We loved her dearly, as well we might, and our family union was complete in every respect. Yet we found that if we gave our lives or even a part of them to the world we could not be in entire accord with her, for she was not "of the world." It was because we appreciated close intimacy with her that we left others for her. I do not wish you to think for a moment that Mamma ever advised us to keep from society. Indeed often I have heard her reproach herself because she had not gone more unto the world *for our sakes.* If, however, she were to devote even a part of her time to visiting, the duties which she would perform in that time must go unfulfilled.

This we plainly saw and now how we can rejoice that she spent every moment of her life in the service of God! Please do not think, however, that Mamma directly influenced me to think of becoming a nun. So far from it, that I remember her saying ever since I was a mere child, "I do hope God will not give you, my children, a religious vocation. If He does I must submit; but I shall never permit you to enter a convent until you are 25 years of age." And in her last illness when she spoke of leaving us, I used to playfully threaten her with, "You had better not go away from us, darling, or else I shall run off to a convent." And, indeed, I then felt and still feel that Mother in Heaven, I must be as near to her as possible on earth....

One addenda and then I have done. I have overdrawn the case at the end of page 3 in saying that I have no longer "*any dislike*" to being under the rule of a woman. Under the rule of some women I should love to be. There was one holy Sponsa Christi *of the world*, whom we were constantly with in Rome. I rejoiced in being in her society, and I felt happy in being led by her. But suppose that I were to be under the rule of a cranky superioress. I shall not *like* it; but don't you think Our Lord would give me the grace to bear all things provided they led to Him? And now, good-bye to self. I am sorry for occupying so much of my good Father's time. If I have been too lengthy please reprove and I shall reform next letter. You give such a delightful prospect in saying, "When I see you." We all shall be so glad to welcome you to St. Michel. We sail for Philadelphia on the 26th of April....

In the limited space here, all of this O'Connor correspondence cannot be recorded. As the letters proceed there seem to be two lines of battle drawn up, the Bishop's insistence that her place was in the world, and Katharine's ever stronger desire for a religious life. Along with this desire was a spirit of penance, a desire to offer sacrifice as a mark of her love.

Leamington, April 18, 1884

... In order to hide nothing from you I must confess that the following luxuries I promised Our Lord not to take if I obtained certain requests. These requests I obtained. The promises each bound me for a year; but as I was never sure that I had entirely abstained, I continue to dock off – Ice cream, Preserves, Cakes, Grapes, Partaking of desserts *before* they are passed. Some years ago I promised never to take candy. Lately I have practiced *not* taking wine, except for sickness. I am practicing not as a general rule to eat between meals. I usually do not take butter except when used in cooking or on toast.

As in one of your letters you kindly proposed overhauling my devotion on reaching home, I shall send you my daily list.

15 minutes Meditation
30 minutes Hearing Mass (I read the Missal)
15 minutes Rosary (5 decades)
10 minutes Other Prayers
15 minutes Office of Children of Mary

... I have reserved an important question for the last. Do you give me permission to go to Holy Communion 4 (four) times a week instead of three times? Would such a course add to my judgement and condemnation in the future life, or would the precious Body and Blood, Soul and Divinity of Jesus strengthen me still more in the difficulties of the pilgrimages? Or would a more frequent reception of the sacrament through my weakness lead to pride and vanity?

In the midst of a summer vacation, Katharine wrote again about the desire in her heart that would not be stifled, this fire of love that would not be quenched.

Long Branch, Seacliff Villa, June, 1884

We return to St. Michel on Monday, making a week's visit here.

This time last year I sat in the same room and wrote to you. I thought then that I should never pay another visit to Mrs. Childs. I expected that God would have called me from the world and unreality, that He would have called me where I could learn to know Him and make it my soul purpose in life to love Him and serve Him. Dear Father, as far as I can read my heart, I am not happy in the world. There is a void in my heart which only God can fill. And can God obtain full possession of my heart whilst I live in the world? I wish that these words of the Good Master applied to my soul, "Sell all thou hast and come, follow Me." For he that follows Christ "walketh not in darkness." Am I not now walking in the darkness? One thing alone consoles me, viz., that if my way is dark I am trying to oppose no obstacle to the rays of the "kindly light" when it is God's will to pour it down upon my soul. Then I shall see the way in which I should walk. I have gone according to your directions. I do not ask Our Lord to select my particular state in life for me. I only ask to do His Divine Will and that He will make known to me in His own good time....

After her father's death in 1885, the desire for the religious life was fired anew.

Long Branch, August, 1885

... The question then, of my state in life resolves itself, it seems to me, into this one. What can I do for God's greater glory and service? ....

I presume He wishes me to be where I can first save my own soul, secondly, to do as much good as He intends with the means Dear Papa has left me. If Our Lord wishes me to go to a convent, I should be an idiot did I not obey the call. If amongst the temptations of the world, it is His will that I should steer my course to Heaven, fiat. It is His strong grace alone which could enable me to keep out of sin in that ocean. I confess the ocean of the world is full of dangers for me, and the route to God *very indirect....*

To tell the truth, it appears to me that God calls me to a religious life. But when is it prudent for me to obey the call? Next week? This Fall? This Winter? In what religious order? Please tell me, dear Father, what I should do to save my own soul, to save as many souls as possible, to devote myself and all that I have to God and to His Church.

You know that I have a leaning to the contemplative life, but you and Father Ardia both say no to that; you know that I yearn to bring the Indians into Mother Church....

The battle went on in letters. Neither position changed. Very definitely, Bishop O'Connor's had not. In the following letter, however, he gives the state of her health as the basis of his decision. His letter must have deepened the agony on Katharine's soul – the agony of an inclination too strong to thwart, and a desire to submit to Bishop O'Connor's direction, too sincere to be passed by.

Omaha, Nebraska, August 29, 1885

The conclusion to which I have come in your case is, that your vocation is not to enter a religious order. The only order to which I could have thought of recommending you, as I more than once told you, is the Sacred Heart; but you have not the health necessary to enable you, to discharge the duties that would devolve on you as a member of society....

But, though God does not will you to a religious order, He has, I am persuaded, a special mission for you in the world. He wishes you, in my opinion, to be in the world, but not of it, and to labor there for your own salvation, and the salvation of others, just as you are now doing.... Living as you do, and as you will continue to live, you will benefit not only Christ's poor, but by your example, the rich of this world also, who after all, are the poorest of the poor. You will benefit your own relatives, and

> perhaps, be the means under God, of bringing some of them back to the faith of their fathers....

There follows a series of letters dealing with Indian missions and the aid Katharine was freely disbursing. On the surface, there appeared to be a calm in the storm. Evidently, Bishop O'Connor concluded, the question was settled and the turbulent waters were still.

> Omaha, Nebraska, March 5, 1887
>
> ... You are making bountiful provision for the most abandoned and forlorn of God's creatures on this continent. You have the means, you have the brains, you have the freedom of action necessary to do this work well. In religion, you could direct your income to this or some other good purpose, but your talents and your energies would be directed by others....
>
> You are doing more for the Indians now, than any religious, or even any religious community has ever done, or perhaps, ever could do for them in this country. Your connection with this and other charitable works has a salutary influence on ladies of the world, that would be, to a great extent lost on them, were you to become a nun....
>
> Omaha, Nebraska, April 21, 1887
>
> ... The question you will bear in mind is, not which of the two states – the religious or the secular – is the better. That was settled long ago. But in which you can give more glory to God, be of more service to your neighbor, and acquire more merit for yourself.
>
> Nor is there any question as to whether or not, you are called to be the bride of Christ. This you can be in the world as well as in religion, and that such is your vocation, I have had, for long, no doubt....
>
> Omaha, Nebraska, May 16, 1888
>
> ... I take all the responsibility for having "kept you out of convent" till now. The more I reflect on the matter, the more I am persuaded that you are where God wishes you to be at present. Should I see any certain indications of His will that you should enter religion, I shall not fail to direct your attention to them. The good work in which you are now engaged calls for all your time and your entire freedom and, as far as I can see, they give more glory to God, and do your neighbor more good, than anything you could accomplish in a religious community....

And then it happened. Katharine's desire soared to a summit. She could not submerge. She could not accept the Bishop's decision. She was more and more aware of that private intercourse between her soul and God, where even a director could not follow. The anguished yearning of her soul had reached the count-down in the firing of the rocket of her desire. Its propelling force was too strong. She disclaimed the Bishop's right to keep her from fulfilling the desire she was sure God had implanted. In this outer space, she was alone with God, and on fire with love to be entirely given to Him in the intimate consecration of the religious vows.

St. Michel, November 26, 1888

May I trouble you to read the enclosed? It was written more than two weeks ago.... The sentiments in it remain the same, and have remained the same, only I am suffering greater anxiety lest Our Lord should deprive me of a life near Him, in union with Him. My God! What can I desire better than this! "If thou wilt be perfect." *I will it.* Our Lord's words ring in my ears. How I wish to spend the rest of my life entirely given to Him by the three vows which would happily consecrate me to Jesus Christ! This night I feel a sadness out of which it is difficult to rally.

It appears to me that Our Lord gives me the right to choose the better part, and I shall try to draw as near to His Heart as possible, that He may so fill me with His love, that all the pains I may endure in the religious life may be cheerfully endured for the love of Jesus, the Lord of Love. Do not, Reverend Father, I beseech you say, "What is to become of your work?" What is to become of it when I shall give it all to Our Lord? Will Our Lord at the day of Judgment condemn me for approaching as near Him as possible by following Him, and then leaving my yearly income to be distributed among the Missions, or for the Missions in some way that I *am sure* could be devised if only Our Lord will free me from all responsibility save that of giving myself to Him? You allowed Louise to take Mr. Morrell. What about *her* income to the poor!

Are you afraid to give me to Jesus Christ? God knows how unworthy I am, and yet can He not supply my unworthiness *if* only He give me a vocation to the religious life? Then joyfully I shall run to Him. I am afraid to receive your answer to this note. It appears to me, Reverend Father, that I am not obliged to *submit* my judgment to yours, as I have been doing for two years, for I feel so sad in doing it, because the world cannot give me peace, so restless because my heart is not rested in God. Will you, Reverend Father, please pardon the rudeness of this last remark, in view of this – that I am trying to tell you the truth?

Katharine won. Bishop O'Connor's opposition ended. His capitulation was sudden and complete. He withdrew all opposition to her religious vocation in one paragraph and in a rapid transition in the next, suggested orders she should consider.

Omaha, Nebraska, November 30, 1888

Yours of the 26th is received. I had come to regard it as certain that Our Lord had chosen you for Himself, but, for reasons with which you are familiar, I inclined to think He wished you to love and serve Him as His spouse, but in society. This letter of yours, and your bearing under the long and severe tests to which I subjected you, as well as your entire restoration to health, and the many spiritual dangers that surround you, make me withdraw all opposition to your entering religion. In all that has passed between us in regard to your vocation, my only aim and anxiety have been to help you to discover God's will in the matter, and that, I

> think, is now sufficiently manifest. Something, too, which I heard, when in the East, a couple of weeks ago, of the well meant plans made by those of your own flesh and blood to entangle you and Lizzie in mere worldly alliances, confirms me in this view of the case. A vocation like any other grace, may be lost, and they who have it should not be too much exposed, or expose themselves needlessly.
>
> The only matter that, now, remains to be determined is, which order you should choose? Have you a decided preference for some one of them?....
>
> There are three orders the rules of which it would be worth your while to examine: The Sacred Heart, the Sisters of Mercy, and the Ursulines of Brown County, Ohio.... Don't be impatient. The matter to be considered is a serious one for you; so, let your motto be; *Festina Lente....*

In her answer of December 15, 1888, Katharine made it quite clear that she was not interested in entering the Ursulines or the Religious of the Sacred Heart. With no intimation at all of the full significance of her words, she wrote "I want a missionary order for the Indians and Colored people." She indicated that she admired the missionary zeal of the Franciscans of Philadelphia, and wanted to investigate their rules. Significantly, the one point she wanted to find out was if daily Communion was in keeping with the Franciscan Rule. All her life, Katharine had yearned for daily Communion.

This Banker's Daughter was always an efficient, practical business woman. Side by side, with her endeavor to settle on a religious community, was her desire to have her financial help to the Indian and Colored missions organized in an ecclesial plan that would be permanent and protective. Along with the planning was the search for the order she should join. The words Pope Leo XIII had spoken to her: "Why not, my child, yourself become a missionary?" had not conveyed to her any intimation that she was to found a community. She did not know what he meant, and her soul at the time was torn over a struggle to find God's will for her. She had no idea she was to be a great apostle to the Indian and Colored races. She wanted to get to a convent quickly, but at the same time make sure that her income would flow to the two races she yearned to help.

> 1503 Walnut Street, February 12, 1889
>
> ... Would it not be well to organize a Bureau for Colored and Indian Missions? To lay aside a fixed salary for the President, Vice President, and *all* members *necessary* for carrying on the work? Let these members live at Washington and let it be their *sole* and soul duty to attend to the affairs of the Bureau. Besides the members who shall reside in Washington, let there be two or more ecclesiastical members whose business it shall be to travel into the various missions and report the conditions of the same, the conduct of school, etc. to the Catholic Indian Bureau. Then, comes the question of the Income put at the disposal of the Bureau for the Colored and Indian Missions. I suggested that *not* my income alone; but also that received from the collection of the 2nd Sunday of Lent, be handed

> over to the Catholic Indian Bureau for distribution. The question then arises, to whom is the Catholic Bureau responsible for the proper distribution of these moneys, to whom shall the accounts be given, how shall the Bureau be prevented from investing the moneys in speculations, etc., etc., who shall investigate each year the economy and prudence of the Bureau? Father Stephan asked me this question. I said, let the accounts of the Bureau be sent annually to the Five Bishops whose representatives the Bureau shall be. Father Stephan, I believe, will think over this matter.... A question involving thought arises here. How put in written form the precise "*purpose* for which money is given?"
>
> ... And now about my own vocation. I concluded that it were best to put myself out of the Indian and Colored plans if I would judge correctly as to what is really best for the cause. God's will be done, whatever it is! I believe that it is His will that I should go to a Convent. Pray in charity to Our Lord to tell me the Order in His own good time. I confess I am very anxious to know whether I can settle all temporal matters, so as to go into a Novitiate this Spring – May 5th – when we close our home, and go abroad. I dread to go with the European party unless Our Lord really wishes me to wait until our return for entering a Novitiate. I dread to expose my vocation to the test of more world.
>
> How would it do to enter a Novitiate on May 5th and leave my income to Lise and Louise, making them trustees for the application of my income in developing the rough plans we haved formed? This will give full time for developing a mature, well-thought-out plan, a plan in which every detail could be considered. Who is to do the considering? Is the plan not sufficiently large to call for an assembly of the Bishops of at least those concerned in the Indian and Colored Missions? Is it not probable that such an assembly could devise methods which I could not think of, or Father Stephan could not think of?
>
> I fear such an assembly of Bishops would not think of the importance of the Indian. There are 7 millions of Colored people in the U.S. and only 600,000 Indians. I would have to devise some method to save these 600,000 souls so that the interests of the Colored 7 million would not prevent speedy help which these 600,000 Indians require in order to fit them for the opening of their reservations in 25 short years....

Now, at long last, it would appear Bishop O'Connor was sure not only of her vocation, but of the specific details of that vocation. The thought had come to him forcibly at Mass that Katharine should found a new order in the Church to work exclusively for the Indian and Colored. After this new and sudden inspiration, everything seemed to fit into one plan in Bishop O'Connor's mind. He lost no time in communicating this decision to Katharine.

> Omaha, Nebraska, February 16, 1889
>
> ... You have decided to become a religious. The next thing for you to determine is, whether you shall establish a new order for the Indian and Colored people, or, leaving your income for their benefit, enter an order already established, which will take more or less interest in these races. If

you establish the new order, you will need all your income, and ten times more, to make it accomplish its object partially. In this hypothesis, then, no need to talk of a committee of administration. Should you enter an order already established, take Louise's advice. Make no final disposition of your income, it would be simply folly to do so, till you shall be read to make vows. In the meantime Lizzie and Louise can administer according to your instructions.

The more I have thought of your case the more convinced I become that God has called you to establish an order for the objects above mentioned. The need for it is patent to everybody. All the help in the established orders can give, in the work, will be needed, but a strong order devoted to it exclusively is also needed. You have the means to make such an establishment. Your social position will draw to it subjects and friends without number. God has put in your heart a great love for the Indians and Negroes. He has given you a taste and capacity for the sort of business which such a foundation would bring with it. All these things point more clearly, than an inspiration or a revelation could, to your duty in the premises.

`... Reflect carefully on what I have told you, and let me know your objections to my decision of your case....

This decision of Bishop O'Connor awakened no ready response in Katharine. She had a very low opinion of herself, her talents, her virtues. She wanted to follow leaders in the spiritual path. She felt utterly deficient in the holiness essential to one who would rule religious. Katharine was a good lawyer for her cause and she pleaded it intelligently and, as she thought, convincingly.

1503 Walnut Street, February 24, 1889

I thank you for your very kind, very patient, very prompt answer to my last letter, and also for the one which preceded it, offering us hospitality at your own home, and the kind offer to accompany us to the Indian Territory. The Indian Territory for us will have to be 1503 Walnut. Lise and I thought the matter out and decided that it would be impossible folly for us to attempt one thing other than the winding up of our affairs for May 5th. And, therefore, trusting in your kindness we ask you whether it would be possible for you to come to us, in company with Father Stephan, or after Father Stephan's return. It seems to me I need a long talk with you, first, and then with him, or with both together, perhaps that is best. I am truly blind, blind as to God's Will with regard to where He wishes me, as to what I am to do with regard to my temporal affairs, etc., etc. I have only to hope in God's mercy that He will make me see the only thing I wish to see — His will — and then grace to do that with all my heart and soul and strength. Please in charity pray for me and for Lise — these two blind men of Jericho....

My reasons for not wishing, or rather for ????? questioning whether I should found an order for Indians and Colored are: 1st. I have never decided whether a life devoted to prayer and contemplation would not be more acceptable to God.... Then in Contemplative orders, daily Communion is permitted and this is not the case in active Orders.... The difference between 7 Communions each week, and 3 or 4 Communions, must be great in God's sight.

Will not those three or four Holy Communions each week in addition to the three or four Communions usual in active Orders give God the Father, Son and Holy Ghost more glory that I could possibly give were I to work and toil in the active life to save souls?

My second reason for not wishing to found an Order for Indians and Colored is that I appreciate that a founder of an Order should be animated with every virtue capable of fitting her to carry out the object of her order. If she has not the right spirit, who should have it? I know the self-sacrifice necessary in the missionary life! I know the privations, the trials, the temptations, and I ask myself, could I go through all these in a manner suitable for edifying the religious of my order? And *if* the founder were not to set an example, were to shrink from the toil and privations, where could you expect to find this example? I have seen my Sisters of St. Francis. Their spirit is my ideal of what a missionary nun should be. I know I have not the courage to put in practice the gospel as they do. Why not be taught by them and follow in their steps by following their rule *(if* I am called to an active life) rather than starting a new rule?

3rdly. Is not an old and tried order more efficient in this Indian and Colored Harvest; because in making new rules there are necessary delays and oppositions not to be met with in an approved order.

4th. Could the Indian and Colored Work not be better done by employing *all* the orders? The Orders to be employed by the Catholic Indian Bureau to which Bureau I would leave all my income....

Rt. Rev'd and dear Father, I hope Our Lord will teach me to do His Will. I see Him thirsty at the well and tired. I wish to slake His thirst, according to His Will and in the manner He wills. I wish to be a docile instrument, etc. If it be His Will for me to found an Order I shall do it. I know Our Lord wished for souls, but does He wish me to *ask* Him for them in prayer and contemplation, or does He wish me to found an order? The responsibility of such a call almost crushes me, because I am so infinitely poor in the virtues necessary. Pray for me, I beseech you, that I may know God's Will and do it....

Bishop O'Connor persisted in his decision. This time he was sure of God's Will for his spiritual child.

Omaha, Nebraska, February 28, 1889

Let me know when Fr. Stephan is to be in Phila. and it will give me great pleasure to go on for the "long talk" you desire.

I was never so quietly sure of any vocation, not even of my own, as I am about yours. If you do not establish the order in question, you will allow to pass an opportunity of doing immense service to the Church, which may not occur again.

Your objections are simply scruples.... Your love of contemplation is just sufficient to sustain you under the distractions of external occupations. No more.

Daily Communion can well and easily be made a rule of the new institute. It is simply a matter of history, that every great need that arose in the Church, called into being a new order. There are intrinsic reasons why this should have been the case. Is not the conversion and civilization of seven million Colored, and of a couple of hundred thousand Indians, a great and pressing need? The "old and tried orders" have done very little to meet it, and what they may do in the future will be, for each community *a side issue.* We will welcome their assistance but it will be far, very far from sufficient to accomplish the work that is waiting for us. We must have an order, and a strong order devoted exclusively to it, and, even then, I fear, it will be little more than half done....

An order established for the Negroes and the Indians will make a much more direct and *economical* use of your money than an Indian Bureau could.

Even as foundress you will have your faults, but God not you will do the work. He often makes use of very weak instruments. The question is not, will you be all that you should be, but does God will that you be His instrument....

I regard it as settled that you are to establish a new order, and I shall go to Philadelphia merely to arrange details. The Church has spoken to you through me, her unworthy organ, and you must hear her or take the consequences. Do you wish for a decree of a general council in this matter, or for a decision ex cathedra of the Pope? ....

To add authority to his decision, he brought Archbishop Ireland into the matter.

Omaha, Nebraska, March 16, 1889

I have just arrived home. Deo Gratias! At Chicago I met Archbishop Ireland. Anxious to hear his opinion of the new enterprise, I gave him in strict confidence, an outline of it. His face brightened up as I spoke. "Why" said he, "it is just the thing we needed. It is a great, an indispensable work. Miss Drexel is just the person to do it, and if she does not undertake it, it will remain undone." He became quite enthusiastic about the matter. I give you his opinion of it to strengthen you against any feeling of diffidence that might come over you in regard to it. I am sure there is not a bishop in the country who, if it were explained to him, would take a different view of it....

Everything in Katharine's character rose up against the idea of founding a community. For years now she had longed to enter religious life, to give herself by vow to God, to learn how to stretch herself to the uttermost capacity of love. She inclined definitely to a cloistered life where by prayer and penance she could, in giving herself entirely to God, help many souls to find their way to Heaven. But finally she bowed to this manifestation of God's will for her.

> 1503 Walnut Street, March 19,1889
>
> The Feast of St. Joseph brought me the grace to give the remainder of my life to the Indians and Colored, to enter fully and entirely into your views and those of Rev'd Stephan as to what is best for the salvation of the souls of these people.
>
> On the 30th of April, Lise said she would accompany me to the Pittsburgh House of Mercy. May I ask you to kindly drop me a line introducing me to the Superior? I wish to ask her what clothing, etc. I must bring with me. I shall not tell Uncle Anthony nor Mr. Childs of *the* "plan" until Louise's return so please keep very secret. They would have every reason to be angry did they hear the news first from strangers. From my heart we thank you for your extremely kind visit. We thoroughly appreciate it. I had a lovely retreat at home. It was only this morning that I could promise Our Lord to please Him by entering fully into your plan of founding an order. As long as I look on self, I cannot. Our Lord gives and will give me the grace always to look at Him. Please, I pray, bless your child....

The important question after her decision was to what community should she turn for her initial novitiate training. Bishop O'Connor decided the Sisters of Mercy in Pittsburgh would supply the most helpful preparation for her educational and social work among the poor. Many years before, his brother Reverend Michael O'Connor, in Rome, had translated the Mercy Rule into Latin for the foundress, Mother McAuley. Later, as Bishop of Pittsburgh, he had brought the first group of Mercy Sisters from Ireland to Pittsburgh where he guided them and helped them establish their Pittsburgh Motherhouse.[2] He had a high opinion of their spirituality and capabilities. Bishop James O'Connor, Katharine's director, shared this opinion. To Pittsburgh then, Katharine planned to go. She and Elizabeth paid a visit there in April, traveling under their mother's name, Langstroth. Only the mothers of the council knew their real identity and the purpose of their visit.[3] Both sisters liked what they saw and definite plans for Katharine's entrance were made.

Before that visit, on March 25, Katharine first revealed her plans to her Uncle Anthony and Mr. Childs, executors of her father's will. Their reactions are recorded in another letter to Bishop O'Connor.

> 1503 Walnut Street, April 6, 1889
>
> ... On the Annunciation I told Uncle Anthony and Mr. Childs of my intentions and future plans. Uncle Anthony dropped four or five tears; but he said he would not oppose anything which would contribute to my happiness. He thinks, however, that I am making the mistake of my life if I become a religious; yet he consents and so does Mr. Childs. I told them both of your plans relative to my establishing an Order for Indians and Colored. They think I can do much more good by helping the Orders

already established. I have told your plans to no one except to Uncle A. and Mr. Childs. We have agreed that it is best to tell the world nothing but this: "I am going to pass the summer with the Sisters of Mercy at Pittsburgh. If I like it there, I shall remain. Please, dear Father, if you are questioned, say nothing more than this, and please say nothing at all until I tell Louise whom I shall not inform until her return home, April 15th....

First, Katharine planned to go to Pittsburgh alone, the very day Louise, her husband, and Elizabeth sailed for Europe. Louise had planned this European trip as a continuing part of their honeymoon, and Elizabeth had not planned to go. Now, however, with Kate entering, she was alone, and the idea of being at St. Michel without either sister seemed, at this point, unbearable. She decided to join Louise and Colonel Morrell in this European tour. The sisters would not hear of Katharine's going unaccompanied to Pittsburgh. Louise, her husband, and Elizabeth went with her on May 6, 1889.[4] The party went directly from Pittsburgh to New York where they sailed for Europe. Uncle Anthony Drexel was on the same boat bound for Karlsbad.

That day, three heroic souls, Katharine and her two sisters, made a heroic offering to God. Family ties are intimate and sacred. They are not broken without pain. The pain in the affectionate soul of Katharine must have been intense. Even St. Theresa of Avila said her pain in leaving her home to enter the convent was like the pain of death. Whatever her emotions, Katharine controlled them. She was strong in the grace which God always gives the baptized soul for the accomplishment of His designs, and rich in the special, efficacious graces He gives to those predestined to signal service. The design into which her life was being fitted was God's, not Katharine's; the courage, strength and vision were God's, not Katharine's. Nothing now, could keep her from the total consecration of herself to God which for years she had wanted to make. Her two sisters shared in her sacrifice. She gave herself; they gave *her* to God. Two weeks later, Elizabeth wrote to a friend:

... Let me assure you that on Kate's account we feel nothing but tranquility and contentment. She went to the Convent with the ardor and joy of one, who at length after long delay, finds the desire, nay the longing of years satisfied. And should these few months' trial prove that she has not mistaken her vocation then we shall regard her choice as not alone wise and good, but one in which she will secure for herself the fullest measure possible of even human joy and peace. To say that we do not miss her and will not, is another matter....[5]

# Chapter 9

# Schooling For The Apostolate

A door had opened and closed on Katharine Drexel. As of May 7, 1889, she was a postulant just like all the other postulants in the Novitiate of the Sisters of Mercy of Pittsburgh. For her, the transition must have been a demanding experience. Everything about this religious life, except its opportunity for recollection and more intimate intercourse with God, was entirely new to her, but from the beginning she was a source of edification to others. One of her companions in the novitiate wrote about her: "The first thing that impressed me was the whole-hearted generosity with which Sister Katharine responded to every demand of her new life. With childlike simplicity she changed over from a life of luxury and ease to which she had been accustomed to the humble self-effacing life of our novitiate. Indeed, she always managed to choose for herself the most menial duties. I recall this example: When the little bell in the novitiate tinkled, calling us to the chapel, it was a regulation of the novitiate that the sewing room in which we had been recreating and mending our clothes was to be left in perfect order. Again and again I saw Sister Katharine, at the sound of that bell, jump up, run and get the pan and brush and be the one to get down on her knees and gather up the scraps that had fallen on the floor."[1]

There had never been anything strained or stilted in Sister Katharine's character. She had a natural gaiety and delightful sense of humor. She took both with her into the convent. Her novitiate companion expressed it this way: "Sister Katharine had a keen sense of humor. She used to laugh most heartily at some of our absurdities. At recreation times when the novices were in the grove out at Saint Xavier Academy, she used to teach and lead us in Indian dances. At recreation she was delightful."[2]

In her early religious life and later all through it, her religious companies would be forcibly struck by her spirit of poverty. It was evident from the beginning: "Her spirit of poverty was evidenced at recreation where we would see her scrupulously mending her clothes, darning her stockings, and once we found her mending something in her lap. We curious novices discovered she was darning the napkin she was using in the refectory, which chanced to be old and frayed on one end. In fact she wasted nothing."[3]

If Sister Katharine could have faced her new life with no other end but her own personal sanctification, her own complete dedication to her Creator, her longing to be entirely given, surrendered to God, it would not have been frightening. But despite her calm, happy exterior, her readiness to accept the most menial tasks which was quickly noted by her companion novices and postulants, alarm broke out again in her soul. One would have to understand Katharine Drexel's temperament, her reticence, her very low opinion of her virtues and her abilities, to sound the depths of the isolation and hesitation surrounding her first days in the novitiate.

She was sincerely determined to be submissive to superiors, to the inspiration of God and the direction of Bishop O'Connor, but she shrank again from the idea of being a Foundress. Just six days after entrance, she opened up the whole question which Bishop O'Connor was so sure he had settled. Not only does the following letter evidence the struggle within her, it also records the intimation she had of the share of Calvary which would be hers as a Foundress of a new order:

> Convent of Mercy, Pittsburgh, May 12, 1889
>
> Yes, dear Father, I have reached this Harbor of Peace! I have read with deep appreciation your two letters of May 8th. You are always extremely kind and full of fatherly thought for this child of yours. May God bless you for it! I know you are anxious to learn how we all bore the good-bye on May 7th. Did I tell you that my two sisters and brother decided to travel to Pittsburgh with me? We parted in the early morning at the train in which they left for New York. The prayers that so many in charity offered for us were heard and we scarcely shed a tear. God will certainly bless these sisters of mine, especially the one that is left *one!* I am indeed grateful to you for your telegram giving them your blessing for the voyage.
>
> I trust those I love feel as comforted as I. This convent life is full of joy for me, and I am taking a most unmortified satisfaction in this respite from responsibility, which brings me peace. There is one thought, however, which causes me uneasiness. It is the thought of why I am here, viz., to prepare me for a future life of responsibility, and what is more, a life which is most apt to be one of opposition, trial, and subjection to criticism, even of the Church. Then, to have the very salvation of so many hang, as it were, upon my instrumentality! The undertaking you propose, Reverend Father, seems enormous, and I shall freely acknowledge that my heart goes down in sorrow when I think of it. To be the head of a new order! New orders always, I think, have to pass through the baptism of the cross!
>
> All these dismal thoughts are *not* generous to Our Lord, and in chapel and meditation I am striving to overcome this selfishness and self seeking, and to look upon the future life you propose for me with cheerfulness, since you say it is the will of Our Lord. But are you *sure* it is God's will for me to establish a new order when there are so many orders fitted for the purpose, which by adding a vow, made by each sister to devote herself to Indians and Colored, could effect the same good?
>
> You ask, Reverend Father, for permission to invite two young ladies to join *your* Indian and Colored Order, or rather to propose their entering the novitiate for that purpose. Do, Reverend Father, *as you think best,*

> and may the will of God be done! Eternity will be too short for me to regret not doing the will of my Creator and my God, to whom I wish every part of my being and life to be as an instrument for fulfilling His divine will.
>
> Please tell me, Reverend Father, what your wishes are with regard to me. Do you wish me to think constantly of my own individual sanctification *irrespective of your future plan*, leaving that to God and to you and those you appoint? Then when I shall have obtained the religious spirit you will tell me what you wish to do? Or on the contrary, do you wish me to learn the religious spirit, continually bearing in mind that I am learning it not only for myself, but for the order you are establishing? ....[4]

Bishop O'Connor's answer was immediate and definite:

> Omaha, Nebraska, May 16, 1889
>
> I cannot consider, and I beg you not to consider for a moment, the proposed foundation an open question. I gave all this matter all the deliberation in my power, and I have never for one instant doubted that the conclusion reached was in accord with the Devine Will. The prelates and heads of religious orders to whom I have spoken on the subject agree with me, some of them enthusiastically. If you expect an angel to be sent to enlighten you in regard to this matter, you may be looking for a little too much.
>
> I am not surprised to find you dreading and shrinking somewhat from the responsibility of the undertaking. If you did not, I should feel very nervous about your success. But you must remember that the work will be God's work, and that you are to be only a weak instrument in His hands. You should distrust yourself, but can you not, in a work of charity, confide in God? ....[5]

His answer to other questions proposed by Katharine gave her definite direction on a prudent course of action then and there. It was well she had this constant and never-failing advice upon which to lean heavily. It was well, too, she had an intimation of the suffering involved. This, too, she was willing to endure if God willed it. In a private retreat she had made under the direction of Father McGoldrick before entering, she had written: "*Resolution:* I shall do the pleasure of God, cost what it may, even to *reproducing in myself each separate agony of Our Lord.* How shall I do this? I will unite myself to the Precious Blood which falls from the wounds of Jesus. The Blessed Virgin and St. John are under the Cross of Jesus; the Precious Blood falls upon them. They are faithful to Jesus because they stand under His Cross where His Blood drops upon them. I am perhaps afraid that the Blood may soil my garments. The Blood is grim, it speaks of death. When I look at myself, I stand at a distance. If I stand anywhere but under the Cross where the Blood of Jesus can fall upon me, I go away from Jesus. This Precious Blood can alone blot out my stains, alone bring me to do the Pleasure of Jesus."[6]

Despite her desire to be unnoticed and treated as an ordinary postulant, certain exceptions were made in her case. She was allowed more time to peruse spiritual books and study religious rules. She was given time also to take care of the mission correspondence and the appeals which continued to flow to her. It was hoped that eventually Louise and Elizabeth would handle this correspondence for her, but at her entrance, they were on their way to Europe. Colonel Morrell would be her able business representative later, and handle many of her affairs. Correspondence with Miss Cassidy shows that she took care of some details for the new postulant, but decisions still had to be made by Sister Katharine. Bishop O'Connor had written her that she could with a safe conscience attend to all this business till Lizzie returned from Europe.[7]

He gave her some very practical advice on the distribution of alms to those who sent repeated requests: "... There are a great many Indian and Negro Missions in this country that need assistance. All you can do for them is to give them a start, leaving it to the bishop in whose diocese they are, and to the priests in charge of them, to provide funds for their maintenance. This can come from the pensions received from the government and the alms of the faithful ....As to yourself and your good sisters, I would recommend you to give no considerable sum to any object of charity or religion which the Catholic public are able and ought to support. You have done enough already in this direction...."[8]

In the novitiate exceptions were made in the matter of food although she admitted to Bishop O'Connor that "convent rations" completely satisfied what she thought was her enormous appetite. One of her letters tells that she was given an orange before breakfast and a dish of strawberries at noon which the others did not have.[9] These exceptions, however, were short lived. As soon as Sister Katharine was aware that they were exceptions she asked to have them stopped.

There were three dominant concerns in her new religious life. First and foremost was her own growth in the perfect love of God which she desired above everything else. Second was an ever deepening knowledge and understanding of spiritual truths and principles of religious life in the Church. Her third concern had to do with the continuance of plans and disbursement of financial assistance to the Indian Missions she was already helping, and to others that continued to appeal to her for assistance. All her long life she would have a keen penetration and broad vision of the apostolic function of the Church, its responsibility, and opportunities in her day. Special graces from God must have enabled her to pursue these three ends as grace intensified the fire of love in her soul and deepened her awareness of the presence of God.

She who was to found an active community would be well grounded herself in the contemplative spirit whose overflowing renders the activity fruitful.[10]

The ease with which she passed from the realms of intimate prayer to the small practicalities of life was very evident in her novitiate days. Mother Sebastian, Superior General of the Sisters of Mercy, and Mother Inez, the Mistress of Novices, made sure that she should have practical experience in the various works of the Congregation. Accordingly, she was given a hospital assignment initiating her into hospital service. She was also introduced to the teaching of very young children. This was something very new to Sister Katharine. She had never been in a classroom. Her only experience with children had been in the Sunday School conducted by the three sisters over the years, at their country home in Torresdale. There are still extant in a notebook she kept in her novitiate, suggestions for teaching decimals, fractions, spelling, and sentence construction.[11] What a comedown for a mind as trained and rich in cultural background as hers! And yet she went at it as if it were a very important assignment, and she recorded minute suggestions for class procedure with the very young. Records show that class disciplining of small children was not exactly in her line. She had difficulties here, but nothing daunted her.

Bishop O'Connor's health began to fail in the late summer of 1889, but his letters did not seem too alarming. October 18, 1889, he wrote Sister Katharine that fifteen delegates from Nebraska would go to Baltimore in November for the centenary celebration of the Foundation of the American Hierarchy. He would be among them and would go to Pittsburgh to assist at her reception scheduled for that month.[12] He must have been torn between the knowledge of the seriousness of his illness and his desire to give his spiritual daughter every possible help.

In the spiritual order, she seemed to have two major problems. The first had to do with the sense of her insufficiency to be the foundress of an order. She continued to shrink from that idea. The second rose from her very clear penetration of the essence of religious poverty. This one point of religious discipline seems to have made more than an ordinary impression on this Banker's Daughter. Throughout her many letters before and after her entrance, she quotes often the unalterable statement of Our Lord: "If thou wilt be perfect, go sell what thou hast, and give to the poor, and thou shalt have treasure in heaven; and come, follow Me" (Matt. 20, 21). She wanted to fulfill it literally. Bishop O'Connor assured her she was literally fulfilling it:

> Omaha, Nebraska, June 5, 1889
>
> ... As for yourself, you are now on the straight path to perfection. I know no more direct road to it, than by the daily practice, *under obedience*, of the spiritual and corporal works of mercy. You had already sold

> what you had, and given to the poor, and you are now following Our Lord. You know, then, what you have to expect.
>
> The highest ambition of "the girl of this period," and even of the great majority of girls, is to go on "a coon hunt" for a husband. This is all very well in its way, but what a poor pursuit it is, compared with the quest to which God has called you! You will thank Him for this grace, all through time and eternity....[13]

In her notes of the private retreat she had made under Father McGoldrick's direction in Philadelphia, in March 1889, two months before her entrance, there is this entry in her own handwriting: "Poverty of Spirit and not alone of spirit but actual abandonment, should He call, to all.... During Mass I gave back to the Eternal Father, that which God gave. I placed it in the hands of the spouse of Jesus, the Church, to hold or not to hold according to His Will. If we possess nothing, then we are not esteemed or praised. We can be humble ....I gave myself and all to Jesus meek and humble of heart, to follow Him fearlessly."[14]

Evidently after this offering, she considered her wealth as given back to God. It was as if it no longer belonged to her. Prudently, Bishop O'Connor had suggested the arrangement of a means of support for the new community:

> Omaha, Nebraska, July 20, 1889
>
> ... In regard to your funds, allow me to remind you that for some years, your community will have no regular revenue. It would then be only prudent to begin now to lay aside, say, fifty thousand dollars a year as a fund for its support. Should the time come when it will not be needed, it can easily be applied for the benefit of those to whose spiritual welfare you will devote your life....[15]

Sister Katharine thought over the suggestion but it disturbed her. She seemed to want to give everything then and there. Then to make sure that financial help would flow to the needy Colored and Indian Missions, she suggested the formation by the hierarchy of the United States of a definite organization which would disburse all funds to both races. She had specific suggestions for the formation of such an organization. She was very anxious to have *it*, and not *herself*, disbursing her wealth. She evidently wanted her new community to start out in strict poverty, whose evangelical spirit she understood so well. This understanding of the essence of poverty and the practice of it that followed, would endure all her life. It was a spirit that she left as a precious legacy to her spiritual daughters who follow today a strict interpretation of the Vow of Poverty.

> Convent of Mercy, Pittsburgh, October 28, 1889
>
> My dear Father in our Lord, my first religious cross seems to be to feel trouble of heart and soul because I do not think I am carrying out the call of God in simply devoting my life exertions and income to a new order for Indians and Colored People....I have meditated on the Flight

into Egypt and the best resolution that I feel Our Lord asks me to make is "Remain there until I tell thee." I have meditated on the Nativity and looked upon the poverty of our Lord in the stable and thought He chose this portion for Himself because poverty was the most honorable to God and the most beneficial to mankind. This thought continues with me, "If you do not attain this perfection, your poverty will not be truly voluntary, nor will it assimilate you to Jesus Christ and unite you to God." And at this my soul will insist upon disturbing me because from the very first, my call to religion seemed to be to become one of the many orders engaged in missionary work.

It makes little difference whether there be a new order for Indians and Colored; but it seems to me to make the greatest difference to have this order start out more wealthy than all the others. I cannot see that God would not be more glorified by making the new order share the fate of all the others who have showed such self-sacrifice in the work. God give us their evangelical spirit of poverty and detachment!

... Imagine an efficient Bureau and several holy men and intelligent men like Father Stephan whose business it would be to see to all the missions, to encourage the zeal of the often despondent missionary, to take up collections for them when necessary, to bind and unite orders (which would follow out, each its own rules) into one grand whole just as the United States is a union of many states. If such an organization were established it would seem to me impossible that the missions would have to *fear* the closing down of the contracts with the Government or the obliterating of their rights, nor that the *Orders* engaged in the missionary work would leave the Indians and Colored and engage in labors amongst the white communities.

Enough of this; I am sure, my Father, you have lost all patience with me. If I thought that you were my ecclesiastical superior and that the Holy Church binds me to obedience, then with all my heart and soul and mind, I shall with God's help obey you in all that the Church demands, and renounce now and forever my opinion and judgment. I do not say this may not be entirely wrong, this persisting in this idea of the union of all missionary orders by means of a Bureau. I simply say my conscience gives me no rest if I abandon this idea as it would give me no rest to entertain it for a second were I disobedient to the Holy Church in so doing.

This evening I enter an eight days' retreat. I hope in charity you will send me your blessing hoping that you will not be offended with me. Reverend Mother announced very good news to me when she told me that Bishop Phelan of his own accord invited you to give me the holy habit. I did not know how much I felt being deprived of that privilege until I felt the happiness of knowing that it was given to me. I did know and do know, however, that I am indeed blessed in having you for a sincere friend, who, thank God, always are a patient father....[16]

Bishop O'Connor's health did not improve. A serious relapse prevented his leaving Omaha. To Sister Katharine's great disappointment, her guide and director, he whose advice she was following and on whose help she was leaning, was not present for her reception. Archbishop Ryan of Philadelphia presided, Bishop Phelan of Pittsburgh, Bishop Brondel of Helena, Montana, Bishop Glorieux of Boise City, Idaho Territory, surrounded by a score of priests, were in the sanctuary.[17] No bride ever looked more beautiful than Katharine Drexel that morning of her reception, November 7, 1889, as she entered the chapel in a white wedding gown trimmed with orange blossoms. There were diamond rings on her fingers and diamonds in her necklace. Eight little girls in white satin dresses, and wearing white silk veils followed her.[18] That day, the Banker's Daughter was a regal bride, the bride of the Lord of Heaven and earth.

Those who witnessed the ceremony, Sisters of Mercy, her close relatives and friends, must have had long deep thoughts as they watched Katharine leave the chapel in the glory of her bridal array, and return shortly after in the habit and white veil of a sister. There were many reactions, many exclamations, many newspaper items about the event. Probably the best summation of the whole ceremony was made by Archbishop Ryan when, a few days after the reception, he addressed the assembled bishops at the Baltimore Centenary:

> "I believe that in the last century we could have done more for the Colored People of the South and the Indian tribes. I am not unmindful of the zeal, with limited resources for its exercise, of the Southern Bishops, nor the great self-sacrifice of Indian missionaries, who, in the spirit of primitive Christianity gave their lives for the noble, but unjustly treated Indians. But as I believe that Negro slavery and the unjust treatment of the Indians are the two great blots upon American civilization, so do I fear that in the Church, also, the most reasonable cause for regret in the past century is the fact that more could have been done for these dependent classes. Let us now come in the name of God and resolve to make reparation for these shortcomings of the past.
>
> On the threshold of the new century, I lately beheld a scene prophetic of this reparation. On Thursday last, in the quiet Convent chapel of the Sisters of Mercy in Pittsburgh, I could well imagine along each side of that chapel the representatives of the different races. On one side the Indians and Colored, on the other the White race that oppressed both. They, the oppressors and oppressed, gazed on each other with little feelings of fraternal love. And then I saw coming out from the ranks of the White race, a fair young virgin. Approaching midway between the contending lines, she knelt before the illumined altar of the God of all the races of men, and offered her great fortune, her life, her love, her hopes, that until the grave shall receive her, all she possesses now or shall possess in the future, may belong to God and to the Indian and Colored races. She hopes that other Christian maidens may unite with her and thus inaugurate the great work of reparation, and help to render it perpetual."[19]

A week after her reception, the new novice received word that her cherished sister, Elizabeth, was engaged to Walter George Smith, a prominent Philadelphia lawyer and an outstanding Catholic layman. Sister Katharine was delighted and very grateful to God that her sister would no longer be alone.[20]

From the correspondence passing between Bishop O'Connor and the new novice it is evident that he planned to go East as soon as he could travel and visit her. All of her questions could not be answered in letters. But the doctors changed that. On November 22, 1889, he wrote that his physicians canceled any idea of an Eastern trip because of the cold, variable climate there, and had urged him to spend the winter somewhere on the Gulf of Mexico. Four days later he left Omaha with the Reverend A. M. Colaneri for St. Louis and then on to the South. The Very Reverend William Choka was appointed administrator during his absence.[21]

He left St. Louis the evening of November 29 and sailed down the Mississippi to New Orleans. From there he went to Mobile. In a letter written there to Sister Katharine on December 21, there was an ominous sentence: "I had improved considerably this week, up to Thursday morning, but then took a turn for the worse, which may have a serious termination...."[22]

It cannot be that God's salvific work has any other source than Calvary. This direction to Calvary, this flow of strength from its source, is characteristic of every great spiritual endeavor. Katharine's progress and the progress of her community could not escape its experience. She understood the portion of Calvary through which her Father in God, Bishop O'Connor, was then passing.

> Convent of Mercy, January 6, 1890
>
> Your letter of January 3rd has made me participate by sympathy with your sufferings. Are these not the hardest and most difficult paths leading to the Divine Will, originating in the Divine Will? Pain brings so many anguishes of body and soul and will with it. If it were in any way agreeable to us it would not be the Cross on which Our Lord hung. Honestly, I shudder at the thought of Calvary. The total extinction and immolation of every faculty of soul and body, and then the grandeur of the eye of the soul, looking above its agony to the pleasure of the Heavenly Father. "The pleasure of the Heavenly Father!" This was also the star which three Wise Men followed and which led them to Bethlehem, and there they found Jesus. I pray, Right Reverend Father, that He may be yours entirely and then no fear, you are strong enough to do all things, to suffer all things.
>
> I can only resign myself to your pains by looking with the eyes of my soul upon the Sacred Heart who has sent you the trials in love. What frightful mystery it is that such things are proofs of His charity. It is very easy, *comparatively* speaking, to see this *on the surface* when one feels as well as I; but in practice is there anything harder than suffering, or anything that can be more meritorious? I wish I could be the means of

> bringing you some consolation. Can I do anything for you, my Right Reverend Father? Please tell me. I beg you not to worry about business. I should have had better sense than to have bothered you when you are unwell. Mother Sebastian tells me she is going to invite you to the hospital here. I sympathize as she does with your desire of being home, if the physician approves....[23]

The darkness and the pain of Calvary deepened around Bishop O'Connor as his answer seemed to indicate:

> Spring Hill, Alabama, Jan. 9 1890
>
> My physician does not approve of my returning North at this season. We leave tonight for St. Augustine. My address there, for the present will be care of Bishop Moore. We were to have left last night, and I was unable to begin the journey.
>
> Depression of spirits is said to be a necessary effect of dyspepsia. I know it to my cost. I feel crushed and forsaken. Faith alone sustains me. Pray that its support be not withdrawn from me....[24]

Sister Katharine's next letter was in a lighter mood. Evidently, she wanted to cheer him up. To that end, she recorded the humorous details of her first attempts at teaching:

> Convent of Mercy, January 14, 1890
>
> ... Yesterday at the Colored school, I replaced one of the sisters who has la grippe. On this occasion things prospered for me so much better than they did when I first taught there as a postulant. Did I tell you how on that occasion, this poor teacher was almost bereft of her senses? A certain little dark one had a whistle. He was a bright little fellow and he seized upon the situation. At a glance, he took in that the postulant knew little about modern methods of primary teaching. He thought it worth while to try her metal by fixing that metal (that tiny piece of tin) in the interior of his large mouth and giving a loud shrill blast. There was something in the horror stricken expression of the teacher that told him she was a regular "tender foot."
>
> The whistle was a signal for general fun among five or six fellows ready for sport. Another whistle shrill and sharp on the other side of the room warned the teacher to go for a rattan. She held it over offender No. 1. "Hold out your hand, sir." He would *not* hold out his hand. Far from it, he folded them firmly, and before the teacher's very face! The whistle being safe within that mouth of his, he let off another whistle.
>
> Then, whistle No. 2 tuned up, and several other urchins indulged in a race around the room, one calling out: "You don't know how to teach. I'll teach you!" And off went two coats and sleeves up, to commence a fist fight among themselves as a side show!
>
> I had seen Sister Loyola controlling her young ones by sitting at the desk and looking a mild rebuke on the assembled pupils, and issuing her reproach slowly and patiently. I did not know how to use the rattan when

> the offenders obstinately refused to put out their hands. I would try Sister Loyola's method.
>
> I took the seat and glared over my eye glasses at them. "Children! No more lessons until there is perfect silence in this room!" Again "a look" which I tried to make like Sister Loyola's. There was a second's silence; but only a second. All the entire class with one accord burst into a hymn rendered at the top of their lungs. This brought Sister Emerentia from the opposite room. She showed me how to restore order, as well as to insure safety in the fireplace where a scoundrel had kindled a rousing fire, while I had been occupied in another disorder.
>
> It was very different yesterday. The children are very interesting. I think, however, hospital work is more improving for me just now.
>
> The good wishes of all the community are yours, Right Reverend Father, and their desire to offer you consolations. They pray that God who alone can do this may be your support and refuge in the trials you are passing through....[25]

The public announcement of the fact that Katharine Drexel was establishing a new Religious Congregation was not made until after her reception. In a letter in which she had written to Bishop O'Connor August 15, 1889, she had stated that she felt the explanation would be due at her reception and if made before, the public might tire of the subject. She mentioned, too, that Reverend Mother Sebastian thought it would be better to have her habited in the dress of the novice before the arrival of postulants.[26] After her reception, without any personal effort on her part, questions about the new order began to come in, and gradually in the course of her novitiate, and after a study of suitability and recommendation, others were accepted to be part of the new community. By the time she would leave the Mercy Novitiate as a professed religious and the first superior of the new congregation, there would be thirteen to accompany her to their new Motherhouse. No distinction was ever made between the different sets of novices and postulants. They were one novitiate family. Sister M. Katharine made no attempt to draw those for her community around her or to give them any direction. She knew that right then, *she* was learning how to tread the paths of holiness.

The determination to aim at perfect love and the perfect giving of herself deepened in her heart and soul. Under the date of December 28, 1889, when she entered a three day retreat, she made this notation in her notebook: "I would be afraid to die because I am naked before God who knows the graces He has given me. I know I shall have to give an account for faith, education, fortune, Sacraments. Point out one Saint in Heaven who has had more aids than I have had."[27] At the end of that retreat she wrote out: "*Fruits of Retreat, Eve of Circumcision*: To please Our Lord at every minute, to be holy as Jesus is holy. This will please Him for He said, 'I am the Way'. Jesus came to do the will of His Father. Have this Divine model of Jesus always before your eyes and continually unite your soul to the soul of Jesus. Jesus is the means of reaching

Jesus. Therefore, on the first of the year, 1890, through the Precious Blood, by the Precious Blood, I leave myself. I give God my nothing and my sins."[28]

She had work to do but she knew that first of all she herself had to be fitted and formed to be the humble instrument in God's hand. She was totally unaware of any advance she may have made in the spiritual life; she sought only to serve God and her neighbor. Her neighbors, the sisters in the novitiate, were the recipients of her many acts of kindness. Mother Inez, the Mistress of Novices, remarked that at the beginning of her novitiate she was far more fervent and advanced in virtue than many who had been long years in religion. To one of the pupils of the Sisters of Mercy who was contemplating joining the new community, Mother M. Inez said, "I have eighty in my novitiate and none can approach, much less equal, Sister M. Katharine in humility."[29]

Day by day, Katharine seemed to sink deeper into this serious business of opening her soul to the sanctifying power of God's grace. Her sister Lizzie's marriage to Walter George Smith, January 7, 1890, at St. Dominic's Church in Holmesburg, near their country home, was a cause of joy and thanksgiving to her.[30] Glowing accounts of the wedding at which Archbishop Ryan officiated, reached her. She rejoiced at her beloved sister's happiness and the goodness of God in directing her choice. The newlyweds took a short trip to New York City, then Buffalo, Niagara Falls and Pittsburgh. After a day in Philadelphia, they left for an extended tour of Europe.[31]

The news of Bishop O'Connor continued to be ominous. A letter of January 27 had very discouraging word. Two days later, Mother Sebastian and Sister Katharine left for St. Augustine, Florida, to see if the very sick Bishop could be brought to the Mercy Hospital in Pittsburgh. On the physician's advice after two weeks, it was decided to bring him North. Sister Katharine was sent to the hospital to help, and was given charge of his medicine and trays.[32] The Bishop did not speak much but his silent endurance of suffering was in itself a course of spirituality. Writing to her sister Louise, Elizabeth had this to say, "I am glad that Kate went to Bishop O'Connor, glad that she should have such words of counsel as he may be able to give. Heaven will not desert our sister, even if it keeps down her beacon. Were it not for this faith and trust, Bishop O'Connor's critical condition would cause me to fear for her as well as sorrow for him. She is all right."[33]

In the midst of the novice's concern for her spiritual father, very distressing news soon reached her from abroad. Her sister, Elizabeth, was stricken seriously ill in Florence, so ill that the last Sacraments were administered. It was a strange intervention in a honeymoon, and alarm rose in the affectionate heart of Sister Katharine. She was very much relieved when after six weeks, her sister was reported restored to health and continuing her journey. A special nurse, a nun of the nursing sisterhood of the Little Company of Mary, was assigned to travel with her and accompany her back to America.[34] This was a great relief to her two sisters. Shortly after, came the glad news that Elizabeth was expecting a child. The deep faith of Elizabeth is noted in a sentence in one of her letters from Europe, "My pious and good little religious sister, Katharine, we count on your prayer to bring ours safely to the waters of Baptism and beyond them through a good and useful life to Heaven."[35]

There was no improvement in Bishop O'Connor's condition and he felt his end was near. He wanted to die in his own diocese. Accordingly, April 16, 1890, with his doctor, Dr. Coffman of Omaha; his secretary, Father Colaneri, and a nurse, he undertook the strain of travel to his Episcopal residence in Omaha, with perfect resignation to the will of God. If he preached obedience to the Will of God during his life, he gave a striking and living example of it in this last illness. He gave up his soul to God May 27, 1890.

The bottom fell out of Sister Katharine's world. Tidal waves of isolation, distress, and anguish broke over her. This time Bishop O'Connor was not there to allay them. Only at his direction had she consented to undertake a foundation for which she felt completely inadequate. For the acceptance of candidates, for the writing of a Rule, for working out the whole plan, she had counted on his direction and assistance. Now she was alone. All her old fears crept back, and her soul was flooded not only by the grief of her loss, but a sense of the futility and inadequacy of any efforts she might make. She may well have concluded his death indicated the whole project was not God's will. She felt she could not go on.

This favored child of God and daughter of the Church was to receive special encouragement from many bishops in the Church as long as she lived. At her death many years later, they would rise up and call her blessed. At this point the Archbishop of Philadelphia, Archbishop Ryan, intimate friend of Bishop O'Connor, came in his friends place to help her. Realizing what this loss would mean to her, Archbishop Ryan lost no time in getting in touch with her.

> May 29, 1890
>
> ... I write a word of sympathy to you on the loss of your kind father and my good friend, Bishop O'Connor.
>
> The memory of his virtue is the truest source of consolation. He had a heart as tender as the most gentle woman, with a splendid intellect and a great acquired learning, but why should I wound you by recalling the greatness of your loss? He should be regarded in future as the founder of your future order.
>
> I will leave here on Monday to attend the funeral in Omaha on Wednesday and shall call to see you on my way home. I cannot say now on what day I shall be in Pittsburgh, but shall certainly call.
>
> *Your friend and father in Christ,*
> P. J. Ryan, ABP.[36]

After officiating at the Requiem Mass in Omaha, Archbishop Ryan went on to Pittsburgh. Frankly, humbly, but in evident distress, the bereaved novice told him she could not go on; she simply could not do it. The Archbishop listened with sympathetic understanding. (He, too, had lost a friend). Then he asked a simple question: "If I share the burden with you, if I help you, can you go on?"[37] Courage and hope flowed back to her troubled soul. Then and there began a spiritual relationship between her Archbishop and herself that would be intimate and fruitful in the years ahead. Archbishop Ryan was to prove truly her father in God.

Archbishop Ryan was no stranger to her. She had had many contacts with him dating from his installation August 20, 1884, when her father had taken her to the ceremonies. First they had stopped at the Episcopal residence where Bishop O'Connor had introduced them to the new Archbishop.[38] He came to know the family well. He said Mass several times at their country home. At the death of Mr. Drexel, he paid high tribute to him. Speaking at the General Quarterly Meeting of the Archdiocesan Conference of St. Vincent de Paul, he said: "Soon after my arrival here I was handed a memorandum in the handwriting of the late Archbishop Wood, which was found with his Will, to the effect that during his life he had always consulted his trusted friend, Mr. Francis A. Drexel, on the temporal affairs of his diocese and had found his advice invaluable to his administration. One of my first acts was also to consult him, as I had entire confidence in his head and heart. The power to inspire confidence is the highest factor in the success of a man like Mr. Drexel."[39]

Just a few days after her entrance, he had written her a very cordial, warm letter. After thanking her for a check for $1,200 for the local Colored Mission, he went on to say:

> How are you in your new home under the same roof as Our dear Lord? You have no idea of the good you have *already* done by taking this step. The whole city is talking about it, and the people are deeply edified. So you begin to win hearts for Him whom you love. … May God grant you holy perseverance. I feel that you will continue to love and serve Him and that now, your heart is 'at home'.
>
> *Always, dear Child, your friend and father in Christ,*[40]
> P. J. Ryan, Archbishop

In October of the same year he had written the novice that things were going well in "our" Colored Mission. He noted, too, that he had had several long conversations with Bishop O'Connor about her future plans. He advised her, however, for the present to devote herself entirely to acquiring a deep interior spirit. He warned her that the activities of the future would depend on that spirit.

Then, too, as her Archbishop, there would be certain matters of business: the location and erection of a Motherhouse, the acceptance of candidates, which she had to take up with him. On Christmas Eve, 1889, she had had a long letter from him answering her many questions. He told her that it was fitting that she should consult him before leaving to found a house in another diocese. At that time Sister Katharine was not quite sure where she wanted to establish the novitiate. Monsignor Stephan had listed four reasons why he thought it would be well to establish her novitiate at St. Boniface, Banning, California.[41] Shortly after that, he called her attention to a ninety-two acre property, three miles outside Washington, which Major Brackett's niece was willing to sell for $20,000.[42] Thus, before Bishop O'Connor's death, there had been many contacts with Archbishop Ryan — contacts of a general nature. His letters to her had always been signed, "Your friend and father in God." From now on they would be signed, "Your father in God."

With the zeal burning in her heart for the salvation of souls and charity weighing and dispersing help to them, she went confidently on cementing her union with God. Death, separation, pain, sorrow — of these this young Drexel woman had an abundant share. Was it that this future apostle of the American Negroes and Indians was being led to a complete renunciation of all, to the point where she could exclaim with St. Paul, "For I determined not to know anything among you except Jesus Christ and Him crucified"? (1 Cor. 2.2).

Elizabeth and her husband had arrived home from their European honeymoon September 7, 1890. She was not well, though she had great hopes for the child she was expecting. Then suddenly September 24 she was stricken. Sister Katharine was notified. When she reached Philadelphia September 26, Elizabeth and her child, prematurely born, were dead. Louise and Colonel Morrell were still on the ocean, homeward bound. Again Katharine's soul was plunged in grief at the loss of a dear one. The casket where Elizabeth with her dead child in her arms seemed asleep, was placed in the oratory of their former country home at St. Michael's. Kneeling there, her mind thronging with memories, the young Foundress restrained her grief and kept a valiant watch. Her mother, her father, Bishop O'Connor, and now her sister, Elizabeth, had each given her an encounter with death, intensifying her grief as each loss cut through her affectionate heart. She who was to lead others in the way of the Cross was given first of all to drink deep of the chalice herself.

Sister Katharine rose above her sorrow. Supported by grace and strengthened by the ever present assistance of Archbishop Ryan, she continued her novitiate and her earnest striving to attain the perfect love and the perfect gift of herself she so ardently desired. In late November Cardinal Gibbons, Archbishop of Baltimore, came with Archbishop Ryan to visit her and the members of the new community. He spoke to them on the need in the Church for the apostolic work to which they were dedicating themselves, "Your work is truly an apostolic one. Be apostles and carry the glad tidings of the Gospel to these neglected races, for 'beautiful are the feet that carry the Gospel to heathen lands'." He then spoke of the training of the Apostles and he likened the novitiate to the Apostolic School, over which Our Lord presided.

The annalist continues the account of this visit: "Our Father in God then spoke to us and told us of the paternal love he had for us, his Baby Community, and how he was to be Our Father in God, that our interests were to be his interests, and how he would remember Sister Katharine and all the pure young hearts who would devote themselves to this work; he would remember them every day at the altar."[43]

Unusual grace must have been given her to keep up with many demands. In addition to the training and the duties of her novitiate life, a constant stream of letters reached her from the various Indian Missions. Father Stephan wrote her long, graphic, distressing accounts from the mission situation and particularly his concern about the ending of the Contract System for the Indian Mission schools. Thomas J. Morgan, Commissioner of Indian Affairs (1889-1893) made no secret of the fact he would work to end the Contract System. His attitude in the matter was a cause of great concern to Father Stephan and Sister Katharine.

Possibly the most urgent question to be settled was the location of a Motherhouse for the new Congregation. In addition to the other suggestions made by Father Stephan, there had been another one made by Bishop Marty. As soon as he had heard of her desire, and before she entered the Novitiate of the Sisters of Mercy, he had suggested the location of the Motherhouse near Sioux Falls, South Dakota. The following letter gives evidence of his great interest in the project and his desire to be of help:

> Sioux Falls, Yankton, Dakota, April 6, 1889
>
> ... Words are unable to express the joy which I felt when three days ago I learned from Right Reverend Bishop O'Connor that on the feast of your holy patron you will leave the world to become a bride of Jesus Christ. After devoting your means to His interests, the salvation of souls, you will henceforth devote your own person and endeavor to win and lead and teach many others to join in the work. This point being reached, I consider it my privilege and my duty, to offer you my humble services in this enterprise. It will be thirty-five years next Easter Sunday since I took the same resolution and received the religious habit on the feast day of another Siennese on the 20th of May. If you place the Motherhouse of the Missionary Sisters near Sioux Falls, I will be able to render you all the services that shall be needed for their formation and success as long as God will let me live; and when I look back upon my past years, it seems to me, that they all had only been a preparation for the most important task of my life, which is now to begin. In Father Stephan we have both the best help one could wish for and in the new position, which thus would be created for him, we might keep him yet for a good number of years.
>
> My plan would be this:
>
> Whilst you are going through your novitiate, Father Stephan would build the convent and gather the little community and build St. Catherine's Chapel, in which at the close of the novitiate you would take the vows of religion and missionary work in that form, which would

suit the circumstances of the case as well as the laws and intentions of Holy Church.

I think I could at the same time or a year later start a Benedictine community of fathers and brothers by its side — a missionary college with a large farm attached to it and its Theological Department at least connected with the seminary of this diocese.

There has been a similar missionary order established in France called the Congregation of P'ayans under the Rule and in the spirit of St. Benedict and you know probably that the Colored Sisters in Baltimore are also Benedictines. The statutes of these and other similar institutions would be an acceptable help in shaping our plans and rules. Now if it is the will of God that we shall thus work together for the salvation of the Colored races, He will inspire you as I think He does me, and we doing our part, He will do His!

Whatever the decision will be, my prayers always belong to you.[44]

After considering the several sites suggested for the location of the Motherhouse and consultation with Archbishop Ryan, a spot nineteen miles outside the city of Philadelphia was finally selected. Sister Katharine had arranged for the purchase of sixty acres of land on a hill twenty-five feet above the Delaware River, running parallel to the Pennsylvania Railroad in Andalusia, later to be called Cornwells Heights, Pennsylvania. Her plans were for a series of buildings in the quaint old Spanish Mission style of New Mexico with their combined Spanish and Italian features. Early in her novitiate, Sister Katharine was permitted to go to Philadelphia to discuss plans with the architects and consult with Colonel Morrell and her uncle Anthony on business matters.[45] Later, near the end of her novitiate, she went again to inspect the progress.

It became very evident that the new Motherhouse would not be ready for occupancy at Sister Katharine's profession, which Archbishop Ryan scheduled for February 12, 1891. Archbishop Ryan made two suggestions here; first, that she should stay at the novitiate in Pittsburgh until the building was completed. He was of the opinion that the longer she stayed at the novitiate, the better for her young community. Then again he suggested that she rent a house in the Colored section of Philadelphia in the area of the school she was supporting there, St. Peter Claver's, and supervise the building from there.[46]

Even as Sister Katharine went into retreat for her Profession Day, a devastating crisis occurred in the Indian territory. A Sioux uprising near Pine Ridge Reservation led to the terrible days of the Wounded Knee Massacre. Holy Rosary Mission which she had built on the Pine Ridge Reservation thus became a cause of painful concern, particularly for the welfare of the Franciscan Sisters teaching there and Father Jutz, S.J., the intrepid missionary in charge. Only God could estimate the effect of this whole bloody affair on the young Foundress preparing in the silence of retreat to dedicate her life by vow to the service of the Indian and Colored races. The title of the new community had been decided on by Archbishop Ryan. "Sisters of the Blessed Sacrament" had been Sister Katharine's choice; for complete identification, the Archbishop had suggested the addition of the two races.[47]

The Foundress of the Sisters of the Blessed Sacrament for Indians and Colored People stormed Heaven for the protection of the missionaries, and went bravely and prayerfully on to complete the offering of herself and all she had for the salvation of souls. In her three day retreat ending January 1, 1891, she recorded some of her desires, and her anguish: "Union with God alone gives *life* and abundance of life. I ask a gift of the Infant Jesus, kneeling before and depending upon my Mother and His. Let me act on this knowledge to God's glory. Fill me with Thy life that I may understand Thee, O Light, the only Light! No creature gives light. *We are not* sufficient in ourselves. My God! How often I have experienced this! Each cross of death, of anxiety ... proving this truth. My soul cries to my Mother to tell her Babe — I am not sufficient in myself. My Mother, pray to Jesus that I may understand and not live as I constantly do as if I were sufficient in myself. When I feel want of help — that aching void and weakness — then, my Mother, obtain for thy child a grace, viz., *Not* to go to creatures to supply my want of life. Their life will decay. They have no life except from Jesus. My superior be he who he may, will point out to me how to unite myself with God."[48]

Such were Sister Katharine's sentiments, with full knowledge of the bloody massacres so near the mission she had built and named in honor of her mother — Holy Rosary. As far back as her recollections of childhood went, she recalled her mother leading the family rosary. The mission was saved when everything else in the area was destroyed. Mother M. Kostka, superior of the mission school, wrote a long letter expressing gratitude to God for His protection. The details had been gory:

> The poor wild, fearful, enraged Indians kept in their hostile lodge, only a quarter of an hour's ride distant from the mission, for almost three weeks. No man, woman or child was to be seen, and all was as still as death. Yet everyone who approached the lodge in civilized dress was shot down. Every sunset the sky was dark with smoke from burning houses. Wherever one looked was fire, and nobody was in sight.[49]

The sisters had been given an opportunity to leave the Mission, but one and all they had decided to stay at their post. Father Stephan had hurried from Washington as soon as the news of the uprising broke to remove the Sisters to safety, but they stayed, and according to Mother M. Kostka's letter, prepared every night for death, resting fully dressed in case their home, too, was set on fire. Prayer and the intervention of Chief Red Cloud, wrote Mother M. Kostka, had saved the Mission and their lives:

> I would like to publish it from the highest mountain that PRAYER and only prayer saved our very dear Mission and all the inmates from harm and injury, by the enraged savages, burning, killing, stealing all

> and everything in the vicinity. Just today we learned from an interview with Chief Red Cloud that those cruel young warriors who set the Government Schools on fire wanted and intended with all force to destroy our Mission and kill us too, but Red Cloud used all his influence to convince them that the Blackrobes always acted kindly toward the Indians.
>
> At this exhortation some of the other Chiefs joined him and said to the young warriors that if they, in spite of Red Cloud's interdiction, harmed the Mission or missionaries, Red Cloud and his tribe would go over to the soldiers and fight against their own nation. As often as we are told of such evidence of protection we repeat with new confidence from the depths of our hearts, "In Te Domine speravi, non confundar in aeternam!"[50]

Red Cloud remembered the three gracious women who had braved the inconveniences of the area, visited the Reservation, made a special visit to his home, and promised to erect a school. They had fulfilled that promise and provided for the education of the children. In the day of the greatest danger to the Mission, he remembered and rose up to prevent its destruction. Thus, at the very beginning of her life as Foundress of a new community in the Church, whose life began with her profession, February 12 1891, she was to have this existential knowledge of a gratitude that would go on deepening in the hearts of the Indian and Colored as long as she lived. It would continue to deepen after her death.

# Chapter 10
# Birth Of A Congregation

February 12, 1891, Katharine Drexel made her profession as the first Sister of the Blessed Sacrament for Indians and Colored People. Bishop Phelan of Pittsburgh celebrated the Mass while Archbishop Ryan received her vows and invested her with the black veil. For the first time she put on the new habit of the Sisters of the Blessed Sacrament differing in many details from that worn by the Sisters of Mercy. In a clear, determined voice, resounding throughout the Motherhouse Chapel of the Sisters of Mercy, the Banker's Daughter vowed herself to God for a period of five years. To the usual vows of poverty, chastity, and obedience she added another: "To be the mother and servant of the Indian and Negro races according to the rule of the Sisters of the Blessed Sacrament; and not to undertake any work which would lead to the neglect or abandonment of the Indian and Colored races."[1]

There were only a few friends at the ceremony as Sister Katharine had no desire for a large attendance and had evidently invited only a few. Archbishop Ryan wrote her January 13, 1891, that he thought she had done well to invite those she had mentioned and then added, "It was hardly polite to tell some not to come. However, they will understand your motive, and will probably go."[2]

The Archbishop had very carefully thought out the form of her vows and specifically her Vow of Poverty. Sister Katharine thought carefully about it too. In a letter of January 6, 1891,[3] he told her very definitely there was no necessity for any form of renunciation and he repeated the statement in another letter, "I do not think any paper is necessary to sign a renunciation of the possessions."[4] It would look as if in her desire to give everything to God, she was anxious to sign it all away on a dotted line. The Archbishop spelled out for her his decision in this matter:

> You retain the possession and the administration, but have to promise *in case of my requiring it*, that you would renounce your possessions. This does not, of course, oblige by law, but from Father Villiger's statement, it appears necessary for a Vow of Poverty. You do not need fixed rules from me as to the mode of administration, for it will remain in your hands. When a general permission is given you need have no scruples about details.[5]

Another note was added the following week: "I think you had better vow to be a member of the new order and I will appoint you Mother for five years."[6] It was well Sister Katharine had a very obedient spirit for she was certainly sailing out into uncharted seas as far as her future was concerned. Her actual relation to her property was clarified in a letter of February 28, 1891:

> As to the mode of holding the property, this should be only until the Motherhouse is completed and you have entered it. *Afterwards,* the property should be in the name of yourself and a few of the sisters, as in the case of the Good Shepherd and other institutions. But there is time enough for this consideration.[7]

After the profession, there was a great note of expectancy among the pioneer members of this new community in the Church. "Where next?" was in everyone's mind. The ground at Andalusia, Pennsylvania, had been purchased, but building operations were still in the planning stage. Two possibilities loomed up: to remain with the sisters of Mercy or to arrange a temporary novitiate in the Drexel country home at Torresdale, unoccupied since the death of Elizabeth. It was the Archbishop who decided on the latter course and set July 1 as the opening date.[8] Mother M. Katharine went on with another sister to make arrangements and get things in order. She was followed shortly by Mother Inez whom the Sisters of Mercy agreed to lend to the new Community as their Mistress of Novices for a period of one year.[9]

Before any other sisters arrived, however, the first distinguished visitor reached Torresdale — Archbishop Janssens of New Orleans.[10] Several months before, he had contacted Mother Katharine about the Colored in New Orleans whom he greatly desired to help.[11] There would follow a long series of friendly and apostolic relations between the Archbishop and the Foundress. For those who want to plumb the record, the evidence is there to show that this shepherd of a diocese in deep financial straits[12] was greatly concerned about the spiritual welfare of the Colored in his flock. This mutual interest was a long and deep bond between him and Mother Katharine who responded generously to his appeals. Her donations flowed through him to the Colored in his Archdiocese from 1891 till his death in 1897.[13]

St. Michael's was an ideal location for a new novitiate. The dream garden Mr. Drexel had planted for his family, the sloping lawns, the variety of flowering trees, all contributed to an atmosphere of quiet beauty in which inner wells of spirituality could be sunk deep. They were a happy, eager group, ten novices and three postulants. Community prayers, classes, laundering, preserving, cooking, the religious instruction of some old Colored women in the area, together with delightful recreations in the beautiful grounds filled their days. A large stable where they stored their preserves, and two cottages on the grounds were put to good use. One was called Holy Family Mission. It was fitted out with a classroom for some children of employees, white and Colored, a dormitory, and a sleeping apartment for a sister.

On the Archbishop's suggestion a priest came from Philadelphia once a month for a conference and direction. Father Scully, S.J., played a strong part in the spiritual formation of these young pioneers whose number increased to twenty-eight by the end of the year 1891.[14]

Shortly after this happy group was established at the new and temporary novitiate, a big project loomed up before them. News of it had come before they left Pittsburgh. In their eyes it assumed the proportions of a national disaster calling, they thought, for their immediate help. It all had to do with St. Stephen's Mission in Wyoming. Misfortune had dogged the progress of this mission from the very first time a Jesuit priest, Father Jutz, landed on its desolate site and formulated plans for the evangelization of the Arapahoe and Shoshone Indians. In the loneliness of his western outpost he must have been delighted to receive a letter from one K. Drexel offering to send a donation to his mission and asking questions about it.

He wrote back immediately, April 10, 1885, addressing his letter to "Mr. K. Drexel." Eagerly he asked "Mr." Drexel if he were the music teacher at Feldkirch where he, Father Jutz, had studied. He seemed quite sure "he" must be the same individual because he had never heard of any other man named Drexel. He begged the writer if "he" were the same gentleman to let him know as soon as possible so that he could carry on his future correspondence in his native language — German. This chatty letter gave a detailed account of his attempt to evangelize the Indians. He had started by planting potatoes and vegetables and hoped to build a school later. He ended with a delightful P.S. in which he asked if it were possible to send him a trumpet. The Indians, he wrote, liked music and he felt he could draw them if he had a trumpet. Before Katharine Drexel finished, she would send much more than a trumpet to St. Stephen's Mission.[15]

His second letter was one of jubilation addressed to "Highly esteemed and most dear daughter in Our Lord, Miss K. M. Drexel:"

> I can hardly tell you, my dearly beloved daughter in Our Lord, what impression your letter made on my heart. For a good while I could not think of anything but "My God, how great is Thy Goodness!" And last night I dreamed of you nearly all night. I saw you and one of your sisters and talked to you, and in the morning, I thought if I would meet you I would even know you. But that was only a dream and I might be mistaken. May Our dear Lord in the love His most Sacred Heart reward you for such an extraordinary benevolence and sympathy for these poor Indians....[16]

From the letter it was evident that Katharine had arranged for a workman to take care of the farm and had offered to pay for the erection of a school and sisters' convent.

But things did not progress normally at St. Stephen's. There was one upset after another, one involvement after another, and disagreement between the contractors and the Jesuit priests in charge. Bishop O'Connor had sent the plans to Father Panziglione, S.J., Father Jutz's successor, and he had signed the contract with the builders. But then troubles began. The foundations were not laid deep enough and the walls threatened to collapse. Another zealous Jesuit missionary, Father Kuppens, took up where Father Panziglione left off. In the midst of all this Bishop O'Connor had written Katharine that she should suggest to Bishop Burke, Bishop of Cheyenne, in whose diocese this mission was, that in view of the money she had already expended, possibly he and the diocese should undertake the additional expenses.

Bishop Burke answered immediately. In his letter one finds a striking expose of the agony of soul endured by these men of God, bishops and priests, struggling to found the Church in the vast and uninhabited stretches of the West. Bishop Burke explained the whole situation minutely as well as the tragic loneliness and poverty of his position. In his long, six page letter he wrote:

> You certainly cannot be expected to do any more.... Our position, however, in Wyoming is not understood, and this fact is to our real disadvantage and embarrassment of all concerned .... I am a bishop in name and title — Maurice Burke, Bishop of Cheyenne. I am here in a vast desert without inhabitants and without any means under heaven to accomplish any work in the interests of the Church or of religion.... If I had the zeal and the ability of St. Paul, I could accomplish nothing here. I am without people, without priests, without any means whatever of living or staying here.

Part of the difficulty, Bishop Burke went on to explain, arose from the fact that it was impossible to get a religious order definitely to accept the mission. At urgent requests they sent priests for periods of months and then changed them. His discouragement is evident throughout the whole letter. He could even see the reasonableness of their refusing to take the mission permanently.

> Why should they come out here from other dioceses to spend their life in the desert under the circumstances in which Wyoming has been placed? I can get no priests to come here to labor, and I have none to whom I can say, "Go here or go there." This could be done in the past but not in the present state of things.
>
> Your work among the Indians has been and is indeed a charity so great that words cannot express it. If a little of what you have done for the poor Red Man of this desert, were done by others who had the means and the power to do it, for the poor whites who are scattered here and there throughout this vast territory like sheep without a shepherd, many souls would be saved that are now lost to the faith....[17]

An insight into the stark heroism, vivid faith, and almost superhuman endurance of the bishops and priests who were themselves the foundation stones of the Catholic Church in the vast stretches of the great Wild West, is revealed in many other letters in the Motherhouse Archives of the Sisters of the Blessed Sacrament. The heroic endurance of great physical discomfort, a burning zeal for the salvation of souls, all this and more is recorded in neatly written letters of these unsung and unheralded pioneers of the spread of the Catholic Church in nineteenth century America.[18]

After many reverses St. Stephen's Mission was finally established and the school was opened by the Sisters of Charity from Leavenworth, Kansas. However, before June 1890 word reached Sister Katharine that the superior general of these sisters would recall them to the Motherhouse because of a shortage of sisters. Four Protestant ladies were hired to teach the following September, but this did not work out. At her profession she learned that the school was closed. The idea of seeing this mission terminated after all it had gone through, after all the obstacles overcome, and all the expense incurred, was a little too much. This set-back was all she needed to fire her zeal anew for the souls of the children involved. Applications were sent to various religious communities for sisters to teach in the school but to her sorrow there were no sisters available.

Shortly after her profession ceremony, she secured the permission of Archbishop Ryan to go out and visit the mission.[19] As far as she was concerned she was going out to prepare the way for her own sisters to take it over. She intended to check supplies and see what was needed. All the pent up zeal of her soul, all the impelling desires of her generous charity to help the American Indian longed for this opportunity dawning, she thought, for her young community. With high hopes and undaunted resolve she and Sister Patrick went West.

She wrote a delightful letter back to the motherless sisters at Torresdale describing, in her unique humorous way, her travel by stage coach. Bishop Burke, greatly encouraged by her promise of help, had met her and traveled in the stage coach with her. According to her letter they crashed along for fifteen miles to an old hovel where they stopped for something to eat and a change of horses. Three miles from the mission they heard the pealing of the bells welcoming the bishop.[20] To get to the one hundred and sixty acre St. Stephen's Mission, they had to cross the rapid current of the Wind River in a small boat. This was real adventure for the young Foundress and recalled vividly her first visit to the Indian missions with Bishop O'Connor and Monsignor Stephan. Then they had encountered practically every kind of physical hardship, and yet they had gone bravely on thrilled with the adventure of it all. In this letter of 1891 she noted she shook hands with William Shakespeare, the Indian guide and interpreter who met them with the priest from the mission, on the other side of the river.

What she saw in the empty building only deepened her enthusiasm to have the place alive again with the sound of children's voices. She asked many questions, took notes on supplies, and made many suggestions. When she left to return East both the bishop and the priest were highly encouraged with their impression that her sisters would soon be out to take over the school.

But on this point the Foundress was in for a big disappointment. She received her first intimation of that when she stopped to visit Mother Sebastian in Pittsburgh on her way back. Quietly Mother Sebastian remarked, "I fear the Archbishop will not permit you to send your sisters to St. Stephen's."[21] That jolted Mother M. Katharine somewhat but not completely. She did not know that Mother Sebastian had expressed her fears about the foundation to Archbishop Ryan. All she knew was that the Archbishop had given her the permission to make the trip which she interpreted as the permission also to make arrangements for staffing the mission. On her way back she had stopped in Chicago and bought all the furniture and supplies needed. Everything was packed, ready to be shipped to St. Stephen's as soon as she notified them of the date of her sisters' departure.

The final blow to her plans came in an interview with the Archbishop when she reached Philadelphia. As soon as she entered the room she asked, "My Reverend Father, do you mean we are not to go to St. Stephen's?"[22] Very casually the Archbishop walked to his writing desk as if he were looking for some paper, and without looking at her said, "No, I think you had better not go." Mother M. Katharine was a woman of strong will and stronger determination. It was not easy for her to see her first missionary plan halted like this, but she accepted it as the will of God.

The young Community at Torresdale, however, took the news as if it were the final scene of a tragedy. Even the youngest postulant wept. Scarcely entered on the way of religious perfection, they were afire to go out and convert the Indians immediately. The know-how, the equipment and the personal spiritual formation seemed so secondary in the face of what they thought was their first great challenge.

This was certainly an incident in which Mother M. Katharine was not planning a prudential course and it was well that wiser heads curtailed her. The immediate urgency of this situation had so impressed and touched her that every other consideration was swept aside temporarily. At that time Mother M. Katharine was the only professed member of her Community; all the others were postulants or novices in need of formation to religious life and discipline. It could well have shattered the new community to have attempted a very difficult mission with a small group of neophytes. Fortunately, the obedience of the Foundress was stronger than her prudence in the matter, for it saved her from a disastrous step. Later, she herself would admit her plan was unwise. Years after when founding new houses, she would sometimes say, "Oh how audacious I was in those days. Almighty God was certainly good to save us from such a mistake. I see now what a wild scheme it was. It would have been the ruination of our little Congregation."[23]

All thought of going to the Indian missions was put aside for the present while the important work of preparing for their apostolate went on. Then came a big day, July 16, 1891, when the whole community put on the new habit of the Sisters of the Blessed Sacrament in the morning, and assisted at the laying of the cornerstone for the new Motherhouse in the afternoon. Mother M. Katharine had worn the habit from the day of her profession, but the rest of the community continued wearing the Mercy habit till all details had been approved. Now everything was in order. That morning Archbishop Ryan said Mass in the convent and the ten novices put on the new habits which he had blessed.[24]

With regard to the new habit it would seem the Banker's Daughter had an eye to spiritual business. Since she was so determined to buy stocks and bonds in the eternal kingdom of Heaven, she wanted to gather as much profit along the way as she could for herself and her community. Through the help of Father Regis Canevin, afterwards Bishop of Pittsburgh, she obtained affiliation with the Benedictine Order, and the privilege was given her Congregation of wearing the Benedictine scapular and sharing in all the merits, privileges, and good works of the Benedictines.[25]

This affiliation did not suffice. Mother M. Katharine had been a member of the Third Order of Franciscans. All her life she had a strong and tender devotion to St. Francis. She ardently desired that her sisters be affiliated with the Franciscan Order. Archbishop Ryan obtained the authorization in Rome. From the date of this clothing, the Franciscan cord became a part of the habit of the new missionary Congregation.[26]

Mr. and Mrs. Morrell sent carriages to drive all the community to the new Motherhouse ceremony in the afternoon. Enthusiasm ran high when Archbishop Ryan with solemn ceremony laid the cornerstone into which had been placed papers, medals, photographs and a Philadelphia newspaper clipping on the death of Mrs. Elizabeth Drexel Smith to whose patron the new Motherhouse was dedicated. Happy in their new habits and carrying lighted candles, the sisters walked around the building in procession.

They would not know till many years later that all was not as serene as it looked on the surface. Feeling against the erection of the Motherhouse was strong among some of the surrounding farmers who were probably the victims of an ignorant prejudice. The day before the ceremony a stick of dynamite was found near the space marked for the cornerstone, and there were rumors in the air that someone had said that all the Catholics who were on the platform would be blown to Hell.[27]

In the course of her long life in which she would erect many buildings for the neglected races of America, this hatred and bigotry would rear its ugly head many times. Never however, would it deter or daunt her. Was it prophetic that the building she was erecting as the base of a nationwide apostolate for the Indians and Colored was for some, the object of prejudice and hatred?

Colonel Morrell, Mr. James M. Burns, the architect, and the Archbishop had been told about the dynamite. It was the Archbishop's command that the sisters should not know it. He did not want them alarmed. A dozen plain clothesmen were stationed on the grounds to prevent possible bomb throwing. The architect concocted a little scheme of his own to frighten whoever the guilty ones were. He bought a dozen broom sticks, placed them in a wooden box and then nailed it shut. On the outside, he wrote in large letters: "HANDS OFF, DO NOT TOUCH, HIGH EXPLOSIVE. NITROGLYCERINE." He had one of the workmen on the grounds guard it all day. He was told to prevent anyone coming near it lest the least vibration should cause an explosion. This little scheme worked perfectly. Word spread rapidly among the farmers, and no one went near the dangerous box nor the platform arranged for guests. Even the workman thought he was guarding an explosive.[28]

Now that Mother M. Katharine was not to open a mission among the Indians and would be at Torresdale with her sisters, Mother Inez was recalled to Pittsburgh.[29] Her health was not good and it seemed best to the Mercy Sisters to bring her home. This was a great disappointment to Mother M. Katharine but she consoled herself with the thought that it was only a temporary arrangement, and that she would come back again to give her valuable help to the novices. But as matters would turn out, she would not be sent back again. Mother M. Katharine herself for seventeen years would serve as superior general and mistress of novices as Archbishop Ryan directed.

A great sorrow fell on the Foundress in the first death of a Sister of the Blessed Sacrament. Three sisters had been professed in September 1891. One of them, Sister M. Patrick, was too ill to attend the ceremonies and pronounced her vows from her sick bed. The year before while nursing in Pittsburgh, she had contracted la grippe. Despite all remedies, she did not seem to rally and went into tuberculosis. Carefully and lovingly the Sisters took care of her wants and were edified by her sentiments of love and resignation as she offered her life willingly to God.

Just one week after her profession while Mother M. Katharine was watching alone at her bedside at night, she died. When a sister came in at midnight to relieve Mother, she was amazed to find Sister fully dressed in her habit, lying on the bed as if asleep. Mother rose from her knees beside the bed and said quietly, "Our Sister Patrick has gone to her Spouse. Her death was very quiet. She passed away about eleven o'clock." The Foundress had arranged her body and for one hour prayed alone for the soul of this spiritual daughter. What passed between her soul and God in this first encounter with death in her religious family, only God knows. There may well have been notes of joy in the realization of the purity and generosity that marked this young life so completely given to God. Sister was buried on the grounds at Torresdale temporarily, till the body could be removed later to the cemetery at the Motherhouse.[30]

Many distinguished visitors were to find their way to the temporary novitiate in the very first year of residence there. Ecclesiastical dignitaries, zealous missionary priests came to consult Mother M. Katharine and to ask for her help. Among the first callers, in addition to Archbishop Janssens, were

Bishop Meerschaert, Vicar Apostolic of Oklahoma and Indian Territory, accompanied by Father Ketcham who would later direct the Bureau of Catholic Indian Missions;[31] Bishop Haid of North Carolina,[32] and Bishop Burke of Cheyenne.[33] The sisters were particularly impressed with one Indian missionary who told them humbly that he felt most unworthy to address them but that he would give his blessing instead. He entered the chapel in his cassock and knelt in very fervent prayer before giving his blessing. His piety made a deep impression. Alas, he turned out to be a bogus priest! Even the keen business woman was taken in. Mother Katharine lamented the fact that she had given him ten dollars to help buy some vestments for his Indians!

The new Motherhouse was to have been ready for occupancy in June 1892, but a serious cave-in prevented their moving in. Later there was danger of a wall collapse in the chapel. The heavy weight of the Spanish tile on the roof had not been taken into consideration in laying the foundations. Stone buttresses had to be erected to carry this weight. Mother M. Katharine capitalized on this situation by reminding the sisters that the same thing would happen in their spiritual lives if the foundations were not properly dug. There were further delays in the construction and another entrance date had to be postponed.

Finally Mother M. Katharine would brook no more delays and announced they would move in December 3. The contractor hired extra workers, and tried to delay the entrance date again. But move in the young community did, even though there were many things still to be taken care of in the building. Water had to be carried in from a pump in buckets; the only light available was from candles and the heating system was not yet operative. But they were happy in their new home and gladly put up with the temporary inconveniences as they advanced in grace and wisdom.

The fifteen children who had occupied "Holy Family" cottage in Torresdale came with the sisters to the unfinished Motherhouse and were domiciled in Holy Providence School, still in the course of erection. The place was wide open to the world with no locks or bars on the doors, but several rooms had been finished off for their occupancy. Mother M. Katharine's plans for the Motherhouse had included this boarding school for poor children. By February 2, 1893, it was completed and opened to further registration; within a short time it was filled to its capacity. The school endures to this day; several additions have been made to the original building and a fair tuition is charged. In the intervening years, thousands of young children have received their elementary education there.

Archbishop Ryan was determined the sisters should not leave the Motherhouse for any mission till they were well steeped in religious principles, and their foundations in holiness were dug deep. He insisted on several more years of preparation. When this preparation ended he would give his consent and his fatherly blessing, and a new community in the Church would operate in the vast mission areas of the United States.

# Chapter 11
# To The Pueblos

Long before white men ever set foot in America, it belonged to people. The gorgeous stretches of its landscapes were homes, hunting grounds, summer and winter resorts for the various tribes who lived on its shores and claimed its lands. There are those who think of them as fierce savages, cruel, murderous people, and yet their various cultures were ages old before the first explorers came. Without the help of a Department of the Interior or a Secretary of Agriculture, they evolved systems of soil cultivation and conservation that served them and their needs quite well. Without graduate courses in art, they developed a pottery making technique, a sand painting perfection which proclaimed to all the world the native artistry implanted in them by their Creator. Without language laboratories, they devised in prehistoric times a universal picture language, and used it to write manuscripts on rocks and directions on stones to endure for ages.[1]

It was to the various tribes of Indians, driven from their homes, despoiled of their hunting grounds, caught in the throes of poverty that Katharine's heart extended. She knew their plight; she had, in her brief visits, experienced the destitution of their existence. Her whole life was to be dedicated to the improvement of their condition and the alleviation, too, of the condition of the Colored throughout this nation.

Centuries before the discovery of gold sparked the grand rush to California, the great Southwest had been the scene of another quest for gold much more limited in its extent and disastrous in its termination. In the early sixteenth century, an alluring story of seven cities of gold had fired Coronado's thirst for gold and incited him in 1540 to organize a brilliant expedition to find and take possession of this untold source of wealth. But there were no cities of gold. His rainbow of hopes vanished into nothingness.

Spanish colonization of this area followed in 1598 and with it, an attempt to force Spanish culture and customs on the natives. Almost a century later in 1680 the Pueblo Indians rose in revolt and killed twenty-one of thirty-three priests in the pueblos, and three hundred and eighty colonists out of a total of about twenty five hundred. The missions and their records were destroyed.[2]

When the revolts were over, a surface peace was effected. The Indians were allowed to remain in their own pueblos and thus establish a continuity in their cultural pursuits. But for a long period, longer than anyone knows, there has resulted an acculturation, a double culture, Spanish Catholic and native pagan. From the first Spanish contacts with these Indians, the Franciscan fathers have labored among them. In the course of time each pueblo would witness the rise of an adobe church named in Spanish after a saint. Their names today make a musical litany: Santa Clara, San Ildefonso, San Juan, San Domingo, San Philipe and Santa Ana. To these Pueblo tribes, living quietly in their remote villages surrounding the city of Santa Fe as so many outposts of quaint beauty, Mother M. Katharine sent her sisters to open the first mission of the new Congregation.[3]

Up to her entrance into religious life there was always a delicate balance in Katharine's life between polar opposites, a poise and counterpoise between the splendor of wealth and the simplicity of holiness. In her young life there was the striking contrast between her enjoyment of riches, and the inner determination of her soul to live close to God and to mortify herself in hidden ways to please Him. After these preparatory years, the dividing line in her life had been obliterated. She was now a religious vowed to poverty, chastity, and obedience, and to the special service of the Indian and Colored. She was no longer to be served, but to serve, to serve the underprivileged of America, the ones who were usually passed by, whose rights were consistently denied. She had given her material wealth; now in a special way she gave herself, her liberty, her whole life. And a long life it was to be. She would still travel, but she would travel in dusty trains, she would take what accommodations she could get, to reach not a welcoming hotel but the wretched homes of the poorest of America's poor. She would establish convents and schools in these areas after she had investigated and made her plans. Where she could not send her Sisters (they were still few and in an infant stage) she would go into areas and offer to help with the foundation of a school or a chapel.

At this stage of her life, there would be perfect coordination between her interior and her exterior occupation. They would both be stamped with the redeeming imprint of the Cross. By the Rule she would draw up for her Sisters and the life she would lead, she would be totally given to God. All, even the least detail, would be surrendered to Him as the motto she chose to have engraved on her ring at her final profession indicated: "My Beloved to me and I to Him." Like her Beloved, having joy set before her, she would endure the Cross. Let us trace the footsteps of this remarkable woman as she starts her long and winding trek across her native land she loved so well. Let us study this simple, valiant woman who rose up to meet bishops and prelates to urge and supply new foundations for the advancement of the Indian and Colored.

St. Catherine's School in Santa Fe was one of the many schools erected by Katharine Drexel before she was a religious. At first, only boys were admitted, but later girls also were enrolled when her own community took over. Archbishop Salpointe of Santa Fe had laid the cornerstone for the building June 17, 1886. Before death came to Archbishop Lamy, he blessed and dedicated the completed building April 11, 1887.[4] It was called St. Catherine's as an expression of gratitude to its donor.

This mission, however, was to run into the same difficulties that many others had encountered — the scarcity of religious personnel. The Sisters of Loretto assisted by three laymen conducted the school for two years and were then withdrawn. The Benedictine Fathers took over the school but they, too, withdrew at the end of the year. Finally, three lay women were employed to continue the classes. But that did not work out either. In June 1893 the school closed with no prospect of reopening. Father Stephan, in distress over losing government contracts and the loss of faith of these young Indian boys, visited the Motherhouse to ask Mother M. Katharine to send her own sisters there. But Archbishop Ryan maintained that the sisters needed at least another year's training.[5]

Archbishop Chapelle of Santa Fe and Bishop Bourgade came to Cornwells Heights too. (The placing of a railroad station at the entrance to the grounds resulted in a new name for that area — Cornwells Heights.) Archbishop Chapelle asked Mother M. Katharine if it would be at all possible for her to take St. Catherine's. Like Father Stephan, he feared that if the school remained closed for the year the government would withdraw the contract. Again Archbishop Ryan said, "No! Let Archbishop Chapelle try to secure another community for the present."[6] He still insisted that the sisters were too young in years and in religious life, and that another year's preparation would be best for all. Bishop Bourgade, Vicar Apostolic of Arizona, expressed his desire for evangelization of the Navajo Indians of Arizona as well as the Pueblo of New Mexico, and hoped for some combined effort for both. But the Sisters of the Blessed Sacrament would evangelize neither the Pueblo nor the Navajo Indians that year.

Mother M. Katharine announced the Archbishop's final decision this way: "Sisters, we can make an act of humility. We are not fit instruments for apostolic labor among the Indians of New Mexico. Do not let this, however, deter us in the work of our sanctification. If we persevere courageously in the uphill work, dying to ourselves and letting God reign in our hearts, He will in His own time choose us to go and work in His vineyard and bring forth fruit that will remain. Let us strive earnestly to grow in all the virtues especially the virtue of humility...."[7]

Mother M. Katharine did not know until the following spring that no teachers had been found for St. Catherine's and the school had been closed. When she learned that, she immediately asked Archbishop Ryan's permission to visit Santa Fe and see what could be done. He gave her the permission now as he had given it to visit St. Stephen's; no further step was discussed at this point. But hope ran high as she and Sr. M. Evangelist set out. Archbishop Chapelle met her at Lamy and greeted her with, "Thank God, my prayer is answered. You are coming to take St. Catherine's."[8] Mother M. Katharine and her companion, Sister M. Evangelist, spent a week in Santa Fe taking an inventory at the school and engaging workmen to restore and make alterations in the building.

Bishop Bourgade of Tucson called on Mother M. Katharine during this visit to Santa Fe and asked her to visit the Papago Indians. With Sister M. Evangelist she accompanied Bishop Bourgade to Tucson, staying there with the Sisters of Saint Joseph. Early the next morning, the three started out for the Papago reservation and visited the old mission of San Xavier del Bac. Mother M. Katharine, a great lover of poverty herself, was keenly edified to find the retired Bishop Salpointe living in a small adobe house. The Archbishop's room had a little iron bed, three yellow chairs, a crucifix on the wall, and that was all. There was no carpet, not even a small rug.[9]

Back in Philadelphia again, Mother M. Katharine sought the Archbishop's permission to send her Sisters to St. Catherine's. This time the permission was given, much to the joy of the Foundress and every sister in the community. Faces were radiant, hearts were filled with anticipation and everyone wondered who the chosen first apostles would be. One by one as they came out of the chapel, Mother beckoned nine sisters appointed to become the first active S.B.S. missionaries in the field. Everybody helped with the preparation for the departures until finally all was in readiness. Four sisters were to go on first; five others were to follow. There was a very close spiritual bond among these young pioneers of a new religious community. Tears flowed at the farewell scene June 13, 1894, at this, the first departure of missionaries from the Motherhouse.

Mother M. Katharine and Sister M. Augustine accompanied the four sisters to Philadelphia to see them off on their travel West. She took care herself of checking the baggage, and bought an alarm clock, a gong to be used as a calling bell, and other odds and ends that she felt would be necessary. While she was taking care of this purchasing, the four missionaries went to the Archbishop's residence to bid him good-bye and to ask his blessing. To Mother M. Evangelist who had been appointed the Superior of the new mission and who was weeping freely, he said, "You seem to feel it very keenly." He went on to tell her of some Franciscan sisters who had come to him when he was Bishop of St. Louis for permission to go to Memphis and help nurse in the yellow fever epidemic. He gave them the permission, he said, and then added, "When they went down the steps from my front door, I knew they were walking into their graves."[10] This attempt at comfort did little to help Mother M. Evangelist restrain her tears. They were still flowing as the train pulled out. But they dried up on the way, and these first four pioneers found the ride through the gorgeous West an exhilarating experience. Their letters gave glowing accounts of the joy of their trip and the welcome awaiting them at the end.

But it was not so with the second group of five who left a week later. Their travel was almost a nightmare. They found themselves in the midst of the violent Pullman Strike of 1894 which tied up all the railroad traffic between Chicago and the West. All went well until they reached Hutchinson,

Kansas, where the strikers unhitched the engine, rode off with it and left the passengers helpless in a stalled train. For eight hours the sisters sat apprehensive in a motionless car. Finally an engine was secured which carried them to Dodge City where the engineer and fireman ran away with that engine. This type of excitement was repeated at La Junta, Colorado, and Raton, New Mexico. In both places they were surrounded by furious mobs.

After a delay of some three days at La Junta, volunteers were requested for a first train West to be manned by the United States Infantry. By this time President Cleveland had ordered federal troops to break up the strike on the ground that it interfered with the passage of the United States mail. The five lonely pioneer missionaries had telegraphed Mother M. Katharine for directions. Her return telegram was to the effect not to continue if there was any danger in doing so. This telegram caused quite a bit of discussion. Some interpreted it as a direction of Obedience that they should not go on. Others felt that Mother did not understand the rail situation and thought they were staying there unnecessarily. Consequently, when two hundred people volunteered to go on the train, these young missionaries, or at least Sister M. Mercedes who was directing them, felt that they should display courage, too, and be among those going on. Despite the dangers of their passage, the sisters felt that God would protect them. As Sister M. Mercedes wrote in one of the many letters sent back by travelers to the Motherhouse, "We all felt sure that Our Lord had not brought us here to meet our deaths unless thereby He would be more glorified and we more prepared then than ever after to render our account."[11] Sister M. Anthony, however, put a handkerchief carefully away with this remark, "I would like Mother to get this and keep it as I am sure we are riding to our deaths."[12]

But Mother M. Katharine herself was deeply concerned and puzzled about the misinterpretation of the telegram which could have resulted so disastrously for the lives of her young religious. She wrote later:

> And by the way, I cannot understand how it was you misunderstood that telegram of July 4. It ran, "If continuing journey seems dangerous REMAIN at La Junta." And in the face of the "REMAIN" Sister M. Mercedes explains that she would go AT ONCE if possible. I know you did not mean to be disobedient, but misunderstood. And later on she says she would go on no matter how dangerous. Good gracious! Child, did you think your Mother imagined you were staying at La Junta for pleasure? It was because I feared your going despite the danger that I telegraphed.
>
> I explain this, not to pain you, but that you may know your Mother better on another occasion. I have offered the judgment you have formed of me in atonement for the many times I have doubted Our Lord's love. Indeed the little penance was well merited and made me understand the Sacred Heart better, and how want of confidence must grieve Him. I know Sister M. Mercedes understood the telegram as well as she could,

> thank God! Striving to act in obedience and to please the Divine Spouse and of course she did please him.[13]

Mother M. Katharine had felt keenly the departure of her first sisters for the West. As a matter of fact, the morning after the second contingent left, she broke into tears at the breakfast table. For the first time, she became ill and was confined to bed for a day, a most unusual happening for her.[14] Her anxiety at the word of the strike was deep.

They misinterpreted the telegram, and went on protected by soldiers in every other seat. It looked as if their preparation for the missions was to include an experience of every kind of terror. They ran into a terrible storm as the train wound over high gorges of rocky mountains. At one point they had just passed over a gorge when the bridge collapsed into the swirling waters. When they reached Lamy Junction, Governor Price of New Mexico met them with the explanation that due to the strike, the only means of transportation to Santa Fe was a freight car. By this time the sisters were ready for anything. It would not have surprised them if they had been asked to carry their luggage and cross the hills on foot.

What a relief St. Catherine's was at the end of the journey, and how warmly the four already there embraced and welcomed them. But despite their eagerness to serve God and be part of the missionary endeavor of the Church, they had human hearts. They were not too encouraged by the fact that just a stone's throw from St. Catherine's were the National and Catholic cemeteries. The first afternoon after their arrival, the funeral of a little child who had wandered away and been lost in the mountains, and the band's playing "Nearer, my God, to Thee" were not exactly suited to raising their spirits.[15]

In September after the Sisters had had time to settle, to get all things in order for the opening of school, and to visit some of the pueblos, Mother M. Katharine started for Santa Fe eager to see this long desired work begin. She wrote her usual delightful letters along the way filled with descriptions of the gorgeous scenes through which they were passing, and interspersed with her deeply spiritual thoughts. In a letter from Kansas we read:

> If we have died to self in life and lived in God's presence, and near Him and with Him, in union with Him in life, surely on that day when eternity shall commence to us, God's own beautiful life will glorify all our thoughts, words and actions because His Will and Light will appear in them and thus they will glorify Him for ever and ever. The splendor will not fade as do the golden tints of these clouds that pass when I'm writing to you. Oh even now they have assumed a leaden hue and they appear but fleeting clouds! So will all self-will, self-seeking, self-judgment be on our day of eternity. Let us do God's will and see God and God's judgment whilst travelling to eternity. Then we need not fear that only

fleeting clouds will remain in our thoughts, words and actions. All these will be laid up in Heaven as a treasure that will not fade.[16]

She arrived in Santa Fe in what she called "starlight" at nearly ten o'clock at night. They knocked and knocked at the door with no results until the hack driver, before they could stop him, got hold of the Angelus bell rope and pulled it for all he was worth, thus notifying all of Santa Fe as well as the sisters that Mother was in town. That threw the windows up on the second floor. In a few moments all were down to welcome her, and the whole house was astir with the joy of their Mother's arrival.

Early the next morning she began her appraisal. It was a great disappointment to her to find that there were only nine boys enrolled in the school. She set out immediately to consult Bishop Chapelle who had promised to have some of the priests visit the families and arrange for students. He set her mind at rest and assured her the students would come. With the student enrollment provided for, after her visit to the Bishop, she studied the whole situation and liked what she saw. She spoke encouragingly to the sisters, and arranged with them the definite plans for the operation of the school for the coming year. She did not remain long, for there were many matters awaiting her at the Motherhouse. On the way East she wrote back to the sisters at St. Catherine's:

Thursday, Sept., 1894

My own darling children at St. Catherine's:

I could do nothing for some minutes after leaving you but pray to Our Lord, your Spouse, to keep my precious treasures and give them grace to be very dear to Him. My last prayer for you in that dear chapel where one feels so much that Jesus is our All, my last prayer in that chapel of St. Catherine's was that the Blessed Sacrament would make you and all of us One in His love. God bless you each and every one!

I loved you before my visit, more since my visit and during it. Even the apple orchard we passed a few minutes ago made me think of you, "My Nine". It was this way — I saw some dear little trees that were burdened with many, many rosy apples, and I thought how pleased the master of the orchard must be to see them bearing fruit so young. Then I thought of the Master of our souls and the pleasure you will bring His own sweet Heart if He beholds your Indian children amidst the branches of virtue in your soul. Indeed as I think of His paternal love, it does not seem improbable to me that He has plucked some of the fruit from you by not permitting the children to come all at once, because He wisely saw they would be too heavy for the slender branches. That is at least now, if they came all at once. Growth must be gradual to be enduring.[17]

The New Year, 1895, started out very auspiciously for the Foundress. On the morning of January 9 in the Motherhouse chapel, before Archbishop Ryan, she pronounced her perpetual vows and received the silver ring which the Sisters of the Blessed Sacrament would wear as a symbol of their perpetual espousal.[18] In it was engraved the motto she had chosen: "My Beloved to me and I to Him." In the years ahead, each sister would choose a motto for the ring she would receive at her final profession. In May of that year, she set out again for Santa Fe and en route wrote scintillating letters back to her daughters at the Motherhouse. One of them was headed "Express train between the two convents of the Blessed Sacrament, St. Elizabeth's and St. Catherine's."[19]

There was the usual joyful reunion with the Sisters at Santa Fe who had not been told beforehand of her coming. The Foundress seemed particularly happy at what she saw at St. Catherine's; everything was running efficiently and there seemed to be an atmosphere of peace, even in the children's quarters. Realizing the fact that the school was growing and the duties were piling up, she had brought two sisters to join the staff. Having inspected everything and made suggestions for the new needs which had arisen, she was preparing to return to the Motherhouse when word reached the convent that a plague had broken out at San Domingo Pueblo. The Indians were dying off, and the doctors sent by the government became victims too.

She wired Archbishop Ryan asking permission for two sisters to go and nurse the sick Indians and then announced to the sisters that she and Mother M. Evangelist had volunteered to go to San Domingo and nurse during the pestilence. She forbade the sisters to write to St. Elizabeth's because she did not wish to make them anxious. She herself had already written and told the Motherhouse she would be away possibly five or six weeks. As the sisters watched helplessly and in horror, trunks were packed with medicines, other accessories, supplies of food. Sister M. Mercedes was placed in charge of the house.[20]

Finally one morning the two started out in a horse and wagon for a long journey to San Domingo. The sisters stormed Heaven for their protection, in the utter helplessness of their position to stop this heroic venture of their Mother Superior. They told their alarm to a friend of the community, Miss Egan, attached to the government Indian school. She wrote immediately to Archbishop Ryan begging him to recall Mother M. Katharine and saying that the government had supplied sufficient nurses and doctors. She added that during the first week several doctors and nurses who knew how to take precautions and avoid infection had fallen victims of the dread malady.

God heard the prayers of the sisters. When the two Mothers, worn out and hungry, reached San Domingo, they were informed they could not enter the Pueblo until the Council of the Pueblo decided to admit them. They had to wait around another day until the Council was assembled and formulated its deliberation. The San Domingo Indians would have none of their assistance and positively refused to let them even visit or see the sick. The governor of the Pueblo came to them, still outside its precinct, and told them they could not nurse the Indians. "You go to the church and pray for them," he said quite definitely. His word was law; there was no higher source to which one could appeal. In other areas one might appeal to a bishop or a cardinal or even to Rome, but in San Domingo the Pueblo governor was the end of the road of all appeals. To the extreme delight of the sisters, the two Mothers came back, their trunks unopened, their zeal unsatisfied.[21]

There would be another time in the future when the sisters would serve as nurses and be acceptable to the Indians. In August 1901 a malarial fever raged in the Cochiti Pueblo. The priest there had done everything he could do but he had no help. The government had sent one male nurse. After three Indian men had died, the Indian agent pleaded for the help of the sisters. Sister M. Loyola and Sister M. Perpetua went in answer to the appeal, well supplied with medicines, beef extracts, broths, and large supplies of oatmeal for gruel. They stayed in nearby Pena Blanca and went to the pueblo each day. Those were tragic days for the pueblo and trying days for the sisters. Despite their care, little children and older Indians died in the ravages of the disease. They stayed there five weeks helping in every way they could until both sisters fell ill with raging temperatures. The physician at Santa Fe insisted they be recalled, for he declared the government had enough money to send out nurses to care for the Indians. The sisters were brought back and eventually they regained their health and the hospital care of the Indians was handed over to the government.[22]

Once the Sisters of the Blessed Sacrament were firmly established at St. Catherine's, it would not be without teachers again. Right down to the present day it would be staffed by a long line of Mother M. Katharine's sisters, who would take the same path but not incur the same danger as the first Sisters of the Blessed Sacrament to go West. The school would be filled yearly with groups of children from the surrounding pueblos who in turn would go back to their pueblos and send their children to receive the same Christian education they had received. Outside of their classroom experience, the Sisters would have many other contacts with the Indians in the pueblos.

In September 1944 the Sisters and the Indians celebrated the Golden Jubilee of the Foundation of St. Catherine's. It was a glorious and a gala day. A Pontifical Mass celebrated by Archbishop Byrne started the ceremonies. The Indians in costume poured in from the surrounding pueblos and exhibited their dancing and skills in a day of never to be forgotten delights. Possibly what pleased the sisters, and Mother M. Katharine back in the convent at the Motherhouse, most was a short speech delivered at the end by Martin Vigil of the Tesuque Pueblo. His speech was not announced on the program but he stood up toward the end of the ceremony and, by a motion of his hand, let it be known he had something to say. He spoke with deep gratitude of the work of the sisters throughout their fifty years in Santa Fe. He paid tribute to them for all they had done for the many pueblo children committed to their care. He emphasized the fact that in that year particularly, they were grateful for the guidance their children had received at St. Catherine's. In that period of war, their sons and daughters were scattered in the armed forces over the face of the earth. It was consoling to the older Indians, said Martin Vigil, that their children had gone into this battle of life fortified by the Christian education they had received at St. Catherine's. He ended his short address by saying, "We will stand by the Sisters as long as we live and when we get to heaven, we hope we will be standing by them still."[23]

What else could the Sisters of the Blessed Sacrament desire? This message gave special joy to Mother M. Katharine whose health at this time did not permit her journeying to the first mission she had founded, the mission she loved so well. *She* would stand by the Indians and Colored her whole life long because she wanted to be standing with them in Heaven. Through her generosity, St. Catherine's would grow in buildings and equipment through the years, dropping the lower grades as government day schools were opened in various pueblos. Today in addition to the seventh and eighth grades St. Catherine's includes a fully accredited high school. Three of its graduates are now Sisters of the Blessed Sacrament. That development alone would be the source of great joy to Mother M. Katharine. One generation after another of Pueblo boys and girls have come to St. Catherine's in the seventy-two years of its existence. Generations of parents, too, have come under the influence of the sisters who include the surrounding pueblos in their visitations, catechetical work, and choir direction.

An outgrowth of the work in Santa Fe was the establishment of another mission from the Pueblo Indians at San Jose, picturesque and quaint Old Laguna, New Mexico. Two sisters were assigned there in 1935.[24] Before that, sisters had gone there in the summer to conduct catechism classes for children and adults. There are four sisters today stationed at the convent adjoining the historic church, San Jose. Their convent, except for its second floor, is just another adobe building in the village, but an intensive missionary program emanates from there.

There are five Pueblo villages surrounding Laguna: Encinal, Mesita, Paguate, Seama and Paraje. In each of them the sisters conduct C.C.D. classes. Two other pueblos of the Acoma Indians, McCartys and Acomita, are also instruction centers and visitation centers for the sisters from Laguna. The Acoma Indians with homes on the four hundred foot heights of the Acoma mesa do their farming and take up their general living in these two pueblos on the plains. San Jose in Laguna is a modern mission in an ancient setting. The sisters must be good drivers to make their rounds, but they are. They must be good musicians too, and they are! The sisters generally supply the organ playing for all Masses. There are two Masses daily in the Laguna chapel; six on Sundays: three in the morning on one route, two on another route in the morning, and one at night. The swift driving down well paved New Mexico roads is a far cry from the tortuous wagon driving in many of Mother M. Katharine's first visits to this area. But she would rejoice at the change, rejoice at the swifter travel to reach the Indians she longed to help.

This catechetical apostolate has been carried on steadily and quietly like the educational apostolate in Santa Fe. But through the years in both centers, Mother M. Katharine's dream has been fulfilled, that her daughters would be the instruments through which the living waters of grace would flow to souls not for a year or a decade but as long as the tribes endure. She dug deep in New Mexico. The fruit is rich and widespread.

More than sixty years after the first group of Sisters of the Blessed Sacrament went to St. Catherine's, Archbishop Byrne of Santa Fe wrote to Mother M. Anselm, then Superior General:

> May 11, 1956
>
> ... I consider the presence of your daughters a distinct benediction for the Church in New Mexico, and it gives me joy to be able to express from time to time my gratitude to God and to them. May the Divine Missioner continue to bless St. Catherine's School for the Indians and may an intense love of souls animate always the spiritual daughters of Mother Drexel, who had fallen in love with immortal souls because she knew their value.[25]

# Chapter 12

# On The River James

All her life Mother M. Katharine had a great capacity for details and the coexistence in her mental horizon of vastly different projects. It was as if she wanted to use every moment, every opportunity to plough into the vast field that opened up before her, and to plough into it in all directions. She had a mission to fulfill and she strained to accomplish it. While she was carefully and exactly checking all details for the opening of her first mission and the sending forth of her first sisters to the Pueblo Indians, she was considering and drawing up plans for another type of activity that she wished to begin at once, this time for the Colored.

From the birth of her community, she was deeply concerned about the higher education of the Colored. She was eager to establish a boarding high school and normal school where young women could live with the sisters for the years of their higher education, and gradually have the Catholic way of living, the Catholic outlook, Catholic culture permeate their whole being. Then, she hoped they could go out and teach in southern schools. She wanted this school placed in an atmosphere that would be conducive to their cultural progress, an atmosphere far removed from the din, the harm, the moral evils in the crowded sections of the cities.

In 1894 Colonel and Mrs. Morrell (Louise Drexel) had purchased at the cost of $28,000 a sixteen hundred acre estate, forty miles northwest of Richmond. The place was called Belmead and was one of four estates belonging to General Philip St. George Cocke.[1] Immediately after the purchases, plans were put into operation for the conversion of existing buildings into school facilities, the reconditioning of shops already on the grounds — the grist and saw mills, the wheelwright and carpenter shops — and the erection of new shops and buildings. It was the very definite plan of both Colonel and Mrs. Morrell to provide an education in trades and agricultural pursuits, so that Colored men of the South would be fitted to make an honorable living at the completion of the course. It was called St. Emma's Industrial and Agricultural Institute. Louise had deliberately chosen the name in memory of her mother, Emma Bouvier Drexel.

This book is being written about Katharine Drexel; but her sisters, Louise and Elizabeth, could each supply material for a separate book on her service to God and her fellow men. Each in her own sphere carried on the generous charity of their mother and father. Louise was deeply interested in the welfare of the Colored. She had already donated large sums to the Josephite Fathers for the erection and maintenance of their seminary buildings. She would until her death and after her death by her will, contribute large sums to the continued improvement of St. Emma's. Like her sister Katharine, she too, had sought a place of secluded beauty and plenty of farm land, where young Colored men in an atmosphere of peace, could be drawn to a love of the good and beautiful while they strove for mastery of some particular trade or skill.

In the course of its history, St. Emma's would be under the supervision of four different groups. It was first placed under the care of the Christian Brothers, 1895-1924.[2] They were followed by a group of laymen, 1924-1929;[3] and they in turn by the Benedictine Fathers of St. Vincent's Abbey, Latrobe, Pennsylvania, in 1929.[4] Each of these groups made a valuable contribution to the development of the school. Since 1947 the Holy Ghost Fathers have been in charge.[5] Mrs. Morrell was quite determined that the school should be a military, vocational school fitting each graduate for a specific trade. Many young men so prepared have gained good livelihoods as a result of their training. But in the course of the years, more and more academic subjects have been added, so that in addition to a skill in a trade, the young Belmead graduate of today is prepared to go on to college should he so desire. The name in recent years was changed to St. Emma's Military Academy. Today at least seventy-five percent of the graduates enter colleges and universities throughout the country.[6] Dormitory buildings, an agricultural building, trade shops, a library and a gymnasium have been added over the years. After the death of Colonel Morrell, Louise Drexel Morrell had a beautiful memorial chapel, St. Edward's, built in his memory. Cardinal Dougherty consecrated it on October 24, 1928.[7] Since its erection it has served as the principal church of the locality. In 1947 it was officially established as a parish church.[8]

The particular charity of Elizabeth Drexel Smith was St. Francis Industrial School in Eddington, Pennsylvania, which she built for orphaned boys of any race so that they would be trained to follow a trade rather than be thrown into society after they finished at the local orphan asylums. This was the first trade school in the state of Pennsylvania; from its foundation it would be ably conducted by the Christian Brothers. There were no local models to guide Elizabeth in her planning. In her tour of Europe with her sisters, she and they had studied and taken notes on the equipment and methods of European trade schools. The cornerstone of the building was laid in the fall of 1886.[9] Archbishop Ryan blessed the completed building July 28, 1888.[10] After the ceremonies, two hundred boys from St. John's Orphan Asylum, Philadelphia, dressed in new suits and straw hats provided by the Drexel sisters, took up residence there. It was a great day in their lives. They had said good-bye to the St. Joseph Sisters, who had mothered them at St. John's and marched to the Girard Avenue Station where they boarded a train for Eddington. A new life began for them.[11]

Elizabeth Drexel Smith died September 26, 1890, before her endowment for St. Francis (named in honor of her father) had been completed. Since they were receiving her part of the father's income, both Mother M. Katharine and Louise Drexel Morrell decided to contribute conjointly for a period of ten years, $120,000 a year, to assure an annual income for the school. [12] Mrs. Morrell assumed Elizabeth's responsibility for the general welfare of the school. One of her happiest days came years later when one of the graduates of St. Francis who had gone on to study for the priesthood was elected Provincial of his order.

In 1945, at the death of Mrs. Morrell, St. Francis was taken over by the archdiocese. In 1965 it was the focus of concentration for the Catholic Charities Appeal of the Archdiocese of Philadelphia. The goal of the Appeal was $2,500,000. One million of this was allocated to St. Francis for a new school building, more shop space, swimming pool, gym, and auditorium.[13] Thus, seventy-nine years after the foundation stone was laid, the people of the Archdiocese generously supplemented the contributions of the Drexels and those of the archdiocese after Mrs. Morrell's death in 1945. Many young men have been helped in this vital institution and many more will continue to receive the best in vocational training in the years ahead. The still imposing original structure rises as a monument to Elizabeth Drexel Smith and her far seeing vision. Seventy-five years after her death, the work she founded goes on with renewed vigor.

Katharine Drexel would have no special school or institution as the object of her charity. Every bit of her income would be spread as far as she could spread it all over the country. It was her sister's glowing account of her purchase of Virginia land for a school for Colored boys that aroused her interest in that area and impressed on her the advantages of this background of quiet scenic beauty. She wrote to Bishop Van De Vyver about entering his diocese. His answer warmly welcoming her was immediate.[14]

She set out at once to investigate the field for a new operation. A week before her second group of sisters left for their adventurous ride to Santa Fe, she hastened to Virginia. She was sure she would find just what she wanted. She found it. Her selection was a six hundred acre estate of a plantation known as Mount Pleasant. It too had originally been one of the four plantations owned by General Cocke. It would hardly be possible to find in America a site more beautiful than the one she purchased. She planned the school should rise on the crest of a hill facing the James River. As she stood on that hill viewing the surrounding country, and looked across the James to the lines of wooded hills curving across the sky, she felt God had made this to order for her plan. Rich fertile meadows skirted the base of the hill down to the brink of the running waters where blankets of violets still cover the emerging earth each spring. Later, when Archbishop Ryan would visit the area, he would exclaim that it was more like Ireland than anything else he had seen in the United States.[15]

Again she would build in a remote spot with the difficulties of bringing in supplies and providing transportation. The only travel approach was on the Chesapeake and Ohio Railroad on the other side of the James River. The only way to cross the river was either a row boat or a wooden flat attached to a cable, operated by an old Negro resident. Only two trains ran daily on the winding railroad. But this is where she built, and built wisely on property adjoining that purchased by her sister, Louise. The two schools were an ideal arrangement and an ideal accomplishment. In both cases the main buildings were planted on top of a hill, twin hills with a half mile of meadow space and a winding creek between them. Mother M. Katharine called her school St. Francis de Sales in memory of her father. Louise had named hers in memory of her mother. Thus, two sisters giving the world an example of unstinted charity, erected two towering monuments to the memory of their parents from whom they had learned the principle and the practice of charity. From many viewpoints, it was well to have these two schools, one for boys and one for girls, within an area of association. The presence of the one and the other has been mutually enriching in opportunities for combined efforts in dramatic and musical arts, and in social life generally.

In July 1895 as the building began to appear above the ground and was ready for a cornerstone laying, Mother M. Katharine made another visit to Rock Castle as the area was then named. Later the Post Office would change the name to Powhatan. Again her companion was Sister M. Mercedes who had been brought back from Santa Fe to have an eye condition treated by a Philadelphia specialist. They had planned to start out the morning of July 10th but that very morning Archbishop Ryan sent word that he and the papal legate, Archbishop Martinelli, would visit the Motherhouse around noon.[16] That changed the traveling plans. Because she did not want to lose any time, Mother arranged to leave Philadelphia the same day on the five o'clock train which was scheduled to reach Richmond at one o'clock in the morning. Being the type who seemed able to adjust herself to any situation, she figured that she and her young companion could stay in the waiting room until it was time to go out for an early Mass. Then they would pick up a breakfast at the station and leave on the nine o'clock train for Rock Castle. Personal comfort never entered her plans. We quote Sister M. Mercedes' account of what happened,:

> … When we reached Richmond, we found that the Bird Street Station closed after the arrival of our train, and that we could not as planned remain in the Waiting Room. Here we were in Richmond, not knowing any sisterhood and not quite sure of the hotels. As we were conferring together, an old Colored gentleman came up to us raised a hat and said, "Are you the ladies that the sisters in Duval Street sent me to meet?" Now we knew there were sisters, English Franciscans, on Duval Street, but we did not know how they could have known we were coming. I said to Mother: "I think our architect, Mr. Dodd, must have been in Richmond to meet us, and finding that we did not come, thought it likely we would take this evening train, and thus notified the sisters." Mother gazed at the old gentleman and his old fashioned carriage with its two horses, and elected to go with him as he seemed safe and reliable.
>
> He stopped at the door of the convent, took our bags up to the porch, rang the bell and said, "This is St. Joseph's Convent, sisters, good night!" and departed.
>
> We rang and rang. After a little while a face came to the grille and looked out and saw that we were two sisters. We said we were Sisters of

> the Blessed Sacrament. She went back and consulted with some other members of the community. Gradually they withdrew the bolts and let us in. We found that they had not been notified in any way and had not told any old gentleman to meet us. On our arrival at Rock Castle we inquired from Mr. Dodd. He had not been in Richmond and knew nothing of the affair. We inquired of the Visitation Sisters thinking perhaps some of their community were to arrive. The answer was "No." They knew nothing about it. Mother said it was St. Joseph who did that lovely act for us because he did not want us to be on the streets of Richmond so late at night.[17]

They were in plenty of time for the train in the morning, and were welcomed in Rock Castle at the home of Mr. and Mrs. Dodd where they were to stay for a week. Each morning they were driven over to the Christian Brothers at Belmead for Mass. The annals record that a *phaeton* called for them each morning and brought them back! They were delighted with what they saw. The surrounding countryside was more beautiful than ever. The building was very definitely progressing.

There would be no rushing through on this building. Carefully and slowly the materials supplied by nature were being fitted and formed into the structure. More than 500,000 bricks had been molded out of Rock Castle clay, shaped in a brick machine, and burned in a brick kiln. All the stone for the foundation and trimmings was quarried on the grounds. With the exception of the dressed lumber, everything else needed was also secured on the grounds. The massive oak and pine trees were felled and sawed at the planing mill.[18] A farmer was hired while they were there and arrangements made for the purchase of some stock. It was a full and busy week, but they returned to the Motherhouse well satisfied.

Finally in the fall of 1889 the school was ready for occupancy. Mother M. Mercedes was appointed the first superior and left the Motherhouse July 17 with Mother M. Katharine to get the convent quarters ready for the arrival of the first community. She was young and the thought of the responsibility of this new undertaking weighed heavily on her. Mr. Mosby, the hired farmer, met them at the railroad station with a sad face and announced, "Mother, I have very, very bad news for you. We have had an awful fire."[19]

In their first moment of concern they thought the entire place had burned down but they found out it was only the barn. And yet, that was enough; it seemed to have been deliberately set on fire. As it was only half covered by insurance, it cost the community around $4,000. Many times in her life, with a heart full of charity for God and man, Mother M. Katharine would initiate building projects and erect institutions with evidence of ill will from surrounding communities. Here in the midst of this beautiful solitude someone had set fire to the new barn.[20] Greatly relieved that the disaster had been no worse, on reaching the new completed building, they set to work to get things in readiness for the sisters and to arrange a small temporary chapel. Mother M. Katharine's approach to opening a new mission was an existential one. In most cases in the early foundations, she went out herself and helped with the cleaning, the unloading and arrangement of furniture, and then was on hand to welcome the sisters as they arrived.

Nine sisters reached Rock Castle July 24, and could hardly believe their eyes when they saw the imposing building set in such scenic splendor. Classes began in October on rather loose schedules until the students could be properly classified. For its first years, St. Francis de Sales functioned as an industrial and normal school. It emerged eventually as a fully accredited high school which today draws students from all over the nation. In the beginning there were no charges at all. Girls of good character with the willingness to learn were accepted on the condition that they would stay at the school until they finished their course. Fees, very small at first, were introduced gradually through the years. Within the last decade the school reached the point of self support. Before that, beginning in 1952 and ending in 1955, a million and a half dollar renovation and additions were made to the buildings by the Sisters of the Blessed Sacrament. They were completed just before Mother M. Katharine's death when her income stopped and the community would not have been able to bear the financial burden.

It was very definitely Mother M. Katharine's desire that whatever missions she founded would engage not only in teaching but in catechetical instruction and in home visitation. Long before Catholic papers clamored with suggestions that sisters should go out among the laity, enter apostolates and establish adult contacts outside their convents, the sisters at Rock Castle, and other missions as they were founded, did exactly that. The very first winter St. Francis de Sales was opened, the sisters went to homes on both sides of the river; hidden, poverty-stricken homes, and helped as they could. They went to the unfortunates in the State Farm and instructed the prisoners. Their first visitation there, December 23, 1902, was to a man condemned to die. They prepared him for his baptism December 29, two days before his execution. In 1904 they opened a small library for the prisoners. Records show that more than two thousand, five hundred books and magazines were borrowed the first year.[21] In 1939 they included the inmates of the women's prison in their apostolate. This prison visitation was continued to 1942.[22]

Down through the years, the sisters have continued their apostolate through the countryside fulfilling Mother M. Katharine's desire to share not only the Faith but also learning skills and culture. The Lyceum Programs featuring outstanding musical artists are shared with people in the area who are invited to come as the guests of the school and the student body. From the beginning, the sisters instructed children in Belmead and in Columbia. This latter had an interesting history.

Very early in 1900, Mother M. Katharine visited Rock Castle and announced that the chapel would be ready for occupancy Holy Thursday. And a beautiful chapel it was to be with its altar of Siena marble and Mexican onyx panels. It was erected, she said, as a memorial to her father. In all her charities she was always aware that she was distributing her father's charities and she tried to acknowledge this publicly by her memorials. During this visit she was asked to go to Lynchburg about the question of a school for the Colored. On the way, as the train stopped at a small station marked *Columbia*, she noticed a gilt cross gleaming through the trees and said to her companion, Mother M. Mercedes, "Do you think that is a Catholic Church?" Mother M. Mercedes replied that she did not think so as she had been told there was no Mass celebrated between Richmond and Lynchburg till the Christian Brothers came to Belmead.

On reaching home, Mother M. Mercedes asked a student from Columbia if there was a Catholic Church in the neighborhood. The girl's answer came as quite a surprise, "Yes, there is. But it is not used anymore. There are a lot of Colored people living around there."[23]

The sisters decided to investigate. A few days later Mother M. Mercedes, Sister Mary of the Sacred Heart and the girl as guide, left on the noon train. In Columbia she directed them to a good frame structure with a seating capacity of two hundred. To their amazement, it was scrupulously clean and there were fresh linens and flowers on the altar. The story emerged that the girl's father, "Uncle Zach Kimbro", was the only Colored Catholic in Columbia and on his own, he took great pride in keeping the church in good order. He had originally belonged to the Wakem family, strong Catholics who were proud of the fact that even in the persecutions of Elizabeth and Cromwell, no Wakem had ever surrendered the faith. Mrs. Wakem had lived in Columbia with one unmarried daughter, and she had built this church for her Sulpician son to say Mass there during his vacation days. She and the unmarried daughter were long since dead and also Father Wakem. A married son someplace out West paid no attention to the chapel. Uncle Zach wept as he exclaimed that he had prayed for years that Mass would be said again in the chapel, and for that purpose he had taken great joy in keeping the chapel in order.[24]

Bishop Van De Vyver was contacted and readily gave permission for the sisters to conduct a Sunday School there. Uncle Zach notified the town. Twenty-five children and seventy-five adults gathered in the church. The children went up to the choir loft for a class while Mother M. Mercedes stood in the church and read the epistle and gospel of the day. As she proceeded to give an explanation, she was wondering about the liturgical procedure of a sister preaching in church. The Bishop, however, assured her it was all right. He suggested that they contact the Josephite Fathers to see if one would be available to say Mass there once a month.

Thus it was that Mass was said there once a month and the fervent prayer of Uncle Zach was answered. Thirty adults and a number of children were baptized there the first year. Two years later a school for the Colored was opened with a capable Catholic woman, Miss O'Hare, in charge.[25] All this and much more developed because Uncle Zach prayed and Mother M.

Katharine's eagle eye saw a cross gleaming through the trees. Now there was another place between Richmond and Lynchburg where Mass was being celebrated.

The Foundress felt a special love for these missionaries at Rock Castle as she had felt for the first missionaries to Santa Fe. In her letter to them for their first Christmas in Virginia, 1899, she had written:

> My very dear children in the Blessed Sacrament at St. Francis de Sales:
>
> You will not be with my flock at St. Elizabeth's this Christmastide. I shall miss each dear child of mine with whom it has been my privilege to be in such close relations in those sweet Christmases of the past. And you too, will miss us, just a little, I hope. This is natural. Our Lord gave us our nature and He will not be displeased with us because we miss each other.... You have left us to bring in imitation of Our Lord, the blessings of redemption to the souls for whom He is born in such poverty, abandonment, and suffering.
>
> See his little arms; they are opened wide to receive the souls you will bring to Him in Virginia. Last year the house of St. Francis de Sales stood as it does now on the rolling hilltop overlooking the James; but to the eyes of Faith, how different now from then. It encloses within the walls, as the case of Bethlehem, its God. And you, His own spouses, are there as St. Joseph and Mary to adore and worship and love Him in His first Christmas at St. Francis de Sales. Really I see little difference in one way, between His birth at Bethlehem and his birth in this land where He has never been before on Christmas Day — that spot where my dear daughters will be at the Midnight Mass of 1899....[26]

Before every other realization, the foundation of a new mission meant to her the building of a new tabernacle of the Blessed Sacrament in a place where one had never been before, and in a place where her own sisters would lead countless souls to know Him in the Blessed Sacrament, to adore and love Him in His Eucharistic Presence. Such has been St. Francis de Sales from the beginning. In the quiet of a beautiful countryside and the solitude of its scenic splendor, she built a church to house the Blessed Sacrament. The *Gloria's* of thousands of Masses and the *O Salutaris* of countless Benedictions have risen before its Tabernacle.

The students of St. Francis de Sales from all parts of the country have shared a rich liturgical life blended with their scholastic and physical education. Graduates of this high school are found in every walk of life throughout the nation, all the richer in mind and soul for the type of education they have received. Their appreciation is evident in the vitality of a very active Alumnae Association.

# Chapter 13
# Navajo Frontiers

This century was two years old when Mother M. Katharine opened a school for Navajos in a land of breathtaking beauty — Arizona. The first white settlers who reached the state gasped at the stark beauty of God's creation and the primitive loveliness of its mountains, mesas, valleys, and deserts. A well-known Arizona poet, Sharlot M. Hall, who came into the state as a young girl with the family caravan, said once in addressing a meeting of the Federated Garden Clubs of Arizona: "No one now living knows just how lovely was Arizona when the first white settlers arrived on horseback, leading their pack horses; and a little later driving ox teams across the mesa and valley, where the grass and wild flowers turned down under the wheels like tall wheat under a mowing machine. There were wild flowers in such variety and profusion that the wettest season now cannot bring them to memory — and the flowering shrubs made a royal flower show of their own from March to November."[1]

In this land of the Painted Desert, the Petrified Forest, Canyon de Chelly, and the Grand Canyon, dwelt the noble tribe of Navajos, poor in earthly possession but rich in their power to appreciate the beautiful. Their pagan chants reflect their instinct for the beautiful. When a new home, a *hogan*, is built the father blesses it by sprinkling a handful of meal as he chants:

May it be beautiful my house
From my head may it be beautiful
To my feet may it be beautiful
Where I lie may it be beautiful
All above me may it be beautiful
All around me may it be beautiful.[2]

The Navajo Maiden Sheep song ends with:

With beauty before me, I sing
With beauty behind me, I sing
With beauty above me, I sing
With beauty below me, I sing

With beauty all around me, I sing
On the trail of beauty I hear
The beautiful voice of my sheep
I sing for my sheep.[3]

To the people with this craving for beauty, Mother M. Katharine yearned to bring the knowledge of Immutable and Absolute Beauty — God. As far back as 1744, two Franciscan Fathers had entered the Navajo country by way of Jemez and reported the Indians willing to hear more about Christianity. The fathers set about to establish four missions among them, but a war between the Navajos and the Utes put an end to this attempt. In 1748 two missions were established in the Laguna area at La Cebolleta and at Encinal. But two years later in 1750, the Navajos revolted, drove out the priests and left the missions.

Historians give conflicting causes for this revolt. The Navajos themselves through their Pueblo interpreters said they had not really wanted Christianity. They did not want to be confined to pueblos nor to any specific place. They wanted to be free as deer to roam. Evidently the attempt to form them to agricultural pursuits was not to their liking. There were three points they made clear after this revolt: they did not want to be tied to a fixed abode; they would listen to the missionaries provided they received gifts; they positively would not permit their children to live with or be instructed by strangers away from their homes.[4]

After this declaration, the Navajos roamed and raided at will, capturing horses and sheep, often at the cost of having their women and children caught and sold as slaves to Mexicans and settlers in New Mexico. Since the Navajos had no central controlling government or council, a peace with groups only, not with the whole tribe, could be established; and the raids continued. It was difficult to defeat the Navajos. Their horses were fleet, the country wide, and the hiding places in secret ravines well know to them and many.

When the United States declared war on Mexico in 1846, she proclaimed sovereignty over all the people within the boundaries of our Southwestern territories, including the Navajos. At first they offered peaceful submission, but a series of unfortunate incidents set them running the warpath again. One Navajo leader described the situation from the viewpoint of the Navajos: "About two hundred years ago, the Spanish came to our country and said they were our boss. In 1846 the United States took our land from the Mexicans and told us we belonged to them. Why these nations, which had so much land of their own, had to fight about our land and take it away from us, is hard for us to understand. When the United States soldiers came, they said we would have to stop fighting. Most of our people did not believe we had to obey these strangers so kept on doing the same as they did before."[5]

The roundup and capture of the Navajos was finally accomplished by Kit Carson who pursued them to their last stronghold, the deep gorges of

Canon de Chelly. They were marched to Fort Sumner and held captive there four unhappy years. Bishop Lamy was very much interested in the Christianization of these Indians, and appointed a young priest and two clerics in minor orders to stay with them at Fort Sumner. The priest died the following year, and this missionary attempt ended. The United States Government turned down Bishop Lamy's request to be assigned the education of the Navajos. It was granted instead to the Presbyterians.[6]

After much suffering, the Navajos finally sent a delegation to Washington to plead with the President for permission to return to their own land. Eventually, by the Treaty of 1868, they were assigned a reservation of 3,500,000 acres in Arizona overlapping Utah, Colorado, and New Mexico, large parts of which were barren waste. Since then, Executive Order Extensions and Congressional Acts have increased the reservation to 15,000,000 acres.[7] The United States agreed to give them seed, sheep, goats, and tools for beginning their life anew. The older Navajos advised the tribe to honor the peace and start another life with their sheep. Their herds increased, they developed remarkable handcrafts, men in silver smithing, the women in blanket weaving, using the wool from their sheep which they learned to card and dye every conceivable color.

Bishop Salpointe, Bishop Lamy's coadjutor and successor, planned a joint endeavor to serve Hopi and Navajo Indians. He was evidently unaware of a cultural antagonism between these two tribes. The attempt never succeeded.[8] As a result of the sporadic and incompleted efforts of the Catholic Church among the Navajos, by the end of the nineteenth century, there was no Catholic mission or school among them, nor was there any background of Catholic influence in the history or the experience of the tribe.

Katharine Drexel had long been interested in the Navajos and eager to supply educational facilities for their children. Her interest was intensified by Father Stephan. In a letter of June 10, 1895, he wrote from Fort Defiance:

> The Navajos are anxious to get Catholic Missionaries. There is a great harvest field in this Reservation. The agent here, an Army officer, Major Williams, an Episcopalian, is a most excellent gentleman and very willing to help us. I am going further into Arizona tomorrow, and after carefully examining the situation, shall return to Santa Fe where we can talk matters over....[9]

The following year, 1896, through Father Stephan, she purchased in Arizona a tract of fertile valley land fed by a spring in a little oasis which the Navajos called Tshohotso.[10] Again there was difficulty of finding missionary priests to attempt a foundation there. The Benedictine Vicar Apostolic of the Indian territory, Rev. Ignatius Jean, in answer to her request for missionaries, wrote her in French, that their entire congregation in all its provinces, Germany, Belgium, Italy, as well as France, had a great interest and willingness to come and evangelize this mission territory.[11] With her practical prudence,

Mother M. Katharine wrote Father Stephan asking if he thought they could accomplish the work, not knowing the language, the American way of life, nor the problems of Industrial school management. Father did suggest they might be brought over and given training in the language and school methods before assigning them to Western missions.[12] But in the end this idea was dropped.

She did a lot of thinking, praying, and investigating about the Navajo Indians. Finally her zealous appeal and promise of help to the Reverend Provincial of the Franciscan Fathers of the Cincinnati Province won from him the promise that these Fathers would go out to the desolate Arizona desert and give their best for the salvation of souls there. The Provincial and some of the fathers visited St. Catherine's in Santa Fe early in March 1898 on their way to California. Mother M. Evangelist writing back to the Motherhouse recorded that they had said the vision of the Navajo Indians had made a striking appeal, particularly to the younger men of this very fervent community. "They are all very energetic religious," she wrote, "Americans who speak our language fluently and are quite talented in every way."[13] Father Stephan had already said the same thing in a letter dated August 12, 1897:

> I spoke to a Franciscan Father of the Province of Cincinnati who are good, pious, and hard working priests, like the Sanguinists. I got real encouragement and hope we may get them for the Navajo Indians. They are mostly Americans and adapted for the work; there is a "go ahead" in them.[14]

Father Stephan's appraisal was very accurate. They have been going ahead ever since. They accepted the charge October 13, 1897; the first three Franciscans, Fathers Juvenal Schnorbus, Anselm Weber, and Brother Placid Buerger, arrived on the scene the following year, October 7, 1898. Father Juvenal, the superior, had made a visit before, to arrange to have a one story stone building on the property, intended originally for a trading post, converted to a place of residence.

Mother M. Katharine had agreed to cover all the cost incurred in the opening of the mission, the house renovation, the travel, the furnishings, a horse and saddle, and she asked for a list of the day to day mission expenses of the fathers. She must have been particularly delighted with the existential living of the Vow of Poverty by these Franciscan Fathers. First of all, she ran into difficulty getting a title to the land because they could not with their interpretation of the Vow of Poverty, take possession of the land by personal ownership which the Homestead Act required. They made it clear to her that although this did tie up the business and add a few complications, it was in accordance with their observance of the Vow of Poverty.[15] When after their arrival she asked for a definite amount that would constitute a fixed salary for them, the Provincial wrote back:

> I would rather leave it entirely to you to contribute toward supporting them.... We propose to observe Holy Poverty and hence will be satisfied with whatever you contribute.[16]

At this point she suggested sending an annual salary of one thousand dollars for the three missionaries, and agreed to renew it each year if it were satisfactory to both parties concerned.[17]

The fathers realized they could do nothing against the language barrier which separated them from these Indians, the majority of whom understood only their own language. With the exception of the initial work of the well-known anthropologist, Dr. Washington Matthews, this language had never been analyzed or written down. The fathers determined to learn it from the ground up. Only in the heavenly account book will there by a definite record of the painstaking effort they made to master the unwritten Navajo language. They originated a new code to record it. With the help of two boys, Charley Day aged nineteen, and Sammy Day, sixteen, they went through Webster from A to Z.

It really was a momentous endeavor. More and more the Navajos watched the progress of these fathers; more and more their use of Navajo terms became intelligible to them. They began to develop a deep admiration for these white men who were willing to put themselves to such inconvenience and long drawn out hard labor to converse with them in their own tongue. The fathers' home became a gathering place for the Indians. They came in small groups and large groups at any hour and at any time. They were always made to feel welcome.

The language study received a big impetus when early in 1900 Frank Walker was hired as a handy man and interpreter. He lived with the fathers, accompanied them on their long treks to isolated homes, and acted on all occasions as their interpreter. An interesting letter by Frank Walker himself, throws some light, not only on his background, but on the mission situation among the Navajos generally.

> Gallup, New Mexico, December 14, 1896
>
> Most Reverand Bishop:
>
> I am fully aware of the kind interest that your Grace takes in the Navajo race, and having heard that you intend to establish in the near future a mission for the Navajos, I take the liberty to give you some information about them.
>
> I am not entirely a stranger to your Grace having had the honor to travel through the reservation with you. My name is Frank Walker. My father John Walker was Irish and my mother Domicia Walker was Navajo; both of them were Catholics. I was baptized in the Catholic church of San Bernardino and when 8 years of age returned to the reservation. I

studied 4 years at Fort Defiance, and became afterwards the interpreter of the post. I held that office for 6 years and 9 months. So much for my pedigree and occupation.

According to the report of that last census taken of the Navajos, they would be only 16,000 which is completely false. That census is a fraud. There must be from 24,000 to 25,000 Navajos. But the Navajos are far from living solely in the reservation, in fact I do not believe that 10,000 of them stay in the reservation, else they would starve.

Out of the 25,000 Navajos, 22,000 live in New Mexico. They have no villages, but camp here and there for the time being looking after pasture for their sheep. They do not live much in Arizona because there is no water for their herds.

The Navajos live in the eastern southern part of the reservation, and around Gallup, at Pino's ranch 12 miles from Gallup; Dubois ranch 19 miles from Gallup; they have ranches near Fort Defiance; but in New Mexico at Tuye, Newman's ranch, both places near Gallup, at San Lorenzo, Mitchell Coolidge, around Wingate, Ramah, la Posta, Alamosa.

There are more Indians coming to Gallup than to any other place of the territory. Rather, few of them live on the Rio San Juan.

The Navajos speak more Spanish than English. Medicine men have no influence on the younger element of the race; their religion is dying out. The Navajos are well disposed to receive the teachings of the Catholic priests. Strange to say, although the reservation has had for many years a great number of Protestant preachers of all denominations there is not, I think, a single Protestant Navajo.

Among all the other Indian races of New Mexico, the Navajos glory themselves not to have obeyed the order of Segundo and to have saved the life of the priest who was living in their midst in the Canon de Chelly, while in all the pueblos the priests were killed.

Should your Grace require more information from me, I always will be at your disposal.[18]

In 1900 a young Franciscan, Father Berard Haile, came to St. Michael's. He threw himself into the language study and contributed new methods of attack. When St. Michael's school opened in 1902, he used a mail order catalogue as his text, and the children as his teachers. He would point to a picture and wait for the child to give him the Navajo name. Through the years, with the help of his confreres, he would master Navajo. A printing press was installed at the fathers' mission in 1909. The following year *An Ethnological Dictionary of the Navajo Language* and *A Navajo-English Catechism of Christian Doctrine for Navajo Children* were printed.[19] Of the first, Dr. Edward Sapir, University of Chicago anthropologist, said, "This volume forms the best introduction we posses to the culture of the Navajo Indians."[20] Of the second, Cardinal Van Rossen, Prefect of the Propaganda in Rome, said that the Cincinnati Franciscans had accomplished more in a dozen years among the Navajos than missionaries elsewhere had done in a century.[21] *A Manual of Navajo Grammar, The Holy Gospels for Sundays and Holy Days, Text and Translation* and a score of works on Navajo language, chants, and culture followed.[22] Christmas 1964 found the fathers using Navajo in the new liturgy of the Mass, a final tribute to their assiduous linguistic labors through the years, and a delight to the Navajos.

With the zealous Franciscans in action, Mother M. Katharine was all set to fulfill a long cherished ambition — to build a boarding school where her own sisters might undertake the education of Navajo youth. She went West in 1900 to visit the mission, to talk over plans, and to make arrangements for the foundation of the school. A point that should be constantly borne in mind in connection with the multitudinous building operations of Mother M. Katharine for her own community and for others, is that most of them were carried on in rather desolate areas. They were far from railroads or shipping points, in places where there were no resident contractors, nor local supplies of vital building materials. She had been fortunate enough to secure a delightful oasis in the desert for the site of her school for the Navajos, but there were many problems still to be faced. After this visit, she engaged her Philadelphia architect to draw up the plans, with special attention to the directions of the Indian Commissioner for the Agency school at Fort Defiance. The commissioner stressed the importance of industrial branches in the education.[23] She agreed to give the contract to Mr. Owens, a building contractor from Minneapolis, who was then finishing the erection of a government school at Keams Canyon. He already had a staff and workmen in the area, a very practical advantage.[24]

There would be a great deal of correspondence and a great deal of discussion until title to the land which she had purchased was finally established. As a matter of fact, parts of this land had to be exchanged for land belonging to the United States Government which could be included in the Homestead Act, as surveyors determined that some portions of it belonged to the railroad, and the railroad would not sell. Actually, in the establishment of all these Indian missions there was a tremendous amount of detail, of research, of land title investigation. The records of all this are safely kept in the Archives of the Sisters of the Blessed Sacrament. One goes through them reverently and carefully, wondering how in the world the Foundress of a new Community was able to enter into the intricate phases involved. Building a school involved for her a careful analysis of all details. It was well the Franciscan Fathers were willing to investigate all points for her and report on details. A few excerpts from her many letters to the Franciscans will illustrate this point.

There was an early call for her sisters but they would not be ready till 1902.

> May 28, 1899
>
> I am very sorry that you think I have very little interest in St. Michael's Mission. On the contrary, I feel the keenest interest in it, and all its concerns, and only wish everything were ripe tomorrow for sending our sisters to the Navajos. But as that cannot be done for at least one year

or more, we will have to be patient and bide the Lord's time and call. The harvest is indeed ripe, but the laborers are not fitted to reap it.[25]

In the meantime, she wanted the fathers to have a suitable residence instead of a transformed trading post.

1900

On Saturday we had a meeting of the Council. I brought before it the consideration of allowing something for the erection of your house at St. Michael's. The decision is as follows: We will pay one half the cost of erection of the building as shown on the last plan you sent me. You stated in your letter the plan would cost several thousand less than the first estimate which, I believe, was $10,000.

We will pay one half the cost if the Province pay the remainder. If you cannot secure this amount from the Province, we will pay the balance. That is we will make up the amount that the Province cannot give. We will then in any case pay one half the cost, and further if you are unable to procure the remaining half from the Province, we will make up the deficit whatever it may be. I am glad to be able to assist you in building your convent this year....[26]

The Franciscan Fathers were patient and obliging missionaries. She trusted them implicitly and counted on their generous cooperation. Her investigations would cover many points.

No date

There is another favor I wish to beg of you. When you go to Gallup, will you please ask the agent there what his instructions are relative to the freight rebate? When Mother Francis Xavier saw the General Freight Agent, he explained as follows: "I will instruct the agent at Gallup to allow 50% rebate on all freight charges on goods delivered at Gallup for St. Michael's Mission, shipped between May 15th and June 30th."[27]

April 4th, 1901

I have been thinking very seriously about the location of the Convent, and I have decided that to build up on the hills will be inconvenient on account of the scant supply of water. Here we get fifty gallons of water a second, and I am afraid the small quantity of water to be procured from the well you wrote about some time ago would never suffice for the school and Convent.[28]

October 14, 1901

... I am rather at sea as to which contractors are really reliable. Do you really think there is a reliable contractor at Gallup, or other near region? The building is pretty large. It takes a large one to house about one hundred pupils and sisters, and chapel, classrooms, etc. I have the plans and specifications of a Philadelphia architect with me; but what are they if I cannot get an honest contractor! Do you know of an Arizona lawyer I could consult for safe signing of the contract? I suppose the Arizona law would have to be followed, and I wish to make the contract in every way binding and legal.[29]

January 9, 1902

No doubt you have by this time received the Valentine Scrip for the 40 acre Day tract. Thanks be to God! That much at least is secured. I am so anxious to begin the building. I can scarcely brook any delay. Will you please purchase the scrip for the remaining Government land, that is 160 acres.[30]

But she was grateful and deeply appreciative of the zeal and untiring efforts of the fathers.

February 26, 1902

Please let me have a bill for your expenses to Prescott and San Juan. If there are any other travelling expenses, please let me know. I cannot express my appreciation of all you have done for us at St. Michael's. It seems almost like an imposition to write this letter to you. Now I know every one of these trips means an expense to you, so please, I beg of you do not hesitate to send me a list of expenses and I shall forward check to cover same.[31]

No consideration was too small for her attention. She overlooked nothing from killing rats to diverting a creek.

April 9, 1902

In one of my private letters I intended asking you if you will be kind enough to procure some "Rough on Rats" and put it around the Days' house in the various rooms, to keep the mice away and prevent them from destroying the furniture when it comes. I am ordering a Reed Bake Oven; it will arrive at Gallup some time this month. Perhaps it could be hauled over to St. Michael's, or else stored away in the Odd Fellows Hall. If there are any mice in this basement do you not think it would be well to distribute some "Rough on Rats"? I know from experience how destructive mice are; in an empty building they usually hold sway.

There is a matter — an important one — I have often thought of but unfortunately neglected to mention to you before this. Does that Creek ever rise so as to come up to the spot I selected for the building? Could you inquire of some old settler, or Mr. and Mrs. Day, and if so, get Mother M. Evangelist to authorize placing the building more to the right, if possible. Or could the Creek's course be diverted in case it were to rise?...[32]

She planned a simple but substantial building for the first Catholic school on the entire Navajo reservation. And she determined it should be called St. Michael's. It was her hope that the school would be ready for occupancy October 15, 1902. Early in that year, she and Mother M. Ignatius started out to look over the situation and see how her carefully drawn up plans were being carried out. The sight that met their gaze as they entered the property at St.

Michael's was not too inviting, though definite progress was being made. The foundations had been completed October 1901; the actual construction had only begun in March, and they were visiting in April.[33] The building area was surrounded by a number of small log huts which the contractor, Mr. Owens, had put up for the men working for him. One of these little shanties had been fitted up roughly for her and her companion. Each morning they walked the mile to the one story house of the fathers where they assisted at Mass. During the day, she went over the building details with Mr. Owens, checking light, ventilation, type of furniture, every conceivable element that would contribute to the foundation of an effective and permanent Catholic missionary endeavor for the Navajos.

On her return to the Motherhouse, she announced the names of the twelve sisters who would be the first S.B.S. apostles to the Navajos. Everyone had been eagerly and hopefully awaiting this word. The evident joy of those selected was great. Today, by jet, the West is reached within hours. Back in 1902 it was a very distant country; to these very young missionaries, it was a new world. Disappointments and back breaking labors would come later; then, they knew only the joy of the anticipated apostolate.

Mother M. Katharine's concern about the progress of the building deepened as the date she had set for occupancy drew nearer. Taking her cousin, Josephine Drexel, as her companion she left for St. Michael's late in the summer of 1902. She had a threefold plan in mind. First she would inspect the building and if possible, try to hurry the men along; then she would tour the Indian mission she had aided in the Indian Territory or what is now known as Oklahoma; finally she would be at St. Michael's for the sisters' arrival. This would be Josephine Drexel's second visit to the West with Mother M. Katharine who wanted her cousin to be interested in the welfare of the Indians, too. Very definitely, she was hoping she might have a vocation to the religious life as she wrote in one of her letters to the Motherhouse.[34] It must have been quite an experience for Josephine, accustomed to the best in travel accommodations, to be the traveling companion of her religious cousin. She may have been highly amused and possibly edified at the spirit of poverty she saw exercised in the selection of travel accommodations.

At Lamy Junction Mother M. Katharine changed partners temporarily, Josephine going on to Santa Fe and Mother M. Ignatius accompanying her to St. Michael's. Once there, she was disappointed to find no part of the building under roof yet. She pursued the builder and tried to induce him to promise that at least five rooms would be ready by October 19. The best she could get from Mr. Owens was a promise that he would try as hard as he could to have five rooms roofed for the occupancy of the Sisters October 19. Though she had expected to spend only a few days there she was detained ten days. That letter she wrote to the Sisters was by the Providence of God. Two days of rain had turned what she thought would be their drinking and washing water into a deep brown liquid. That necessitated arranging for machinery and pipes to test for underground water. As she waited for results she wrote:

> Shall we find limpid waters? That depends on your prayers. Today we visited the little church at Newton, and I told Our Lord the truth when I said to Him it was easy for Him to give you all to drink. Then I thought of Him at the well .... Do you remember how He said: "*If* thou didst know the gift of God ... thou wouldst rather have asked of Him living waters"? I feel a reproach for asking Him to give these temporal waters when I could have asked for living waters springing up into Eternal Life, waters abundant of grace for the missionaries, waters of Baptism for the poor pagan Navajos.
>
> I told Our Lord that better would it be for us to drink muddy temporal waters always in this short span of life, provided that He gave us His own pure living waters. With that great gift we shall never thirst, and the Navajos will never thirst, but will become God's own most dear children with Jesus in the Blessed Sacrament to them as *the* gift of God dwelling in their hearts, as in a sanctuary. Yet Our Lord can give us, if He wish, both the spiritual and temporal waters.[35]

With a very indefinite promise about the readiness of the building, she brought Mother M. Ignatius back to Santa Fe where she picked up Miss Drexel and both of them started out to visit the Indian Territory. Mother's vast contributions had been given to institutions spread over a wide area. Except through occasional letters, she had no way of knowing the progress of individual missions. Because of this, she had decided while in the West to visit those in the Indian Territory.

Every detail of these visits was recorded in her letters back to the sisters. She began her correspondence on this trip by a very special letter just for the sisters at Santa Fe. These were her very first missionaries and she had a special love for them. Both her affection for them and her humble opinion of herself as their spiritual mother are very much evidence.

> It is five thirty P.M. and my heart is really lonely for you — there is a weight there and has been since we parted. I feel keenly your sweet daughterly affection for me, that charity so precious because it is from Our Lord and for His sake. You could not have been kinder nor more lovingly thoughtful, one and all. I hope Our Lord may reward you for it. Here is one of the causes of my heart-ache.
>
> I would so much have loved to help you and encourage you on, in your beautiful lives; to have been some little comfort to you. I know I have failed in this. I am always so ambitious for the spiritual progress of my dear ones, that in striving to show them a more excellent way, I discourage them. At Lamy, I felt such remorse that I said the rosary to obtain from Our Lord, through His own Love for you, that He Himself would supply for all my failures. I placed you all in His Sacred Wounds, and your superior especially in His Heart. I thought of your hands and

feet, moving so continually by and in obedience, and I united them to those dear wounded Hands and Feet.

I greatly rejoice that Our Lord is served by you, that you are body and soul, given to Him. I think of those one hundred and forty-five children you bring daily to your Eucharistic King, and how your lives are devoted to serving Christ in them, feeding them, clothing them, spiritually and corporally....

Please, dear daughters, pardon then, all my very many faults in being less a mother than I ought. If sorrow could make me a better mother, I would be so now from this moment. Yet I have nothing to rely on but her who is your own Mother, Mary, who will be more a Mother because she pities you in having the mother on earth. Tomorrow, my every prayer and fifteen decades of the rosary will be for you, that Mary may show herself a Mother to you, and that Our Lord may be your All. At the Forty Hours Devotion, I shall pray through Our Lord in the Blessed Sacrament, pray for you individually. Pray, dear ones, for me....[36]

Her first stop in the Indian Territory was Purcell which they reached at the unearthly hour of 12:45 A.M. They met the five Franciscan Sisters who had left Philadelphia for that mission fourteen years before. Mother M. Katharine had been particularly interested in this school, but she wrote that she was horrified when watching the children file into the church and saw not one Indian face among them. All, she mentioned, were as white as she was. Interviewing the children individually with the superior's permission, she was to find out that all of them, whether their hair was light and eyes blue, were claiming some Indian blood. She received answers like: "Yes, my mother was a Creek, half-breed"; or "My father is a Chickasaw, not full-blood"; "My grandfather was a Chocktaw." She was not encouraged when she found out that any child who had any Choctaw or Chickasaw blood, no matter how little, if it could be proven, was entitled to three hundred and sixty acres of land. In addition to that, any surplus land was to be sold and the money which it brought, to be given or invested for the child. Mother M. Katharine was not at all happy about this situation, for she felt that the full-blooded Indians would not receive that which was really theirs. From Purcell they went to Ardmore. Here the same situation faced her with children as white as she, and in most instances very few of them claiming Indian blood.[37]

In the Chickasaw territory she was to be disappointed again. There were only about eleven boarders, all white, and about one hundred day pupils. Mother M. Katharine was convinced that only a few of these had any Indian blood. There was to be some comfort in the trip for her, however, when they reached Anadarko, and talked with full-blooded Indians in an Indian camp on the Comanche Reservation. St. Patrick's Mission on this reservation had been built to accommodate one hundred Indian boys and girls. There were only twenty-six in the school then.

At Sacred Heart School for Potawatomi Indians, she notes in her letter: "There is not an India-looking girl in the whole school. As at Purcell I went from child to child, asking where the Indian blood came in, to find every child claimed a Potawatomi relative of some kind, making them half, one-eighth, or one-sixteenth Indian."[38] At the nearby Benedictine Monastery she found a school of thirty-eight Potawatomi half-breed boys.

Mother M. Katharine was interested not only in the Indian blood of these pupils before her, but also in the whole school, its supplies, its arrangements, etc. For these details in all the schools visited, she had the highest praise. They were poor, they were working with little equipment, but everything was neat and clean and the children were well disciplined. She noted particularly at Sacred Heart, the Potawatomi Mission, the ages of the boys: one fifteen year old was in the Third Reader; boys thirteen were in an addition class; none of them, as far as she could see, had reached the fraction stage.

Their next stop was Guthrie where they visited a small school for the Colored. Up to that point, only thirty children had been enrolled in the school as this was still cotton-picking-time, and the area was rich in cotton. Only five were in attendance the day of her visit as Buffalo Bill's show was parading through the town. Mother noted carefully that there were three thousand Colored in Guthrie, only sixty of whom were Catholic. She also met the priest and Sisters stationed at a school for the Colored in Langston.[39]

Their journey through the Osage Nation was made in a large wagon high enough to carry them across the Arkansas River without getting too wet. The water, however, did sweep over the floor as the horses struggled against the current. Once the river was crossed, they enjoyed the fifteen mile drive to St. John's Mission. She spent two or three hours in a classroom there interviewing and questioning the thirty-nine Osage boys attending the school.[40] At St. Louis School in Pawhuska they found seventy-two girls all full-bloods, in attendance. In Vinita in the Cherokee Nation, four Sisters of Mount Carmel were teaching a day school for whites and the one-eighth blood Indians. There were forty-two day pupils of whom sixteen only, were either one-eighth or one-sixteenth blood Indians.[41]

At Muskogee, they visited St. Joseph's Mission; only two of its boarders were one-thirty second blood Indian. It must be noted here that Mother made this tour in September and early October. The gathering and assembling of children for the fall term in the Indian territory involved many details and could not be accomplished as definitely and specifically as in a modern parochial school. You just did not say to Indians that classes would be resumed at a specific day, and registration closed a few days later. You kept on registering as they came. Consequently, for another month or so these children would be drifting in. But the fundamental fact would remain that the native Indians, full bloods, in whom she was particularly interested did not seem to be faring too well in these missionary educational institutions she had supported.

As an advocate of integration, Mother M. Katharine, it would seem, was way ahead of her time. She and her community were dedicated to the intellectual and moral preparation of both Indian and Colored races to the full enjoyment of their rights and privileges as American citizens. Her aim was to prepare them for effective citizenship of this world and of the next. Her sentiments in this direction are well stated in the close of a letter she wrote to her community at the end of this traveling October 15, 1902:

> ... I am still dazed at the discovery made in one trip to the Indians, where in their own land, their own specially reserved territory, so few Indians, comparatively, are to be seen. White people and white people always, and white Indians, except in the unbeaten paths. In the Cherokee Nation alone, there are 28,000 one-quarter, one-eighth, one-thirty second breeds, and only 7,000 full-bloods. I do not know, nor have any means of knowing the population of full-bloods in the other tribes. Of Osages there are, I believe, 1,500 only.
>
> Please, please mail to me at St. Michael's Mission, Fort Defiance, a Government report of the Five Civilized Tribes. I believe you will find a copy in the press or bookcase in the Superior's office. Miss Josephine and I both want to read about these Nations or what is left of them. We both burn with a desire to bring the full-bloods, what is left of them, somehow to the Church, to educate them so that they may not be cheated out of their land by the teeming population of whites, so that they, too, may be fit to intermarry with good Catholic whites, and not the worst white element. Thus they may be saved unto generation and generation, soul and body, mingled as Normans and Saxons were, so that future generations may not be able to discern differences of nationality, but that mingled into one Nation, all may serve God on earth and praise Him eternally in Heaven. If an awful effort be not made to save the full-bloods, they must inevitably become paupers and die out. These are my impressions which I long to communicate to Father Ketcham, that he who has lived so long in the Indian Territory, may tell if they be true impressions or not.[42]

Adhering closely to her schedule and her determination to have the sisters installed at St. Michael's October 19, she and Josephine Drexel, having completed their Indian tour, reached St. Catherine's October 17. The following day she set out for St. Michael's with three sisters including Mother M. Evangelist. Miss Drexel and six sisters came on later. On their arrival Mother M. Katharine announced that Sister M. Agatha was to accompany Miss Drexel on a tour of the reservation to get acquainted with Navajo life and possibly to help secure students for the school.

Father Anselm Weber conducted the party. The trip occupied ten days and was a delightful experience both for young Sister M. Agatha and Josephine. Their destination was Canon de Chelly and the deep ravines there where Navajos lived. They made the trip in two stages driving thirty-five miles first to Mr. Hubble's Trading Store; then going on the following day, thirty-seven more miles to Mr. Day's house at Chin Lee. Sister M. Agatha's letters at the time record the breathtaking scenery along the way, and the intriguing and interesting encounters with the individual Navajos.[43] Father Weber used this opportunity to investigate the possibility of founding a branch mission at Chin Lee which later materialized.

At this point the school was nearing completion; four rooms only were under roof; the Sisters were installed, the Community life begun; and the money was available to support this new missionary endeavor. But the main problem was the students. Navajos had never been interested in the education of their children, particularly education away from hogans. Then too, January 7, 1900, Mother M. Evangelist, Superior at St. Catherine's, had asked Father Anselm and the Franciscan Fathers if they could gather some Navajo children for St. Catherine's in Santa Fe.[44] Mother M. Katharine had repeated the request in a letter of August 30, 1900. She had expressed the hope that at least ten Navajo boys could be obtained for St. Catherine's.[45] She earnestly desired their Catholic education. That presented more problems than she was aware of: not only long treks across deserts to interview the parents, but it involved also a terrific effort on the part of Father Anselm to answer the very definite objections of the Navajos to sending their children away to any kind of boarding school. It was a long drawn out and strenuous effort for the Franciscan Fathers, but eventually seven Navajo students were promised. Five of them reached Santa Fe, and were entered as students at St. Catherine's.

It had been difficult to gather those students. It would be doubly difficult to collect enough for a new school. Anticipating this difficulty, Father Anselm had arranged back in 1900 a meeting of Mother M. Katharine and all the Head Men on the Navajo Reservation. He had written her to come on to St. Michael's and be there when the famous Mountain Chant was concluded.[46] He invited the leaders gathered for the Chant to meet her at St. Michael's. A feast was prepared for them, after which a very interesting meeting took place in the open.

The Indian leaders expressed strong and definite opposition. Some were of the opinion that education had hurt rather than helped them. The arguments went on for a long time until Father Anselm explained that the education being planned would include training in manual arts as well as in prayers which would be a great advantage to their children. Mother M. Katharine in a gracious and pleasing way pointed out the definite advantages to them and to their children of the type of education that would be given at St. Michael's when the building was erected. They could not doubt the sincerity of her desire when she explained how much she wanted to help them.

Their strongest objection had to do with the health of their children. The Navajo had his own view of how to preserve health and how to take care of sick children. That view included bringing the child home, no matter how sick, to his own medicine men. It took some long arguing on the part of Father

Anselm to make them see that in many instances this could be dis-astrous for a sick child, particularly in the biting cold of an Arizona winter. The whole interview, however, seemed to have ended with an acknowledgement by a group of the leaders that this would be a good thing to try out. They promised that some of their children would be in attendance. But all this was two years before the school was built.

When the time for opening St. Michael's came around, getting the children to attend was another matter. Father Anselm took to his saddle again and spent long, uncounted hours crossing the desert and arguing with parents. By the opening day, December 3, he had gathered forty-seven Navajos. A few more would be brought in later. It was an exciting time for everybody. Parents, who in many instances had come with their children, stayed around for about two weeks. They went outside to sleep in their blankets at night, but all day long they followed the sisters and children watching everything. They wanted to make sure their children would be well treated. Finally they were satisfied at what they saw. One Indian leader, before he left, told Mother M. Evangelist that the Indians were pleased and willing to leave their children with the sisters. He noted particularly that the girls and boys were kept separate. That was what the Navajos wanted.[47]

The children, of course, brought nothing with them. There were no tuition or board fees, there were no clothing lists they had to supply. As a matter of fact, some arrived with practically none. For years on years, these children would be given everything at St. Michael's. The first year was an extremely difficult one for both sisters and students. The winter was the coldest known in that area for years; the fires in various rooms were weak because the chimneys would not draw. The children were all ages, but none of them above third grade level. For a month they were all grouped together till their individual capacities could be determined. To add to the difficulties of the situation, the children spoke no English, and the sisters, no Navajo. For weeks, the children like their parents before them, just watched the sisters but said nothing. They too, had to be satisfied before they took any chances with these women, to them, so strangely dressed. They thawed out after a few weeks and a mutual attempt at communication began.

The parents and their children must have been satisfied, for in the following year the registration doubled. It dropped to fifty in the third year but after that it took a steady rise till it reached around one hundred and fifty, the limit of the school's capacity in the earlier years. Up until 1946 it remained just a grammar school of eight grades. More and more the Indians saw the advantages of this fundamental Christian education; but each year for lack of space many children had to be turned away. Then the tables turned. Instead of Mother M. Katharine pleading with them to send their children to be educated, they pleaded with her to enlarge her facilities so that more and more children could be admitted.

St. Michaels, Arizona
February 23, 1925

Rev. Mother Catherine:

Owing to the limited capacity of the school at Saint Michaels which is conducted by you, we the Navajo Indians humbly petition you to grant our request. We realize the good that is being done by this school and would like to see this influence spread. All of us are anxious to bring our children to your school but since it is filled our children are turned away and we are forced to take them to other places against our will. It may not be possible for you to enlarge the school at Saint Michaels, in that case could you not consider the matter of opening a school some place else, for all of us appreciate what you are doing for us and we would like all our children to attend a school like the one at Saint Michaels, Arizona.

We humbly request you again and again to enlarge the school at Saint Michaels and hope that you will grant our petition. This is not the request of one or the other but of many who have talked about the school at Saint Michaels, and listed below will be found a few signatures of our people, who hope to see the school enlarged and able to give their children a Catholic Education when they are brought to your school at Saint Michaels, Arizona.

This letter was signed by outstanding tribe leaders: Chee Dodge, Henry Taliman, Thomas Curley, Dan Kinlichini, Votuth Broh, John Gohino, Sam Jones, James Comman, John Morgan, Mark Burnaide.[48]

With the many demands on her from her missions for Colored and Indian, stretching by this time, across the country, Mother M. Katharine could not see her way clear then to enlarge St. Michael's although a gymnasium and several buildings were added in the course of the years. However, in 1946 a high school department was opened, and that definitely required an additional outlay in buildings and equipment. Consequently in 1948, a general reconstruction of the original plant was begun. The entire plant was redesigned and renovated. A completely new high school of modern architectural design was built of the same native stone as the other buildings.[49] Driving over route 666 some thirty miles from Gallup, and turning left at route 87, one comes suddenly on an imposing group of buildings settled comfortably in the sunken oasis which Mother M. Katharine had selected as the secluded and protected site of her missionary endeavor for the Navajos. One hardly suspects it is there till one is almost upon it, looking down at it from the vantage point of the highway.

The accomplishment and the hidden seclusion of St. Michael's are in some way typical of Mother M. Katharine's apostolate in the American mission field. She gave away millions, and was the instrument of education for hundreds of thousands of the underprivileged. She did it all quietly and without fanfare. She shunned publicity and sought only the glory of God. She burned with desire to bring all Americans to full membership in the Mystical Body of Christ. Across the country from North to South and East to West, institutions sprang up from her munificence; but the world knew little of her accomplishments because for herself, she sought the secluded valley of prayer and service.

Today two buses go out daily to gather day students from the first grade through high school. The plan originally was to take only boarders. But today, by means of buses those within reasonable distance can be brought in. Boarding accommodations are given only to those who live too far away. In that way St. Michael's can accommodate a larger number. Between day and boarding students, the registration at St. Michael's, as this book goes to print, is four hundred and sixty. There were no charges at all in the beginning, but gradually as the Navajos' economic condition improved in the course of years, small fees were established. Today specific tuition and boarding fees are higher, but they are still far below the actual cost of running St. Michael's. The deficit must be annually supplied by the Sisters of the Blessed Sacrament.[50]

Many waters have flowed through the arroyos since the Franciscan Fathers and the Sisters of the Blessed Sacrament first opened a mission and a school for these delightful children of the desert. In the eddying past of arroyo currents during the intervening sixty-three years, many changes have come to the Navajo. As a matter of fact, many changes have come to all the Indians. One reads with interest that in 1964 The United States Indian Claims Commission awarded over thirty-eight million dollars to Indian tribes. This much was awarded in judgements to eight Indian tribes. "Judgment funds from land claims settlements are held in trust for the tribes by the Bureau of Indian Affairs. Programs for the use of the funds are developed by tribal governing bodies and approved by the Secretary of the Interior. The Indian Claims Commission, an independent tribunal, was created by Congress in 1946 to hear and determine claims of tribes, bands, and other identifiable groups of American Indians living in the United States. More than 850 claims have been filed since, of which about 25 per cent have finally adjudicated. Awards totaling nearly $140 million have been granted."[51]

Tribal income from oil and gas leases, together with vanadium-uranium leases and royalties have mounted considerably, but not enough to remove poverty from the entire tribe nearing today the one hundred thousand mark. Very definitely, poverty has not been eradicated from the reservation by these new developments any more than a Congressional Anti-Poverty Bill will remove poverty from all places on American shores. The Navajo and other Indians have come a long way in securing the help and direction of the American Government for their basic rights and their basic claims. But poverty still has deep roots in parts of the Navajo reservation. The fathers still go out from Franciscan headquarters at St. Michael's and their forty-three mission centers to desolate homes in desolate places. Children still come in to St. Michael's who can afford no board or tuition. The result of all this is that there still exists a Navajo problem. An item in the *Navajo Times* puts it this way:

> The Navajos are many years behind the rest of the civilized world and the only solution for this nation is education. I'll say that 70% of this nation cannot read or write. There are some that have the education that the average white man has. And in the years to come there will be thousands of boys and girls (this in spite of the dropouts) ready for high schools, colleges, and business training schools. In order to get these future students the proper education they will need in order to compete with their brothers, they will need money. Therefore the tribal money invested for this purpose will be an investment that in the long run will pay dividends. I say education is the only solution. The old men and women and the uneducated will not be here always. They are the "Vanishing Americans", but in their places is appearing on the horizon a new nation of Navajos who will come out of the chaos of the present poverty and primitive state.[52]

If the *Navajo Times* can publish this in 1964, one can imagine what the situation was in 1902 when St. Michael's School opened its doors to these children of the desert. The plan put into execution that year was the fulfillment of long standing desires in the heart of Mother M. Katharine, specific desires for the evangelization of the Navajos. She passed those desires on to her spiritual daughters for all the years to come. In 1903 after visiting St. Michael's and seeking the fruits of the first year's harvest, she wrote back to the sisters:

> I wish I had some more days to spend with you. I much feared I failed to express the real consolation my visit was to me. Do you know it seemed like the realization of years, yes, longings of the last fifteen years? When I looked at you, the virgin mothers of the poor Navajos, my heart was full of gratitude to God because He had beyond all expectation, fulfilled the desires He Himself had given me, to do something for these poor pagans. You know God gave me this desire one or two years before I entered religion or ever dreamed that God would permit me to be a sister.
>
> And so, on this visit I looked up in wonder at God's wonderful ways and thought how little we imagine what may be the result of listening and acting on a desire He puts into the heart. If He puts it into the heart, He will bless it, if we try to act upon it, and great will be the effect before God. It will be success before God, even if it be not so to our weak understanding. For God means that which He breathes into the soul should bring forth fruit to eternal life. God in His great condescension to my weakness has let me see with my own eyes the good results of this desire of fifteen years ago. When one is strong in the spiritual life He does not always permit this. He makes us adore without understanding.
>
> How fifteen years ago, could I have believed that eleven of my own spiritual daughters would be amongst the Navajos and that each one of them would have a mother's heart for them. That, God has given to you,

> along with big earnest desires for the salvation of your spiritual children, the Navajos. These are the desires God has placed in your hearts and great will be the effect if you continue as you do, to nourish these desires and act upon them. He will fulfill your desires with good things far beyond your expectations, especially as you have so cheerfully endured with sacrifices of this foundation of this Convent.... With God's help you were able to get through last winter's privations. Years ago you would not have believed you would have had the strength. Who gave you the strength? God! He will give you more strength this year....[53]

The desires endure; the strength and the grace of God continue to flow to St. Michael's and through it, to the loneliest hogan on the far flung Navajo Reservation.

# Chapter 14
# A Mission To Fulfill

The beginning of Mother M. Katharine's interest in the Indian missions is well marked and definitely recorded. The missions she built and those she helped are by this time, matters of historical record. The organization of the Bureau of Catholic Indian Missions gave her a specific medium through which to disburse her wealth. Through it and beyond it, she distributed millions. With regard to the Colored, however, the situation was different. That field was marked by a paucity of laborers and the absence of a widely organized Catholic effort among the teeming millions set free without the implements to use their freedom. It must be borne in mind too, that with the exception of Louisiana, the South was largely Protestant. Of the 59,000 churches listed in the states of the Confederacy, only 2,200 were Catholic.[1]

Despite a lack of personnel and a lack of funds, the Catholic Church was deeply concerned about the plight of the freed Negroes. As Bishops were preparing for the Second Plenary Council of Baltimore in 1866 (Katharine at that time was eight years old), Archbishop Spalding of Baltimore wrote to Archbishop McCloskey of New York: "Four millions of these unfortunates are thrown on our Charity, and they silently but eloquently appeal to us for help."[2] Bishop Verot of Savannah wrote a pastoral letter on the subject which was quoted throughout the country. The editor of the *Baltimore Sun* referred to it as an indication that "The intellectual, moral, and religious culture of the Southern Negroes would engage the earnest attention of his Church."[3] Very definitely, it did. Included in the decrees of this Second Plenary Council was a chapter dealing with the spiritual care of the Negroes, and the personal and serious attention bishops should give this pressing situation.[4] Bishop Verot was appointed to write The Society of the Propagation of the Faith in France for monetary assistance.[5]

Like the Papal call for volunteers for Latin America today, this council too, sent out a call for laborers, for the establishment of religious communities to take up this work, for priests to dedicate themselves to it. Answers to the call were few. As of January 1965 the Catholic Church in the United States has sent a total of 4,091 priests, sisters, and lay apostles to work in various countries of South America.[6] What a harvest for the Church would have been realized if anything approaching this number had been available for the apostolate to the Colored of the South. In addition to the scarcity of laborers for this field, there was another road block to the progress of this apostolate. A prevalent sense of race superiority and a bitter resentment of Civil War losses militated against the spirit of brotherhood vital to any effort to help the freed Negro enjoy the liberty that springs from his nature as man, and his origin as a child of God. Prejudice sank its roots deep in many areas where former slaves were set free.

Not only American bishops were concerned about this situation; Rome was more than concerned. Word had reached there that Negroes were humiliated at the treatment given them in some Catholic centers in the South. Cardinal Gotti, Prefect of the Propaganda, had asked the papal legate to communicate the concern of the Holy See to Cardinal Gibbons so that, if the report were true, remedial steps could be taken by the American Bishops.[7] At the meeting of the Archbishops, April 14, 1904, it was decided to send a copy of Cardinal Gotti's letter to all bishops, requesting the correction of the abuses if they existed. But the abuses went on, and unshepherded millions were not reached.

In 1905 Archbishop Ryan, urged on by Mother M. Katharine, suggested the establishment of a bureau with a priest in charge, for Colored Missions, similar to that for Indian Missions. His recommendation included a committee of bishops from the North and the South to be named by Cardinal Gibbons as chairman. The Cardinal was also to select and supervise a priest to be in charge. Accordingly, the Catholic Board for Mission Work among the Colored People was formed with Cardinal Gibbons as chairman, and the committee including Archbishops Ryan and Farley, Bishop Byrne of Nashville, and Bishop Allen of Mobile. Rev. John B. Burke, pastor of St. Benedict the Moor's in New York was named as director.[8]

The untutored millions of Colored People struck a responsive chord in the soul of Mother M. Katharine, so sensitive to the needs of the poor and the underprivileged. In the course of her religious life, she would give millions for the education of Colored Americans, give these millions so quietly and unostentatiously that not many would be aware they were being given. The beginnings of her contributions to the Colored are not so distinctly marked nor clearly discernible, even though they are definitely true and as accurately historical as her contributions to the Indians. May 10, 1889, just four days after she became a postulant in the Mercy Novitiate in Pittsburgh, Archbishop Ryan wrote to congratulate her on the good she had already accomplished just by her example in entering the religious life. He noted that her action had made a tremendous impression on the Philadelphia area.[9] In the same letter he thanked her for the check for $1,200 for the Colored mission in Philadelphia which would later develop into St. Peter Claver's Parish. In 1886 she had purchased a spacious three story house at 832 Pine Street which the Sisters of Notre Dame opened as a school for the Colored.[10]

In 1893 Archbishop Ryan wrote Mother M. Katharine from New Orleans that he had visited all Archbishop Janssen's schools and institutions for the Colored and found everything satisfactory.[11] He had visited these areas because it was her donations that had enabled Archbishop Janssen to found various works for the Colored members of his flock in whom he was deeply and zealously interested. From the very beginning of her community, many appeals reached Mother M. Katharine from the South for the construction or reconstruction of churches. She gave help always on the condition that an aisle would be reserved for the Colored. She was not at all interested in a roped off back pew; she expected a definite promise that a whole aisle from transept to door would be reserved. She received many pledges to this effect as she sent check after check in answer to a long line of appeals that came to her daily, appeals for both churches and schools. By 1904 she had disbursed in smaller donations ranging from $200 to $6,000 more than $100,000 in the states of Arkansas, Florida, Georgia, Kentucky, Louisiana, Mississippi, North Carolina, Ohio, South Carolina, and Tennessee.[12] She wanted to see what had been done with her donations and for that purpose, she and Mother M. James left Rock Castle March 19, 1904, for a quick visit to the South. As far as the fulfillment of her hopes for the Colored was concerned, she was in for a series of disappointments.

Their first stop was Charlotte, North Carolina. In a letter to the Motherhouse March 22, she described the church in detail and noted that the windows were good specimens of American glass. But the object of her special attention was the reserved pews:

> Unnecessary to state, my eyes made it a duty to watch that row of twenty to twenty-five pews reserved for the Colored and to observe how many would occupy the seats. With great expectancy I watched until the Mass commenced. I counted and recounted. Only six and no more came in to swell the number. All of the church was filled with the exception of that row of twenty to twenty-five pews occupied by *the* precious *six*. Not a white member of the congregation, however, sat in one of the vacant pews reserved for the Colored....[13]

In Belmont they visited Bishop Haid who welcomed them warmly. He explained that in the Cathedral he had reserved for the Colored a whole row of pews from the top to the bottom of the edifice, but only twenty-five attended Mass on Sundays. The two mothers attended a magnificent pontifical vespers during their visit there. As Mother M. Katharine admired the fine wrought golden chasuble and cope, the gothic altar, the Bishop on his throne, the storied windows of magnificent Munich glass, she thought the scene one of heavenly splendor and longed to have the Colored share it. In the same letter she wrote that not a single Colored man or woman occupied the row of pews, and that they reminded her of the vacant seats awaiting us in the Kingdom of Heaven *if* only we win them.[14] It was very evident to her that reserving pews was not enough; much more was needed to have them filled. It was not that the Colored would not come. More zealous apostles were needed to invite them.

It was amazing the ground she covered and the number of churches and schools she visited. Probably more amazing still is the record she kept of every place visited. In a small notebook still preserved at the Motherhouse, she carefully noted down what she saw, and she saw plenty. She heard plenty, too, of the treatment sometimes accorded Negroes. She was under no delusion about the situation. Hidden away in the pages of this notebook in her clear pencil handwriting is a very keen and enlightening analysis of the race situation in many churches and schools she visited. Of course, it was not possible for her at that time to visit all the places she had helped, but she visited enough to let her know in what directions the currents were flowing. Her notebook is a mine of information, a behind-the-scene picture of a tragic condition. She took notes on everything: the size of the churches and schools, the number attending, the equipment, the type of teaching, the future prospects of the Colored students, the course of study and type of text books used.[15]

She seemed to have been a very clear reader of character. Some of those she met puzzled her and we run across entries like this:

> My impression is that it is an immense risk to help Father X, a real spiritual speculation because Father X is very speculative. His motives, however, I really think, being all AMDG. [She was very careful to preserve charity in her notations on the conditions as she found them. The notations were made only in connection with her donations and the use to which they had been put.] The zeal of his Father's house, will, I fear, eat up more than Father X. I think his imprudent zeal will bring on him such persecutions even from the good that many saints have endured. I think if we pray for him, he will, with God's help, come out spiritually reformed on account of his charity. He that dwelleth in charity, dwelleth in God....[16]

As she made this self-conducted tour through parts of the South, her heart must have sunk at the lack of facilities both in churches and schools, and the baffling incidents she noted in the course of her travel. But she was a person conscious of a mission. In a retreat she had made just before entering religion, she recorded this resolution in her notes on the meditation, The Finding and Manifestation of Our Lord in the Temple:

> Ask the Eternal Father what He wants of you. Vocation — all right. New Order — all right. Does God wish me to do anything better, or leave undone what I do?
>
> Resolve: Generously with no half-hearted, timorous dread of the opinions of Church and men to *manifest my mission.* To speak only and when it pleases God; but to lose no opportunity of speaking before priests and bearded men. Manifest yourself. You have no time to occupy your thoughts with that complacency or consideration of what others will think. Your business is simply, "What will my Father in Heaven think."[17]

By the vows of religious life Mother M. Katharine had dedicated herself, her fortune, her life to God, for the Indian and Colored races. She would never go back on that dedication. These were the underprivileged, the ones not accepted, but all she had would be given to them. She knew the situation in the South. She knew the opposition she would face in any attempt to penetrate it, but once she had accepted her dedication to that penetration, as the Will of God for her, nothing could hold her back. Alone, when her community was small and young, she planned Catholic schools and churches for the Colored. In some instances, she answered requests for help; in others, she went to bishops and offered to build a school or help with a church so that the Colored could enjoy every educational and spiritual help. She was a woman given a mission by God. No matter what difficulties rose up in her path — and it was well strewn with obstacles — she would persist in meeting the difficulties head on. Long before modern exigencies inflamed a hope that burst into the song, *We Shall Overcome*, she sang that song in her heart.

The notes she recorded on this trip were made for her own information and guidance in future donations. Some of them provide interesting background for present day situations. Under a heading, *Montgomery,* she wrote:

> We passed through a Colored section of town in a carriage. There is a large Colored population here, but no Colored school in the city of Montgomery. The Sisters of Loretto would, I believe, with help in the way of payment of sisters' salary, be willing to undertake a Colored day school. They seem kindly disposed to the Colored and have dealt with them in their Motherhouse in Kentucky and taught them in Lebanon.
>
> I inquired from Bishop Allen if he thought it would be advisable to start a Colored day school in Montgomery. He said he thought Selma and Birmingham would be better fields of labor because in Selma and especially in Birmingham there was less prejudice among the whites.[18]

As this chapter is being written, newspaper headlines on Birmingham and Selma could indicate this attitude has changed. It may be better though to conclude that the bombings, the murders, the brutality inflicted there on Negroes and those who wanted to help them, were the work of a deluded and ignorant fringe, not of the respectable citizenry of these American cities.

When she returned North and the inspection was completed, her notebook was a small encyclopedia of facts on the religious and educational status of the Negro in the South. Places were minutely described, methods appraised, suggestions recorded where help could be bestowed and how it could be used.[19] She must have had a keener realization than ever, of the tremendous effort it would take to lift this weight of ignorance and intolerance. But she could not be daunted and her enthusiasm ran higher than ever. She knew her mission, she knew all it entailed, but she also knew the power of God. She trusted in that power, not in herself.

There are prophetic lines in a letter Mother M. Katharine had received shortly after she had brought her young community to the temporary novitiate at Torresdale. The writer was the first Colored priest in the United States, Reverend John A. Tolton, a diocesan priest of the Archdiocese of Chicago.[20]

> 3554 Dearborn St., Chicago, Illinois, June 5, 1891
>
> Dear Mother Catherine,
>
> I deem it necessary to write you this letter to ask you to please forgive me for vexing you. A priest wrote me stating that all of us fathers in the Colored Missions were almost setting you crazy, that you had too many to tend to. Of course, I, for one, cannot tell how to conduct myself when I see one person at least, showing her love for the Colored race. One thing I do know: it took the Catholic Church 100 years here in America to show forth such a person as yourself. That is the reason why you have so much bother now and so many extending their hands to get a lift.
>
> In the whole History of the Church in America we cannot find one person that has sworn to give her treasury for the sole benefit of the Colored and Indians. As I stand alone as the first Negro priest of America, so you, Mother Catherine, stand alone as the first one to make such a sacrifice for the cause of a down-trodden race. Hence the South looks on with an angry eye. The North in many places is criticizing every act, just as it is watching every move I make. I suppose that is the reason why we had no Negro priests before this day. They watch us just the same as the Pharisees did Our Lord. They watched Him. I really feel that there will be a stir all over the United States when I begin my church. I shall work and pull at it as long as God gives me life, for I see that I have principalities to resist anywhere and everywhere I go.
>
> The world is indeed a great book and I have read all of its pages. So this letter is to ask you to excuse me if I have bothered you. I know that you have a lot to do, for I am sure you have letters from all parts of America and even outside of it....[21]

Mother M. Katharine would never consider herself bothered by any request to help the Indian and Colored. She would give every help she could. There are many pages in her private notes when she reproached herself for not having answered every request, though she knew that was not possible. Her position was unique. As a society leader, she would have been acclaimed and honored. But she cast her lot with the poorest of the poor; her only desire was to please God and help His neglected children. As she moved across America in the twentieth century, establishing her sisters in a line of missions from East to West to North to South, she would meet an opposition against her efforts, difficult to explain and more difficult to experience. But she knew her mission. All things to the contrary notwithstanding, she followed it through.

# Chapter 15
# To The South

The growth of the Community of the Sisters of the Blessed Sacrament was gradual but steady. By 1904 there were one hundred and four sisters functioning in the Motherhouse, in Santa Fe, Rock Castle, and St. Michael's, Arizona.[1] In June of that year, Bishop Byrne of Nashville, who was deeply concerned about the Colored, asked Mother M. Katharine if her Sisters could undertake a school in his diocese.[2] He had been in contact with her by correspondence since 1900 when she had sent him a check for $2,667 to pay one third of the cost of a church for the Colored.[3] At that point she did not feel she could undertake another mission and staff it with sisters but she offered to give $3,000 for establishing a school and suggested that maybe the Dominican Sisters would be able to staff it.[4]

In the fall of that same year, however, in a personal meeting with her, Bishop Byrne managed to change her mind. She was on her way West for her annual visitation. Her plan had been to go to St. Catherine's first and help the sisters there who were besieged with an outbreak of diphtheria. On the way to the train she stopped to see Archbishop Ryan; he told her she was to go first to St. Michael's and then go on to St. Catherine's when the diphtheria was over. That was a big disappointment to her. Somehow or other she never got around to the nursing. Despite all her good will the Archbishop always saw that she was shunted on to something else or to some other place. Good, faithful Archbishop Ryan really watched over her and protected her from her over-eager desires to be of service.

In this particular trip West because of a wash out near Kansas City, the repair of which would take more days than she could spend waiting, her railroad travel was routed through El Paso, Texas. From there she wrote to the Motherhouse giving the details of her meeting with Bishop Byrne:

> ... At St. Louis, I had to stop off at a convent on business, and whom should I meet there by the decree of Providence, but Right Reverend Bishop Byrne who chanced to be visiting the convent. As you know, he is the Bishop of Nashville who wrote that very zealous appeal for the Colored and Indian Lenten Collection which I read to you last spring. He

is also the Bishop who has asked our Sisters to teach a Colored school in Nashville when he establishes one.

"Why Bishop Byrne," said I, "how did you get here?" I discovered he was on his way to Santa Fe for his health.

"Mother," he said, "I want to have a talk with you, but I'll see you in Santa Fe."

I told him I would not be there for two weeks and he said: "I'll be away from there by that time, but I can come up and see you at St. Michael's, if you invite me." Which, of course, I did on the spot, provided His Lordship promised to be satisfied with missionary fare, and a thirty mile drive in a market wagon, to which he agreed. I am to write him and appoint a specific day and explain the route from the Santa Fe Sanatorium where he is to stay...."[5]

From Santa Fe, Bishop Byrne wrote her:

October 18, 1904

... Last Sunday afternoon, Archbishop Bourgade and I went for walk and called at St. Catherine's. I was a little surprised at seeing your school there, so flourishing is it, and I rejoiced to meet your sisters. They seem so cheerful and content, but it must be an uphill work. The thought that came to my mind and which I expressed to them was that they would surely some day, not very distant either, be in Nashville. It seemed an inspiration and I hope it is prophetic.

There is a beautiful property in a desirable part of the city, but in the opposite direction from the present Church of the Holy Family, and within a short distance of a large Negro settlement containing possibly some three or four acres and a splendid house that could be had on easy terms and at moderate price, say $18,000. It would be an admirable place for an industrial school and a second mission for the Negroes of that quarter of the city. The good to be done, my dear Mother, is incomparable. But we must have your sisters to carry it on. After seeing your sisters, I feel enthusiastic at the prospect of what can be done, and there is no place like Nashville for beginning such a work and for a centre of operation. Will you think it over, Mother, and pray and get prayers for its success?....[6]

The interview that took place at St. Michael's, Arizona, between Bishop Byrne and Mother M. Katharine covered many points: the property in Nashville, the type of education, the courses, etc. The Bishop made it very clear that the property he had in mind was owned by a wealthy southern banker who was not particularly known either for an interest in, or a love for the Negro. If his property were to be purchased, great caution would have to be used. They arranged that when an option of thirty or sixty days was placed upon it, the Bishop would notify her at once, and that in the meantime he would keep an agent on the lookout so that she could be notified in time to go to Nashville and have a look at the building before purchasing it.[7]

Back at the Motherhouse, she discussed with her Council the points of her interview with Bishop Byrne. In a long letter written to him December 7, 1904,[8] she gave their very definite views, and hers too, on two important items. Bishop Byrne had desired that the school should be limited to Catholics only. Mother M. Katharine could not agree with this and she wrote her reason: "Our Congregation is consecrated to God for the conversion of the Negro and Indian races. A missionary congregation should not make this distinction." The second item had to do with a measure then being considered by the Nashville City Council. They proposed to abolish high school education for the Negro and substitute a common school and industrial education for them. She who would build the first and only Catholic college for Negroes when other Catholic colleges were not open to them, definitely disagreed with this proposal. "I must confess," she writes in this same letter, "I cannot share these views with regard to the education of the Race. I feel that if among our Colored People we find individuals gifted with capabilities, with those sterling qualities which constitute character, our Holy Mother the Church who fosters and develops the intellect only that it may give God more glory and be of benefit to others, should also concede to the Negro this privilege of higher education."

The following January, Father Plunkett, the zealous priest in charge of the church for the Colored in Nashville, notified Mother M. Katharine that an option of sixty days had been taken on the property at $25,000. With Mother M. Mercedes she left the Motherhouse for Nashville to examine the place and estimate its suitability. She had to view it, however, from a closed carriage in which the Bishop also rode.[9] All she saw was a glimpse of a very large house in the center of a spacious lawn. In view of the hostility that would be aroused at the purchase of this building for the Colored, no closer inspection was deemed advisable.

It was well Mother M. Katharine had a strong constitution. In the extent of her mission travels, the inconveniences on the way were many. There is a very interesting account in the Community Annals of the incidental happenings of this particular visit.[10] Their lunch box had given out at noon the day they were to arrive in Nashville. They reached there at eleven P.M. instead of seven. Mother was so embarrassed at disturbing the Dominican Sisters at this hour of the night, that she would not take anything to eat though they had a supper prepared for her. On her way to Mass the next morning she remembered it was fast day — the eve of the Purification — and she whispered the information to Mother M. Mercedes. To the dismay of the Sister who had prepared a substantial breakfast for them, they took only a cup of coffee and a piece of bread. The Sister consoled herself by telling them that she was going to call up St. Thomas where they were to have dinner and tell the Sisters there they had neither supper nor breakfast. "Anyway", she added, "the Bishop will be with you and there will be a grand dinner."

But an unusual thing happened that day, an unusual thing for Nashville; it snowed and snowed heavily. After they had secretly viewed the estate and were on their way with the Bishop to St. Thomas where it had been arranged they would discuss the pros and cons of the purchase, driving through the snow became a little difficult. Finally after a half hour of driving, the drifts were so high that the driver announced he could not make St. Thomas. The Bishop then decided they would go to his house for dinner. The annalist describes the dinner with the Bishop at the head of the table and a Sister on either side of him. "The housekeeper brought in a piece of steak that would be a fair portion for one person, a bread plate with four slices of bread, a butter dish with a fair quantity of butter, a small tea pot and cream pitcher. Then she placed the desert on the table – three apples." Talking about it years later, Mother M. Mercedes said, "The sight of that dinner maddens me yet, but it was usual fare for the good holy Bishop and, of course, he did not know his guests had been without supper or breakfast."

But the end was not yet. At supper time they were back at the Dominican Convent. The gracious Sister who had served them at breakfast, greeted them with, "Mother, as it is one of your community's fast days, I knew you wouldn't eat supper, as you had a good dinner at St. Thomas. I have prepared just a little collation for you!" The two sat down to bread, butter, tea and cake. The annalist, Mother M. Mercedes, concludes the account with, "For the first time in years, Mother M. Katharine consumed two pieces of cake!"

After a full discussion of the estate, Mother M. Katharine at first offered $18,000 for the property. There was a great deal of business astir and many phone calls through the real estate agent, W.P. Ready. But the Nashville banker who owned the property would not even consider a purchase sale of $18,000. Clever bargaining business woman that she was, the Foundress raised it to $24,000 and said she would not give another cent. At this point the Bishop said he would give the $1,000 additional. February 2, 1905, a Nashville attorney, Thomas J. Tyne, acting for Mother M. Katharine, negotiated the purchase of the property. On February 11, the owner executed and delivered the deed to Attorney Thomas Tyne, who the same day conveyed the property to the Sisters of the Blessed Sacrament.[11] All was calm till on February 13, *The Banner of Nashville* printed the account of the real purchasers of the property and the end for which they bought it. Startled residents of Nashville read that it would be used as an Industrial Academy for Colored Girls with a basic grammar school course and several years of high school, that renovations and additions would be made the following summer and the school opened for the fall session.

The article was ordinary newspaper reporting with no intimation of dissatisfaction, but with its publication, a storm broke over Nashville. The owner was indignant that his home should have been bought for such a purpose. He was further indignant for his neighbors whose property, he was sure, would be devaluated if Colored girls were admitted to the area. He wrote a long letter to *The Banner* explaining step by step, the details of the sale and his ignorance of the real purchasers or their intentions. He appealed to the newspaper for help. He wrote a series of letters to the attorney, to the Bishop and to Mother M. Katharine requesting that the trade be rescinded, and offering to give back the entire purchase price and also commission he had made on the sale.[12]

With the calm and dignity of the cultured woman she was, Mother M. Katharine answered his letter to her:

St. Elizabeth's, Maud P.O., Pa.

My Dear Sir:

I am just in receipt of your letter of February 17th, transmitted to me from Drexel & Company. I hasten to answer it, and to express to you my regret that you and your neighbors should feel as you do concerning the purchase of the property. I think there is some misapprehension on the part of you and your neighbors which I should like to remove. The Sisters of the Blessed Sacrament, who have purchased the property, are religious, of the same race as yourself. We will always endeavor in every way to be neighborly to any white neighbors in the vicinity; we have every reason to hope we may receive from our white neighbors the cordial courtesy for which the Southern people are so justly noted.

It is true we intend to open an industrial school and academy for Colored girls, but the girls who will come there will be only day scholars. In coming to the academy and returning to their homes, I am confident they will be orderly and cause no annoyance.

I observed very carefully when in Nashville, that the property which we purchased was within very few blocks of numerous houses occupied by Colored families, and therefore, even were the property to be the residence of Colored teachers, which it is not, I think no just exception could be taken to the locality selected.

I can fully realize, I think, how you feel about your old and revered home, around which so many attachments of the past — the sweet relations of home life — hover. I acknowledge I feel the same with regard to mine, and confess that some time ago, when passing it in the trolley cars, when I saw a bill of sale on it, a whole crowd of fond recollections of father and mother and sisters, etc., came vividly to my imagination. Then I more than ever realized how all things temporal pass away, and that there is but one home, strictly speaking, that eternal home where we all hope to meet our own, and where there will be no separation any more. And so temporal things, after all, are only to be valued, inasmuch as they bring us and many others — as many as possible — to the same eternal joys for which we were all created.

With warmest trust that all misapprehension be removed, believe me,

Very sincerely yours,
M.M. Katharine (Drexel)[13]

The agitation continued. By newspaper articles, letters, speeches, the owner kept the issues alive, making every possible offer he could think of. In a letter to Bishop Byrne he even offered a donation of $2,500 to any other type of Catholic organization that would buy it, and he suggested the Little Sisters of the Poor. The Bishop answered in a letter similar in tone to that which Mother M. Katharine had written.[14] When everything else failed, the owner started an agitation to have Central Street run right through the property.

This property had in Civil War days been owned by Orville Ewing. July 17, 1863, he had written a letter to General Rosecrans, in which he stated he expected to continue as a loyal citizen of the United States as long as Tennessee formed a part of the domain. He proposed leasing to the Federal Government part of his property on condition that the part to be used would be cut off by a fence and that protection would be accorded his property. The lease was made January 25, 1865; peace was declared shortly after. A U.S. engineer made a plan for the Ewing property which showed it enclosed by the government fence. By some error in computation or oversight, his plan showed Central Street continued right through the Orville Ewing home place and through the center of the old residence as well. Naturally no street was ever run through the home. In discovering this document, however, the owner clung to what was his last hope. He requested that the original document be fulfilled and a street put through his home. Fifty people signed a petition to that effect to the Mayor and the City Council.[15]

Then to Mother M. Katharine's embarrassment, he published her letter to him. Evidently the paper would not accept it as correspondence; it appeared as a paid advertisement.[16] In a letter to Bishop Byrne, her sentiment on the matter is clearly expressed. There was no rancor, no indignation, no desire to make her position clear to the public. She had been given a mission by God; she wanted to fulfill it quietly and as perfectly as she could.

St. Elizabeth's, Maud P.O., Pa., July 14, 1905

… I cannot tell you how I regret that any letter of mine on the subject should appear in print. The very best thing to do is to let the whole affair die out — at least in the press if it won't die out before the Mayor and the City Council. If the Apostles were sent as sheep in the midst of the wolves, they were told, *therefore*, to be wise as serpents and harmless as doves. To have this matter stirred up in the press is only to fan the flame. I have resolved not to answer another letter sent me by any of these parties, since they come out in the press. It seems but prudence to protect our cause by being very quiet, since there seems to be a certain prejudice

> which I hope will blow over by quietly minding our preservation of the good we have undertaken without any aggressiveness....
>
> It is certainly encouraging to meet some opposition in *your* work and ours. It is so appropriate for a Convent of the Blessed Sacrament—Christ dwelling with us—and the School of the Immaculate Mother, to have people of the city have no room for our precious Charge. They say "There is another place on the city's outskirts" for our educational work. How truly was the Cave of Bethlehem *the* great educator of the World! This was indeed the School of the Immaculate Mother.
>
> May the Holy Family teach us how to look out for the interests of the Father according to the Pattern given. My God! how much light can be wasted when the darkness does not comprehend it....[17]

The tempest continued to rage. May 29th, she and Sister M. Juliana went to Nashville to examine the house, make lists of needed furniture and supplies, and also to visit some Negro institutions. During this visit she went over the whole situation and decided the new school would be called Immaculate Mother Academy and Industrial School, and that it would include grades from the fourth through the third year high school. Shortly after her return to the Motherhouse, she received another petition, this time from a group in Nashville of women who endeavored politely to make her see that the opening of a Negro school would depreciate the value of their property. Their peroration was a classic:

> ... In conclusion, we beg to say that we highly appreciate and cordially commend your worthy enterprise among the Colored People. There are a number of localities in and around the city where Colored People live, and where no objection would be made to the location of your school. On the contrary, it would be welcomed as a distinct good and a social blessings.[18]

The inference was that if she wanted to open a convent for her sisters in a run down section of the city and put up a school in a dilapidated neighborhood, they would have no objections.

Despite the opposition, she went ahead quietly with her plans. The best rooms in the house were fitted out as classrooms; one room was prepared as a chapel, and the sisters' quarters were arranged in the rear and the attic. September 5, 1905, Bishop Byrne opened the school term with the celebration of the Mass of the Holy Ghost in the small chapel. Twenty-eight students were on hand the first day with eighteen music pupils and eight who applied for the Domestic Art courses. It was a good beginning.[19]

It looked as if the struggle was ended and the new school would proceed on the road to growth and development. But at this point strong and vociferous opposition arose from another source, and an unexpected source — the Negro ministers. From their pulpits they preached against the Sisters, the school, and any Negro parents who would send their children there.[20] In their non-ecumenical day they were evidently alarmed at what seemed to them an invasion by Catholic Sisters.

But Mother M. Katharine had sent her Sisters to stay. They could not be daunted. The attendance grew. By the end of the first year the registration was over a hundred and the building was too small. Again Mother's Philadelphia architect drew up plans and by the spring of 1907 a new school building was ready. A few rooms were reserved in the old building for Domestic Art and Music lessons. In a few years even the new building was filled. Three sisters were stricken with the typhoid in 1908 and one, the youngest, died. At that time the sisters were to experience a kindness and a helpfulness, especially from the sisters of the city, that overshadowed any other recollections. In this same year, three years after its purchase, the original building was condemned. The Sisters used the school auditorium while Mother M. Katharine went in the building process again, this time for a combined high school and convent. Thus on the original property the Sisters continued to teach at Holy Family Parochial School and Immaculate Mother High School until July 1954. Integration went into effect then, and arrangements were made for Catholic students to attend Cathedral School and Father Ryan High School.[21]

In 1933 Bishop Smith, Bishop Byrne's successor, opened a chapel in North Nashville for the Catholic students at Fisk University and Meharry Medical School and Dental College. A few classrooms were fitted out on the second floor above the temporary chapel. Two Sisters of the Blessed Sacrament coming daily from the other side of the city, thus started St. Vincent's School. Today there is a thriving parish there with rectory, church, school, and convent.

The original property at Immaculate Mother's contributed to various types of historical development from Civil War days to the present. When Bishop Adrian arranged for the integration of Catholic schools, the two separate schools on the grounds were no longer needed nor was Holy Family Church. Bishop Adrian wrote Mother M. Anselm, then Superior General of the Sisters of the Blessed Sacrament, that one of the Catholic bankers in the city had made an offer to purchase all the property, one-third of which belonged to the Diocese. Arrangements were made and the sale completed. The purchasers this time, too, did not want their identity known, and did not reveal it for several months. The purchasers were Sears Roebuck and Company. The buildings meant nothing to them and they were razed. Two wealthy parties had invested in the same property for vastly different ends.

There was never anything startling about the missionary work at Immaculate Mother's in Nashville. It was steady through the years, sinking the roots of Faith if not over a large area, at least into solid foundations. Mother M. Katharine's consuming desire was to save souls and provide a God-centered education for the Indians and the Colored. She was content to work hard and consistently toward this end as long as there were fields to be cultivated, and to move on to other pastures when her mission in one area was fulfilled.

# Chapter 16

# The Poorest Nun In The World

Newspapers at home and abroad had a habit of running every now and then, a feature article with banner headlines on The Richest Nun in the World, Mother Katharine Drexel. There were certain static features about the recurring articles: she had an income of a thousand dollars a day. She slept on an old iron bedstead. Any time you dropped in, you might find her scrubbing floors! One article announced she lived on a dollar a day: another reduced her daily expense to forty-five cents!

The articles, however, were in high praise of her endeavors. A *Boston Post* writer recorded: "Mother Katharine is the daughter of Francis Drexel, one-time partner of J. Pierpont Morgan Company, in the old firm of Drexel and Morgan. She is linked by the closest family ties to all the socially powerful of the multi-millionaire clan of the Philadelphia Drexels.... While family background offers, in a measure, some explanation of the career of Mother Katharine, it fails to satisfy one's curiosity as to why this woman foreswore social position, her natural birthright, for the grind and toil that go with the life of a religieuse. If we would understand this remarkable figure, we must try to remember two facts: there have been at all times men and women who have given their lives to saving the souls of their fellows. Every human being has a soul worth saving."[1]

Such articles were very distasteful to Mother M. Katharine who shunned all publicity, and distasteful to her Community. The details were fantastic, and they gave a picture of unlimited wealth. Usually after an article made its appearance, a flood of appeals found its way to the Motherhouse. A young man in dental school would ask for help to continue his course, a child would ask for a cow for a sick grandmother, etc.

If in the realm of finance any title were to be given to Mother M. Katharine, paradoxical as it may seem, the best would have been *The Poorest Nun in the World*, or *A Millionaire in Poverty*. She was terrifically impressed with Christ's call to poverty. She would have understood well Cardinal Lercaro's Declaration on Poverty at the First Session of the Vatican Council: "I mean that the Mystery of Christ in the Church is always, but particularly today, the Mystery of Christ in the poor, since the Church, as our Holy Father Pope John XXIII has said, is truly the Church of all, but is particularly The Church of the Poor.... In its future deliberations, let the Council give not merely some attention, but pride of place, so to speak, to the development of the Gospel doctrine of the holy poverty of Christ in the Church."[2] She would have read with eagerness the statement on Poverty in Vatican Council II's Constitution, *De Ecclesia*: "Just as Christ carried out the works of Redemption in poverty and oppression, so the Church is called to follow the same route, that it might communicate the fruits of salvation to men. Christ Jesus 'though He was by nature God ... emptied Himself taking the nature of a slave' (Phil 22: 6-7) and 'being rich, became poor (2Cor. II: 8-9) for our sakes' .... Christ was sent by the Father 'to bring good news to the poor, to heal the contrite of heart' (Luke 4: 18)."[3]

It was the direction of Christ to the rich young man that convinced this rich young woman that she must be poor to follow Christ who chose to be poor and enjoined poverty on His closest followers, "If thou wilt be perfect," He said, "go sell what thou hast, and give to the poor, and thou shalt have treasure in Heaven; and come follow me." (Matt. 19: 21) Her understanding, her motive, her ideal of poverty were grounded in this statement of Eternal Wisdom. The renouncement involved seemed to her a condition sine qua non of attaining perfect love.

Even as a postulant she had wanted to give all her wealth away. She was troubled when Bishop O'Connor suggested she lay aside $50,000 a year for her community which in the beginning would have no income. Christ's words kept ringing in her ears: "Give it to the Poor." She thought her community should start out in poverty. She was disturbed. After her profession, when her community was well on the way to permanency, she was still inclined to give her wealth away and let her sisters depend on Divine Providence. In addition to her personal practice of poverty, she wanted her congregation to be poor. The thought of putting money away for their support, that could be used here and now to relieve the poor, troubled her. She did so want to serve God perfectly. When she was formulating the Rule for her congregation, she decided to seek advice in this vital matter. She wanted to be sure of the extent of poverty God wanted her to practice and prescribe for her sisters.

She evidently had great confidence in Father Pantanella, S.J., of the College of the Sacred Heart of Denver, Colorado. On her visitation of the Western missions in the fall of 1903, she made a special trip to Denver to seek his help. As a result of the interview he was evidently so impressed with the sincerity and stark simplicity of her desire to be poor as Christ was poor, that he told her to follow her light, not to endow the works of the community, but to leave them to the Providence of God.[4] She went back to the Motherhouse fortified with his advice to follow her inspirations and what she felt was God's direction to her. She explained it to her Council and asked for their approval.

Her Council did not agree with her, and a very detailed discussion followed.[5] The argument that finally altered her viewpoint was their explanation of the fact that none of the Bishops of the dioceses where she had founded schools could support them then, while she lived. They would definitely not be able to support them after her death. She would simply leave them unprovided for and under the necessity of being abandoned. Since her only object was to help as much and in as many directions as she could, she gave in and agreed to establish a partial endowment fund for the Motherhouse, the education and the formation of the Sisters, plus some support for the four missions then established. It was a temporary plan for a temporary need. At that point in the history of the congregation, she could not have envisaged the extent of mission development and the increase of the number of missions in the long years ahead in which the Sisters of the Blessed Sacrament would carry on their apostolate.

As far as her personal living was concerned, she followed a very strict interpretation of the Vow of Poverty. She would take no exception in anything. She, who had traveled extensively with luxurious accommodations, chose as a religious the cheapest way. She took upper berths to save money. In the days when Pullmans had coaches attached, she rode coach till it was time to take a sleeper at night. She carried her lunch with her or left the train at stopovers to get a sandwich and a cup of coffee at a cheap counter in a railroad station. She had her shoes mended and re-mended till there was little of the originals left. She cut off small pieces of unused paper at the ends of the letters she received, and used them for her notes and jottings. Even in the retirement of her old age, she was meticulously careful about conserving electricity and water. Foolish? Eccentric? If she were a very poor woman like the millions of homeless and half fed in the world today, she would have to take these precautions. She was a very poor woman who chose a life of poverty rather than one of great wealth. The Son of God had not whereon to lay His head. She wanted nothing but to give God pleasure and to help save souls.

She did not interpret poverty according to the norms of the century in which she lived, nor was she inclined to substitute a vow of common life for the evangelical Vow of Poverty. She interpreted it in the light of the Incarnation and Redemption where in stark poverty the Son of God became man, and in stark poverty died naked on Calvary, and was buried in the tomb of another. This may well be heroic poverty which not every religious attains or seeks.[6] It would seem, however, to be in line with a view on the matter expressed by Pope Paul VI: "Religious must surpass all others by their example of true evangelical Poverty. It is not enough for the religious to depend merely on the superior's decision with regard to their use of material things. Let religious of their own will be content with the things that are needed for properly fulfilling their way of life, shunning those little extras and luxuries which weaken religious life."[7]

After her death in 1955, *L'Osservatore Romano* published a long article on her life with the significant title: The Daughter of Millionaire Drexel Gives Away Millions To Live a Life of Poverty. No title could have been more accurate. Included in the article, however, is a statement to the effect that the only mistake she made — if it can be called a mistake — was that she did not try to modify her father's will in favor of her community. But that was exactly what she would not do even though she knew that at her death, her community's income from the $14,000,000 Trust Fund established by her father would cease, and the entire fund would be distributed in the proportions her father had arranged. The recipients would be a long list of parishes, hospitals, institutions in and around Philadelphia. Her community would not be among the beneficiaries of her father's estate.

Her view of religious poverty had been consistent since the day she took the Vow. She would not alter it at the end. For years before her death, in the staggering expense of a nationwide program, she strove assiduously to have many of her missions supported in their local dioceses; she appealed for help to organizations within the Church. The will, however, she would not attack though it might not have been impossible to prove that this arrangement would not have been the will of her father, or his wish had he known that she was going to found a congregation dedicated to the service of the underprivileged.

As a banker treasures wealth, this Banker's Daughter treasured poverty, not for itself, for she loved life and all it held, but for the resemblance to Christ it effected. She gladly used her wealth to lead men to God. For herself she chose the stark simplicity of Bethlehem and the complete surrender of Calvary, not only in the entire relinquishment of her material possessions but in her willingness to endure contempt and humiliations — the lot of the poor.

The relinquishment by vow of the personal use of her material possessions was no act of ordinary poverty to this millionaire's daughter. While it meant introducing her to a life-long existential practice of pure evangelical poverty, it meant also the enrichment of numerous efforts of the Catholic Church for the Colored and Indian races. She despoiled herself voluntarily of her millions, to distribute them freely and magnanimously to the two races to whom she also dedicated her life.

To gather all her donations and estimate her total contribution would be a long drawn out and difficult process. Her gift to the Church and through the Church to the Colored and Indian races was her entire income through the years.[8] She gave reports reluctantly; she never wanted her total donations known. Her motives here were both spiritual and material. Because she loved God so much and her fellow men so intensely, she gave her wealth away freely. The pure love of God and the desire to please Him were her motives. She was not interested in anything else and she shrank from any recognition. Thus far, her motive was spiritual. Being as she was, however, a very keen business woman she felt that if her donations were publicized, the missions might suffer, Catholics who should help the cause might be inclined to think that all the missions were well cared for. She distributed her wealth in a systematic and pre-arranged way asking in each case for a signed agreement that the money donated would be used specifically for the purpose named and specifically stating that if the property should ever be used for any other purpose, then the money she donated would either be refunded to the community or be used by the bishop of the particular locale for the Indian or Colored there. In her, the love of God and the wisdom of God guided her to an apostolate whose extent is difficult to measure.

Some idea of how far she spread her millions, in her simple retiring way, can be gleaned from the following lists. Before she founded her congregation she had generously aided missions in the following places:

> ARIZONA: Fort Defiance, San Xavier del Bac, Tucson; CALIFORNIA: San Diego, Banning; DAKOTA TERRITORY: Bad River, Chapel of St. Francis, Crow Creek, Elbowoods, Fort Totten, Grand River, Pine Ridge, Rosebud, Standing Rock, Turtle Mountain; IDAHO: Lewiston; INDIAN TERRITORY: Anadarko, Hominy Creek, Pawhuska, Purcell; INDIANA: Rensselaer, Sacred Heart, St. Michael's; MICHIGAN: Cross Village, Harbor Springs; MINNESOTA: Graceville, Red Lake, White Earth; MONTANA: St. Peter's (Jesuits), St. Xavier's, St. Paul's, Holy Family, St. Peter's (Ursulines); NEVADA: Reno; NEW MEXICO: Santa Fe, Acoma, Albuquerque, Bernalillo, Jemez, Laguna; OREGON: Umatilla Reservation; WASHINGTON TERRITORY: Tacoma, North Yakima; WISCONSIN: Baraga, Bayfield, Courtes Oreilles, Keshena, Lac de Flambeau, Odanah; WYOMING TERRITORY: St. Stephen's.[9]

Once her congregation was founded, her help continued to flow to missions outside it. She sent aid to Colored missions in the following places:

> ALABAMA: Mobile, Montgomery, Birmingham, Prichard, Tuscaloosa, Selma, Chastang; ARKANSAS: Pine Bluff, Little Rock, Fort Smith; DELAWARE: Clayton; FLORIDA: Ybor City, St. Augustine, Tampa; GEORGIA: Savannah, Augusta, Atlanta, Macon; ILLINOIS: Cairo, East St. Louis; KANSAS: Leavenworth; KENTUCKY: Louisville, Lebanon, Bardstown; LOUISIANA: Lafayette, Opelousas, Alexandria, Hickory Hill, New Orleans, Isle Breville, East Baton Rouge, Cameron, Marksville, Shreveport, New Iberia, Le Beau, Point a la Hache, West Point a la Hache, Lake Charles, City Price, Algiers, Plattenville, Rideau, Breaux Bridge, Coulee Croche, Paillet Town, Port Barre, Thibodeaux, Broussard, Donaldsonville, Scott, Crowley, Napoleonville, Bertrandville, Mamou, Mallet, Abbeville, Prairie Basse, Carencro, Leonville, St. Martinville, Madisonville, Church Point, Edgard; Franklin, Julien Hill, Eunice, Rayne, Reserve, Glencoe, Klotzville; MARYLAND: Baltimore, Bryantown, St. Mary's , Ridge; MICHIGAN: Detroit; MISSISSIPPI: Natchez, Vicksburg, Scranton, Jackson, Pascagoula, Meridian, Pass Christian, Greenville, Biloxi, Jefferson County, Gulfport; MISSOURI: Kansas City , St. Louis; NEW JERSEY: Highwood; NEW YORK: Brooklyn, New York City; NORTH CAROLINA: Charlotte, Belmont, Newton Grove, New Bern, Rocky Mountain, Near Raleigh, Gastonia, Wilmington, Spencer; OHIO: Cincinnati, Carthage, Columbus, Cleveland; OKLAHOMA: Guthrie, Okmulgee, Oklahoma City; PENNSYLVANIA: Philadelphia, Germantown; SOUTH CAROLINA: Cross Roads, Georgetown, Charleston; SOUTH DAKOTA: Cascade;

> TENNESSEE: Memphis, Jackson, Nashville; TEXAS: Houston, Beaumont, Corpus Christi, San Antonio, Galveston, Dallas, Ames, Pear Orchard, Austin, Orange; VIRGINIA: Richmond, Norfolk, Alexandria, Lynchburg; WASHINGTON, D. C.; WISCONSIN: Milwaukee.[10]

In addition to the Colored Missions above, she gave generously to many Indian Missions outside her own Congregation:

> ARIZONA: Tucson, Komatke, Anegan, Pisenemo, Gombadi Village, Topawa; CALIFORNIA: Banning; FLORDIA: Old Town; IDAHO: Boise City, St. Joseph; MINNESOTA: Cloquet, White Earth (Calloway), White Earth Reservation; MONTANA: St. Ignatius; NEW MEXICO: Mescalero, Tohatchi, Santa Fe, Ship Rock, Laguna, Pena Blanca; NEW YORK: Hogansbury; NORTH DAKOTA: Fort Yates; OKLAHOMA: Pawhuska, Purcell, Vinita, Antlers, Ardmore, Tulsa, Grayson, Anadarko, Chickasha, Boley, Muskogee, Hominy Creek, Boswell, Quapaw; OREGON: Grand Ronde; PENNSYLVANIA: Carlisle; SOUTH DAKOTA: Corn Creek, Medicine Route, Rosebud Reservation; WASHINGTON STATE: Tacoma, Tulalip, Barnaby, Colville Reservation; WISCONSIN: Odanah, Oneida, Reserve; WYOMING: St. Stephen's.[11]

Even Colored and Indian Missions in foreign countries were the recipients of her aid:

> AFRICA: Bathurst, Uganda, E. Africa, Sierra Leone, Free Town, Omitcha, South Nigeria, Nyenga, Nsambya, B.E.A., Marianhill, Natal, South Africa; BRITISH HONDURAS: Benque Viejo; CUBA: Cardenas, Havana; CANAL ZONE: Gatun, Frijoles, Cristobal; ITALY: Monte Cassino; B. WEST INDIES: Jamaica, Trinidad, Cedros; CANADA: Duck Lake, Oblate Missions.[12]

Quietly and unobtrusively her wealth was disbursed not only to these many missions conducted by other communities, but to the houses and missions of her own congregation as well. The Congregation of the Sisters of the Blessed Sacrament did not have a phenomenal growth. At her death in 1955 the Community numbered 501 and her establishments had spread across the country from Massachusetts to Texas, and from Virginia to California. Many times she would cross and re-cross the United States to found and later visit the missions of her own community. The beginnings of the earliest missions have been recorded in this book; it would take volumes to record all the foundations with their interesting and fascinating details. By 1955 from 51 convents the Sisters of the Blessed Sacrament were conducting 49 elementary schools, 12 high schools, Xavier University in New Orleans, 3 houses of social service and a house of studies in Washington, D.C.

The line of missions was a long one:

> ALABAMA: Montgomery; ARIZONA: St. Michaels, Houck; CALIFORNIA: Fresno; GEORGIA: Atlanta, Macon; ILLINOIS: Chicago; INDIANA: Gary; LOUISIANA: New Orleans, Lake Charles, New Iberia, Church Point, Eunice, Rayne, St. Martinville, Carencro, MASSACHUSETTS: Boston; MISSOURI: St. Louis; MISSISSIPPI: Biloxi, Gulfport; OHIO: Columbus, Cleveland, Cincinnati; OKLAHOMA: Pawhuska; PENNSYLVANIA: Philadelphia, Carlisle; NEBRASKA: Winnebago, NEW JERSEY: Camden; NEW MEXICO: Santa Fe, Laguna; SOUTH DAKOTA: Marty; TENNESSEE: Nashville; TEXAS: Orange, Port Arthur, Beaumont; VIRGINIA: Rock Castle; WASHINGTON, D.C.[13]

Despite her inheritance, the financial burden of the missions caused her to seek help from the Church she had helped. In the late twenties she began to devise ways and means of making some of the missions self supporting or supported by the Church in the local area. In many cases this was done. Other plans would mature in the course of time. But her Indian missions and Xavier University in New Orleans would always be beyond the pale of her Community's resources. For help here, she appealed to the *Commission for Catholic Missions among the Colored People and the Indians* which administers the funds derived from the annual collection for the Negro and Indian Missions; and to *The American Board of Catholic Missions* which, acting for the hierarchy of the United States, receives the home mission quota from the *Society for the Propagation of the Faith* and distributes it to the home missions. For some thirty years now, both groups have allocated annually substantial amounts that have greatly aided the continuance of the works of the Sisters of the Blessed Sacrament.[14]

Unlike the rich young man in the Gospel, this rich young woman had not turned away from Christ because she had great possessions. Rather, she laid the wealth at His feet completely, utterly. She asked only the grace to please Him and to be His instrument in the salvation of souls. She stripped herself of everything to follow Christ poor. She studied His poverty in Bethlehem and Calvary. She lived it. She kept nothing for herself. By His grace and for His love she became the poorest nun in the world.

# Chapter 17
# A Rule To Live By

From the time the foundation of a new community was first presented to her, the question of the Rule loomed large in Katharine's mental horizon. She felt utterly incapable of writing one, of formulating a way of life for others. She had gone on because she knew she could count on Bishop O'Connor's help and direction. When he died shortly after her Reception, even though Archbishop Ryan offered immediately to take his place, she suffered intensely not only from the loss of this counselor and friend, but also from the loss of a certain sense of direction which she had confidently expected him to give. More than once in her letters to him she had referred to "our" community. The plan was his; she had expected that the formulation of the Rule would very definitely be his.

In the novitiate, her immediate concern had been the perfect observance of the Rule she was following then — the Rule of the Sisters of Mercy. There would be no question of writing another until she had completely absorbed and lived this one. Writing to her just before her Profession, Archbishop Ryan had put it this way: "The understanding is that the Rules are those of the Sisters of Mercy with such modifications as shall be deemed necessary for your peculiar work."[1] Accordingly, for the first three years after the actual foundation of her community, February 12, 1891, the Sisters of the Blessed Sacrament studied and lived the Mercy Rule with a few incidental changes to fit their apostolate. There was plenty to do in this organizational period, plenty to study in the essence and principles of religious living.

Early in 1894 Mother M. Katharine began working on the Rules and Constitutions for her Community. At Archbishop Ryan's suggestion, she had written to different communities for copies of their Rule. These she studied carefully and about them she asked many questions. The Rule of the Holy Ghost Fathers made a special appeal to her as they were engaged in so much missionary and educational work at home and abroad, and they had what she thought was a well established plan of government. After a careful study of the Jesuit Rule, she wondered about the possibility of adopting it entirely, thus forming something like a feminine branch of the Order. Archbishop Ryan wrote her a very short note on the matter in which he stated he did not think the Jesuits wanted a female addition.[2] In all this investigation and the prayer and study involved, she was guided by her father in God, Archbishop Ryan. No question of hers was too insignificant for his consideration. He wanted to help her in every possible way. He said to his secretary, Monsignor Cavanaugh,

"Mother Katharine needs me, she needs my supervision and counsel in the most minute details, for she is planning now for the future and that future must rest on very secure foundations."[3]

This work and study on the Rule would go on for years and be intensified and completed in 1906 and 1907. Very definite encouragement came to her and a great joy to her community when Rome sent a Decree of Praise on the Community in 1897. This usual first step to an authoritative sanction by the Church of newly established congregations, gave the Foundress renewed courage and hope. She wanted to be entirely circumscribed by the authority of the Church, and active only within its jurisdiction. She never thought of what she was doing as her work, but she thought of herself as an instrument at the disposal of the Church.

The Decree was dated February 16, 1897. Cardinal Satolli, Apostolic Delegate to the United States from 1893 to 1896, was at that time back in Rome. On three different occasions he had come in contact with the work of the Sisters of the Blessed Sacrament. In October 1895 he had been present for the conferring of the pallium on Archbishop Chapelle at the Cathedral in Santa Fe. After the ceremony, Cardinal Gibbons, Cardinal Satolli, Archbishops Corrigan of New York and Ryan of Philadelphia accompanied Archbishop Chapelle and other prelates to St. Catherine's where the Sisters served a dinner.[4] The Roman Cardinal was back again in March 1896. Archbishop Chapelle had asked him to stop over at Santa Fe on his return from San Antonio. This time he was the special guest of honor and the sisters arranged an elaborate Indian festival for him. In full regalia and costumes the Indians came in from the surrounding pueblos and danced for him. Everyone seemed very happy about the whole affair. Cardinal Satolli addressed them at the close and told the Indians they did not have to give up their customs, if only they would be faithful to their religion. That pleased the old Indians very much.[5]

A week later Archbishop Chapelle wrote to Mother M. Katharine:

> Santa Fe, New Mexico, March 12, 1896
>
> ... Cardinal Satolli was delighted with the reception given him at St. Catharine's, and well he might be, for it was truly princely. He told me that on his return to Rome he intended obtaining from the Pope a Brief in favor of yourself, your Community, and your work. I have no doubt that this will be a great consolation and encouragement to you and yours, for an Apostolic Brief will bring with it Our Lord's approbation and blessing on all your endeavors for the salvation of the poor Indian and Negro. If necessary, I shall not fail to remind the Cardinal of his promise....[6]

A month before this second visit to Santa Fe, Cardinal Satolli spent several days in Philadelphia as the guest of Mr. Walter George Smith. From there he visited Eden Hall, the Convent of the Sacred Heart in Torresdale; St.

Francis Industrial School in Eddington; and the Motherhouse of the Sisters of the Blessed Sacrament in Cornwells Heights where the children had prepared a musical entertainment for him. Before he left, the Cardinal spoke to all the sisters who had assembled in the community room. He remarked that the new and flourishing Order of the Sisters of the Blessed Sacrament had already accomplished much for the Catholic Church on behalf of the Negroes and Indians and he hoped it would continue to grow and flourish. He added he was sure that Pope Leo XIII would be especially pleased when he gave His Holiness an account of the work in which the Community was engaged.[7] There were grateful thoughts of Cardinal Satolli when the Decree of Praise came through.

Archbishop Ryan wrote his congratulations to Mother M. Katharine and all the community saying that the approval of the Holy Father proclaimed the institute to be God's work for His most neglected children, and that all that remained to be done was to have the Rule translated by Father Sabetti and sent to Rome.[8] This was done within the year. About this time in Rome Cardinal Gotti was compiling the Normae, a summary of directions for communities of men and women. The only message that came back from Rome was a very brief cablegram, "Conform to the Normae." This meant seeking new counsel and going over the whole Rule again.

At this point the Foundress had come to the definite conclusion that of all the rules she had studied, the one best suited to the works of her congregation was the one she had originally followed — the Rule of the Sisters of Mercy. She decided to take that then and permanently as the basis of hers. Like St. Theresa of Avila, Mother M. Katharine gloried in being a child of the Church. She yearned to have membership in the Mystical Body of Christ extended all over the world, especially to the Indians and Colored of America. She was conscious always that she was working for the Church under the direction of Church authorities, that she was an instrument of the Church.

The Church in turn, blessed her apostolate, consecrated her efforts and fired her zeal to ever deepening intensities. In the matter of help and direction from Church authorities she was more than fortunate. It was as if God sent her the help she needed to fulfill His demands of her. Two members of the hierarchy had cradled the community in its infancy. In the writing of the Rule, help came to her from many sources. Father Scully, S.J., the community confessor, gave her the benefit of his experience and sent other questions she had to the Woodstock theologian, Father Sabetti, S.J., Father (later Bishop) O'Gorman of the Holy Ghost Fathers gave her valuable help and suggestions. In 1900 Archbishop Ryan appointed Father Heuser, theology professor at Overbrook, the diocesan seminary, to help her work out all details in conformity with Canon Law. This scholarly priest would work faithfully and steadfastly with her in all details till the final approval of the Rule was attained. In 1904 the archbishop appointed Father Wissel, C.Ss.R., to put the Rule in Latin. Mother M.

Clement, Superior General of the Sisters of St. Joseph at Chestnut Hill, whose Rule had been approved, gave helpful advice.[9]

Near the end of 1903 Mother M. Katharine read to all the Sisters at the Motherhouse and the three missions, the Rule as she had it summarized then. Every Sister was asked to sign it if she approved. In 1904, however, other ideas began to formulate in her mind and she made alterations in certain chapters. In the fall of that year she sent a list of these changes to each house and asked the superior to read them to the assembled Sisters and have each and every sister in the community sign her name if she approved of the changes. The papers were written out in longhand giving the heading of the chapter and the new additions. For example, under The Vow of Poverty, Section VIII, she called their attention to the fact that the original statement read: "In the spirit of Holy Poverty, the sisters shall rely wholly and entirely on Divine Providence for all that pertains to their holy calling and the means of fulfilling it, being strongly convinced that their Heavenly Father will never abandon them if they confide in Him with a steadfast confidence.... They should not endow their institutes and works to the neglect and abandonment of the present needs of the Indians and Colored People...."

In very large handwriting the next line announces: "NOW THIS IS CHANGED. It reads 'The Sisters shall rely on Divine Providence, etc.' It leaves out, '*wholly* and *entirely*'. All the rest, 'They shall not endow, etc.' is also to be omitted." Evidently her discussion with her Council following her visit to Father Pantanella, S.J., had wrought decided changes in her first plans. In two other chapters on the Powers of the Superior General and the Council General, there was a statement to the effect that the decision to help works for the Indian and Colored which the community itself could not undertake, was to be made by the Superior General with the deliberative vote of the Council. Another paragraph posited an annual investment to supply an income for the Motherhouse, Holy Providence, and the three missions then established.[10] All her religious life the Foundress would stress the necessity of her Sisters relying on Divine Providence. At this point neither she nor her Council could have envisaged that at her death in 1955, the Sisters of the Blessed Sacrament would be established in more than fifty missions stretching from Massachusetts to Texas and from Virginia to California. No endowment of hers could possibly extend to them all. Her Sisters would have need in the years ahead to be mindful of her direction to rely on Divine Providence.

After the changes had been approved by all the Sisters, and Father Heuser had made sure of the conformity of each detail to Canon Law, Archbishop Ryan approved the Rule and sent it to Cardinal Falconio then Apostolic Delegate who had offered to send it to Rome. The Cardinal sent it back requesting that it be accompanied by a complete financial account of the expenses of her own foundations and the amounts she had contributed to different dioceses. It took some time to get all this together. Finally, December 10, 1904, everything was on its way to Rome including the assistance given to the Dioceses of Cheyenne, Nashville, Mobile, Boise, Charleston, S. C., Covington, Galveston, Fargo, Helena, Lead, Louisville, Los Angeles, Natchez, Mesqually, Ogdensburg, Omaha, Pittsburgh, Savannah, St. Augustine, Sioux Falls, Tucson, Wilmington, Delaware; Vicariate-Apostolic of Indian Territory and North Carolina. Archdioceses of Philadelphia, Baltimore, and Santa Fe.[11]

But there would be still more revision. Monsignor Kennedy, on a visit to the United States in January 1905 called at the Motherhouse with some further points of discussion; and further work on the rule continued through the year. During the Novena of Grace in March 1906 Mother M. Katharine asked the Council General to be relieved of all duties to make a retreat so that in solitude with God she could know His Will with regard to every point of the Constitutions. After the twelve days retreat, Father Heuser checked all points again. Everything seemed in order. At this point a very interesting interview took place.

One day as Mother M. Katharine was taking care of some correspondence a very distinguished visitor was announced — Mother Cabrini, Foundress of the Missionary Sisters of the Sacred Heart of Jesus. She could not think of any religious whom she would rather meet just then. One of the Sisters living still at the Motherhouse who served them dinner remembers that they got together like two life-long friends though they had never met before. These were two very similar souls on fire with zeal for souls, neglected souls. Mother Cabrini explained that she had come to thank Mother M. Katharine personally for the hospitality she had given two Sisters whom she had sent to that area when they knew no one there.

Mother M. Katharine brought the conversation around to the Rule, her big absorption at that moment. She was aware that Mother Cabrini knew Rome, and she asked for any suggestions she might make about getting the Rule approved at Rome without a long delay. The conversation went like this:[12]

"You see, it is like this," began Mother Cabrini. "You get a lot of mail every day. Some of it you must take care of immediately. Other items are important but you put them on the shelf to take care of tomorrow. Then tomorrow, something else demanding attention comes in and you leave the other letter still on the shelf. Before you know it, there are a lot of other items before it. It is like that in Rome. Things get shelved even though they are important. If you want to get your Rule approved, you go yourself to Rome and take it with you."

Mother M. Katharine gasped, "Oh, I don't think the Archbishop would give me that permission. I am mistress of novices too."

"Well, ask him," continued Mother Cabrini, "ask him and see."

Mother M. Katharine did ask him and the Archbishop thought it a splendid idea. Father Heuser thought it was just the thing to clinch matters. It was not long before final plans were made and she was ready to sail for Rome with the completed English copy Father Heuser had worked out with her; and another copy in Latin which Father Dever also of St. Charles Seminary had done with some alterations and additions he suggested. It was agreed by the

Archbishop and Mother M. Katharine that she would show the English one first and if it was approved have that one put into Latin.

May 11, 1907, she and Mother M. James set sail on the *Konigin Luise* for the Eternal City. Letters the Archbishop had written to Cardinal Merry del Val, Cardinal Satolli and Monsignor Kennedy, Rector of the American College in Rome, had gone on before her. She had arranged for second class reservations, but Mrs. Morrell and the Archbishop changed that and they went first class. In his bon voyage note to her, the Archbishop wrote: "You have the reward of poverty and the comfort of affluence. It is providential especially as Mother M. James is not strong."[13] Then began the flow of her delightful letters, spontaneous, beautiful, reflective, reminiscent of her earlier European travels.

This letter writing was native to her. The emphasis on letter writing and composition writing in her earliest days had given her a facile, gifted pen, and a luminous style. Her letters on this voyage and stay in Rome are many, letters to the Archbishop, to Father Heuser, to her religious daughters. Mother M. James wrote long letters too, filling in the details on days when the Foundress was all absorbed in writings or in a ten day retreat she made under the direction of the Superior General of the Blessed Sacrament Fathers in Rome. From these many delightful letters we can put together the saga of this visit to Rome.[14] There was no priest on board. They had hoped to land in Spain with time enough for a visit to a Church but when they reached Gibraltar they knew that was not possible. The Foundress' letter to her daughters at this point had a special reference to Africa:

> Behold me on the upper deck of the Konigin Luise looking on the land of Africa. I had been standing on the opposite side of the vessel with the coast of Spain laid out before me, at least that part near Gibraltar when Mother M. James came to me and said: "Mother, come and see Africa." It sent a thrill through me as I had not expected to have my eyes rest in this trip on any portion of that Continent.
>
> With an indescribable attraction I crossed quickly over to see that land where there live two hundred million of those for whose salvation our Congregation is instituted. Of course, "they" these two hundred million live far away from the two rolling points of land which even as I write are becoming more and more distant. Yet this land is part of the great African Continent and the sight of it brings questions into my heart: Shall I ever live on that Continent? Shall you?[15]

They disembarked at Naples on the morning of May 24 and after checking their baggage went to St. Peter's Church for Mass, and then to the station for breakfast and the 9:50 A.M. train for Rome. Monsignor Kennedy had someone meet them there and take them to the Cenacle where he had arranged for them to stay. Mother M. Katharine's first reaction there was one of delight when she learned the Sisters of the Cenacle had daily exposition of the Blessed Sacrament. They arrived just in time for lunch and immediately after, set out for Monsignor Kennedy. One hour after she reached Rome, the

Foundress started out on her business. This was typical of her. There was a drive in her that was difficult to emulate and at times, difficult to follow.

Monsignor Kennedy received them kindly but explained that at the moment he could do nothing. He had only returned three days before from the United States, there was an ordination the next day and also the departure of eleven newly ordained priests. Then too, the priest he had expected to employ in translating the Rule had died; and at the moment he could not think of one who could converse with her in English and have the command of Latin to translate into that language. He asked her to come back in several days. The Foundress who was all for going straight and quickly ahead was really disappointed, especially when the Monsignor asked her if there were any hurry. This woman of fabulous plans and fabulous operations always wanted to drive things through. It was possibly part of the equipment God gave her for the vast undertaking He assigned her, fraught as it would be with difficulties and opposition.

She wrote the Archbishop that she felt like a stranger in Rome with her one and only friend not able to help her just then. In her distress she called on her patron, St. Catherine of Sienna. She went to the Minerva and knelt in prayer where the figure of St. Catherine lies in her Dominican habit under the main altar. She reminded her patron that since she knew so many holy men while she was on earth, she must realize her need then and help find a holy man suited for the work on the Rule. Two days later Monsignor Kennedy sent for her. He had found the holy man. A special letter to her councilors gave the details:

> We were summoned to the American College to meet Very Rev. Father Schwartz, C.Ss.R. , formerly Provincial in the United States and now a member of the Council General in Rome. We arrived ahead of time and Monsignor Kennedy explained how it all came about.
>
> "Mother, it must have been the effect of prayer. At dinner after the ordination, Father Schwartz remarked with a deep sigh, 'Well, I have just gotten through one of the worries of my life. I have just put the Constitution of the Franciscans of Philadelphia in the hands of the printer.'"
>
> Then Monsignor explained about us. Father Schwartz is a Philadelphian and knew all about the sum my father left to St. Peter's in his will. *In consideration of this*, he undertook to go over our Constitutions. He has entered fully and entirely into the spirit of Father Heuser's version and altered nothing substantially. He seems to like it....
>
> Every morning from 9:15 to 11:30 or else in the afternoon from 4 to 7:45 we meet Father Schwartz in a private room in the American College. He corrects and we go over every word together. We copy the corrections and then daily carry the corrected sheets to the English Col-

lege where a Reverend Dr. Cronin is translating them into Latin. He has been especially recommended to us.

Her letter went on to explain that Father told her the Normae required a separate chapter on each work and that "aiding needy priests, etc.," was a separate work and it did not belong under the duties of the Superior General, "Not there, but somewhere else." She prayed about this:

> I said: "My God strike that out, if You want it out. I don't want anything. If it is for Your Glory, keep it in. Then while I was thus leaving it to God, my own vocation to the religious life came to me. When my spiritual director refused my becoming a religious, but said just as Father Schwartz did with regard to this point in the constitutions, "Not now," I would pray to Our Lord and say: "I do not wish to be a religious unless you wish me." I never did ask for it except *once.* Behold the next time I went to Confession my confessor said immediately, "Why don't you become a religious?"
>
> Then it came to me, "Why don't you ask Our Lord now to grant us to be the Servants of the Servants of God, to assist those who are engaged in work for Indians and Colored?" So the next Mass I attended I asked for it if it was for the Glory of God. It is the first time I ever remember asking for it. After dinner, I went to the chapel, took a notebook and pencil and I just looked at the Sacred Host exposed there. I assure you there was no inspiration, just *hard thinking.* It is only a few lines but there is a chapter on "Aiding Works Outside the Congregation."[16]

A special private interview with Pope Pius X was arranged for her by Monsignor Kennedy who accompanied the two Mothers and acted as an interpreter. The Foundress was thrilled with the benevolent kindness of the Pope who blessed her, the Rule, the whole congregation and their relatives, and at her special request, everyone of the Colored and Indian races. Mother M. James carried a tray with religious articles for the Papal blessing. Included there was a medal of Our Lady of Good Counsel for every Sister in the Congregation.

If Mother M. Katharine felt at her arrival in Rome she had but one friend there — Monsignor Kennedy — she would know otherwise in a very short time. In her first report from Rome to Archbishop Ryan she wrote:

> ... Very Reverend Father Schwartz kindly undertook to go over every word of Father Heuser's version and pass on it, and at the same time he has procured for us an English Doctor to translate the pages....
>
> We have not been quite three weeks in Rome and now all the Constitutions have been corrected; part of them is being printed and every page is translated. The printer is being supplied with the pages as fast as he can print them, which is not so very fast, for Father does not expect them to be through the press till about June 22.
>
> And now for the marvelous effect of your letter. When we called on His Eminence, Cardinal Satolli he told us he had just received a letter

> from our Archbishop and then he said: "Mother, it is the eve of the Feast of the Sacred Heart, and I want to console you by telling you that fifteen days after you present your Constitutions to me, they will be approved, and if *you wait in Rome* for them you will go home with them in your hands." I have been advised by two Foundresses here that if I wanted to obtain anything in Rome, to wait until I got the papers I needed, and to be sure *not to return without them* or they will be filed for a distant future. So, of course I am going to wait. His Eminence told me you had given him just the information he needed, and most fortunately your letter reached him just one day before I called. I am sure I would have had a different fate had not your own sweet fatherly care encompassed me just in my hour of need. It is so near the time when the Sacred Congregation of Rites ceases to take in any new matter for consideration for this term, indeed I believe the right time is passed already, that it is a great privilege to have a promise that the Constitution will be examined immediately on presentation. Very Reverend Schwartz has corrected very little of Reverend Father Heuser's version....[17]

Matters moved well and fast for the Foundress even though with her customary speed ahead and direct lines of action, she may have thought the movement slow. But she had a spiritual holiday in Rome. The many letters that crossed the ocean gave most intimate details of their visits to Churches and Shrines, and the delight of her soul in the privilege of many Masses and many hours of adoration before the Blessed Sacrament. This experience of Rome would linger all her days. In the heart of Christendom there, she knew hours of very intimate contact with the Sacred Heart of the Divine Missioner. She experienced the loving concern and the pastoral solicitude of those appointed by the Divine Shepherd of souls to take His place and feed His lambs and His sheep. She knew Rome but never before had she come so close to its heart pulsating with Infinite Love.

July 5, Cardinal Satolli told Mother M. Katharine that the following day the Cardinals of the Sacred Congregation would meet and pass on her Constitutions. "We shall meet from 10:30 to 12:00," he said. "I am telling you the hour. Pray then."[18] Besides having Masses said at different places in Rome, Mother M. Katharine and Mother M. James went to St. Peter's and from 9:30 to 12:00 assisted at a Mass every half hour. The following Tuesday Cardinal Satolli told them the Rule had been approved and there was but one more step, to have the Pope add his approval to that of the Congregation. The Cardinal told them to remember that it was on the last day of the Octave of St. Peter that the Sacred Congregation met and approved the Constitutions. "St. Peter," he said, "joined your Congregation especially to the Church on the last day of the octave of his feast. Do not forget that."[19]

Shortly after this interview, Monsignor Kennedy sent for them. The Pope had given his approval. No substantial change had been made in the Rule. A cablegram was sent immediately to Archbishop Ryan asking him to communicate the news to the Sisters. This was the Decree of Definitive Approbation of the Congregation and Experimental of the Constitutions. In the wisdom of Rome, the Decree is given for five years so that the Rule can be tested in the lives of the religious and amended by a General Chapter of the Congregation before Rome sets its definitive seal on it.

The jubilant Foundress made immediate arrangements for the home passage on the *Re d'Italia* of the Lloyd Sabaudo Line scheduled to sail July 18. She chose the line because it advertised a chapel and she was thus sure of Mass on the passage, and it also offered reduced rates to religious. In her letters to the Motherhouse she insisted that no one should come to New York to meet them because this line was frequently late and they would be greatly inconvenienced if they had to wait around New York. She would telegraph them she wrote, immediately on landing and let them know the train on which they would arrive at Cornwells Heights. She was right about the time of the landing. It was due July 31, but did not reach the harbor of New York till August 3.

Two days before landing, she wrote her last letter to the Archbishop giving him the final details of their stay in Rome and telling him particularly of the day spent in Naples before sailing. One item in this letter is especially interesting as it showed the very close bond that existed between the two:

> The day before we set sail for New York, we stopped at Naples to see the great Cathedral of Saint Januarius. All the way up the Cathedral, on each side of the pillars supporting the arches, the main aisle has bas-reliefs of bishops of Naples who were all saints. I could scarcely believe my eyes that so many who had occupied that See had been canonized, and I looked very particularly to see whether "Saint" was before their name. When I saw that is was, I fell on my knees and asked God in as fervent a prayer as I could, that the Archbishop of Philadelphia would be a Saint. Just think how many saints they have in the European cities and in the United States not one yet. For God's glory, my father, you have to be that saint....[20]

The home-coming was a glorious one. The whole community assembled in the picturesque quadrangle of the Motherhouse. As the two mothers entered the chapel and knelt in silent prayer before the tabernacle, the whole community intoned "Holy God We Praise Thy Name" and followed it with a jubilant "Laudate Dominum Omnes Gentes". All hearts were overflowing with gratitude and joy that their mother was back with them, safe, and that the Rule she carried was sealed with the approbation of Rome, activating all who followed it to a more intimate and fruitful membership in the Mystical Body of Christ.

The first General Chapter of the Congregation was announced for November 23, for the general elections of officers and the promulgation of the Rule. Father Schwartz wrote the Foundress from Rome:

> Rome, Sant' Alfonso, Via Merulana
> October 28, 1907
>
> ... You may rest assured that I will pray for you and your community very earnestly to Our Blessed Mother that she may direct you in all your deliberations at your next General Chapter. I would suggest that you note carefully all propositions made by the members of the Chapter. Try to follow them out in practice the next five years. After that time, you can in your application ask for the modifications and additions to the Rule suggested by the Chapter and proved by experience as practicable....[21]

Archbishop Ryan presided at the elections and announced to the Sisters that Mother M. Katharine was elected Superior General by this first Chapter General of the Congregation. There was no note of surprise in that election, only deeper joy. Following the new Constitutions another sister, Sr. M. Juliana, was appointed Mistress of Novices which office the Foundress, at the Archbishop's wish, had filled from the very beginning. At her profession, Katharine Drexel had been appointed and named Mother Superior by Archbishop Ryan. After this general election, her title was changed to Superior General and her community began a new era as daughters of the Church.

# Chapter 18
# Loss And Gain

The final approbation of the Rule would come in 1913. By that time, Archbishop Ryan, on whom the Foundress depended so minutely, and who in turn took care of her smallest need, had gone home to God. He had traveled with her every step of the way and his loss was keenly felt. He had visited the community for the last time November 26, 1910, although no one could have surmised this would be his last visit. In his short talk to the Sisters he asked them to redouble their prayers for him as he was approaching eighty. The first intimation that his health was failing came the following January when Sr. Mary Edith Pardee was professed. She was the former Superior General of the Anglican Sisterhood of St. Mary's in Peekskill, New York, one of a group of Anglican converts who made their submission to Rome.

After her conversion Archbishop Ryan had asked Mother M. Katharine to give her hospitality at the Motherhouse which she did gladly. Later when Mother Edith asked to join the community, she was accepted and warmly welcomed. Mother M. Katharine recognized the eminent stature of the holiness of this woman even as she sensed the anguish of soul her decision had cost her. The Archbishop had very definitely intended to preside at her profession, but the state of his health would not permit it.

He appointed Rev. W. I. McGarvey, a former Anglican minister, recently ordained a Catholic priest, to receive her vows. The ceremony was private and no invitations were issued except to a few former Anglican ministers, friends of Sister Edith, and some interested clergy. The three principal actors in this profession ceremony had formerly been united in similar ceremonies in the Anglican Church. Father McGarvey had been the ecclesiastical superior of the Anglican Community and as such had received their vows in Peekskill. Father Cowl, who said this Profession Mass, had formerly been the spiritual director of the Sisters at St. Mary's while Mother Edith was the Superior General there. Rev. S. Fay, who preached the sermon, had years before preached a retreat for the Anglican Sisters. This was indeed a triumphant ecumenical occasion.[1]

Early in January 1911 Mother M. Katharine and Sister M. Bernardine left the Motherhouse for a visitation of the Carlisle Mission. Since 1906, six Sisters of the Blessed Sacrament had been living there giving catechetical instructions to some 300 Catholic Indians attending the Government School for Indians. They also conducted a small school for Colored children. On her third day there, Mother M. Katharine was notified by phone that the

Archbishop's condition was grave. She returned to Philadelphia immediately. She had no confidence in herself and had leaned heavily on the Archbishop's support and counsel. The news of his condition frightened and saddened her. The bond between them was very intimate and sacred. That bond was recognized by his secretary, Father Kavanagh and she was permitted to see him almost every day. In letters to her sister, Louise, then in Florida with Colonel Morrell, she wrote interesting details of her privileged visits with the Archbishop and commented on the special blessings they were.

In one letter she noted that she treasured especially what he said one day when he was very ill: "You are the Foundress and *I am the Founder with you.*"[2] These last words, she wrote, he addressed to her alone in a lower tone of voice and then added, "I always look on it as my congregation." In another letter she wrote that he asked her if she ever said the Our Father in honor of the Passion. When she shook her head he took a crucifix in his hand and said: "Let us think of that wonderful prayer of Christ and through the Sacred Head of Our Lord crowned with thorns, that Divine Intellect of Our Lord's, through the physical and mental suffering of that Head, we say: 'Our Father who art in Heaven, hallowed be Thy Name'. Through the two outstretched Arms and Sacred Hands nailed to the Cross, and through the wound in the pierced Heart, pierced for love of us, 'Thy Kingdom come, Thy Will be done on earth as it is in Heaven.' At His Feet, the place for beggars, those pierced Feet, we kneel and cry out, 'Give us this day our daily bread.' Then lifting up our eyes once more to that open side, close to the Sacred Heart, we say: 'Thy Kingdom come' — Thy Kingdom, infinite as Thy all embracing Love. 'Thy Will be done on earth as it is in Heaven' Again descending to the pierced Feet, in penitential love, we plead: 'Forgive us our trespasses, as we forgive those who trespass against us, and lead us not into temptation, but deliver us from evil. Amen.'"[3]

On her last visit to him she recalled all his kindness and her debt of gratitude to him. "You are the founder," she said, "If it had not been for your interest, I could not have gone on. Do you remember how you came to me in Pittsburgh after Bishop O'Connor's death?" According to her companion, Mother M. Francis Xavier, a light came into his eyes: "I do remember, my child, I do indeed remember." Then he turned his dying eyes to her in a look of love and depth of meaning. He said, "I remember something else you told me that time too!" Mother M. Katharine made a strong effort to control her grief. Once outside she said, "Is it not wonderful he remembered? I know he added that little remark to assure me that the incident was quite fresh in his mind. I told him something that day that nobody but God and myself know."[4] To this day nobody but God and herself knows what it was!

February 11, 1911, Archbishop Ryan gave up his soul to God. Mother M. Katharine was unable to restrain her grief. She stayed until after the funeral at Our Lady of the Blessed Sacrament Convent in North Philadelphia which she had opened in 1909. The Sisters were distressed as her tears flowed constantly. During supper, in a broken voice, she asked the Sisters' pardon, and added that she did not want them to think she was unhappy about her vocation, but she could not stop the tears.[5] God had given her two mighty counselors; both of them He had now taken home. Later archbishops of Philadelphia including Cardinal Dougherty and Cardinal O'Hara, would befriend her and the congregation, but never again would she know the very intimate and loving fatherhood of Archbishop Ryan whom she had first met in her father's company.

The year following Archbishop Ryan's death was the fifth and final year of the testing period of the Rule. Early that year, 1912, Bishop Kennedy wrote her from Rome that she should bring the Rule herself, but not to come to Rome till he notified her. It was a tremendously busy year for the Foundress. There were invitations to open missions in Columbus, New York and Chicago. Early that year she and Mother M. James visited Columbus, Ohio, to go over the plans for a school the Bishop intended to build on property he had bought. He was very anxious to get the school on its way as there were thirty thousand Colored in the city, but as far as he knew, not one Catholic. The Council General agreed to give the financial help needed. It was expected the school would be ready for occupancy the following fall.

The teeming neighborhoods of Harlem made a strong appeal to Mother M. Katharine's zeal. After returning from her Western visitation in May, she and Mother M. Ignatius took what they called "a missionary journey" to New York to look for a suitable location. She and her companion spent several days in the summer heat tramping the streets of Harlem, inspecting one building after another suitable for a school and a convent. The search was unsuccessful and they returned to the Motherhouse in time for retreat. Mother M. Katharine was under heavy pressure at the time. Mrs. Morrell's health was in a very delicate state. She was on the verge of a breakdown and was under the care of specialists in Bar Harbor, Maine. Her husband and her sister, Mother M. Katharine, were deeply concerned.

As soon as her retreat was over they went back again to New York, staying while there with the Religious of the Sacred Heart at Manhattanville. They scoured the whole district from W. 125th Street to W. 142nd Street looking for two suitable houses, one to start a school and the other to domicile the Sisters. They climbed stairs in apartment houses and private houses from the cellar to the fourth story and down again, then up again. They trudged around in the broiling sun of a hot July. From 8 o'clock in the morning till nearly six, they were marching in the streets of Harlem. Her companion, Mother M. Ignatius, remarked later that she felt she could never again go through this hunting expedition and experience. Long before anyone thought of marching in Harlem, Mother M. Katharine Drexel marched through the streets there looking for a suitable site to lease for the benefit of Harlem children. In the more than fifty years since, her sisters have kept marching there. They are marching in the streets of Harlem still, to schools in five parishes: St. Mark's St. Charles, St. Joseph's, All Saints, St. Thomas.

At length on W. 134 Street she found two houses which she thought would serve her purpose. They were on opposite sides of the street. One was in very good condition and was designated for the school; the smaller one seemed badly in need of every kind of repair, painting, papering, fumigating. The Foundress went over everything this house needed and decided that with the renovations it could be used as a convent. She signed a lease on both houses for a year and a half occupancy. She did not want to buy the buildings outright as she intended erecting a school when she found a suitable site. After arrangements were made for occupying the building several sisters came on from the Motherhouse, and the cleaning and renovation process went on. Mother M. Katharine insisted on working with the Sisters from morning to evening, going down into the lower cellar and superintending men who were cleaning out the refuse of years.[6] There was no restraining her from labors that were beyond her physical strength. Later events would show that the unceasing labors of the summer of 1912 were too much even for her heroic resistance.

After a short stay at the Motherhouse she went on with other sisters to Columbus to prepare for the opening of that house. Fortunately this was a new house needing none of the kind of attention she had given the New York residence. From there she went on to Chicago and again went through the process of cleaning up an old house which was turned into St. Monica's Convent. All the new furniture arrived while she was there and the rooms were attractively arranged before she left to return to the Motherhouse for the Reception and Profession ceremonies. But complications arose in Chicago. The plans had been that the old Armory on 37th Street would be remodeled for a school but unexpired leases turned up which prevented that. There was nothing else to do for a time but fit up some classrooms in the convent. But 160 children could not be squeezed into the few rooms and a nearby laundry was added and remodeled.

In the midst of all this mission foundation, Bishop Kennedy wrote from Rome saying that everything would be in readiness for the final approbation of the Rule and that she herself should take it to Rome and reach there about November first. When, after the Reception and Profession ceremonies, Mother M. Katharine began to make preparations for a visitation of St. Catherine's in Santa Fe with a stop over on the way for the new school in Chicago, the councilors tried to intervene. They tried to prevail on her to let any further missionary visits go for the rest of the year so that she would be in a condition to start for Rome in mid-October. But she insisted all was well with her and that since they had been asked to open a house in Cincinnati, she wanted to look over the situation there before going on to Santa Fe. Confident that all was well, she went right ahead with her plans and left for the West. Then it happened.

September 24 Mother M. James received a telegram from her in Santa Fe asking the Sisters to pray very hard for a special intention which she would tell them later. Four days later the Motherhouse was thrown into a state of consternation by another telegram announcing she had developed a cold and the doctor had found her upper left lung slightly congested. She tried to make light of the matter and continued that with the doctor's advice she had decided to come down from the seven-thousand-foot altitude and go to the Albuquerque Sanitarium. Then she added gently that the doctor found she had incipient typhoid fever. She tried to assure them all would be well soon. Mother Loyola had come with her from Santa Fe; she had a trained nurse and a good doctor who would add his report to the lettergram. She forbade any of them coming to her on what would be a five day journey, for she was sure she would be better by that time, and no more could be done for her than was being done.[7] She submitted beautifully to everything. When the doctor left her after announcing the typhoid, she drew the covers around her and said, "Well, I feel perfect peace on an occasion like this, as this is certainly not according to my plans, and it must be God's Will."[8]

The suddenness of it all threw an atmosphere of pain and anxiety about the Motherhouse. Definitely the visit to Rome was off for that year. Mother M. James, herself ill at the time, sent Mother M. Mercedes to Archbishop Prendergast to ask his permission to send two sisters despite the order. He felt it would displease her and do more harm than good. In his fatherly concern, however, he promised that he himself would go if it became necessary. Telegrams were sent to all the houses imploring the help of their prayers. As the word circulated through the nation, letters from bishops and priests, from missionaries all over the country flowed into the Motherhouse expressing sorrow at her illness and promising prayers. It would not have been possible to compute the prayers and the number of Masses offered for her recovery in all parts of the United States.

Daily reports flowed into the Motherhouse from the patient, the doctor, and long detailed letters from Mother M. Loyola. The one who climaxed the whole affair and proved the most helpful was Colonel Morrell. The Annals state: "The gratitude of the community to Colonel Morrell cannot be told in words. He had always done everything in his power for the Congregation, but now he seemed the only ray of hope, or as one sister expressed it, 'the safety plank in the general sea of gloom in which we were all enveloped.'"[9] Her sisters had been told not to come. Colonel Morrell left for Albuquerque immediately, arranging beforehand that the patient was not to be notified of his coming. He did not want that known until he actually arrived. October 4 he wired back to the Motherhouse: "I have just seen Kate — much gratified at my arrival — Typhoid symptoms rapidly decreasing and lung clearing up — Have arranged to return by low grade cut-off to Chicago — Temperature normal, pulse good — sends love."[10]

He really took over. He found good nursing and every attention being given his sister-in-law but certain tests had not been taken and he insisted these should be made. A week after his arrival he wired Mrs. Morrell: "Am pushing very hard to get Kate out of here as this climate is bad for pneumonia, expect to have her up in a day or two, will rush car through without stopping at Chicago."[11] With the doctors' consent her departure was finally arranged for October 16. Colonel Morrell commandeered a private car of the Atchison, Topeka, and Santa Fe Railroad and the journey was taken low-grade down through Texas. Mother Loyola, Sister Patrick, a Sister of Charity — Sister Rose Agatha, Doctor Reidy, and Colonel Morrell traveled with her. The Colonel seemed to think of everything. He had a large oxygen tank installed and all kinds of restoratives on the train, just in case they were needed. But the trip was made without incident and she reached the Motherhouse no worse for the long travel.

In one of the letters Mother Loyola had written the Motherhouse from the hospital she noted that everyone was wondering where in the world Mother M. Katharine had contracted typhoid. The patient herself could not account for it; it had come so suddenly, a day after she reached Santa Fe. But the sisters who had seen her cleaning in Chicago and those who had tried in vain to stop her supervising the cleaning out of refuse in the house in New York, were pretty sure they knew where the germs had come from and what had caused her weakened condition. Two eminent specialists were called in by Colonel Morrell. Their general conclusion was that she had been and was still a very sick woman; that she really had typhoid and bronchial pneumonia; that her heart had a slight functional disturbance and that she was suffering from an incipient nervous breakdown.[12] They insisted that only complete, absolute rest would restore her perfectly to health.

She was a submissive patient. The doctors laid down the requirement; she calmly and quietly followed them. She was not to walk even to the chapel; she was to transact no business nor see anyone except the nurses attending her. She was at first inclined to make light of the whole affair and told the doctor it was a joke for her to be in the infirmary. She asked him what she would do if she were a tramp. He answered her solemnly: "Mother, if you were a tramp you would be in a certain department in Blockley where people have a very serious disease."[13] She was tired out and this collapse was a serious blow to her. But she accepted it as she did everything else from the hands of God.

Mother M. Katharine's recovery was slow but steady. By early December the Sisters were allowed to visit her and she was privileged to assist at Mass. There was a slight alarm when signs of yellow jaundice appeared but they were quickly disposed of by Dr. Moylan who had just the right remedies. At the end of the year she was beginning to feel completely restored and all traces of her illness had disappeared. The visit to Rome with the Holy Rule was planned definitely for April. The strong bond of affection she had for all her religious daughters had been deepened by this experience of their loving concern for her welfare. In a Christmas letter to the Sisters at St. Michael's she had written: "Of all the Christmases in the past, this is the Christmas in which it behooves me to show you the efficacy of your prayers *through Our Lord in the Blessed Sacrament.* Your prayers have made me well, thank God...."[14]

Mission developments were happening fast as the year 1913 dawned. The January meetings of the Council dealt with pressing problems. They went over the entire Rule again and noted suggestions. They voted to purchase four lots adjoining St. Mark's Church in New York City for a future school and convent. Mr. Perrot was asked to prepare plans for a building large enough for five hundred children and a convent for fifteen sisters. They received word that the combination church and school they were erecting at Atlanta as a memorial to Archbishop Ryan was almost completed. As Father Lissner had requested that Sisters of the Blessed Sacrament conduct the school it was agreed to open it in the fall under the patronage of Our Lady of Lourdes. Cardinal O'Connell wrote from Boston inviting the Sisters to take up some kind of work for the Colored of his Archdiocese. He asked Mother M. Katharine to come to Boston to discuss the matter with him. The doctor forbade her making that trip. Mother M. James and Mother M. Mercedes went in her stead. The interview was a very pleasant one; general plans for social service and catechetical work were discussed. The following year a house was rented at 21 Worcester Square and a catechetical program was inaugurated. In 1922 they moved to 691 Massachusetts Avenue which was used for some twenty years as a center of home visitations and religious instructions. In 1935 the present commodious Blessed Sacrament Mission at 60 Vernon Street was completed to serve as it does today an extensive catechetical and home visitation apostolate. It was Cardinal O'Connell's invitation in January 1913 that brought the Sisters of the Blessed Sacrament to Boston. From the beginning, however, his Propagation of the Faith Director, Father (later Bishop) Cushing, would take a special interest in the apostolate of this mission. Cardinal Cushing as Archbishop of Boston has befriended many causes and inspired many apostolates. His stand on Race Relations and the dignity of all people has been consistently clear and forceful.

Having settled all these immediate matters, Mother M. Katharine planned to sail for Rome April 5. Bishop Schrembs was heading a pilgrimage that day and she decided to join it. He was the new Bishop of the newly organized Diocese of Toledo and he decided to follow the custom of olden days, making his Ad Limina visit to Rome in company with his priests and people. The Toledo Pilgrimage had been widely advertised. As soon as she heard about it, that was the way she wanted to go to Rome. She knew they would have the Blessed Sacrament on board, and with many priests in the party, there would be the opportunity of hearing Masses daily. General goodbyes were said at the Motherhouse early in the morning of April 5, 1913. She and Mother M. Mercedes took a 7:13 train from Cornwells Heights and before noon boarded the *Ivernia* in New York.

With her health restored and the prospect of another visit to Rome, the Foundress was in very good spirits. She was delighted to know there were seventy lay people in the Bishop's group and eighteen priests. Shortly after the liner started Bishop Schrembs introduced himself to her and the priests came over to meet them, the only two Sisters on board. The voyage was to prove a very restful one for her with her Eucharistic desires satisfied. To her delight there were many Masses every day, and on Sunday the Blessed Sacrament was reserved in the Bishop's cabin during the day for Vespers and Benediction in the evening. They had a little Corpus Christi procession of their own on Sunday. One of the priests in cassock and surplice, preceded by one of the pilgrims with a lighted candle and bell carried the Blessed Sacrament from the salon were Mass was said daily, right through the center of the ship to the Bishop's cabin on deck B in the morning, and then back again the same way in the evening after Benediction. There was a little concern in Mother M. Mercedes' heart when she noticed that Mother M. Katharine spent two hours kneeling before the Blessed Sacrament in the cabin. Nothing could draw her away. The Blessed Sacrament was really her life.

When she found out the boat was to have a prolonged stay at Madeira she decided to visit her first cousin, Madam Jardin who lived in Funchal. They stopped first at the Cathedral and then went on to her cousin's home where they had a delightful reunion. Together they recalled many happy incidents of their childhood, their merry days of play at their weekly visit to their grandmother. Mother M. Mercedes was quite interested in a picture of the former Katharine Drexel in a prominent place on the mantelpiece. Mother M. Katharine noted with pleasure pictures of her grandfather, grandmother and one of her aunts on the walls.

After the visit Mr. Jardin accompanied them back to the liner and saw them safely on board. Mother gave him a copy of "The Call", a vocational piece the Community had just published, and sent with him for the children a miniature tin basket that Miss Polly Damrosch had given her on the passage. The famous conductor, Walter Damrosch, incidentally, was on board with his family en route to Switzerland for the summer.

Once in Rome the two Mothers took up their residence in the Cenacle. Mother M. Katharine's cousin, Mrs. Dahlgren, and her children were also in Rome and had leased apartments at the Barberini Palace. As soon as she knew her cousin was in town, Mrs. Dahlgren called on her and placed at her disposal, any time, any hour, her chauffeur and her limousine. Her daughter, Lucy, offered her services as a companion, guide, or in any capacity at all that would be helpful. Then Mrs. Dahlgren pleaded with them to take up residence with her at the Palace explaining there was a little off-corner of the main building admirably suited for their purpose, with two bedrooms and a bath, a private entrance where they could live apart from the family and go and come as they desired. In addition she offered an Italian maid to serve their meals any time they were ready. She pointed out that just a short walk across the garden would bring them to the sanctuary of the Church of the Capuchins. As a last inducement she mentioned it would be a means of saving money as there would be no board to pay.

All of this was very inviting to Mother especially since her spirit of poverty had been appealed to. Mother M. Mercedes thought the idea of hot baths, meals a la America without incessant deluges of olive oil made the invitation attractive. The Foundress weighed the pros and cons as Mother Mercedes pointed out all the advantages and Mrs. Dahlgren listed them again. Finally, Mother brought it down to a final question: "What about precedence? Will any of my sisters feel they should partake of the hospitality of their friends because my example in Rome would lead them to infer I approved such a step?"[15] She had almost been won around to taking up their residence at the Barberini Palace but this last thought bothered her. With an expression of deep gratitude to her cousin for her generous offer, she decided to remain at the Cenacle.

Another offer of hospitality was to come from the Mother General of the Franciscan Sisters who pressed them to stay at their new Motherhouse from which they could get by cab to any part of the city. As they saw it, Mother M. Katharine's presence in Rome gave them an opportunity to return the kindness she had shown their community. Once a year the Franciscan Sisters had come to Philadelphia from their provincial house in Canada to sell vestments and laces. They had always been welcomed at Our Lady of the Blessed Sacrament Convent. In addition Mother had helped them establish an orphanage for the Colored in Savannah. Very definitely Mother Katharine did not want to change her residence but when the Franciscan Superior General said they could not partake of her hospitality again if she would not accept theirs, she gave in and the two Mothers spent the last three weeks with the Franciscan Sisters.[16] To Mother's delight she found they had exposition of the Blessed Sacrament day and night. Mother M. Mercedes wrote that their rooms were lovely, they had plenty of water, and meals cooked in American style.

On this trip it was Mother M. Mercedes who did most of the letter writing while Mother M. Katharine did the interviewing and checked the points and suggestions on the Rule. In addition to the help of Father Schwartz, Father Elliot Ross, the well known Paulist who had been in Rome three years, was appointed by Monsignor Caroli to work in conjunction with him on the Rule and to go over the material with the Foundress. He gave valuable help. When she attempted to give him some remuneration, he would have none of it. Instead before she left Rome, she sent him a grateful letter and enclosed a medal. His reply was typical. He wrote from the Collegio Lambardo:

> ... Of course, I shall wear constantly the little medal you so kindly sent. It will be one of my precious souvenirs of Rome, as having met

> the Sisters of the Blessed Sacrament here will be one of my pleasantest memories.... Certainly as a priest and as a Southerner whose forbears held slaves for generations (but did not rob and exterminate the Indians as the Yankees), I feel a special responsibility toward the Negroes. And so if I can ever do anything for you in the future, I want you to be sure to give me that pleasure....[17]

In between the session on the Rule and the business involved there, the Mothers were able to fit in visits to many points of interest. Lucy Dahlgren knew the city well, its holy places and historic monuments, and she was delighted to serve as their guide. The glad tidings that the Cardinals in session had given their final approval to the Rule came May 15. In this case as in the case of all congregations and orders approved by the Church, a statement in *The Constitution of the Church* of Vatican Council II was actualized: "The Hierarchy following with docility the promptings of the Holy Spirit, accepts the rules presented by outstanding men and women, and authentically approves these rules after further necessary adjustments. It also aids by its vigilant and safeguarding authority those institutes variously established for the building up of Christ's body, in order that these same institutes may grow and flourish according to the spirit of the founders."

Now that her Roman business was terminated, the Foundress had a strong desire to make her retreat in Rome; it had been so ideal six years before. This time she put aside the desire as she felt she was needed in America. However, she had one more project to carry out — a search for possible vocations for the ever-widening American Mission Field. She determined to visit some religious centers in Germany and Ireland in the hope of meeting possible vocations or those who might help to make her community known. Already two vocations had come from Europe: Madeleine Lissner (Sister M. Ignatia) had come from Alsace Lorraine to enter the community in 1909. Her uncle, Father Ignatius Lissner, American Provincial of the Society of African Missions had told her about the American Missions. Marie Mariench (Sister M. Bernadette) had come from Germany in 1912.

The last night they were in Rome, although they had visited the churches in the afternoon, the Foundress, to Mother Mercedes' surprise, called for a cab and they went back for a last good-bye to the Tomb of St. Peter the Apostle and after that they skirted around and made another visit to the Minerva. As they passed the Trevi Fountain, she gave Mother Mercedes a penny to throw in. The saying runs that anyone who throws a penny into the Fountain is sure to return to Rome again!

Leaving Rome May 29, 1913, they headed for Assisi, a place especially dear to Mother M. Katharine whose devotion to the poor man of Assisi ran through all the days of her life. After that they made brief stops at Florence and Milan, and then took a train for Basle, Switzerland, where they were able to interview the priests of two large churches one of whom was director of a very active sodality. At Speyer, Germany, they visited the school of the Dominican Sisters where they met Canon Schwind who acted as their interpreter from the French which Mother M. Katharine used. Two vocations would ultimately come from this visit. Marie Windecker (Sister M. Hildegard) a senior then at Speyer, came the following year. She made the voyage alone across a submarine infested Ocean. Seven years later Elizabeth Schmitt (Sister M. Cecily) under the guidance of Canon Schwind followed her to Cornwells Heights.

From Speyer they went to Steyl to the Motherhouse of the Sisters of the Holy Ghost where summer retreats were in session and where they had an opportunity to visit their normal school and novitiate and also the contemplative branch of the order known as Sisters of Divine Love.

Their next destination was Ireland. They stopped a day in London to give Mother M. Mercedes an opportunity to see some sights, especially Westminster Abbey. After the usual trip through Wales to Holyhead, they crossed the Irish Sea to Dublin and were soon in contact with Father Murphy, a Holy Ghost Father and an old friend of the Community, who had offered to be their guide and to speak their cause in whatever schools in Ireland they could fit into their short stay. They were to find out that Ireland at that time was overrun with traveling nuns seeking vocations from the land so rich in faith. The hospitality of the various communities operating the schools was heavily pressured under the many requests, but it never gave out.

The two American Mothers accompanied by Father Murphy visited schools in Dublin, Killarney, Kilkenny, Cork, Waterford and Lismore. At the Presentation Convent in Lismore they were given an especially warm welcome by Mother Peter, the sister of Archbishop Prendergast of Philadelphia. Two vocations resulted from this trek through parts of Ireland: Augusta O'Brien (Sister M. Brendan) followed shortly from Lismore, and Bridget Rogers (Sister M. Incarnata), from Waterford. In later years from 1931 to 1939 two Sisters of the Blessed Sacrament would visit Ireland annually and bring back many rich vocations for the American Colored and Indian missions.

As beautiful as Ireland was and as pleasant as their visits to schools proved to be, both Mothers were glad to turn their steps home and board the *S.S. Cedric* bound for New York. There was no priest aboard and they missed the daily Mass. The Foundress expressed their sense of loss in a letter to the Motherhouse:

> ... It rarely happens, so they say, that there is not a priest or two on the vessel. We must bless Our Lord for all the Masses He has let us hear in the past. I want this deprivation to be as a penance — though nothing less than the Precious Blood could take this away — for all my faults in life in hearing Mass. How good God has been to us on this journey,

> how many graces! We feel your prayers for us, my dear ones. I think Our Lord has made me perfectly well....[18]

The return voyage was restful. There were no business matters to be arranged, her mission was accomplished, her health was restored, and the Rule she carried back to her Sisters bore the stamp of Rome's final approval. Explosive joy and thanksgiving marked the homecoming, June 29, as the Te Deum rang through the chapel. A new era began that day. The Rule was finally approved, the missions were spreading throughout the country, and the Foundress had a new lease on life. It was indeed a day of great gladness and an occasion calling for renewed consecration and deeper love for the entire Congregation.

# Chapter 19
# Deep River Gateway

Missionary efforts go back far in the history of Louisiana. Priests accompanied the first Spanish explorers in their ill-fated expeditions; Negroes were brought in with the first settlers. The best and the worst of the Spaniards and the French found their way to early Louisiana. The Code Noir of the French and similar provisions of the Spanish attempted to assure instruction in the Faith, Baptism, and opportunity to share Catholic services, for Negro and Indian slaves. Many vicissitudes and deterring influences hampered the foundation of the Catholic Church but were impotent to prevent its growth and extension.

From the beginning, the city of New Orleans with its commanding position near the mouth of the Mississippi River, was destined to take a place of distinction among American cities. Today, blending in its art and its culture the best elements of Spanish, French, and American civilizations, the polarity of its achievements as a city of the Old World and a metropolis of the New, makes it a big drawing card for tourists. Travel pieces stress the fact that there is a great deal to see and much to enjoy in "The City That Care Forgot." There are museums, antique shops, lovely parks, expansive lake fronts, famous restaurants, and a little corner of Old France itself in the famous Vieux Carre. Whether the tourist follows the Azalea Trail through the heart of the city on fabulous St. Charles Avenue, or drives leisurely through the Garden Section verdant all year around, he is struck by the natural beauty that has been incorporated into the structure of the city.

But all New Orleans is not Azalea Trails, Garden Sections and Lake Front opulence. It has its Negro ghettos with its unpaved streets even though much has been done in the way of housing projects in recent years. Tourists see one face of New Orleans, missionaries, another. Mother M. Katharine brought her Sisters to New Orleans in 1915. She went into that city so rich in culture, well aware of the fact that the people who built New Orleans and contributed to its culture were not all white; nor had all the Negroes in Louisiana been slaves. One historian has this to say about it:

> As a result of the slave insurrection in Santo Domingo in 1791, the gripping events of which clustered about the dauntless figure of Toussaint L'Ouverture, some ten thousand refugees, by 1809, settled at New Orleans. These newcomers, one-third of whom were slaves, included whites as well as a considerable number of free Negroes, some of mixed blood, but probably others of pure African stock as well. They were in

many instances persons of culture and affluence, and they brought with them customs and traditions peculiar to their former home....[1]

These free men of color who sent their children to be educated to France, to the North, or even to schools privately arranged in New Orleans, had much to contribute to the development of New World civilization in Louisiana. Many of them were well qualified to accept and hold positions of responsibility and honor in the Reconstruction Period. But the intrigues, the mistakes, the unfortunate operations of that period left Race Relations split wide open in this state. Even down to our contemporary life they are still split wide open in some parts of the state despite the valiant leadership of Archbishop Rummel and his successors.[2] The Archbishops fought segregation head on, and stressed again and again the equality of all men in their creation by God and their Redemption by the Eternal Son of God. The very positive act of Pope Paul VI, October 2, 1965, in naming Bishop Perry, a Negro, Auxiliary Bishop of New Orleans, highlighted the position of the Church on the universal brotherhood of man. In his sermon at his installation as Archbishop of New Orleans, Archbishop Hannon lit some new torches and opened new roads. "I know I express the sentiments of all," he said, "when I express gratitude to the Holy Father for this nomination. Bishop Perry will make in his new office a great contribution to the cause of Christ."

Although Mother M. Katharine did not bring her Sisters to New Orleans till 1915, her contacts go back to the very foundation of the Community. The first visitor to the temporary novitiate in Torresdale in 1891 was Archbishop Janssens of New Orleans. There had been correspondence between them before, and he had come to discuss his problems with her. In the course of the years, an intimate bond, a mutual understanding, and mutual encouragement would develop between them.

Archbishop Janssens was a missionary at heart. Born in Holland, ordained at Ghent, Belgium, he had come to Richmond, Virginia, September 1868, with an intense desire to serve the American missions. Bishop McGill made him his secretary, and later, Cardinal Gibbons appointed him his Vicar. In 1881 he was chosen as Bishop of Natchez. Seven years later, he was named Archbishop of New Orleans at a time when the Archdiocesan debt was $324,759, a staggering amount in those days. The reduction of that debt would involve much of his efforts in collaboration with his priests and people. He was a man of tremendous activity and plunged immediately into the major problems of his new episcopacy, one of the first major ones being the recruitment of seminarians. Up until then seminarians had come from Rome. He felt that there was no reason in the world why Louisiana could not supply its own vocations and he worked hard for the establishment of a diocesan seminary, turning to the Benedictine Fathers in St. Meinrad for cooperation. In 1894 he had twenty-two native Louisianans studying for the priesthood.[3] In this emerging diocese he was beset with problems on every side, one of which sprang from his deep concern for the Colored. It was this interest that brought him in contact with Mother M. Katharine.

In the Motherhouse Archives in Cornwells Heights, there are over sixty handwritten letters of this zealous archbishop to her. Over a period of six years until his death in 1897, correspondence would flow between them. He had turned to her for help because he was deeply concerned about the preservation of the Faith among the Colored members of his flock. In one of his first appeals to her March 14, 1891, he had written that he felt a great responsibility for preserving the faith among the Catholic Negroes. He mentioned the Colored population was about 85,000 in the Diocese of New Orleans and that unfortunately many had left the Church and others were still leaving. His plea was simple but effectively placed, "If you can help us, for that sake of these poor people and for the sake of Our Blessed Lord, do so. You will perform a most meritorious work and deserve our prayers and the prayers of those whom you benefit."[4] As he presented one need after another to her against the background of his heavy diocesan debt, she continued to send financial help.

His letters supply historical perspective and insight into the conditions of his time. July 4, 1891, he wrote her that he had thirty-two schools in operation for the Colored, two asylums, and four schools in the planning stage for building.[5] The following year he wrote after visiting St. Joseph's School, that he thought she should come with her Sisters and take over that school. He urged her to visit Louisiana and see for herself the work already done and that still to be done.[6] Most of his letters urge her to send her Sisters to his diocese. His letter of March 1, 1893, mentions that two hundred Colored children would receive their first Holy Communion at the Cathedral the following Sunday. He was alarmed at the leakage from the Church:

> August 8, 1893
>
> ... There is nothing in my administration of the diocese that worries me more than our Colored People. I cannot find the means to counteract those who try to capture them. In other dioceses they look out for conversions of the Colored People and I have to look out against perversions. I often feel discouraged. With your kindness to our diocese in the way of pecuniary help, please add the prayers of the community for me....

Later the same year difficulties of another nature arose:

> October 7, 1893
>
> ... The Lord has visited us terribly this summer; I lost six priests by death in three months. Four churches and one convent were totally wrecked by a cyclone and two churches very badly damaged. Two thousand people drowned by the late disaster, most all Catholics and ill prepared to meet so sudden and terrible a death. I am downcast and feel sick

> at heart. But the name of the Lord be blessed. You and the Sisters must pray a little more for me....

A very interesting section of this Archbishop's correspondence has to do with the establishment of St. Katharine's Church as a separate church for the Colored in New Orleans. When St. Joseph's Church needed to be expanded and a new church was erected, the Archdiocese purchased the original church with the intention of trying out a church for the Colored. Mother M. Katharine was asked to contribute to the furnishing and renovation of the building. After quite a bit of correspondence as to why a separate church was being provided, she donated $5,000 for the refurnishing. Sunday, May 15, 1895, Archbishop Janssens presided at the solemn pontifical Mass in the church packed to the doors. Colored altar boys served and a Colored choir provided the music.[7] In honor of Mother M. Katharine, the Archbishop changed the name of St. Joseph's to St. Katharine.

Nine years later, 1904, when the Foundress made a tour of the South to investigate how the money her Community had donated to various schools and churches was being used, one of the places she visited was St. Katharine's in New Orleans. She carried a small notebook with her — still preserved at the Motherhouse — in which she wrote out brief reports and summaries of how matters were progressing in each. Under the heading *St. Katharine's,* this is her entry:

> We attended the ten o'clock Mass. There were about seventy-five devout adults present. The choir was not good. The organist was one of the White teachers of St. Katharine's School. We were told that on Sodality Sunday the Church is crowded. It seems that on Sundays, the Colored prefer to go to Church with the Whites. They are given pews or rent them in all the churches in New Orleans. I am told the priests do not wish to give up their Colored congregations because they efficiently aid in the support of the churches. Before Archbishop Janssens purchased St. Katharine's, the Colored asked for a separate Church. Then they retracted but he held them to this first demand.[8]

We do not have any other evidence of this request made by some of the Colored people themselves for a separate church, but a woman as exact and painstaking as Mother M. Katharine would never have written this unless she had definite facts to justify it.

The Archbishop conscientiously sought the most effective way of serving his flock, the way that would be most helpful then and there. His dilemma is evident in another letter:

> November 11, 1893
>
> ... Our white Catholics are unwilling to help the Negro for Church and school purposes; and many of the influential Negroes, especially Mulattoes, are opposed to special Colored churches, not because they go to church themselves, but because they imagine the different churches

> will tend to a greater social separation. I tell them they keep all the privileges they have and that they can continue to go to the white churches, but they do not want to understand it. A separate congregation is a trial, and I think here, where we have two-thirds of all the Colored Catholics of the United States, this ought to be given a fair trial. If we succeed we will have far less difficulty with the following; and if we, after giving it a fair trial, fail, we will simply give it up for the future; and console ourselves with the thought that we tried, did our best and could do no better. If these reasons seem good to you, please, be so kind as to lay them before Archbishop Ryan, saving me the trouble of writing the same thing twice. I hope I do not bother you too much; you know I do it because I want to do my duty toward the colored people....[9]

Before making a trial of a Church for the Colored (as far as he was concerned it was only a trial) he weighed the matter and pondered it well. Many another dedicated apostle would wrestle with this same question. In different instances the Colored themselves would ask for a separate church where they could form their own societies with the privileges such a church would afford them. Colored Catholics petitioned Cardinal Cushing for a separate church in Boston — St. Richard's — and he gave it because they asked for it. However, a recent decision on the construction of a throughway required its demolition and ended that separate church. In 1922 a group of Colored Catholics living in Cleveland sent Bishop Schrembs a request for a separate church, and they were given Our Lady of the Blessed Sacrament. In their rather long petition, this statement is found:

> ... The undersigned committee, representing a social and charitable organization composed solely of members of this racial group of your flock, are mindful of the recent unwarranted attack made upon your Lordship by a minority group of Colored Catholics, who voiced the sentiment that we do not desire a church of our own in this city, on the supposition that such would in some way militate against the civic well-being of the race.
>
> We protest that such is untrue and unfounded, and do incline to the conviction that a Catholic Church and priest consecrated to the needs and service of our race could be none other than a very potent factor in the material uplift as well as of untold spiritual blessing to the race and to the community....[10]

In our day, separate churches, separate schools will disappear one by one. The Catholic Church and every order and congregation within the Church will work for their complete eradication. But in fairness to the apostolates that have been zealously and generously carried on through the years, it would seem evident that under the circumstances in which they arose, especially in New Orleans, the separate churches and the separate schools preserved the Faith of thousands. It was not that the Church wanted it this way, but the Church did it this way in some areas to safeguard the Faith.

Until the end, Archbishop Janssens would keep his concern for his Colored flock prominently in view. But he had many other problems. By 1897 with the splendid cooperation of his priests and people he had reduced the archdiocesan debt to $100,000. The strain of many problems had weakened his health. He suffered from fainting spells but he continued to work disregarding his health. He had determined that year to make a trip to Europe to see if he could arrange for a final settlement of the $100,000 debt. Because the condition of his health seemed dangerous, his secretary and others tried to dissuade him from this effort. His determination was not to be changed. June 9, with his chancellor, Father Joseph A. Thebault, he left New Orleans on the steamer *Creole* bound for New York where he intended to take a liner for Europe. That evening while the steamer was still in the Gulf, he was stricken with a heart attack. Father Thebault administered the last sacraments before he died. His letter to Mother M. Katharine gives intimate details of his going home to God:

> July 7, 1897
>
> ... I assisted the Archbishop during his last night on the steamship *Creole*, heard his confession, gave him Extreme Unction and the Indulgence for a happy death. But never have I been so touched; he died like a true Christian, making the sacrifice of his life like a Saint kneeling on the floor, looking at the Heavens and pronouncing these words: "My God, I am ready." It was the *Fiat* and the *Consummatum Est* of Jesus....
>
> Dear Mother, pray for me who have been so afflicted. I have lost a father full of love for me....[11]
>
> J.A. Thebault

Archbishop Janssens' last letter to her reached Mother M. Katharine after his death. She knew and understood his deep desires for the welfare of all his flock. She knew too, something of the needs and conditions in Louisiana. But it would be many years before she would bring her own Sisters to Louisiana. It would be a very special need that would draw her then.

# Chapter 20
# Into The Deep South

After the chaotic days of the Reconstruction, schools in Louisiana and in other southern states fell into well defined patterns of segregation which southern legislatures forced and established by law as their "way of life." The unfortunate Plessy vs. Ferguson decision of the Supreme Court cemented to a certain degree into the South a cleavage not only in education, but in travel, housing, hotel accommodations, restaurants, recreational facilities as well. The decree of the legality of separate but equal facilities would be applied to almost every phase of human existence. The South went stolidly ahead and provided separate facilities with nothing equal about them. In the field of education, this cleavage was particularly harmful, denying the Negro in many instances the opportunities of better schools and better teachers.

Educational facilities, standards, and programs developed slowly in Louisiana for both Colored and white. By 1913 the State Board of Education had gotten around to listing six requirements for high school teachers. Teachers for state approved high schools had to fulfill one of the six.[1] The standards were low. Thomas H. Harris, who was appointed State Superintendent of Education, stated that the period from 1880 to 1904 "is usually considered a dreary waste in Louisiana's educational history."[2] He listed as the contributing factors: "poverty, lack of leadership, and lack of legislation." If facilities for the whites were poor, they were worse for the Colored. In a parish superintendent report from Franklin, April 16, 1900, we read, "White schools have sessions ranging from four to eight months; Colored schools from three to six months."[3]

The Federal Government felt responsible to some extent for the education of the new citizens of our country. Chiefly through the Land Grant College Program, it extended the benefits of higher education, leaving to the state the organization of the common education. In addition to the Government contributions, Protestant missionary groups went into the South and erected colleges for the Negro. It took years for many of these to develop into full fledged colleges, but they gave the Negro the benefits of a limited higher education he otherwise would not have had. Opportunities for higher education of the Colored were opened early in the post Civil War period in New Orleans. The State Legislature by Act 87, chartered a University for the Colored in New Orleans which had been approved during the Constitutional Convention of 1878. It was called Southern University, and was selected to be the "land grant college" for Negroes under the Morrill Act.[4] Its limited curriculum would expand with time.

The city also saw the rise of three Protestant colleges at a very early period. The Methodist Episcopal Church with the Freedmen's Act Society began Union Normal for Negroes July 8, 1869. A legislative act of March 22, 1873 broadened it into New Orleans University. Straight University sponsored by the American Missionary Association was granted a charter by the State June 12, 1869.[5] Leland University, a Baptist institution incorporated in 1870, opened four years later. Despite their inadequacies and insufficiencies, these institutions provided a long background of higher education.

For the Catholic Colored students, however, there were distressing features about these institutions. They were predominantly Protestant and required attendance at chapel exercises. Over the years, this resulted in a leakage from the Faith. Of the four institutions, many Catholic parents chose Southern University for their children. Though the presidents were frequently Baptist ministers and the environment was Baptist, it was a state institution and could not require chapel attendance. A zealous Josephite priest, Rev. P. O. Labeau, was very much concerned about this lack of Catholic higher education for New Orleans Negroes. He himself had come from a well known Southern family and had joined the Josephites with the intention of making what reparation he could for the sins of the South against the Negro by dedicating his life to their service. After his ordination, he offered himself to the Archbishop of New Orleans but was assigned to Palmetto, which would later be named Labeau in his honor. Eventually he was appointed pastor of the Colored parish of St. Dominic's in New Orleans, and he became more keenly aware of the necessity of Catholic effort in higher education. What he thought was an ideal opening came when the State Legislature moved Southern University to Scotlandville, near Baton Rouge.

The commodious and imposing structure of Southern University had been erected near the outskirts of New Orleans not far from the Mississippi. But in the course of time a middle class white population had settled around it. They resented the Colored students in the area and petitioned the removal of the university. Colored Catholics fought the move but were unable to prevent it. Of the four institutions combining high school and college courses, they thought Southern presented the least danger to the Faith of their children. They valiantly raised funds for legal fees; they took every step they could but they lost the battle. In 1912 the State Legislature ordered the removal of Southern University to its present site near Baton Rouge; the transfer was made the following year. The large building in New Orleans stood majestically in emptiness and idleness.

In 1915 it was made known that the main building, grounds and smaller buildings of the abandoned university were to be sold. To Father Labeau this seemed a providential opportunity for a Catholic venture in higher education for the Colored in Louisiana. He talked the matter over with his Superior

General, Reverend Justin McCarthy, S.S.J., and urged him to discuss the situation with Mother M. Katharine. Her reaction was one of immediate interest. Then Father McCarthy presented the plan and the possibilities to Archbishop Blenk who favored it enthusiastically and invited Mother M. Katharine to undertake the project. Other invitations had been extended to her before, to bring her Sisters to New Orleans, but she had not accepted them. She had watched with interest and loving concern the work of the Sisters of the Holy Family, the Colored Sisterhood, with their Motherhouse in New Orleans. She hesitated to take up any work there already being done by these Sisters. But this was another situation involving possibly a development into a college and university which at that time the Sisters of the Holy Family were not able to handle. This invitation she would accept.

In addition to the denominational high schools in New Orleans, there was a private academy for girls — St. Mary's — conducted by the Sisters of the Holy Family. This Academy had been opened in 1882 with eight elementary grades and three years of high school. In 1902 they added a fourth year to the high school department.[6] The average attendance including all grades was around 350. No more could be accommodated. Thousands of Catholic boys and girls had no opportunity for a higher education under Catholic auspices in an educational system that was segregated by state law. Those of grammar school age were no better off. In some instances they were roaming the streets in the area of overcrowded and poorly supplied schools.

Archbishop Blenk wrote Mother M. Katharine in March 1915 that the property of the vacated Southern University was going to be put up for auction early in April, and he thought it could be secured at a bargain price.[7] She and Mother M. Mercedes left for New Orleans April 5. They stayed with the Sisters of Perpetual Adoration and had several interviews with the Archbishop. He introduced them to several men he thought could be of assistance to them, particularly Mr. McInerney who was willing to make the purchase for them. The two Mothers visited the property and asked a member of the board busy in one of the offices if they could look around. He gave them a careless "Yes" and went on with his work never dreaming that these were potential purchasers. They were more than satisfied with what they saw, a very substantial and beautiful building in the center of a square city block with shading oak trees from antebellum days. At public auction the next day, Mr. McInerney bought it, including a smaller mechanical arts structure and a three room wooden cottage on the grounds, for $18,000. It was a remarkable buy. In addition to six large classrooms and offices on the first floor, there was an auditorium capable of seating five hundred on the second floor and additional rooms on the second and third floor. Her plans were made immediately. Until a convent would be built, the third floor would serve for the sisters and the auditorium for a chapel for the students and any Colored in the neighborhood who wanted to come. The Archbishop approved of starting a parish there and the Josephite Fathers, at Mother M. Katharine's suggestion to the Archbishop, were asked to take charge. A very zealous and holy young priest, Father John Clarke, whose name and memory are still revered in New Orleans, was sent down to lay the foundation of a new parish which used the auditorium temporarily until a separate church was built — Blessed Sacrament Church.

Alterations and repairs were begun immediately and definite plans formulated for the opening of classes in the fall. Going through the rooms with her eagle eye for details, Mother M. Katharine had found in an old basket covered with dust a pile of Southern University catalogues from 1905 to 1913 giving the student registrations for each year and the complete course of studies. That was exactly what she wanted as she desired to continue where Southern left off, but to establish as the core of her program the knowledge of God and the responsibilities and principles of Christian living. Surprise and resentment was the neighborhood reaction when the real purchasers were publicly known. After all the efforts, including those of the State Legislature to have the Colored students removed from this neighborhood, here they were again more securely than ever before, and with renewed vigor. But it was too late now to have anything done about it. Shortly, the word "Southern" cut into the stone near the roof of the building would be replaced with another cutting and for all passerby to read; this would be "Xavier University." Archbishop Blenk was more than pleased with the whole development. In a letter of June 29, 1915, he wrote to Mother M. Katharine:

> ... There is an immense field for good work to be done in this Diocese. Pray most fervently that God's designs in behalf of these people whom he bought with His Blood, may be realized.
>
> At long last, a burden that was weighing very heavily upon me is beginning to be lifted somewhat, and you have been the providential instrument to remove some of this great burden. I hope that more and more attention and care will be given to our Colored Catholics and that those not belonging to the Fold will be brought into it as a reward for your efforts and that of others in their behalf. God bless you and your Community; may your retreat kindle into renewed ardor and zeal all those who are associated with you in taking care of and providing for God's children and bringing them safely to the feet of our Divine Lord....[8]

The archdiocesan paper — *The Morning Star* — paid a gracious tribute to the purchase:

> This splendid accession to Catholic educational activities in the Archdiocese of New Orleans is but another debt to Mother M. Katharine Drexel, in whom its Archbishops have ever found a ready friend in their great needs in caring for the Colored People....[9]

As the alterations and repairs at the newly acquired property were considerable, and registration had been set for September 21, Mother M. Mercedes and Sister M. Frances were sent to New Orleans August 15 to hurry matters along and have everything in readiness. Sister M. Frances was appointed directress of studies for the new scholastic venture; the arrangements, the planning of the curriculum, the grade placement of students and other details were entrusted to her. It had been decided prudently to start with four grades, seventh, eighth, ninth, and tenth, and to integrate the faculty from the beginning. Mother M. Katharine had learned that a young woman teaching the 8th grade at Lafon Colored School was considered one of the best teachers in the vicinity. After an interview she agreed to leave Lafon and enter the employ of the Sisters. Four other Negro teachers were engaged, one for home economics, Miss Coravigne Wilson; and three for the boys: Mr. Albert Boucree in carpentry, Mr. William Lewis in mechanical drawing, Mr. Ernest Du Conge in masonry.

Less than two weeks before opening, the Lafon teacher, despite her contract, decided not to come, and the Sisters were greatly inconvenienced at that late date to get another teacher. Finally at Mother M. Katharine's urging, Sister M. Frances wrote to her sister, a fully qualified teacher in Nebraska, asking her to come South. Her answer was telegraphed immediately. "Coming." She did more than come. She stayed, and the following year entered the Community. She came back later as Sister M. Juanita to resume teaching on the Xavier faculty.

As applicants poured in on registration day it became evident they would need more classes and that particularly they would have to add an eleventh grade. Thirty-four students who had been unwilling to attend any other local high school when Southern was vacated, pleaded for that grade and their wish was granted. In addition to more than three hundred full time students, there were over a hundred in late afternoon and evening classes in sewing and typewriting. Besides these, Sister M. Frances organized several classes on a normal school level for a small group of high school graduates who had registered. Five Sisters and six lay teachers completed the teaching staff. In their letters to the Motherhouse, the Sisters noted there was no question of discipline with these young students. They were refined, attentive, and courteous. The numbers kept increasing as the sisters were reluctant to turn away any of these so eager for a Catholic education. There was an enthusiasm, a desire to progress that kept the whole educational endeavor moving forward briskly. The twelfth grade was added in 1916, but there could be no stopping there. In 1917 a two year Normal Course was inaugurated. This became a necessity, not only because the students wanted to continue to study, but also because the State that year decreed that Negro teachers must complete a two year Normal Course. Up to that time, this was required of white public school teachers, but all that was required of the Negro was graduation from a high school and the passing of a test.

The Sisters will speak of the joy, the enthusiasm, the gratitude of the Colored Catholics of New Orleans for this opportunity opened up to their children. They gave unstinted support and cooperation to the Sisters in everything. The Sisters, in turn, were on the alert to add and incorporate ever widening opportunities. As many students desired to work for a college degree, Xavier in 1924 began a realignment of its Normal courses into regular College courses. By 1925 Xavier was established as a College of Liberal Arts and Sciences. The conferring of the first degrees took place in 1928. In the meantime an addition to the original main building supplied much-needed space for classrooms, laboratories, and a library. Resolved to give young men and women the best of every opportunity, Xavier added a College of Pharmacy in 1927. The first and only Catholic College for the Negro in this country attracted students from many parts of the United States, from the Caribbean Islands, and from Africa. In the course of time its graduates would find their way to positions of leadership at home and abroad.

Within a few years it was evident that the college would have to separate from the high school building and find a much more extensive foundation. The purchase of suitable property went through the usual blockade experience Mother M. Katharine would know in most of her real estate transactions. Two properties she had desired to buy in different sections of New Orleans were made impossible for her by long lists of signed petitions objecting to having a contiguous Negro institution. She finally had to go into an unzoned area to build the bigger and greater Xavier University. In 1929 she bought an extensive piece of property stretching over five blocks with an open canal in front of it, an open canal and a railroad in back of it. Some of it was entirely undeveloped as it had been occupied by a lumber company. Grading and filling were the first steps and the young men of the college helped out here. Eventually, out of this drab unsightly land, the campus of the new university would rise with its Indiana limestone administration building, well equipped science wing and a convent for the Sisters. Bleachers and a football stadium completed the original layout. A library, men's dormitory, student center, and women's dormitory would follow in the course of the years. Classes and faculty moved across the city to the new unit in September 1932; the dedication ceremonies were held October 12 with Cardinal Dougherty presiding. Archbishop Shaw dedicated the buildings.

For the first time Mother M. Katharine agreed to be interviewed by the Press. The *Times Picayune* in its October 15 issue, under the heading *Little Girl of Long Ago Grows up To Be Foundress of Religious Order,* printed the interview given to Gwen Bristow. The article had a unique opening paragraph:

> While writers of the 1860's were setting down the closing events of the war that nearly ripped America apart, a little girl sat curled up in a red plush chair in one of the great houses of Philadelphia and read, with careful spelling of every word, a primer account of how Columbus discovered America.
>
> ...The primer had a big picture of Columbus and his followers disembarking, with a group of curious Indians staring big-eyed at the pale faced invaders.... Between the picture and the catechism little Kate

> Drexel of Philadelphia settled forever in her own mind, at least, the reason for Columbus' discovery — to bring the gift of Faith to the Indians....

After recalling the other foundations of the Sisters of the Blessed Sacrament in Louisiana; New Iberia, Lake Charles and six parochial schools in New Orleans, she concluded:

> And for all this Louisiana has to thank the little girl who saw the picture of Columbus landing on the shores of the New World, and the Indians peering at him from the woods — the little girl who remembered that America was as rich in undiscovered souls as it was in undiscovered wealth. So it was very fitting, after all, that Xavier University, built by the Reverend Mother, who used to be little Kate Drexel, was dedicated to the service of the Negroes of New Orleans on Columbus Day.

When the university moved across town, the registration was 247. It would mount gradually through the years reaching over a thousand in the war years with the influx of GI's, and leveling off to its present average of over nine hundred. In 1934 in answer to the pleas of the alumni, teachers who wanted the opportunity to study for an M.A. — white local colleges were closed to them — a Graduate School was organized offering M.A.'s in Education, History, and English. Today not only Xavier and other graduates, but many white Sisters, Brothers, and Priests are availing themselves of this opportunity for graduate work at Xavier. Summer sessions and Saturday classes have been especially arranged for their convenience.

After the Supreme Court outlawed the doctrine of separate but equal education in the Brown vs. Board of Education of Topeka case in 1954, Xavier University reorganized its charter to include all students without regard to race, creed or color. Protestant students have always been welcomed at Xavier. As a matter of fact, at least one third of the student body from the beginning has been Protestant. It is the definite policy of the University clearly stated in its catalogue, that all students must take the theology and philosophy courses. This knowledge of God and Christian living, this understanding of the universe and the nature of man, Mother M. Katharine considered the basic foundation of a complete education. Long before the present stress on ecumenism, it was practiced at Xavier. Protestant students were never required to attend a Catholic service, and their right to follow their beliefs has always been respected.

Xavier University would be the crowning point of all the endeavors of the Sisters of the Blessed Sacrament. At a time when Catholic colleges of the South were closed to them by state laws, it would give to young Colored men and women the opportunity of a complete and fully accredited Catholic college education. In the midst of planning for new property and new buildings, Pope Pius XI's encyclical: *Christian Education of Youth* was issued December 31, 1929. It contained a very definite statement against co-education. Sensitive as she was to the least wish and suggestion of the Church, Mother M. Katharine went to see the Apostolic Delegate in Washington about building a co-educational college. He laid her fears to rest by assuring her no other course was open to her under the circumstances. He assured her she would have the full approval of the Church. She had explained to him that if the Sisters of the Blessed Sacrament did not admit Colored young men, their only recourse in the South would be a secular education. But she made sure she was following the mind of the Church before she went on.

The measure of any educational institution's success is ordinarily the success of its graduates. The accomplishments of Xavier Alumni have been distinctive and numerous. In the field of education they have made outstanding contributions. Forty percent of the teachers in the New Orleans Public School System (Negro) are Xavier graduates, as are also four out of six high school principals, seven out of eight junior high school principals, and thirty out of forty-two elementary school principals. There are twenty-five principals in other schools throughout Louisiana and some three hundred teachers. In addition the graduates are teaching in schools all over the United States as well as in Africa, Central and South America, the Bahamas, Panama, the Virgin Islands and the West Indies.

To many other areas besides teaching, Xavier graduates have brought the benefits of their professional and Christian training. In the fields of social work, commerce, business, and industry where Kennedy's promise of equal job opportunity has come to full bloom, in government and international spheres, in the professions of medicine, law, dentistry, they are holding positions of responsibility and leadership. They have been very successful in the pharmaceutical fields. Xavier pharmacists find gainful employment in industries, private drug stores, and hospitals.

The Xavier College of Pharmacy has maintained its accreditation by the American Council on Pharmaceutical Education since 1933. In 1964 the only other college of pharmacy in New Orleans lost its accreditation and decided to expand other areas and drop the college. This left Xavier with the only college of pharmacy in New Orleans. It was ready, well equipped and staffed, and willing to integrate. But the segregationists in New Orleans totally ignored its existence, gave a banquet to members of the State Legislature to induce them to authorize the building of a college of pharmacy under the aegis of Louisiana State U's Medical School so that New Orleans would not be without one! Action on this is still pending as this is being written. Thus in big and little movements, in humble and massive operations, the Sisters of the Blessed Sacrament watch the tides of opposition rise and fall, knowing that some day the ocean of the brotherhood of man will engulf them all.

Exceptional gifts in arts and music abound in Xavier graduates and their contributions to the development of American culture have been marked. For too many years the latent abilities of the Race, the restrained wells of their culture have waited to pour their riches into American life. Now is their day. In music particularly the wealth of their talents and the quality of their

God-given gifts have won recognition. Organized by a Sister who had been trained herself in opera, the music department with high praise from the music critics has annually since 1935 presented a grand opera on the Xavier stage with young voices remarkably rich in tonal qualities. Graduates of the Music Department are professional singers and pianists throughout the country. One is a leading Mezzo-Soprano at Aachen Statsoperhaus, Aachen, Germany; another a leading Soprano-Deutschoperhaus, Berlin, Germany; and another a Tenor with the Denver Symphony. The list is long and impressive.

The well organized Art Department is supplying trained artists for many professional and commercial positions: freelance illustrator with the City Planning Commission, South Bend, Indiana; lamp designer in California; head of a university art department; nationally known sculptor, the recipient of a Fulbright Scholarship for study in Munich, Germany, and later of a Danish Government grant for study at Copenhagen. Three hold advanced degrees in art from Notre Dame University. The Xavier Art Guild executes liturgical art pieces for churches and schools.

In the arts, in the professions, in pure intellectuality, Xavier graduates share honors with the best throughout the country. Fulbright Scholars, graduates of Xavier, have made their mark at University of Copenhagen, Denmark; University of Wurtzburg, Germany; Munich School of Fine Arts, Munich, Germany; In France: University Aix en Provence, University of Bordeaux, University of Dijon, University of Grenoble, and the University of Paris. Their areas of concentration were many. Other graduates have enrolled in institutions abroad: National University of Mexico; Universidad de Santo Domingo; Royal College of Surgeons, Dublin; University of Ottawa, Canada. There has been a long, far-reaching development from the original classes at Xavier. Mother M. Katharine took the bare framework of an abandoned university and breathed into it a life and spirit that continue to glow all over America and countries abroad. Her love and understanding of her fellow man were such that she saw and believed in the potentialities of all men regardless of the color of their skin.

Louisiana has claimed the largest part of the apostolate of the Sisters of the Blessed Sacrament. In 1950 the old Southern building housing Xavier Prep began to show dangerous signs of sagging and was condemned. The pine piles had stiffened and begun to crack when the water was drained from that part of the city. The whole stately building had to be torn down, while in makeshift rooms, classes continued. Finally a new modern and spacious building rose in its place. The average attendance is over seven hundred. In addition to six thriving parochial schools in New Orleans, the Sisters are engaged in New Iberia, Lake Charles, Rayne, Eunice, Carencro, Church Point, and St. Martinville.

Mother M. Katharine's penetration of the educational needs of the Colored in Louisiana would affect them at their highest tide and their lowest ebb. The lowest educational ebb in Louisiana was in the rural areas where there was deep poverty for the whites, and misery for the Negroes. It was a rather unusual missionary who called her attention to the plight of the Colored in the backwoods rural sections of Southern Louisiana. Father Jean Marie Girault de la Corgnais came from a noble French family and dedicated his life and everything he had to the poor trappers and hunters who had settled along the bayous and the banks of the Mississippi. A visit to that area while he was assistant pastor at St. Louis Cathedral had brought him in contact with the material and spiritual needs of a forgotten people. He sought and received the permission to live in their midst and help them in every possible way. Many of these were French speaking people and he met them in their own language. He gave them more than the service of a priest. He became a Father to whom they turned in every need and every problem. He served them as a doctor, an attorney at law, a druggist, a coroner, a probation officer, even mayor. Every need of theirs was his concern.

His headquarters was at St. Thomas Church in Pointe-a-la-Hache. From there he took care of missions at Jesuit Bend, Myrtle Grove, Belle Chasse, West Pointe-a-la-Hache, City Price, Grand Bayou, Happy Jack, Bertrandville, East Pointe-a-la-Hache, and Bohemia. His mode of transportation was a boat, the *St. Thomas*, which made its way up and down the Mississippi, in and out the winding bayous. He carried a bell and a gun and used either to let his parishioners know he had landed. The gun would be fired in the air and before anyone knew it he would be surrounded by his eager flock, both Colored and white. In a letter to Mother M. Katharine, Archbishop Shaw told her he had bought the boat for Father Girault so that "he could cross the River at all times, and be able to respond to every call of his poor flock and especially say Mass for them on Sundays."[10]

When this stalwart missionary appealed to Mother M. Katharine for aid to build a church and school for the neglected Colored of City Price, she decided to see the situation first hand and took a trip with Mother M. Francis Xavier on the famous *St. Thomas*. She enjoyed herself immensely – the firing of Father's gun, the crowds of people who answered it, but what she saw in the interior sickened her. Poor little shabby huts in some places given the names of schools. In many places, not even these for the education of Colored children. In other places opportunities for education were offered only two or three months in the year. She could size up Father Girault. Here was a real apostle, a man who had put aside the wealth and the prestige of his family position, not only to give his life to God, but to give it also to the poorest of the poor in Southern Louisiana. With the big heart of a missionary, he wanted to help the Negroes also. Two apostles were of one mind on the solution.

Mother M. Katharine's approach to the Negro problem in the beginning and at the end was the same. It was an approach through Christian education. She was firmly convinced that the educated man or woman was anyone's equal and if the education was deeply permeated with Christian principles, the individual possessing it had the best possible equipment for life.

She moved into a segregated society which she could not change, but which she knew instinctively some day would have to be changed. She worked within its limitations, as best she could. This need of the poorest Negro children in Louisiana was to her a very vital one and one that would have to be met. It seemed as important to her to start these children on the road to life with a fundamental background as it was to send the finished product out from her university to take a distinctive place in life.

Archbishop Shaw writing to her about City Price, had mentioned he had learned from Father Girault that the Colored children there had had only one month's schooling a year for several years.[11] That was an appeal she could not resist. She sent a check to the Archbishop to enable Father Girault to build a church for the Colored as he desired at City Price. He planned to use the building during the week as a school. Archbishop Shaw's letter showed deep gratitude:

> Archbishop's House, New Orleans
> October 28, 1919
>
> ... I also avail myself of this opportunity to express to you my grateful appreciation of your charity in the generous donation you have given good Father Girault de la Corgnais of Pointe a la Hache for the Colored Church and School at City Price. The good Father was beside himself with joy over the prospect of such a blessing for his poor people. He has already started to get all the material for the building. We are sanguine that he will be able with the help of his people in the way of manual labor to keep within your donation....[12]

This church-school dedicated to St. Paulinus served its purpose well. Religious instruction would be a vital part of its daily life, placed in the first period in the morning. It was this religious atmosphere that would permeate the work of all the rural schools to be erected by Mother M. Katharine — an atmosphere that would be carried from the schoolhouse into the home.[13] St. Paulinus was the first of a chain of rural schools erected by Mother M. Katharine. When she saw the need, she envisioned a line of these schools to help as many Colored children as possible. With this in mind, she wrote for direction to Bishop Jeanmard in whose Diocese of Lafayette most of this neglected area was situated. He was more than interested and offered to arrange a tour and accompany her himself. Then he wrote a letter to all his priests:

> Bishop's House, Lafayette
> March 24, 1923
>
> ... Mother Katharine Drexel, who has done, and is doing so much for our Colored people, will be here during Easter week to look over the field and see what more can be done towards making better provision for them in our churches and in educational lines. After acquainting herself fully with the situation, she hopes to be able to enlist the help of wealthy Catholics in the North and East, toward raising a fund necessary to finance the building or enlarging of churches, the building of

> small schools, the providing of teachers, etc. If she is successful — and she is very sanguine of success — it will mean much for our Diocese. She recognizes that the Diocese of Lafayette on account of its large Catholic population, offers a most promising field for the work she has so much at heart, and she believes that her first duty is to the children of the household, that is, the Catholic Negroes, who must be held at all cost within the pale of the Church....[14]

Mother M. Katharine on her part was delighted with the security and blessing of traveling with the Bishop for a cause in which they were both deeply concerned.

> March 21, 1923
>
> ... Now with regard to our spiritual Excursion in the rural districts, first, let me thank you, Bishop, for Your great kindness in offering to accompany us. I was so delighted and overwhelmed when you offered to come I could not speak. It was just what I wished for, but I had not the temerity to ask. I wish I could tell you the joy it gave me to know that Your Lordship will be with us. God's blessing will surely attend the trip, since we have His representative, the Shepherd of His Flock along.
>
> Years ago when I was a young girl, the Bishop of Omaha, then Dr. O'Connor, pastor of the church I attended, was my spiritual director. He accompanied me on a tour through the Indian Reservations of the Northwest. When you suggested coming with us, it made me think of that other excursion, and what came of it for the salvation of souls.
>
> I am praying God to bless this visit to the rural districts, that such good may come from it for His glory, and the Salvation of souls. Again I thank Your Lordship for your great kindness....[15]

It was not long before her new apostolate was under way and twenty-four new simple rural schools were erected throughout Louisiana, at costs ranging from $2,000 to $4,000 each: City Price, Point-a-la-Hache, Broussard, Glencoe, Rayne, Julien Hill, Abbeville, Bertrandville, Thibodeaux, Coulee Crouche, Prairie Basse, Church Point, Leonville, Mallet, Duson, Reserve, Mamou, St. Martinville, West Point-a-la-Hache, Tyrone, Edgard, and Eunice.[16] She arranged to have two graduate students of Xavier in charge of each school, and made careful provision for their board and also for the supervision of the schools. She paid the salaries of teachers in these schools and also arranged to pay additional four or five months salaries for teachers in schools where the state provided education for the Negro only for a few months. Thus she tried to overcome what had been the chief obstacles to educational progress for the Colored in those areas: economic deprivation, lack of qualified personnel, insufficient and ineffective administration and supervision, racial discrimination.[17] The fourth obstacle, racial discrimination, she could at least work against.

Today there are thriving and complete parish units at some of these locations with church, school, rectory, and convent. Thousands of children have come out of these areas to continue their higher education and assume responsible positions. But most important of all was the Faith that was saved. Mother M. Katharine did not plant the Faith there; other zealous missionaries had done that before, but these Catholic schools were instrumental in strengthening the Faith, rebuilding hope and reenkindling charity in the poverty-stricken areas where the fires were burning low.

# Chapter 21
# The Willing Spirit

The fruitful and apostolic years of Mother M. Katharine's life flowed on without any lessening of her labors or diminution of her zeal. There were always new fields to be cultivated, or old ones to be reorganized and refurnished. By the time she reached her seventy-seventh year, the Sisters of the Blessed Sacrament were engaged in thirty-four missions and the Foundress was as busy as ever visiting them all each year. She maintained a personal intimate contact with her own missions and also with those she was helping to support. The drive in her was phenomenal. Where many a younger person would tire out, she kept on with no thought at all of herself or her need of rest and refreshment. On top of everything else, the correspondence in which she engaged was voluminous. The Archive files at the Motherhouse from 1885 to the years of her retirement, include some seventeen thousand incoming letters from bishops, from priests, from those who were organizing or were engaged in apostolates and missions among the Indian and Colored. They give us an authentic, inner view of the extent of her operations and the achievements of her zeal. The last person she ever thought of was Katharine Drexel. Toward others, she would be considerate, she would make exceptions, she would be tenderly solicitous. For herself, she sought nothing but God's grace and love.

In addition to the demands of her intense apostolate, it must also be borne in mind that she lived a very penitential life which she concealed from others. No one could be so consumed with the love of God, so deeply concerned with the spread of the fruits of Redemption to all souls for which He died naked on the Cross, without attempting in some way to resemble Him in physical suffering and to offer to Him the reparation of physical pain. The Memoirs of Mother M. Mercedes, her intimate companion through the years, her Vicar, and the second Superior General of the Congregation give a very definite account of the penances the Foundress imposed on herself, unknown to others.[1] Among other items, she recorded that frequently when all the Sisters had left the chapel, Mother M. Katharine would kneel in a space behind the altar with her arms extended in the form of a cross and her eyes riveted on a fourteen foot crucifix above the altar. She would remain thus in prayer for long periods of time. There were times when a Sister sacristan would return later to take care of some item she had forgotten and be amazed to find the Foundress still on her knees, her eyes fixed on the crucifix, and tears streaming down her face.[2] She had a deep devotion to the Passion. At times like this when she would give full vent to the ardor of her love, her realization of the suffering of the Crucified and her deep love overcame her. The amazing fact was that she never noticed the presence of the Sister, but seemed caught up in another world.[3]

As the number of the missions of the Sisters of the Blessed Sacrament increased and the financial burdens grew heavy, she tried to devise ways and means of making them self supporting. She endeavored too, to direct missions she was helping, to self sufficiency, or to other sources of income. In 1935 she decided after her visitation of her southern missions, to visit St. Mary's Indian Mission at Omak in the state of Washington. Mother M. Agatha, President of Xavier University, was her companion. She had already written Father Caldi, the Jesuit missionary in charge of St. Mary's, that they were coming out to see if the eighty boys and girls boarding there could not be placed in day schools so that the Sisters of the Blessed Sacrament could be relieved of the expense of lodging, feeding, and clothing them.[4]

The ground they covered in this travel, the schedule they followed would have been hard on young women; it must have been particularly fatiguing for both the Mothers. The southern visitation had terminated at Port Arthur, Texas. Their next stop after a day and night of travel, was Gallup, New Mexico at 1:45 A.M. There was an auto waiting for them as the plans were to meet Mother M. Pauline and Father Arnold, O.F.M., later in the day about the possibility of the Sisters going out by car from St. Michael's and Tekakwitha Mission in Houck to visit the Indians.

Late that afternoon they were on a train riding West. The following night at 10:30 they transferred from the train to a boat to San Francisco where they stayed with the Sisters of Charity. Early the next morning after a six o'clock Mass they were on their way to Portland, another twenty-four hour travel which terminated at 6:30 A.M. Here they changed cars, headed for Seattle, and reached there at 2:30 P.M. Father Caldi was at the station to meet them and drove them to the convent of the Sisters of St. Joseph opposite the Cathedral. Here they had some hours of respite before they boarded a 9:50 train for Wenatchee, the nearest station to St. Mary's. They arrived there at 1:25 A.M. One of the Sisters from the mission accompanied by a little Indian girl met them with a car. They drove four hours first in the dark of night, then in the earliest glimmers of dawn, and eventually through a glorious sunrise which colored all the surrounding mountains. The steady grind of travel must have been exhausting. They reached the mission just before six, in time for Mass. Nothing could have prepared them for the method of assisting at the Mass. The Indian children gave the responses in Latin. As the Mass proceeded to the Gospel, the children began to recite the Ten Commandments and followed them with the six Precepts of the Church. Near the Consecration, one of the Sisters recited the Memorare to the Blessed Virgin.

At the Consecration she began: "I promise that...." and the children recited the twelve promises of the Sacred Heart to St. Margaret Mary!

After Mass and a refreshing breakfast, the Sisters wanted them to rest for the remaining part of the day but Mother M. Katharine and her companion were up again at 2:30 to investigate the mission and its surroundings. With her keen vision she took in everything: the Sisters' refectory, the meals, the children, the sleeping quarters. The following day was Sunday and they were told Mass would be at nine o'clock; but it did not begin till around eleven. The priest had a long line of confessions to hear as it was the closing day and the children wanted to receive the Sacrament of Penance before they went home for the summer. At the Mass there was a long sermon. Mother M. Katharine had moved up to the front of the Church to make sure she would hear it. She was always avid for the Word of God, eager to hear explanations of Divine Truths. As the sermon proceeded, she heard every word of it but understood not one, as it was delivered in an Indian language. Shortly after noon, the missionary began it all over again in English! She was deeply impressed with his fervor as she knew the long years he had spent on the Indian missions. Before she had become a religious, a Father Cataldo, S.J., who had come from Italy with this Father Caldi to work for the Indians, had called at the Drexel summer home. He was seeking help. The Drexel sisters invited him to dinner and listened eagerly to his plans. They had just returned from visiting Italy and knew the beauty of Italy near Sorrento from whence he had come. Mother M. Katharine recalled that she had said to herself at the time, "My God, he left that beautiful Italy to come here among savage Indians to live in a desert."

Very soon Mother M. Katharine got down to the business of her coming and asked about the possibility of having these children attend a day school. Father answered that the nearest day school was six miles away, over a mountain and that in winter it would take the Sisters at least a day to get there. He offered to take them over the mountain to the school, and over the mountain to the school they went, through a forest of huge pine trees. The road they followed was a very tortuous one and the Mothers found the frequent turns bringing on a slight nausea. They came down the other side of the mountain and moved along the Columbia River where they met a missionary who spoke sixteen different languages. The day school was located at his mission. She remarked to her Sisters later, "He was an old priest, but think of it, knowing sixteen languages. There he was, just administering to these Indians."[5] They visited the little day school in which they found a combination of Indian and white children. There were other rides and other small missions visited and then she went to see the Bishop. Father Caldi drove them through the mountains as fast as he could, to Spokane. Her effort to have the Bishop take over the support of this and other missions was unsuccessful, as he said the best he could do would be to raise $2,000 which would not go very far.

In her chatty account of this visit to the Sisters at the Motherhouse later, she made an interesting comment: "If the people in the United States only knew of the possibilities of these missions! The Indians as such will pass away,--less red, less red, less red, white; the same of the Colored, — black, less black, less black, white! In myself there is some Anglo-Saxon, and some Roman. There are not many pure blooded people of any one race."[6] Was the Foundress looking down a long line of the future to a disappearance of racial colors in America? When this northwest trip was over, the Mothers were glad to take a homeward bound train after what had proven to be a very exhausting trip. It had been rough riding most of the way.

That year of 1935 was a particularly full and busy one. Mother M. Katharine began to look worn out and the Sisters were concerned. In August while praying at the bedside of Sister M. Bernadette who was dying in a hospital in Philadelphia, she had a slight heart attack but passed it off as nothing. However in the Fall, she was off again for the visitation of the Indian missions in the West. She was particularly concerned about a Sister who for many years had served as superior in both Navajo and Pueblo missions. Different reports had reached her that this sister was showing signs of mental breakdown. Somehow or other she was disinclined to believe the reports. She knew the individual well, had a high esteem of her virtue and a sympathy for her sufferings from an arthritic condition. The whole thing posed a difficult situation for the Sisters.

In an attempt to find a solution, the Foundress changed the Sisters to Tekakwitha Mission in Houck, Arizona to teach a small first grade there and to get as much rest as possible. But when she visited her at Houck, she knew something was the matter and she brought her to a hospital in Gallup for check-up and rest. She herself, went on to St. Michael's to continue her visitation. She made this trip by auto and although she was going through scenery that had always been a cause of delight to her, she was listless and found the drive fatiguing. Shortly after arriving at St. Michael's, while dictating a letter to her secretary, Mother Mary of the Visitation, she had a dizzy spell and dropped to the floor. A young government doctor treating some children at the school was hurriedly called. He hesitated to give a diagnosis and said one of the older doctors from Fort Defiance should be sent for. He did make it forcibly clear, however, that it would be extremely dangerous for her to resume her traveling the next day as she planned, and that a rest was imperative. But this woman whose spirit was too willing, would brook no delay and she prepared to leave for St. Catharine's the following day. It may well have been she had an intuition this would be her last trip West and she wanted to finish it.

In the midst of her visitation of St. Catharine's, word reached her that her sick Sister had not been helped by a stay in the hospital in Gallup and that her condition had grown much worse. Immediately two Sisters were sent to bring the sick Sister by train to Lamy. Mother M. Katharine decided to take the train there and bring her to Chicago where she thought she could get the best medical help. There was something pathetic about her drive from Santa Fe to Lamy, New Mexico. The Indian who drove her told a Sister later that he sensed something was amiss and he kept watching the Foundress from his mirror. When they reached the open road, he reported, she turned around as if to take in the whole sweep of the scenery and then sat up straight, threw her head back and closed her eyes as if giving it all up.

Once in Chicago, she entrusted the patient to the superior at St. Elizabeth's and instructed her to get the best specialists available. Then she and Mother Mary of the Visitation went on to St. Paul's Mission in Marty, South Dakota. She was interested in a very special project at Marty. For over a year, Father Sylvester had been in correspondence with her about the formation of a religious community for Indian girls. The Sisters of the Blessed Sacrament had staffed the mission from its foundation and were engaged in both the grammar and high school there. There were many Indian settlements in the region accessible to St. Paul's Mission which this intrepid missionary of the Sioux Indians wanted to contact. Since the operation of the boarding school consumed all the energy of the Sisters of the Blessed Sacrament there, Father Sylvester had dreamed of a community of Indian girls with their headquarters at Marty and their fields of operation in the surrounding country. He had been encouraged in this desire by statements of pupils at St. Paul's who wished to belong to an Indian Community. Mother M. Katharine and her council were very much interested in the project.

It was Father's wish that the new community should be formed and directed by the Sisters of the Blessed Sacrament until such a time as they were prepared to guide and direct themselves. Accordingly, Mother Mary of Lourdes was appointed the Mistress of Novices. She had been superior at Marty and knew the Indians well. On reaching Marty, Mother M. Katharine was concerned that only two Indian girls had made application, and her first impulse was to withdraw Mother Mary of Lourdes. Before she left, however, five more were accepted and with this nucleus of seven, the Oblate Sisters of the Blessed Sacrament were organized. The original intention was that only Indian girls would be admitted, but the ruling has been changed to admit any qualified young women desirous of dedicating their lives to Indian missions.

In the midst of all this planning and discussion, Mother M. Katharine had another weak spell. She continued to be worried about the Sister she had left in Chicago, especially when she was informed the case was mental and could not be kept at the hospital. Next in her plans had been the St. Louis Mission. Now she decided to take the sick Sister with her and place her at St. Vincent's Sanatorium in that city, which she did. She visited her there several times and before leaving to return to Chicago and complete her visitation, she gave herself an extra hour before train time to pay her a last visit. Then it happened. She had a very serious heart attack and was put to bed there immediately. The Motherhouse was notified and plans were made to bring her home. The doctors there permitted her to travel two days later. The superior of the hospital, Sister Ann, one of their most efficient nurses accompanied Mother and her secretary home. Her devoted Jewish doctor, Dr. Max Herrman, who had been expecting something like this to happen was on hand and arranged for her to go to St. Joseph's Hospital. Before she left to return to St. Louis, Sister Ann spoke very candidly to Mother M. Mercedes and told her the Foundress was in a most serious condition and if anything had to be attended to, it should be done very promptly. Her heart, she said, had marked dilatation and serious artery trouble; she could succumb at any time and the Community had better be prepared.[7] Their only reliance, their only surety was prayer.

The tired heart had almost given out at last. The long wearisome journey to Omak earlier in the year had made great inroads on her strength, but this situation of one of her cherished superiors had probably eaten deep into her sensitive soul. She had not believed the reports that were sent to her, not that she thought the Sisters were misrepresenting them but because it seemed to her that it was something that could not happen. The realization of all this when she finally saw the condition of the Sister had evidently swept her past the breaking point. She was concerned too, about the case and remarked to one of the Sisters how deeply she regretted that she had brought this Sister East a few years before to receive special injections for her very painful arthritis. She had come to the conclusion that the injections had caused mental damage.

This was the end of apostolic wanderings and apostolic plannings. Her doctor and a heart specialist, Dr. Stephens, corroborated the decisions of the doctors in St. Louis. They said everything was in Mother M. Katharine's own hands. If she would cut down on her work, if she let other people look after the details, she might live for many years. But if she did not, there was no hope. Dr. Stephens gave this verdict very plainly to the patient and told her she owed it to her Community and to the community at large to take the steps to prolong her life for the sake of her work. Undaunted and unafraid of the situation, she replied simply, "Nobody is necessary for God's work. God can do the work without any of His creatures." Dr. Stephens, a Unitarian, replied dryly, "Certainly, Mother, I agree with you, but ordinarily He does not."[8]

She was kept at the hospital till December 7 and was then permitted to return to the Motherhouse under the strictest regulations of diet, absolute rest, etc. To prevent any legal difficulties later, she made another will with the help of Honorable John Sullivan, the legal advisor of the Congregation. She had made one many years before, but all her witnesses were dead as well as those by whom it had been drawn up. Letters were sent to all the houses explaining her condition and asking the help of prayers. No one could know then that this almost consumed missionary with the weakened heart and strained arteries would continue to live for twenty years with the help of God, the loving care of her Sisters and the unfailing ministrations of Dr. Herrman. Mother M. Mercedes wrote encouragingly to the Sisters throughout the country, "The doctors will not be able to give her a new arterial system, but they say that with care and dispensing with all this running around, and heavy mental pressure that we all know is superhuman in her case, Reverend Mother may live for some years...."[9]

Her cherished sister, Mrs. Louise Morrell, was deeply concerned. In a letter to Mother M. Mercedes, she wrote: "Truly the zeal of God's house has consumed Mother. It is well nigh impossible in the span of our life to cover such a vast extent of ground and influence so many lives. Of course the ardent cooperation of her dear daughters has been an incalculable assistance in bringing about these results."[10]

Mother M. Katharine always had the facility to fit into any situation and to accommodate herself to any circumstance. She realized the full gravity of her condition and she was content to permit Mother M. Mercedes to take over the general planning and the details. It was a terrific change for a person of the Foundress' capacities and experience. She made the transition without a tremor, without the least show of disappointment or concern. She loved the travel to the missions; she loved the visitations of her convents. She would never do either again. Naturally her advice and direction were sought, but the handling of details was taken care of lovingly by Mother M. Mercedes and the Council General. It was amazing to witness the calm, the peace, the serenity with which she changed from a spiritual executive who traveled and directed constantly, to a lone, aging woman whose territory would be confined to several rooms of the infirmary on the second floor of the Motherhouse. Occasionally in a wheelchair, she would be brought downstairs for a community gathering. This Foundress of flaming activity and arduous supervision relinquished it all with the quiet and calm of an unruffled sea. Early in 1936 she had another attack after walking down the hall to dictate a letter to a Sister. At this point Mrs. Morrell engaged a very efficient trained nurse, Miss Super, to be with her constantly during the day. It was arranged that a Sister would be with her during the night.

She was well enough Foundation Day, February 12, 1936, to be wheeled down to the Community Room for a program arranged by the novices and postulants. She was delighted with everything and spoke affectionately after it to the Sisters: "It just thrills me to see you. How can we ever thank God for our religious vocation! People out in the world think we are doing something great in giving ourselves to God. That is not the case at all. It is God who is great in giving us the chance to be His spouses. It all seems too good to be true.... We have enough graces to make us saints because we have Mass every single day. We are the privileged ones of our Lord. He has chosen us, as Archbishop Ryan so often said when he came here. Often in his sermons he repeated, 'You have not chosen Me, but I have chosen you.' He reminded us often that God had chosen us. Why? We have often met people out in the world who have done more heroic things than we have ever done. We have done nothing heroic. Yet He chose us; He picked us out to be His spouses.

"I have enjoyed this entertainment. I thank everyone of you for giving it to me. I am grateful to the Mothers for letting me come down. I have enjoyed every part of it."[11]

Mother M. Katharine was Superior General of the Congregation until a Chapter met in 1937. She dictated the letter sent to all the houses August 14, 1937, announcing the calling together of the Chapter and the election of delegates. In it, she reminded them she would soon be seventy-nine years of age and at that age it would be impossible to have the health demanded by the fatigue of that position. She included the details of her condition: "My heart action both regards disturbances in rhythm and inefficiency of the myocardiac muscle, renders me subject to a condition either of a stroke of paralysis which would incapacitate me, or of instant death. This is the answer the doctor gave me when I asked for the absolute truth about my condition." She ended the letter by begging their prayers that she would remain "Ever a true Sister of the Blessed Sacrament, and live and die a faithful child of Our Holy Mother, the Church, for both of which graces I rely on the Mercy of God and the prayers of the Sisters."[12]

It was no surprise to anyone that Mother M. Mercedes was elected the second Superior General of the Congregation. In the very first days she had, as a postulant, accompanied Mother M. Katharine to the temporary novitiate in Torresdale. In later years, she had served as her vicar. Now the titles were changed and Mother M. Katharine was elected her vicar. The Chapter General, however, passed a special mandate creating the Foundress the First Sister of the Blessed Sacrament who was to take the first place everywhere as long as she lived. In a simple child-like way she addressed the assembled delegates and told them she would do all she could to help Mother M. Mercedes and serve her as vicar. Her only regret, she said, was that she did not have more physical strength to give to her new task.[13] This Banker's Daughter so rich in grace, so full of missionary experience, so completely dedicated to the service of the Blessed Sacrament and the service of the Indian and Colored races, stepped from the first to the second place in the Congregation she had founded with graceful ease. She would easily have stepped down to the last.

Mother M. Mercedes, assisted by the advice and approval of her vicar, gave firm guidance and sure direction to the Community. She had been part of the growth of the Sisterhood from its infancy; all through the years, she had been closely associated with the Foundress. Now as Superior General, she discussed all her plans with her. She decided to establish a publicity department and to resume publication of the community magazine, *Mission Fields at Home,* and she told the Sister appointed to the task, to discuss every detail with Mother M. Katharine who was so vitally interested and concerned, and to see that accounts of projects and plans reached her. She made sure that Mother M. Katharine would be kept in touch with details and share the joy of each new development. Though her steps were slowed down and her activity curtailed, her keen mind was wide awake for all developments affecting the Church. With the rest of the world she tuned in a radio for the election of a new Pope in 1939 and she listened while Romans waited for white smoke to emerge from the Vatican. Her nurse went in to find her praying with hands clasped, "Oh may it be Cardinal Pacelli, Oh may it be Cardinal Pacelli." When the word "Eugenio" came over the air she added very fervently and with evident joy, "Pacelli." She brought her hands together in thanksgiving and said not another word though joy was written all over her countenance.[14]

Another incident that may serve to demonstrate her general interest in things ecclesial and salvific came out of a clear blue sky. A novice was dusting around her room one day and was suddenly stopped in the midst of her operation. Mother M. Katharine handed her a clipping which she herself had cut out of a newspaper. "Sister," she said, "go down to the Tribune and with your arms outstretched, pray for the conversion of this man. He should be one of us." The picture and the article was about Louis Budenz.[15] Her vision was a wide one. She took in the whole horizon of souls in the United States, and in the world while she was at it.

It became evident in a short period of time that Mother M. Mercedes' health was failing, and her illness was diagnosed as cancer. If the Foundress of the Community had given an example of perfect forgetfulness of self and lifelong consideration of others, her example would be followed and given by her successor. Mother M. Mercedes' last official act of business was on March 2, 1940, when she went to her office to interview Mr. Emile Perrot, the architect for the new building for Holy Providence School she had planned. She visited the Blessed Sacrament after that and spent a few quiet moments in her chapel stall. Then she walked slowly and painfully to the chapel exit and took the elevator to the second floor. She was utterly exhausted and would never come down again. There was a month of intense suffering ahead of her.

No one ever heard a word of complaint from her. Only the look of pain in her eyes indicated the agony through which she was passing. When Sisters came in to stay with her or relieve her nurse, she would ask them questions about the children and the Sisters. She wanted to know if everything was all right, if the children had all the food they needed, if Mr. Lawler (a very fine Christian gentleman who had contributed his services as a general handyman to the community) needed anything. Was his clothing warm enough? When one of the Sisters after answering her question, remarked to her, "Mother, you are always asking about others, never a word about yourself," she simply sighed and said, "well what good would that do?"

Mother M. Katharine tried to do what little things she could for her. She made sure everything she could use was near her. She checked and rechecked and visited her frequently. She prayed with her and read to her from books she herself had found helpful. It was a study to watch them both, to see the quiet, calm resignation of this tried missionary, and the loving concern and silent grief of the Foundress. There were many little incidents that could be recorded. One day, Mother M. Katharine was wheeled down to Mother M. Mercedes' room. At the door she stepped lightly out of the chair and made her way to the corner of the room while the patient slept. She had a little white shawl wrapped around her and sat as if trying to withdraw into space while she prayed fervently. It was not long before Mother M. Mercedes opened her eyes and saw the Foundress in the corner. Very softly she said, "Mother, please go back to your room." Mother M. Katharine moved to the foot of the bed and answered pleadingly, "Please let me stay, I want to pray for you, I want to help you." Quietly but decisively, the patient answered, "Mother, the Community does not need me, but it needs you. Please go back to your room." Without another word, Mother went out quietly, got into her wheel chair, and was moved back to her room.[16]

The agony of pain beyond the power of sedatives, the deep share in the redemptive suffering of the Crucified went on till April 9, 1940. That morning as the rising bell called the Sisters to another day in the divine service, all the days of earthly service ended for the valiant soul of Mother M. Mercedes. There was general grief in the Congregation particularly in the heart of Mother M. Katharine. This was one of the last links with the foundation days and she had leaned heavily on this support. This was another encounter with death, with the death of one intimately part of her life. A long letter giving all the details of her illness and her last days on earth was sent to all the houses of the Congregation. Mother M. Katharine included ever item in it with a message that meant most to the Sisters:

> Before closing, I must tell you this one beautiful thing. One day when I went to visit Mother just a few days before she died and when she was perfectly conscious, I told her of an incident that was attendant on the death of my own dear Mother, and of a request I had made of her at that time. When she was dying I asked her if she would pray for me when she went to Heaven. She looked at me with such tender affection and said in tones of tenderest love: "I will pray for you, and pray for you, and never cease praying for you till you come there too."
>
> Then I said to Mother Mercedes: "You are not like my Mother who had only three children to think of, but you have so many, four hundred or more. Will you promise to pray for each one of them as my dear Mother promised to pray for me? For just a second Mother seemed to ponder over the thought. Then with her hands clasped and her eyes raised toward Heaven in very strong and distinct tones she said: "Yes, I will; I will promise to do this." So be assured that Mother will be praying for you and will never cease praying till you come. Isn't that a beautiful consolation?[17]

The death of the second Superior General required a Chapter General for another election. This Chapter was called for the twenty-sixth of June, and presided over by Cardinal Dougherty. Mother Mary of the Visitation, who had previously served as Mother M. Katharine's secretary, was elected the third Superior General. Mother M. Philip Neri was elected her vicar. It was deemed best for Mother M. Katharine's health to relieve her of all administrative responsibilities. The bond between the new Superior General and the first one would always be very close. Mother M. Katharine would be a source of help and inspiration to her as she had been to Mother M. Mercedes. God saw fit to take both of these superior generals to Himself before Mother M. Katharine's death. In the loving Providence of God she would live to her ninety-seventh year. Mother Mary of the Visitation died in 1952 and was succeeded by Mother M. Anselm who was Superior General when God took Mother M. Katharine home.

# Chapter 22
# Jubilee Interlude

There was a very pleasant and a very colorful interlude in Mother M. Katharine's long period of retirement, an interlude of particular joy and delight to her. As the Community neared the opening of the year 1941, there were suggestions and discussions of a jubilee celebration, since February 12, 1941, would mark the fiftieth anniversary of the foundation of the Congregation. On that day, fifty years before, in the chapel of the Sisters of Mercy in Pittsburgh, Katharine Drexel had made her vows as a Sister of the Blessed Sacrament. Immediately after, Archbishop Ryan had appointed her the first superior of a new Congregation in the Church. It seemed fitting the day should be commemorated and Almighty God thanked for the rivers of grace that had flowed over all the activities of the sisterhood in the eventful passage of fifty fruitful years. The first reaction of the Foundress was one of opposition to any plan for a public celebration. She who always wanted to be in the background, who fled any public recognition and disdained any public renown, saw no reason at all for celebrating a fiftieth anniversary. But Cardinal Dougherty changed her mind and her attitude on the question when he let it be known that public thanksgiving to God for all the graces of those years was perfectly in order and something to be desired. She laid aside her objections and entered wholeheartedly and enthusiastically into the plans for the celebration.

Since the Cardinal would be out of town in February, the dates were set for April 18, 19, 20, with a day for Priests, another for Sisters, and a third for the laity. The Community had its own private celebration on the actual day itself, February 12, and a special program by the Sisters was prepared. Father Nugent, the chaplain, Father Garrity, his assistant, and Father Stanton, C.S.Sp. were three priest guests on the occasion. No one else was included but the Sisters. It was a great joy to all that Mother M. Katharine attended by her faithful nurse, Miss Super, came down to the large parlor where the community had assembled. An address, recitations, and musical numbers comprised the program. Mother M. Francis Xavier who as a postulant had been the cross bearer at Mother M. Katharine's profession in Pittsburgh, gave an inspiring account of that blessed occasion. The choicest item on the whole program was the talk by the Foundress herself to the assembled professed Sisters, novices and postulants:

> I just want to say a word to the Sisters. I want to say that I thank God I am a child of the Church. I thank God it was my privilege to meet many of the great missionaries of the Church and to have

had the prayers of those great missionaries like Monsignor Stephan and Bishop Marty. We have been reading about them in the refectory.... I saw them in their agony. I saw them in their agony, those great souls! I thank God He gave me the grace to see their lives. They are a part of the Church of God, and I thank God like the great St. Theresa that I, too, am a child of the Church.[1]

No one was happier or more jubilant than Mother M. Katharine when the three days of the actual celebration arrived. Bishops, Priests, Brothers, Sisters, friends from far and near gathered for the occasion. The program each day began with a solemn pontifical Mass, Bishop Lamb celebrating the first day, Bishop O'Hara, the second, and Cardinal Dougherty, the third. The sermons at these Masses were given respectively by Father La Farge, S. J., Father Murphy, S.S.J., and Bishop Corrigan, Rector of the Catholic University of America. Bishops from all parts of the country and priests who were not able to attend, sent in their salutations and their greetings. They fill an entire volume in the Motherhouse Archives. Groups of students, too, came from different parts of the United States: Pueblo and Navajo Indians in their colorful costumes; the whole Torreador scene of the opera, *Carmen*, from the Xavier University Music Department; the glee clubs from St. Francis de Sales, Rock Castle, Virginia; St. Elizabeth High School, Chicago, and St. Emma Institute, Rock Castle. If ever one wanted to see a cross section of the American Missions, that cross section was visible at this celebration. It was particularly visible at the community Mass in the early morning before the festivities of the different days began. Following the long line of Sisters to the Communion rail were groups of these students, young Indian children and older ones, young Colored students of Holy Providence and mature students of Xavier University.

In the midst of this jubilation the mind of the Foundress must have gone back over the fifty years of her Congregation's existence; she must have seen again the enthusiasm, the eagerness, the burning zeal with which her first Sisters traveled the difficult way to Santa Fe. She must have lingered again on the beautiful hill top facing the James River where she had stood and planned a boarding high school for girls at Rock Castle, Virginia. She must have known again the longing of her soul to do something to bring the Faith to the roaming Navajo in the deserts and byways of Arizona. She may have recalled the difficulties, the opposition, the race prejudice she had met head on, in establishing so many of her missions. But all these were memories, milestones now passed. Her Congregation was well established, her Sisters were carrying on their Eucharistic apostolate in the North, South, East, and West. It would seem God had especially arranged this interlude, this jubilee celebration to give her a taste of the hundredfold promised in this life to those who leave all to follow Him.

This was the one time she had to listen to tributes paid to her, but she did not regard them as meant for herself. She accepted them simply as tributes to the Community. There was a striking similarity in the various encomiums. They stressed not that she gave her wealth, but that she gave herself to the work of the Church. Preaching at the Pontifical Mass celebrated by Cardinal Dougherty, Bishop Corrigan, Rector of the Catholic University of America, laid emphasis on the fact that her gift of herself had inspired hundreds of other women to enrich the Church with their service, and that her sacrifice for others had lessened the national shame at the white man's treatment of the Indian and Negro. He noted that a distinguished representation of the Church of America were gathered there "To make nobly splendid the glory of the Church of Philadelphia whose high priest offers here today the living sacrifice of the Victim of Calvary, of the Body once spent on the Cross for all men, in thanksgiving for her who in fifty years of loving labor, finds her own frail body spent but her soul gloriously young with the youth of eternal life."[2]

Cardinal Dougherty wrote the Foreword for the Jubilee Book which the Sisters published in connection with the celebration. In it he reviewed the events of her life and the fullness of her service. "If she had never done anything else," he wrote, "than set such an example to a frivolous, self-seeking world, she should be regarded as a benefactress of the human race. She gave her immense fortune to her work. She did still more by giving herself to it; and she has done this for fifty years. She has done it without the blare of trumpets; her picture never appears on the front page of our papers; her name is not found in the lists of great women ... for the world knows only its own. Yet she is a shining glory, not only of Philadelphia, but also of our whole nation. Whilst others persecute and revile Indians and Negroes as if they are mere hewers of wood and drawers of water, rather than God's children for whom our Savior's Blood was shed, she, a refined lady of culture, takes them to her heart and makes their cause her own."[3]

Cardinal Cushing, then Bishop and Director of the Society for the Propagation of the Faith in Boston, wrote a special booklet for the occasion.[4] In it he recorded: "What after all is the greatest contribution that Mother Katharine Drexel has made to the Church of God and neglected souls? Is it the money she gave from the family treasury, the buildings she erected, the misery she was instrumental in relieving? Not at all. Her greatest contribution was the sacrifice of herself, stripped of self, to become part and parcel of God's plan to redeem the Negro and Indian of the United States. Greater love than this no one hath. And her personal example of childlike simplicity, of diffusive sanctity, and Christlike devotion to the Cause of the Negroes and Indians, when their friends were comparatively few, were the fruits of that sacrifice that have immortalized her in my memory and that of many others as the foremost individual benefactress of missionary work of the Catholic Church in North America."[5]

There were many laudatory greetings from lay people, from alumni and students of the Sisters of the Blessed Sacrament. A typical expression of Indian appreciation was made by Mr. Joseph Padilla, a former student of St.

Catherine's Indian School and at the time of the Jubilee, a graduate of St. Louis University. He wrote after the ceremonies:

> Everything that was beautiful was in the life of Reverend Mother M. Katharine. Hers was a flaming desire to dream lofty dreams, an ideal of what you and I could be, a vision that promised what you and I should be. After fifty years of lofty dreaming, dazzling realities were unveiled at the Motherhouse of the Sisters of the Blessed Sacrament, so dazzling that neither poet nor painter, sculptor nor scientist could sound them all, nor fittingly record their complete inspiration. The classic opera of the Xavier students, the play of the little children of Holy Providence, the Navajo with his Yei-Be-Chain dance, the Pueblo imitating the noble eagle, all together formed a harmonious patter never produced by painter, never described by poet, never sung by musicians. The added allurement of the Navajo sand painting, the hand craft of the Indian youth, the ingenious artistry of the Colored youth completed a perfect mosaic of mission accomplishment. We are glad we came from the far West to see this realization of Reverend Mother Katharine's dream. God-like Charity, God-inspired Faith, God-sustained Hope inspired her dream and brought it to this never to be forgotten fulfillment.[6]

A senior at St. Francis de Sales High School, Rock Castle, Virginia, expressed her appreciation in a poem she entitled, Jubilate.

DARKNESS lay on the bayou—
DARKNESS lay on the fields—
DARKNESS lay in the souls of black folk
DARKNESS lay in the minds of black folk
DARKNESS in cotton fields.
"NO HOPE" moaned the wind o'er the meadow
"NO HOPE" sobbed the winds round the lea
"NO HOPE" wept the trees in the forest
"NO HOPE" said the Christ, "Save in Me!"
A woman walked on the bayou
A woman walked in the fields
A woman prayed for the souls of black folk
A woman wept for the minds of black folk
A woman—in cotton fields.
"Sweet Lord, here is land for a harvest,
Dear God, here are souls for Thee.
Sweet Saviour," she whispered, "please answer
If the work of these fields be for me."
The answer was given, "Go child."
She went—through cloistered portals

She went—as a nun—for the souls of black folk
She went—as a nun—for the minds of black folk
She went to bring God to mortals.
"Here's hope" sang the wind o'er the meadow
"Here's hope" hummed the wind round the lea
"Here's hope" laughed the trees in the forest
"Here's hope" said Christ, "Come to Me."
FIFTY YEARS worked the nuns on the bayou
FIFTY YEARS worked the nuns in the fields
FIFTY YEARS they prayed for the souls of black folk
FIFTY YEARS—in mission fields.
"LIGHT" cried the wind o'er the meadow
"LIGHT" laughed the wind round the lea
"LIGHT" sang the trees in the forest
"LIGHT" said Christ, "leads to Me."
SUNSHINE lay on the bayou
SUNSHINE lay on the fields,
SUNSHINE lay in the souls of black folk
SUNSHINE lay in the minds of black folk
SUNSHINE lay on mission fields.
"JUBILATE" cried the wind o'er the meadow
"JUBILATE" laughed the wind round the lea
"JUBILATE" sang the trees in the forest—
"JUBILATE" 'Tis God's work, JUBILEE!"
Hazel Thomas.

A lengthy letter of congratulation and commendation came to her from Pope Pius XII, a copy of which will be found in the Appendix. When she heard that the Pope had been notified of the Jubilee and that a letter of congratulation would be sent to her, she requested that it would include a very special blessing for the members of the Auxiliary Society of the Sisters of the Blessed Sacrament. Years back, when she had begun seriously to devise ways and means of providing a future source of income for the Community, one of the ideas that came to her was an organization of Catholic lay people throughout the United States who would be willing to donate at least a dollar a year for mission support. She intended from the beginning there would be a close association between these lay helpers and the Sisters. She was quite ahead of her time in her eagerness to have lay people partake of and assist in the work of the American missions. As an expression of the Sisters' gratitude, she arranged with all the houses of the Congregation that these auxiliaries were to be specifically included in the community prayers.

She had completed the plans for this Society in 1928 and then handed it over to Mother M. Mercedes for its organization and spread. A long letter from Pope Pius XI in 1932 included a very special blessing for the Auxiliary Society and recommended it to all Catholics. As Mother M. Mercedes' duties were multiplying, the Foundress asked Sr. M. Xavier to take over the arrangements for the Auxiliary Society. Mother M. Katharine was a woman of big plans and big ideas. She had expected that this Society would grow to include possibly millions of Catholics in the United States. As a matter of fact, when she handed the business organization to Sister M. Xavier she said, "Here it is. Now do what you can with it. Try to get at least a million members." She walked down the hall a few paces and then turned back and added, "No. You had better make it 20 million because I believe there are that many Catholics in the United States and Our Holy Father, Pope Pius XI, has recommended the Auxiliary Society to all Catholics."[7] It would never, of course, assume anything like the dimension she had planned and hoped but she was grateful for whatever assistance came. The Society still holds today an attraction for those who are not only interested in the work of the missions but who appreciate particularly the help of the prayers, very definite ones offered for them by the Community of the Sisters of the Blessed Sacrament.

Another set of developments emerged from the Jubilee celebration — the conferring of a series of honorary degrees on Mother M. Katharine. Ordinarily these would be the last things in the world that would appeal to her. A letter addressed to her in October 1939 by Bishop Corrigan, Rector of the Catholic University, asked her if she would accept an honorary doctorate — the first the University ever offered to a woman. "The motivation," he wrote, "will be the unique place you hold in the history of Catholicity in these United States and your splendidly Catholic contribution to the Nation through your untiring devotion to the two races whom you and your Sisters serve."[8]

After consulting her Council she wrote back that she would accept the degree provided she did not have to attend the ceremony. She noted also why she accepted it: "I gratefully accede to this request with feelings of deep appreciation because I think that this declaration on the part of the Catholic University of America in esteem for work among the Colored and Indian People of the United States will give an added impetus and encouragement to this work."[9]

She had no idea then that other honorary degrees would follow in 1941. Sr. M. Berenice and Sr. M. Dolores accepted the degree in her name at the Catholic University Golden Jubilee convocation, November thirteenth. A few days later, Bishop Corrigan came to the Motherhouse to extend his personal congratulations. He was a good friend of Mother M. Katharine and a good friend of the Community. As she came into the parlor with her nurse he rose to greet her with, "Oh, Doctor Kate!" She was highly amused.

These separate doctorates were conferred on her in the Jubilee year of 1941. In April 1941 Very Reverend George J. Collins, C.SS.Sp., Provincial of the Holy Ghost Fathers wrote that the Holy Ghost Fathers were celebrating solemn Masses at Duquesne University, at Cornwells Heights, Ridgefield, and Ferndale and holding special services in their other houses and missions commemorating the Jubilee. He included word that Duquesne would present Mother M. Katharine with an honorary Doctor of Pedagogy degree "In part recognition of her heroic work for religion, education and charity, and in part for that of her religious daughters during the past fifty fruitful years." In May, Emmanuel College, Boston, conferred on Mother M. Katharine its first honorary degree – Doctor of Humane Letters. St. Joseph's College in Philadelphia conferred an honorary Doctor of Laws degree on her in June. This conferring was a particularly joyful one to the Foundress because there were two Doctor of Laws degrees given, one to her cherished sister, Louise. In Louise Drexel Morrell's life had been fulfilled the ideal that Bishop O'Connor had originally thought would be the type of life Katharine Drexel was to follow. Louise had maintained her place in society, she had disbursed her father's inheritance in magnanimous gifts, particularly to aid the Colored. The citation for this degree listed her general gifts to the Josephite Fathers, St. Emma's Institute, St. Francis Industrial School, St. Michael's Shrine of the True Cross and Retreat House, the Interracial Review, and countless White and Colored to whom she supplied food, clothing and medical aid.

It was all a very new experience for Mother M. Katharine – this acceptance of honorary degrees. The day after she received the degree from St. Joseph's, one of the Sisters stopped in the doorway of her room and said, "Our Mother is a doctor." With a merry twinkle in her eye she replied, "Oh, I am a lot of doctors now!" These honors were like so many rivers gliding past. She watched them flow on while she herself went deeper into the heart of God.

# Chapter 23
# Apostolic Contemplative

All of God's dealings with men are marked by the imprint of His Love and the outpouring of His Mercy. This seems to be particularly true of the life of the Foundress of the Sisters of the Blessed Sacrament. In 1935 at the age of seventy-eight, she was obliged to lay aside practically all business and to live a life of retirement at the Motherhouse in Cornwells Heights, Pennsylvania. When this series of heart attacks first came to her, her mind was still in its original vigor, filled with plans for the future extension of the apostolate, and eager to arrange all details in the way that would contribute most to the glory of God and the salvation of souls. These two objectives had been the impelling motives of her life; she wanted to serve God perfectly herself; she wanted to bring to His knowledge and love as many souls as her congregation could contact, and beyond that, the souls of the whole world.

When the attraction to religious life first came to her during the terminal illness of her mother, her desire was to enter a contemplative community. From her childhood, she had been drawn to the Blessed Sacrament and had pleaded to be able to make her First Holy Communion years before the practice of that day permitted. When Bishop O'Connor had finally come to the decision that she had a religious vocation, her first desire was to enter a contemplative order where everything else would be taken away; in her case, given away, and her days would be spent in adoration of the Blessed Sacrament. Her private notes that have come down to us, indicate that from her earliest days she led a rich and deep interior life, that despite the pleasures and the attractions of the world in which she moved as a millionaire's daughter, her quiet communion with God deepened through the years. The activity in which she engaged as the Superior General of a missionary community was manifold and time consuming. And yet to the Sisters who knew her life of prayer, who heard her pray in the Motherhouse chapel, and in the chapels of the local houses throughout the country, she gave every evidence of a contemplative spirit so deep and so rich, that in it was consecrated all her activity, and from it flowed its efficacy.

But in the Providence of God, Katharine Drexel was to know a contemplative life. It would seem that God had so arranged the long years of her life that twenty of them would be spent almost completely in prayer. The years of her retirement were lived in two rooms on the second floor of the Motherhouse. One of them had a small window which could be opened on the chapel and also a ramp leading to a tribune. This tribune is a mezzanine floor rising from the sanctuary and separated from it by a beautifully executed iron grill. While she was still able to move around freely or be wheeled in a chair, she spent a large part of her day in that tribune. The rest of the day she spent in prayer in one of the rooms. She had given everything she had to God; she had worked with a willing spirit until her physical frame could no longer bear the pressure or sustain the weight. There was no other occupation for her now than to pray almost unceasingly for the needs of the Church, for souls, for missions.

With the area of the whole world the object of her prayer and concern, this Banker's Daughter still intellectually rich in a capacity for details, built herself a program by which she was sure to remember everything. On small slips of paper, she wrote out and checked off in her firm, clear pencil handwriting, the different prayers as she said them. This was evidently an aid to her memory so that none would be omitted. In addition to the community prayers, these small papers day after day recorded an amazing number of prayers of ejaculations. All the major litanies are recorded there, fifteen mysteries of the Rosary in the morning and again in the afternoon, many Stations of the Cross, hours of meditation, and countless ejaculations.

In addition to listing her prayers, she also kept notes on her meditations with comments and thoughts as they struck her. These, too, must have been a means of helping her remember and of checking resolutions. Among these notes we find this entry, "Oh my God, what thanks can I offer you for the permissions to spend an hour of adoration in bed at night. True it is not in the presence of the Sacred Host but I am associated by offering." Evidently, the day was not long enough; on top of everything else during the day, she spent an hour of meditation during the night. Of this meditation, too, she kept short notes. But in praying during the night she found it difficult to keep track of time. Scattered throughout her notes are entries like these: (She uses NA for nocturnal adoration.)

> It is now 1:15 A.M. I have been on this NA since 11:15, about two hours. I shall say the Morning Offering and retire for the night!
>
> One hour and forty minutes over the NA.
>
> I looked at my watch and to my great surprise the hands of the watch say 10 to 3. The meditation was supposed to be from 1:10 to 2:10. I must stop at once.
>
> It is now 36 minutes over the hour of my NA. See how slow I am in contemplation.

Often in the quiet of the night her thoughts would go back to the many graces that had come to her in the course of her life. Some of these thoughts are dated; others are not:

> *Feast of Our Lady of Lourdes,* 1942. I am in spirit in Lourdes with Lisa and Louise kneeling at the Grotto.... Oh dearest Mother, what are the graces you have poured into my soul since that pilgrimage when I took the bath in the waters that cold crisp morning some months after the

shock of my dear father's death which left me with the seeds of disease that was cured by that bath some months after we returned home. Our Lord was calling me to the religious life but my spiritual director, Bishop O'Connor, said: "No. Wait, wait." How wonderful are God's ways, so full of Mercy. My life is a moving picture of scenes which recall His wonderful Providence in my regard.

*February 12, 1942.* 51 years ago I was received into the religious life to be the mother and servant of the Indian and Colored races. In imagination I kneel in the Mercy Convent at the feet of Archbishop Ryan. I remember what passed as I told him all. Then I remember the night before the Reception and the morning I pronounced my vows as Archbishop Ryan held the Sacred Host in his hands. Each day of the 51 years since then has been a day of the Mercy and Love of my Divine Spouse. I have every reason to rely on Divine Providence in all that relates to my and our calling.

*September 6, 1942.* Blessed indeed am I who have seen and heard what I have heard from childhood as a member of Holy Mother the Church, partaking of her sacraments. It is deplorable that I cannot bring forth one hundred fold; it is too late now to reach this but I can strive for a penitential life and not let one small opportunity pass.

These prayers of hers running through the days and the nights were stamped with the mark of the Universality of the Church. She remembered everyone and included the whole world:

*After Reading the Address of Pope Pius XII to the National Eucharistic Congress in Peru.* In my annotation I underlined several passages which especially struck my soul. The Holy Father is like St. Gertrude in a crescendo of prayers. He never ceases till he includes every human being of every station of life in the entire world, and he begs for vocations to the priesthood. Then there is a crescendo that they be zealous priests, then another crescendo and he puts his request in the Eucharistic Heart through Mary His Mother. I am going to try this crescendo in my heart to heart talks with Jesus.

And try it she did. This is particularly evident in her notes on nocturnal adoration in the years of World War II. While the country slept she prayed for those in danger and those in anguish:

*June 27, 1944.* One hour NA placing every soldier, every one bombed into the Divine Love of the Sacred Heart. I tried to follow the words and advice of St. Margaret Mary to offer the prayer of Our Lord Jesus Christ to supply for mine. While doing this, I said one hundred Hail Marys and ten Our Fathers on my indulgence rosary giving the indulgences for them and the twenty thousand German prisoners who are to be exchanged for our soldiers and allies.

*June 28, 1944.* My soul is sorrowful at what is going on now in the bombed cities of Calais, of Normandy, and the suffering and anguish

> of France and Italy. Oh, if we here in our convent motherhouse were to suffer as they. But here in the United States we have been spared miraculously. But our youth are being killed by the thousands, and fathers, mothers, wives, etc., are in anguish of soul. Jesus had to grieve over the sins of the whole world and it is sin which has wrought this world war.
>
> *June 29, 1944.* The altar of the Sacred Heart is in the room where my Jesus, both priest and victim, offers Himself up six times each week and is as really offered as upon the Cross on Calvary. There on the Cross, He looks out over all the world and sees only souls to save. I have the immense privilege of having the priest offer it up for all our valiant soldiers, their salvations, their chaplains, and for all those who die now by being bombed, for all the Germans, even for Hitler, even for myself. Father, forgive them.

In these long prayerful years she was aware that God had used her as an instrument, although she was very firmly convinced that she had been a very weak instrument without which the work could just as well have been accomplished. Her life of apostolic activity was ended, but her life of Eucharist contemplation absorbed more and more of her days and nights. With an ecclesial interest as wide as hers, she became almost a living prayer in the Mystical Body of Christ. Everyday at dinner, a Sister read to her, at her request, the Epistle and Gospel for the next day as if she would set the climate for the afternoons by directing her thoughts to the Mass of the following morning. She enjoyed these readings and listened with avid attention. Sometimes, as the sister would start the Gospel, she would exclaim, "Wait, Sister, wait; let me see if I can tell you what the Gospel is!" She was so familiar with the Masses that she knew what Gospel would follow in the Mass.

In the ensuing years of quiet and peace, a physical crisis arose now and then in which her life seemed in danger. But she survived these as they came along and in a remarkable way seemed to be sustained by a special Providence and the constant prayers of the Sisters. In 1943, however, there was grave concern for her life. During the season of Lent she was in great pain for which there seemed no relief. April 29th, the eve of her feast day with hundreds of greeting cards coming in the mail, and decorations in readiness for her room, she had another attack and Dr. Herrman ordered her to the hospital immediately where it was found that an operation was imperative. It as an ordeal at her age and had to be performed with a local anesthetic.

There was an anxious week after it but once again, all was well. Cardinal Dougherty visited her shortly after her arrival at the hospital – St. Joseph's – and gave her the privilege of having Mass said in her room. He arranged for a portable altar to be brought in immediately. Several days later it was replaced by a permanent one. This special dispensation was a cause of great joy to her, a joy she would experience for the rest of her life. Cardinal Dougherty renewed the permission on her return to the Motherhouse.[1] A wooden altar was installed in her room opposite her bed. It was the chaste, simple altar at which she and her sister had received their First Holy Communion at the convent of the Religious of the Sacred Heart in Philadelphia. The Religious had sent it to the Motherhouse. There on the altar where she had received her Eucharistic God for the first time, until the end of her life, Mass would be celebrated daily and God would come to her again with all His strengthening, purifying, and consuming graces. This life into which He poured strong Eucharistic attraction in the beginning, would near its end be drawn by that attraction into an ever deepening union with Infinite Love.

As the years wore on, her memory might fail, her recognition of Sisters might not be accurate; she would speak of those she had known in her childhood. She would say, "This is Johanna's shawl," or point to a comfortable arm chair, "That is my father's special chair." These details of a weakening memory and a weakening body she might temporarily confuse. But the truths of her Faith, the Hope of salvation for herself and for all souls, her Love of God and her neighbor would never be confused. Her prayer life penetrated her nights as well as her days. While other bankers daughters might consider nights as special times of relaxation or worldly delights, to Katharine they were times of more intimate prayer, more undisturbed union with God. The Sister who was in the room with her during the night had to enter into the prayer life too. There was Sister nurse on call during the night, and during the last years, another Sister who slept in the large room with her. Sister Monica recalls in her memoirs that after they were both in bed, Mother would call to her, "Now, Sister, let us say our prayers." The first one was usually, "Lord of the Harvest, send laborers into the Vineyard." This prayer they said together many times during the night.

Another Sister nurse records that the Foundress never complained of not being able to sleep, but with great reverence and devotion she recited rosary after rosary and said many aspirations.[2] If, while saying the rosary she felt any drowsiness coming on, instead of letting herself sleep she would raise her arms so they would not rest on the bed, and in this way overcome sleep until she finished the rosary. One night this Sister noted she was having a great difficulty keeping her arms up and her eyes open after the sixth rosary they had said together.

"Mother," she said, "Let me finish this rosary and you go to sleep."

Mother hesitated, but in a few moments she answered,

"All right, it is the third sorrowful mystery. When you have finished that, say another rosary in reparation!" Evidently she was following a system in her rosary intentions. One night to the surprise of the nurse she said, "We'll offer this rosary for the dying Sister." It was 9:30 P.M. and a seriously ill sister across the hall in the infirmary was sleeping peacefully with no evident sign of death. But at 11 P.M. the Sister rang her bell; the nurse hurried in to find her struggling for breath and in a dying condition. The priest was called and she died shortly after.[3] Throughout these years of seclusion, the bond between Mother M. Katharine and her sister, Louise Drexel Morrell, was close and deep. Once a week Louise came from her home in Torresdale for a brief visit with her cherished sister. The visit was always a delight to both of them though it lasted just about a half hour. Louise usually carried a basket with her filled with jellies, fruits and freshly cut flowers. There was much business discussed in these visits as both sisters were dispersing still the charities of their father and both were vitally interested in the race situation and in the interracial groups springing up throughout the country. To the Catholic Interracial Group in New York, they gave financial assistance over the years and kept in very close touch with Father La Farge, S.J., its moving spirit.

Mother M. Katharine was to have another encounter with the death of a dearly loved one. Louise died quite unexpectedly November 5, 1943. She had suffered a cerebral hemorrhage at ten in the morning and died at five that evening. Cautiously, Mother Philip Neri had told Mother M. Katharine that her sister was ill. Mother Mary of the Visitation, Superior General, was in Columbus at the time but a telephone call started her on her way home. The news was kept from the Foundress till the following morning.

As Mother Philip Neri went into her room then, she asked eagerly, "How is my little sister?" Mother tried to break it gently by telling her that she was with God and far removed from all suffering.

But Mother M. Katharine got the full impact immediately and was almost overcome by her grief. "God, my God", she said between her tears, "I cannot believe that life is taken from me. Oh I cannot believe it.... Wait .... Wait .... I must .... Oh my God, my God, I cannot .... I cannot." The struggle to hold on to the Will of God was very evident. "It is not that I want anything different from what God wants.... I cannot believe it."

When Mother Mary of the Visitation entered the room, the Foundress clung to her exclaiming, "Oh Mother, oh my Mother."[4] She was the last of her family; her mother, father, Elizabeth, and Louise were all with God. This final separation from the one who had always been her "little sister" cut deep into her affectionate heart. But as the day wore on composure came and complete submission to the Will of God. The calm expression of her face was evidence of the triumph of grace.

As the years wore on, her prayer life was intensified and her concern for others found many expressions. She would say to the nurse at night, "Are the children cold? You can take the blanket from my bed and give it to that poor, little fellow. I know he is cold and I don't need a blanket."

When the nurse assured her that the children had blankets on their bed she would ask, "Well, are they warm blankets like the ones on my bed?"[5] This concern for others, this compassion for the poor would mark all her days. Right up to the end of her life she wanted to share whatever she had with them and they must have had a prominent place in her countless prayers. Sometimes at night when all was very quiet and still, she would fold her hands, fix her eyes on a certain spot, and for a half hour or more she would seem to be saying something in a very low whisper. You would feel sure she was having a very pleasant vision. Nothing could distract her. You could pass her bed several times, or go right near it, but she kept her gaze fixed on that one place. What did she see? It is hard to tell.

One evening a Sister went in around seven o'clock and found her like this looking up to the ceiling in the corner of the room with a very peaceful and joyful expression on her face. She turned to the Sister and said: "Did you see them?"

"See what?" asked the Sister who could see nothing.

"The children," she replied. The next morning she said to the same Sister, "Oh all the children were there, all going past, so many of them. And the Pope was there too in all his regalia, and so many children. They were all there."[6] She pointed up to the same spot on the ceiling. One had to be very much on the alert to catch anything like this from this Foundress. Whatever unusual experiences she had, or rich graces she enjoyed, she kept very secretly to herself. But both the night nurse and the Sister had the very definite impression that she had a vision of many children passing by, who may well have represented the thousands and thousands of children brought to the saving waters of Baptism by her Congregation. Many years before when she had shrunk from the idea of founding a community Bishop O'Connor said to her, "It's all right, Kate. It's like an invitation to a wedding; you don't have to take it if you don't want to. But if you do take it, it may mean that thousands of souls will know God who otherwise could never have known Him."[7] Did she see some of those thousands then?

# Chapter 24

# The Bridegroom Comes

For twenty grace-filled and divinely-supported years, this life of retirement and prayer went on for Mother M. Katharine. As her ninetieth birthday approached, the day became a feast day, one of general thanksgiving throughout the Community and a first class holiday. Hers were unusual birthdays, one more blessed than the other and each one another cause for deep gratitude to God and great joy of heart to all. It is rather unusual for a religious community to celebrate the birthdays of the Foundress, but these were special birthdays, and each one called for a separate celebration.

There was no change in her way of life; her prayers continued day and night as the years mounted. She grew weaker each year and every once in awhile there would be another cause for alarm. But each time she came through and the life of prayer went on and on. Her interest in mission developments kept pace with her prayers and she listened eagerly to every new detail of the Sister's activity. Visitors were reduced to a minimum and everything was done to relieve her of any stress or strain. All the while, the Congregation knew a peace and contentment in the realization that many visits would wear her out; they were content to know just that she was there and that her prayers for them and the works of the Congregation were ascending almost unceasingly to God.

In those long years of prayer when her activity was ended, her apostolate accomplished, and her will perfectly at one with God, the thought of death came to her frequently. In earlier years, she had prepared for the foundation of the Community and for the opening of this mission or that. Now she knew she was preparing for death. There are many references to it in her notes:

> *The Storm on the Lake.* Every word of this text is beautiful. "Why are you fearful, oh you of little faith?" I fear the death struggle on which so much depends for eternity. Jesus will be with me in that struggle. He can rebuke the wind and the sea, and there will come a great calm.[1]
>
> *Sunday, April 26, 1944,* Palm Sunday. Jesus come and cure my soul. Today may it sing "Hosannah in the highest. Blessed is He who comes in the name of the Lord." I am not worthy that you should enter under my roof. I shall say these words in about eight hours from now when the priest will place you on my tongue. What humiliation and love on your part. Today the priest will bring You into my room, under the roof, the roof of religion where I took my final vows, the roof of the chapel where

I stay nearly all day long. The little window opening into the chapel is closed off only by a door of wood, one and a half inch thick. Here I live and see the dear sisters who come to visit me so devotedly, so kindly.

Today is retreat Sunday, a day of special preparation for death where all mankind pass to eternal life. "May the Body of Our Lord Jesus Christ preserve your soul to eternal life" the priest says as he places the Sacred Host on my tongue. This morning I shall have in my hand the blessed palm which Sr. Monica will bring me from the chapel. The palm is a sign of Christian victory. I am going to have it on my bed as I receive Holy Communion as if I were receiving it on my death bed.

May my death be a happy one. Lord, into Thy hands I commend my death. Come it must and it must be near, I dread it. It is the punishment of sin.... The Martyrs wore the palm of victory. May I be victorious in the martyrdom of the death struggle, conscious or unconscious. Lord, into Thy hands I commend my spirit. Oh God, relying on Thy infinite goodness I hope to obtain the pardon of all my sins and life everlasting, through the merits of Our Lord and Savior Jesus Christ. Amen[2]

But hers too was the confidence that must certainly have been with her the moment death came to her after her long years of waiting. She had counted on the assistance of the Mother of God:

Mary is our advocate at death. I am her child. She will be there bending over my death bed like a mother over the cradle of her infant. "During life," she said to St. Gertrude, "I pledge myself to obtain all necessary graces for my servants, but at death I come to them in person, and with one look, I put to flight all the powers of Hell."

Oh Mary, how often in our Little Office we plead many times daily:

"Oh happy Mary chose to be
Mother of grace and clemency,
Protect us at the hour of death
And bear to Heaven our parting breath!"[3]

But God had to take her home sometime. In the end, in her ninety-seventh year, her death came quietly and unexpectedly. She had given the community quite a scare February 20, 1955, following a definite weak spell. Dr. McFadden, who had been taking care of her after the death of Dr. Herrman three years previously, was summoned and diagnosed her condition as lobar pneumonia. There was general fear that because of her advanced age this might prove fatal, but within a very short time she was much better. Within the next two weeks she not only held her own but seemed to be improving. Dr. McFadden announced that she had completely recovered from the lobar pneumonia but that a very definite heart murmur was still evident.

On the evening of March 2 just after Benediction, her nurse, Sister Clement, sent hurriedly for Reverend Mother M. Anselm, the Superior General, as the Foundress appeared to be strangling from a severe coughing spell. She had recovered before she reached the room, but her respiration was very rapid and again the faithful doctor was called. An oxygen tent was hurriedly installed by the Bucks County Rescue Squad. All this time, Mother M. Katharine said nothing; she watched the oxygen tent being put in place and smiled sweetly at all present. At 4 A.M., everything seemed fine and the tent was removed. She ate her usual good breakfast at 8, and the doctor was notified she was much better. But the relief was brief. At 8:30, the respiration again became rapid and this time the oxygen tent did not help. It was very evident she was actually dying. The priest and the doctor were called, and the Sisters gathered around the room in prayer. With Father Nugent, the faithful community chaplain through many years, and Doctor McFadden in attendance, and the Sisters kneeling in prayer, Mother M. Katharine gave up her soul to God at 9:05 A. M., March 3, 1955, without a struggle, calmly and peacefully. Her long years of prayer had made her will so completely one with God, her many meditations on death had prepared her so well for the final act itself, that she slipped away as quietly as a child nestling in its mother's arms.

She was gone, gone home to God. The Community was stunned. The wires of the nation brought the announcement within a few minutes to the whole Congregation. In their grief, in their deep sense of loss, the Sisters knew they had cause for deep gratitude to God for the many long years He had spared her to them, long years of leadership, inspiration and direction. They knew too, they had not lost her at this point. They were all aware of the full implications of the words in the Preface of the Requiem Mass: "Life is changed, not taken away." In a much more intimate union with God than she had ever known on earth, she was their mother still. Her prayers for them would continue, and greater help than ever she would send them.

On receiving the word, Archbishop O'Hara of Philadelphia, later Cardinal, offered the Cathedral for the funeral Mass and said he would get in touch immediately with the Apostolic Delegate, with Cardinal Stritch, and Cardinal Spellman. For a little lady who shunned publicity and withdrew from any element of acclaim, Mother M. Katharine had a most unusual funeral. Mother M. Anselm, Superior General at the time, decided to bring home to the Motherhouse sixty of the Senior Sisters from the various missions, as it was not possible to bring all. The body of the Foundress was brought to the Motherhouse chapel. It is the ordinary practice of the Sisters of the Blessed Sacrament that the body of a deceased Sister remains in the chapel over the night preceding the burial, but as there were so many coming from all directions; Bishops, Clergy, friends, and former students; it was decided to have the body remain in the chapel two days. To the amazement of the Sisters, crowds of people appeared, desirous of viewing the remains of this woman whose reputation was so widespread in her own city.

In addition to four Sisters who continually recited the rosary, four Sisters were stationed at the head and foot of the casket when it was noticed some were seeking relics. The weather was miserable, very cold and very wet with teeming rain, but it had no effect on the crowds. They came in overwhelming numbers and passed in single file around the casket, to take a last look and say a short prayer for one whose story was well known to them. Old people hobbling along with the help of canes, young children with their hands clasped in those of their parents, teenagers in subdued reverence, slowly and solemnly passed by.

Since the people were not allowed to touch the casket, the four Sisters obligingly took religious articles from them and touched them to the body. One old man took out a worn booklet and said, "It's all I have, but I want it there." There were many remarks as the crowds passed by. One man, the father of five, walked past with them saying that he wanted his children to be able to say in the future that they had looked on the face of Mother Katharine in death. Another man said, "I want Reverend Mother to remember the family of Nobles." His name was Noble and he was a graduate of St. Emma's in Rock Castle, Virginia. Former students came from every direction to pay silent and prayerful tribute. Another exclaimed, "We came to look upon a saint. She surely was a saint to live the life she did." One man held up his little son and said to the lad, "Take a good look at that nun, my son. Someday you can say that you looked upon a saint."[4] Many parents had evidently brought their children with the same purpose in mind. The crowds grew so large that the police came to direct the flow of traffic.

It was midnight before the chapel could be closed with the streams of people pouring through. The following morning, a low Mass for the repose of her soul was said in the Motherhouse chapel. All the Sisters, the children of Holy Providence School, and many parishioners of nearby St. Charles Parish filled every available space. During the day, the crowds came again. White, Colored, Indian, they came paying silent, prayerful honor to one they revered not only for what she had done for many of them, but for what she was to them. Tuesday, the day of the funeral, there was another low community Mass in the Motherhouse chapel at 5:30 A.M. At 7:50 A.M., the Sisters were ready to take their places in the funeral cortege to Philadelphia. They followed the casket to the waiting cars. A police escort headed the funeral procession as it wended its way at an even twenty-five mile speed through red and green lights to the Cathedral in Philadelphia. Down the main aisle of the Cathedral, the Sisters of the Blessed Sacrament walked behind the casket to the front places reserved for them. Long before the cortege from Cornwells Heights had reached the Cathedral, it was filled almost to its capacity with every available place taken. The crowds had overflowed to the aisles and many had to stand outside after the Mass just to get a glimpse of the funeral procession of this daughter of Philadelphia.

It was a stupendous gathering. More than 250 prelates, priests and brothers assisted at the Mass which was said by Archbishop O'Hara. According to the *Catholic Standard and Times* of March 11, 1955, an archbishop, six bishops, a prefect apostolic, an arch abbot, the provincials of a dozen religious orders and a sanctuary full of prelates and priests overflowed into the pews.

Bishop McShea, Auxiliary Bishop of Philadelphia, preached the sermon, a magnificent tribute to the spirit and accomplishments of this woman of simple desires and total consecration. He traced the events of her life from birth to death. Two passages particularly, struck the keynote of it all.

> First and foremost, in youth and old age, in health and in sickness, with friends and with strangers, the beloved soul of Mother M. Katharine was activated, inspired, and impelled by an insatiable love of God and by a complete subjection to His adorable Will. Hers was not a humanitarianism that stops where true love should begin. She was not a mere social reformer, educator, or philanthropist striving to better the condition of her fellow man while permitting him to ignore God. Hers was a love primarily of God, practiced with her whole heart, her whole soul, and her whole mind, because she accepted and lived by the fundamental principles that govern the relationship of creatures to God, their Infinite Creator and Master....[5]
>
> It was this same love of God that inspired her to place herself and her religious family under the protective mantle of Jesus, ever living, and ever loving and nourishing the souls of men, in the ineffable Sacrament of the Holy Eucharist. Nor is it unfitting to mention that in her last years of venerable old age, when a mind fatigued and exhausted had lost the resilience and perception of youth, she awakened each morning with a renewed brightness of spirit when witnessing the Holy Sacrifice of the Mass and in receiving the Body and Blood of Jesus Christ in Holy Communion.[6]

Immediately after the Mass and just before the final absolution, Archbishop O'Hara came to the pews where the Sisters of the Blessed Sacrament were standing and offered again his deepest sympathy. As Mother Anselm thanked him for his considerate generosity in making the arrangement for the funeral at the Cathedral, he said, "You see, even this church is not large enough for this funeral."[7] There were throngs standing outside who had not been able to enter.

After the final absolution, the procession of Sisters formed again and followed the mortal remains of Mother M. Katharine down the main aisle of the Cathedral so familiar to her all her life. As a little girl, Katie Drexel had come there Sunday after Sunday with her father to assist at the ten o'clock Mass. She often recalled those days in conversation with the Sisters in later years, the joy she felt as she marched down that long aisle with her hand clasped in that of her father, the added joy she would know when the organist would ask her father to supply his place at the organ. Her youngest days had been spent in this sacred environment. Down the same aisle she had trod lightly as a child, her consumed body was carried by representatives of the Indian, Colored, and white races to its burial, surrounded by honors and attended with a reverence she could never dreamed would be given her.

Through the foresight of the former Superior General, Mother Mary of the Visitation, and with the consent of Cardinal Dougherty, a burial crypt for Mother M. Katharine had been arranged years before in the basement of the Motherhouse, underneath the chapel. That is where the Sisters wanted her remains to rest; that is where her body was interred. To this last resting place of her mortal remains, the funeral cortege wended its way back to the Motherhouse.

Since the Religious of the Sacred Heart with whom Mother M. Katharine had many precious and intimate relations all through her life could not attend the funeral, they requested that on the return to the Motherhouse a detour be made through the grounds at Eden Hall in Torresdale. The Religious and their students lined the driveway as the funeral cortege passed silently through the grounds. The children from St. Catherine's grade school recited the rosary, the students of the Academy sang *In Paradiso*, and the Religious stood with lighted candles in front of their building, all paying a final and loving tribute to Mother M. Katharine. There was something very appropriate in this passage through the hallowed grounds of the Religious of the Sacred Heart at Torresdale. The grounds were very well known to the Foundress. Her mother's sister, Mother Bouvier, had lived there many years. She had many recollections of the associations with Religious of the Sacred Heart both at Torresdale and in Philadelphia. There are some interesting references in her notes on one of her Night Adorations:

> I kneel in spirit in the form of a Cross on the earth and there rejoice in that tenderness of the Sacred Heart of Jesus which gave me Mary as my Mother. Oh what a tender and loving mother she has been to me. Once in my childhood when my Father went to see Bishop Wood as he often did after the ten o'clock Sunday Mass, the Bishop gave me a large silver medal. On it, under a bunch of lilies, was engraved: "Monstra Te Esse Matrem." I treasured it and I think now that the Bishop gave this little child — I was then about eight years old — this medal with the desire that this little daughter of my father would keep her Baptismal innocence unspotted and as pure as the lilies.
>
> It was Bishop Wood who confirmed me and gave me my first Holy Communion in the chapel of the Religious of the Sacred Heart. It was again the tenderness of the love of Jesus that he gave me my dear mamma, one reared in the school of these same Religious of the Sacred Heart, and whom God so mercifully gave me to be my mother and after the mother who gave me birth died. I was the cause of her death. The day of my first Holy Communion was spent in the convent of these religious at their Arch Street house....[8]

Both Katharine Drexel and her sisters knew the chapel at Eden Hall well. They used to assist at daily Mass there when the family was in the country home at Torresdale. One of the Religious of the Sacred Heart holding a lighted candle as her funeral procession passed by, had been a student at the Academy when the Drexel sisters came there to Mass. One incident came to her forcibly as she watched this procession. She sent an account of it to the Motherhouse later:

> When I was fifteen years old I saw the Misses Drexel come almost daily for Holy Mass in Eden Hall's Chapel and they went frequently to Holy Communion.
>
> One day they came, Elizabeth and Louise in the buggy, and Katharine on horseback.
>
> At Breakfast Mere Huguet told us "en Francais" (no recreation unless French was spoken) that Miss Katharine had fainted after Mass. She had fallen on dismounting, but said nothing of the pain as she did not wish to lose Holy Communion. They found she had broken her collar bone![9]

There were many memories of Katharine Drexel at Eden Hall. This was indeed a fitting detour for her funeral cortege.

Messages of sympathy poured into the Motherhouse from Pope Pius XII, from Cardinals, Bishops, Priests, relatives, former students. They came from all parts of the world, from countless religious communities, from members of the laity, from missionaries. The Masses offered for her by the many grateful recipients of her charity, as well as priests and prelates throughout the country were innumerable.

One editorial attempted to summarize the impact of Katharine Drexel this way:

> One of the most remarkable women in the history of America was called home to God yesterday. The priests and people of the Archdiocese of Philadelphia have been proud to claim her as their own, and yet she belonged so truly to all America, but especially to the poor and forgotten people of America – our Indians and Negroes. Reverend Mother Katharine Drexel belonged to Philadelphia and to America, but one cannot help seeing in the story of her life that she belonged to God....[10]

In her death, God took His possession home. She had helped in more missions than can be enumerated; she had given her millions away for their support, but greater than all these gifts, she gave herself. Humbly, joyfully she sealed her gifts, she perfected her oblation in death. Willingly, she gave back to God the life He had given her.

# Chapter 25
# A Daughter Of The Church

To understand Katharine Drexel we must understand the milieu of her life from birth to death. This book has attempted to reproduce that. She was brought up in luxury but she understood poverty and chose to experience it. All the gilded doors of society swung open to her, but she lifted the latches on the doors of the poor instead. She knew the comfort of luxurious travel through the scenic glories of Europe, but she scheduled her itineraries through the little traveled places on the American scene. She was American in the fullest interpretation of the term. Her ancestry goes back far to the beginnings of American history. Her activities in behalf of her fellow men, her understanding of the principles of constitutional democracy, her desires to secure the blessings of liberty for all Americans, stemmed from a patriotism and love of country that would be difficult to surpass.

She knew America, its glories and its tragedies. She knew the Race Problem. She never wrote a book on the subject though she was well qualified to do so. She never aired her views in newspapers or magazines, but she organized and put into execution a racial plan in 65 centers in 21 states. Where few seemed to care, she was solicitous; where few seemed to bother, she contributed a dynamic personal effort; where few seemed concerned, this valiant woman gave her life's service and invited hundreds of American women and some from abroad to work with her in righting a great wrong done to racial minorities in this country. God gave her an unusually lengthy life as if He wanted to grant her as many years as possible to inspire, guide, and assist her apostolate.

The Congregation of the Sisters of the Blessed Sacrament founded by Mother M. Katharine, is a Eucharistic one; its apostolate is a Eucharistic apostolate. It has been pointed out before in this book that the foundation of every new mission meant to Mother M. Katharine the construction of a new house of worship, a new place for the adoration of the Blessed Sacrament, a place where it had never been adored before. She wanted everyone to know the mystery of the Eucharist, to share its graces, to be fed with its munificence. She understood well St. Thomas' explanation of the fact that not only do we receive in the Eucharist under the appearance of bread and wine, the Body and the Blood, Soul and Divinity of Christ by virtue of the sacrament, and by concomitance, but the very reception incorporates us more intimately into the Mystical Body of Christ. In other words, a special effect of the reception of the Eucharist is the formation of the Church, the Mystical Body of Christ.

Like the grains of wheat in bread or in the white Host, all become one. That, under God, was her ambition and desire. That ambition and desire must ever remain the impelling motive of her Congregation.

Mother M. Katharine is gone, but her program lives and functions. Over six hundred Sisters of the Blessed Sacrament in 65 different centers are continuing the apostolate she organized and directed. They are well aware as the Foundress was aware, that this is not an apostolate of an individual or a particular group. This is an apostolate of the Catholic Church in the United States. Before everything else, Mother M. Katharine considered herself a daughter of the Church. It would have never occurred to her that as an individual she was founding an order or organizing a program or furthering a particular type of work. Two members of the American hierarchy sponsored the foundation of her community; in its development, Bishops throughout the country were her directors; priests were her co-workers and organizers. Her missions and her endeavors connected with them were truly the endeavors of the Catholic Church in action.

In this mixed up and confused age in which we live, scientifically equipped to blast nations off the face of the earth or carry men to the moon or the depths of the seas, the clamor for freedom of action, freedom of expression, stirs a restive citizenry. Strange accusations are hurled. Latecomers in the field of racial justice spurred on by the restlessness of this age, in some instances criticize the Church for neglecting to play the part it should play or should have played in the evangelization of the Indian and Colored. True, many opportunities were missed, many plans might have been sooner and better organized. The Church, after all, is made up of human beings with human failings that are often evident. But those who criticize the inactivity of the Church or what appears to them as inactivity, who unwittingly spread further discontent among a people who have many causes and reasons for discontent, might well study the part the Church played through the activity of Mother M. Katharine, to say nothing of the widespread activities of whole congregations like the Josephite Fathers, the Fathers of the Society of the Divine Word, the Holy Ghost Fathers, etc.

Mother M. Katharine channeled her efforts through the apostolic involvements of the Church. Everything she did, everything her community accomplished, all the efforts of other communities in the field are the evidences of the Catholic Church in action in America. She would be the last person in the world to want her work recognized as the work of Katharine Drexel. First, last, and always, she was a child of the Church; she labored in that capacity. To have been used by the Church as its instrument is her life's achievement; to have died a daughter of the Church was the fulfillment of her deepest longing.

If great reparation was needed for all the wrongs, all the injustices, all the years of neglect and dishonor through which both the Indians and the Colored have passed in the development and full flowering of the mighty nation, the whole involvement of Katharine Drexel was part of that reparation.

Back in November 1889, three days after he had officiated at her religious reception in the Mercy Convent in Pittsburgh, Archbishop Ryan addressed the assembled Bishops of the nation attending the Baltimore Centenary celebration. He made specific reference to this element of reparation in the course of his address already quoted in chapter 9 of this book.[1] This call to reparation echoes down the years to the present day. Every American has a part to play in this reparation, a part that will substitute consideration for oppression, understanding for prejudice, and justice for injury.

The national reparation spiraled from the forceful thrust of President Kennedy, the first President since Lincoln to state publicly that racial segregation was morally indefensible.[2] Robert Kennedy as Attorney General, was to emphasize the same basic fact many times as he and his deputy, Burke Marshall, brought legal action in the South to assure every citizen's right to vote.[3] Today, led by President Johnson whose forthright statements on the moral evil of race segregation have been broadcast throughout the country, the American nation faces the task of helping all citizens to a full enjoyment of their basic rights and privileges. The Congressional passage of Civil Rights Bills culminating in the Civil Rights Bill of 1964 and the Voting Rights Bill of 1965, has chartered the course of a national reparation.

The race problem, however, is still with us. Social, economic, educational injustices still abound. As long as there are Indian and Negro neighborhoods or needs in the United States, the Sisters of Blessed Sacrament will spread themselves to serve them. Already areas are being integrated that were never integrated before, and the Sisters find themselves with White as well as Indian and Colored children in their classrooms. What the future will bring in this development remains to be seen. It was for this eventual integration that Mother M. Katharine founded her Community of the Sisters of the Blessed Sacrament, and toward it the Sisters have directed their labors. Where opportunities were denied the Indians and Colored, the Sisters offered them; where doors were closed, they opened them. Their place in United States History has been on the other side of the color line. No one will rejoice more than they if that line eventually disappears. Their work has been a remote preparation for that day.

What will be the ultimate resolution of their aim — the evangelization of the Indian and Colored races — will be solved by the Community at that day and in those circumstances when the evangelization is completed. Very wisely, and with that foresight that was so essentially part of her character, Mother M. Katharine requested that the title Rome had translated "For Indians and Negroes" be changed to "Indians and Colored People." That change was made in the Decree of Definitive Approbation of the Constitution given May 25, 1913. Will that include all the Colored races of the world? That remains to be seen.

The life of Mother M. Katharine was much more than a series of apostolic adventures and educational foundations at every intellectual level. It was the gradual development and progression through long years of a deep seated holiness evident to many. Cardinal Cushing, outstanding missionary himself, wrote of her: "She was a missionary at the foot of the Cross by prayer and sacrifice. She was a missionary among her sisters by the extraordinary example she gave them. She was also the greatest individual benefactress of the missions among the Indians and Colored in the history of the Church in America.... I have never met anyone during my forty years in the Holy Priesthood like Mother Katharine Drexel. She was unique. All the virtues that one would expect in a valiant woman and in one of the elect of God, gentleness, patience, prayerful perseverance, and abiding confidence in the Lord, were preeminent in her gentle character.... The lasting impressions that I gained as a result of the various meetings I had with Mother Katharine in Boston and also at the Motherhouse of the Community at Cornwells Heights, Pennsylvania, are many and inspiring. They are characteristic of a chosen soul who was raised by God to an extraordinary degree of Christian perfection and personal sanctity."[4]

Hers was a holiness grounded as all holiness must be, in the theological and moral virtues. All her life she prayed for a firm faith for herself and for others. It was firm, a living vital acceptance of God and his Revelation. Because she believed so strongly in the teaching of the Church, the mysteries, the efficacy of the sacraments, she wanted others to have the unerring guide and strong support of faith in their lives. She wanted to share the best thing she had—her faith.

She walked through many disappointments and rose above harsh opposition. She faced situations that seemed impossible, but her hope was undaunted. Often it was the most destitute, those who seemed to have little grounds for hope, that she wanted to help. She was conscious of her own weakness but she knew well the unlimited power of grace for herself and for others. Her hope grew as difficulties mounted.

The greatest of the virtues, St. Paul tells us, is charity. In the unending joy of the Beatific Vision, faith and hope, will be no more for their ends will have been attained. But charity endures forever. The simple untarnished facts of Katharine Drexel's life testify to her love of God and her all embracing love of her fellow man. She wanted to help others not only materially and intellectually but spiritually as well, so that those deprived of material wealth might know and experience a far more enduring spiritual wealth. A God-centered and a God-directed education was the core of her apostolate.

The moral virtues; prudence, justice, temperance, and fortitude are woven clearly and unmistakenly into the pattern of her life and exemplified in many incidents. She followed no ordinary way, but prudence set and guided her course. She was beset with difficult circumstances and worn to weariness in the demands and problems that faced her, but the virtue of the fortitude sustained and strengthened her. Temperance in the matter of food was a lifelong practice with her. She had a keen perception of the obligations and privileges of justice, distributive, commutative, and legal. If all Americans had her sense of justice informed by charity, there would be no Race Problem in America. She fought all her life for justice for the Negro and the Indian.

But above everything else was her charity. By the end of her life she had reduced everything to love. In one of her last meditation notes she wrote:

> Practical Conclusion: Love! Love! Let us give ourselves to real pure love. Devotion to the Sacred Heart is a devotion which alone can banish the coldness of our time. The renewal which I seek and which we all seek is a work of love and can be accomplished by love alone.[5]

There were many facets of her spirituality as there were many facets to her character and personality. No one was more approachable, no one simpler in her tastes or more unpretentious in manner. There was a definite personal charm about her in which candor, simplicity, reserve and kindness mingled together. The general picture she presented, the picture that remains with the Sisters is a picture of joy. For all the toil, the journeyings, the difficulties, the hardships of the way, she abounded in joy. She evidenced this particular fruit of the Holy Spirit so well in life that it radiates still through the life of the Community. So many people remark the spirit of joy in the various houses of the Community. It is part of her legacy to the Sisters. Her sacrifice of praise, her surrender to the Trinity was offered in joy. In the Mass of her life, the closing prayer of the Canon would seem to have sealed the direction of her offering: "Through Him, and with Him, and in Him, be to Thee Father and Spirit, all honor and glory."

And now the Church she served so well has entered on a study of her life and virtues. February 27, 1964, nine years after her death, Archbishop Krol of Philadelphia announced the beginning of the ordinary process toward the cause of the Beatification of Mother Katharine Drexel. Father Nicholas B. Ferrante, C.Ss.R. stations in Rome at Sant' Alfonso, the Motherhouse of the Redemptorist Fathers, was named the postulator and Father Francis J. Litz, C.Ss.R. of St. Peter's Church, Philadelphia, vice-postulator.

Katharine Drexel's mortal life, striking in contrasts and startling in achievements, is ended. In a life of contemplative prayer and apostolic endeavor she pioneered the great movements of contemporary American civilization. Her direction was to New Frontiers of grace and education for the neglected and overlooked; her concern was for the building of a Great Society with membership for all in the Communion of Saints. Hers was a life of love, labor, and light.

She knew great joy in the total gift of herself to God; she knew too, the agony of the soul sharing in the redemptive process. February 12, 1941, on the festive occasion of the Community celebration of the Golden Jubilee of the Congregation whose existence started with her profession in 1891, she spoke briefly to the assembled Sisters. She artfully shifted their attention from herself whose jubilee it really was, and directed it to the intrepid missionaries who had first made her aware of the desperate needs of the Indian missions. "I saw them in their agony," she said, and then slowly repeated the statement: "I saw them in their agony."

She did not recall their triumphs, nor the immeasurable extent of their labors; she remembered their agony of soul in the obstacles they overcame to extend the redemptive graces to the neglected races of America and to forge an honorable place for them in this land of prosperity. Redemption she knew well had taken place on Calvary. Those who would spread its saving effects to men willing to accept them must approach that Calvary and take up their share of that Redemption. Like St. Paul, they too, must fill up the things that are wanting in the Passion of Christ. She never referred to her own agony but she sounded its depths in the lives of others.

All men follow the same pattern from the agony of Calvary to the ecstasy of the Resurrection. The Paschal mysteries are a whole and cannot be separated. Emerging millions in America today have known the agony of prejudice and hatred. These millions were the objects of her deepest concern.

Katharine Drexel dug a new highway through America, lit a new light in its darkest corners because she loved God with her whole heart and mind and soul, and her neighbors – all her neighbors – as herself. She knew that peace could not be established without tranquility of order. She wanted to help establish that order. "You must love peace," said Pope Paul in his memorable homily delivered during the Mass for Peace at Yankee Stadium. She would have understood his message well: "Peace is not a state which can be acquired and made permanent. PEACE MUST BE BUILT: it must be built up every day by works of peace.... Peace must be like a garden, in which public and private beneficence cultivates the choicest flowers of friendship, of solidarity, of charity and love." Katharine Drexel was a builder in the literal and metaphorical sense of the word. The flowers of friendship, of solidarity, of charity, and love, will continue to grow in the gardens she planted all over the land of her birth.

Mother Mary Katharine Drexel

(1858-1955)

PRAYER

GOD: Father, Son and Spirit We rejoice in Your servant,

KATHARINE DREXEL

who was filled with love for You and reverence for Your image in the Indian and Black people. In creative, compassionate urgency she walked as a prophetic witness for equality and as an apostle for justice among the poor and oppressed. She gave herself totally and founded a community to share the message of the Gospel, and the life of the Eucharist among Your people, recognizing in the Eucharist the source and bond of our unity. May she be honored in Your church so that You may be glorified and that we may strive for greater unity, justice, and peace.

NIHIL OBSTAT: James McGrath
*Censor Librorum*
Philadelphia, March 10, 1987

IMPRIMATUR: John Cardinal Krol
*Archbishop of Philadelphia*
Philadelphia, March 12, 1987

(Please report any favors received through Mother M. Katharine's intercession, to: SISTERS of the BLESSED SACRAMENT, Motherhouse, 1663 Bristol Pike, Bensalem, Pa. 19020.)

# Appendix I

Drexel - Langstroth - Bouvier Who's Who

DREXEL Francis Martin - Founder of Philadelphia Drexels

***Born*** in Dornbirn, Austria, April 7, 1792, and came to Philadelphia, Pa., 1817.

***Married*** Catherine Hookey, April 23, 1821, who died in Philadel phia, Pa., September 21, 1870.

***Died*** in Philadelphia Pa., June 6, 1863.

***Children*** of Francis M. Drexel and Catherine Hookey

Mary Johanna (Mrs. John Lankenau)
Francis Anthony
Anthony Joseph
Joseph Wilhelm
Heloise (Mrs. James Smith)
Caroline (Mrs. John Watmough)

DREXEL Francis Anthony - Born Philadelphia, Pa., January 20, 1824.

***Married*** Hannah J. Langstroth, September, 1854, who died in Phila delphia, Pa., December 30, 1858.

***Married*** Emma Mary Bouvier, April 10, 1860, who died in Philadel phia, Pa., January 29, 1883.

***Died*** in Philadelphia, Pa., February 15, 1885.

***Children*** of Francis A. Drexel and Hannah J. Langstroth

Elizabeth Langstroth, born on August 27, 1855.
Katharine Mary, born November 26, 1858.

***Child*** of Francis A. Drexel and Emma M. Bouvier

Louise Bouvier, born on October 2, 1863.

Elizabeth Langstroth Drexel married Walter George Smith, January 7, 1890; Died September 26, 1890.

Katharine Mary Drexel founded The Sisters of the Blessed Sacra ment, February 12, 1891.

Louise Bouvier Drexel married Edward Morrell, January 17, 1889; Died November 4, 1943.

LANGSTROTH Piscator - ***Born***, Falls of Schuylkill, Pa., May 27, 1791.

***Married*** Eliza Lehman, December 12, 1819, who died in German town, Pa., January 23, 1877.

***Died*** in Germantown, Pa., August 14, 1861.

***Children*** of Piscator Langstroth and Eliza Lehman

Benjamin Lehman

Elizabeth (Mrs. Fortunato J. Figueira)
James Fassitt
Hannah Jane (Mrs. Francis A. Drexel)

BOUVIER Michel - ***Born***, Pont St. Esprit, France, March 2, 1792.
***Married*** Sarah Ann Pierson, 1823, who died in Philadelphia, Pa., December 26, 1826.
***Married*** Louise C. Vernou, May 29, 1828, who died in Philadelphia, Pa., October 5, 1872.
***Died*** in Philadelphia, Pa., June 9, 1874.
***Children*** of Michel Bouvier and Sarah Ann Pierson
Eustache
Therese (Mrs. Jonathan Patterson)
***Children*** of Michel Bouvier and Louise C. Vernou
Elizabeth (Mrs. Joseph Dixon)
Louise (Madame Louise Bouvier, RSCJ)
Emma Mary (Mrs. Francis A. Drexel)
Zenaide Sara
Alexine Eugenie
Mary Howell
John Vernou (Great grandfather of Jacqueline Bouvi er Kennedy)
Josephine
Michel Charles
Joseph

# Appendix II

*To Our Beloved Daughter in Christ*
*Katharine Drexel*
*Foundress*
*of the Sisters of the Most Blessed Sacrament*
POPE PIUS XII
*Beloved Daughter in Christ*
*Health and Apostolic Blessing*

It was with profound joy and heartfelt satisfaction that We learned that you are about to observe the fiftieth anniversary of your religious profession and We hasten to extend to you, beloved daughter, and to all the Sisters of the Most Blessed Sacrament, Our cordial felicitations. With what consolation and spiritual gratification you may now look back over those years! For they have, indeed, been years dedicated to the service of Almighty God; a half century given with self-sacrificing zeal and devotion to the propagation of Christ's Kingdom among Indians and Negroes of the United States. The history of your work and of the uninterrupted progress made by the Sisters of the Most Blessed Sacrament, who have served as your devoted handmaids in the magnificent mission, bears ample testimony to the fruitfulness of your labors.

With the paternal encouragement of Our predecessor, Leo XIII, of happy memory, and under the guidance of James O'Connor, Bishop of Omaha and Patrick John Ryan, Archbishop of Philadelphia, you courageously renounced a life of worldly comfort and pleasure in order to insure that, through your missionary efforts, others might share with you the joys and consolations of a higher and nobler life in Christ. With thirteen devoted companions, the first Sisters of the Most Blessed Sacrament, you set forth to bring the Word of God to countless thousands who had until then, through no fault of their own, been deprived of that inestimable privilege. We know that you and your associates have spared neither effort nor expense in extending your apostolate. We realize, too, that the trials were many and the labors difficult; for you were among the pioneers – Christ's pioneers in the North American desert. And yet, from that day, in the year 1894, when a small band of Sisters established the first mission among the Pueblo Indians at Santa Fe, you have persevered with courage and confidence, undaunted by the many obstacles and difficulties which lay in your path. But your beloved apostolate was favored by Almighty God and encouraged by the bishops and priests of your own country; and today, as a result, that inspiring work continues in twenty-one dioceses. From that small beginning at St. Catherine's Mission, you and your eager associates have extended your field of endeavor to include sixty-nine schools, in which each year more than fifteen thousand Indian and Negro children receive the light of Christian teaching and are rescued from pagan darkness.

We have already, on many occasions, expressed Our very especial interest in the welfare of the Colored and Indian people and We have exhorted Our beloved children in the United States-those devoted children who, in their loving charity, have willingly, nay joyfully and magnanimously espoused every worthy cause – to support this apostolate with love and enthusiasm. While joyfully congratulating you, beloved daughter, on the outstanding service which you and the Sisters of the Most Blessed Sacrament have rendered, We gladly avail Ourselves of this happy occasion to renew the expression of Our interest in your mission and to call upon Our American children to give to you and your Community the encouraging support which this great work so justly merits. It is, especially, to Our Venerable Brethren, the Bishops of the United States, and to the Clergy of your country that We make this commendation, in the hope that through their kindly leadership the faithful may insure the perpetuation of that splendid work which has already written so glorious a page in the annals of the Church in the United States. In this regard, We should like to recommend to one and all, with heartfelt solicitude, the "Auxiliary Society of the Sisters of the Most Blessed Sacrament," whose members are assisting so nobly in this truly American undertaking.

We earnestly beseech Almighty God to bless your work in ever more abundant measure, that it may continue to prosper for His greater honor and glory and for the spiritual and material advancement of the more neglected of Our beloved American children.

While joining in spirit with you and the Sisters of the Most Blessed Sacrament on this joyful occasion of your two-fold anniversary, We bestow upon you and them, and upon all the members of the Auxiliary, Our affectionate Apostolic Blessing, that it may be an assurance of Our paternal benevolence and a pledge of abundant heavenly recompense.

**PIUS pp. XII**

Given at Rome, at St. Peter's, Palm Sunday, the sixth day of April in the year of Our Lord nineteen hundred and forty-one.

*Mother Katharine Drexel*

# Footnotes

## FOOTNOTES TO CHAPTER I

1. ASBS. Archives of the Sisters of the Blessed Sacrament. (abbreviated as ASBS.)
2. Ibid.
3. Ibid
4. *Life of Francis Martin Drexel.* Typed copy to 1826 in ASBS.
5. SBS An., 1-9. (Annals)
6. Ibid
7. Sister M. Dolores Letterhouse, S.B.S., *The Francis A. Drexel Family* (Camden, 1939). p. 7. (This book was written by Sister M. Dolores at the request of Louise Drexel Morrell who supplied and verified the contents, and had it privately printed.)
8. SBS An., 1-9
9. ASBS, Drexel & Company, Newcomen Society Address by Edward Hopkinson, Jr., November 25, 1952.
10. The banking data herein is found in a December, 1933 copy of *The Girard Letter* in an article: *Francis Martin Drexel and Philadelphia Leadership in International Finance.*
11. Letterhouse, op. cit., p. 9.
12. Ibid. In 1756 a daughter of the Levering family married Peter Keyser, whose daughter Elizabeth married Benjamin Lehman, whose daughter Elizabeth married Piscator Langstroth, whose daughter Hannah Jane married Francis Anthony Drexel.

## FOOTNOTES TO CHAPTER II

1. Sister M. Dolores Letterhouse, *The Francis A. Drexel Family* (Camden, 1939) , p. 12.
2. Ibid., p. 15.
3. Ibid., p. 17.
4. Ibid., p. 187.
5. ASBS.
6. Ibid.
7. Ibid.
8. Ibid.
9. Ibid.
10. Letterhouse, op. cit., p. 40.
11. ASBS.
12. SBS An., 1-31.
13. Ibid., 1-26.
14. Ibid., 1-27.
15. Letterhouse, op. cit., p. 22.
16. Ibid., p. 42.
17. Ibid., p. 43
18. Ibid., p. 44.

## FOOTNOTES TO CHAPTER III

1. Sister M. Dolores Letterhouse, *The Francis A. Drexel Family* (Camden, 1939) , p. 77.
2. ASBS.
3. Ibid.
4. Letterhouse, op. cit., p. 52.
5. ASBS.
6. SBS An., 1-144.

## FOOTNOTES TO CHAPTER IV

1. Sister M. Dolores Letterhouse, *The Francis A. Drexel Family* (Camden, 1939) , p. 107.
2. Ibid., p. 105.
3. Ibid., p. 107.
4. Ibid., p. 108 ff.
5. SBS An., 1-45.
6. Letterhouse, op. cit., p. 61.
7. ASBS. All the following quotations in this chapter are taken from these notebooks.

## FOOTNOTES TO CHAPTER V

1. O'Connor-Drexel Correspondence.
2. Ibid.
3. ASBS.
4. Ibid.
5. Ibid.
6. Ibid.
7. Ibid.
8. Ibid.
9. SBS. An., 1-215.
10. Ibid., 1-230.
11. Ibid., 1-229.
12. Ibid., 1-230.
13. Sister M. Dolores Letterhouse, *The Francis A. Drexel Family* (Camden, 1939) , p. 219.
14. Ibid., p. 220.
15. Ibid., p. 223.
16. ASBS.
17. Ibid.

## FOOTNOTES TO CHAPTER VI

1. Sister M. Dolores Letterhouse, *The Francis A. Drexel Family* (Camden, 1939) , p. 242.
2. Ibid., p. 337.
3. Ibid., p. 338.
4. Ibid., p. 316.
5. Rev. William H. Ketcham, "Bureau of Catholic Indian Missions," *Catholic Encyclopedia*, Vol. VII, p. 745.
6. Ibid.
7. ASBS.
8. ASBS.
9. Ketchum, op. cit., p. 745.
10. Peter J. Rahill, *The Catholic Indian Missions and Grant's Peace Policy* 1870-1884 (Wash-

ington, D. C., 1953) , p. 322.
11. Ibid., p. 320.
12. Ibid., p. 321.
13. Ibid., p. 323.
14. Ibid.
15. Ketchum, op. cit.
16. ASBS.
17. ASBS, Drexel Correspondence.
18. ASBS, Drexel Correspondence.

## FOOTNOTES TO CHAPTER VII

1. Sister M. Dolores Letterhouse, *The Francis A. Drexel Family* (Camden, 1939) , p. 242.
2. Ibid., p. 243.
3. Ibid., p. 246.
4. ASBS.
5. ASBS.
6. Letterhouse, op. cit., p. 303.
7. Ibid., p. 304.
8. Saint Therese of Lisieux, *Autobiography* (New York, 1926) , p. 114.
9. Letterhouse, op. cit., p. 313.
10. ASBS.
11. Letterhouse, op. cit., p. 321.
12. Ibid., p. 322.
13. Ibid., p. 324.
14. Ibid., p. 325.
15. SBS An., 2-198.
16. Letterhouse, op. cit., p. 326.
17. Ibid., p. 327.
18. This incident was told to the writer by Mother M. Katharine herself.

## FOOTNOTES TO CHAPTER VIII

1. This letter and all the letters in this chapter between Bishop O'Connor and Katharine Drexel are in the O'Connor-Drexel Correspondence in the Motherhouse Archives of the Sisters of the Blessed Sacrament.
2. ASBS.
3. ASBS.
4. ASBS.
5. Sister M. Dolores Letterhouse, *The Francis A. Drexel Family* (Camden, 1939) , p. 358.

## FOOTNOTES TO CHAPTER IX

1. Testimony written by Mother M. Irenaeus Dougherty of the Sisters of Mercy of Pittsburgh for the Vice Postulator of the Cause of Mother M. Katharine Drexel, April 27, 1964. Mother Irenaeus was a novice at Old St. Mary's in Pittsburgh when Katharine Drexel entered the Novitiate there.
2. Ibid.
3. Ibid.
4. O'Connor-Drexel Correspondence.
5. Ibid.

6. ASBS.
7. Ibid.
8. O'Connor-Drexel Correspondence.
9. ASBS.
10. SUMMA, II-II, q. 188, a. 6.
11. ASBS.
12. O'Connor-Drexel Correspondence.
13. Ibid.
14. ASBS.
15. O'Connor-Drexel Correspondence.
16. Ibid.
17. SBS An., 2-259.
18. Katharine Burton, *Three Generations* (New York: 1947) , p. 276.
19. SBS An., 2-273-275.
20. Ibid.
21. OCA. (Omaha Chancery Archives) .
22. O'Connor-Drexel Correspondence.
23. Ibid.
24. Ibid.
25. Ibid.
26. Ibid.
27. ASBS.
28. Ibid.
29. SBS An., 2-271. Mother M. Mercedes, who wrote this item in the Annals, was the pupil of the Sisters of Mercy to whom Mother Inez made this statement.
30. Ibid., 3-7.
31. Ibid., 3-14.
32. Ibid., 3-17.
33. Ibid., 3-22.
34. Ibid., 3-18-19.
35. Ibid., 3-65.
36. Ryan-Drexel Correspondence.
37. SBS. An., 3-110.
38. Ibid., 1-250.
39. Ibid., 2-169.
40. Ryan-Drexel Correspondence.
41. ASBS, Father Stephan to Sister Katharine, May 5, 1890.
42. Ibid., May 18, 1890.
43. SBS An., 3-109.
44. ASBS.
45. SBS An., 3-20.
46. Ryan-Drexel Correspondence.
47. Ibid.
48. ASBS
49. ASBS, Mother M. Kostka, O.S.F. to Sister Katharine, February 20, 1891.
50. Ibid.

## FOOTNOTES TO CHAPTER X

1. SBS An., 3-126.
2. Ryan-Drexel Correspondence.
3. Ibid.
4. Ibid.
5. Ibid.
6. Ibid.
7. Ibid.
8. SBS An., 3-146.
9. Ibid., 3-169.
10. Ibid., 3-174.
11. ASBS.
12. John Tracy Ellis , *The Life of James Cardinal Gibbons*, I (Milwaukee, 1952), pp. 273, 274, 281. In 1879 the staggering debt was $590,000. Archbishop Leroy as Coadjustor, reduced it in three years by $140,000, but finally he was about to declare bankruptcy and put the Archdiocese in the hands of a receiver. He died in France, September, 1887. The following July, Archbishop Janssens was appointed to New Orleans.
13. ASBS.
14. SBS An., 3-237.
17. ASBS.
16. Ibid.
17. Ibid.
18. Ibid. Countless hand written letters from Indian missionaries and about Indian missions have been carefully preserved in chronological order and are now part of the Archives of the Sisters of the Blessed Sacrament. Before the foundation of the Community and after, Katharine Drexel preserved these letters possibly as records of the development, progress and needs of the many missions she was helping.
19. ASBS.
20. SBS. An., 3-189.
21. Ibid., 3-185.
22. Ibid., 3-186.
23. Ibid., 3-188.
24. Ibid., 3-189.
25. Ibid., 3-160.
26. Ibid., 3-163. Some years later when a question about this affiliation arose, Mother M. Katharine in Rome at the time, looked up the center of affiliation and made sure her Congregation was registered in the Church of the Holy Apostles and belonged to the conventual branch of the Franciscans.
27. Ibid., 3-190.
28. Ibid., 3-191.
29. Ibid., 3-203.
30. Ibid., 3-220.
31. Ibid., 3-224.
32. Ibid., 3-226.
33. Ibid., 3-256.

## FOOTNOTES TO CHAPTER XI

1. William Coxon, "Ancient Manuscripts on American Stones," *Arizona Highways*, (September, 1964) , p. 1-4 ff.
2. Edward M. Spicer, Editor, *Perspectives in American Indian Culture Change* (Chicago, 1961) , p. 134.
3. The Spanish called these Indians "Pueblos" because they lived in towns (pueblos). The name is applied to the tribe and to the towns in which they live.
4. Local House Annals.
5. SBS An., 4-19.
6. Ibid., 4-20.
7. Ibid.
8. Ibid., 4-60.
9. Ibid., 4-61.
10. Ibid.
11. Ibid, 4-119.
12. Ibid.
13. Ibid, 4-127.
14. Ibid., 4-87.
15. Ibid., 4-84.
16. Ibid., 4-146.
17. Ibid., 4-154.
18. Ibid., 4-205.
19. Ibid., 4-257.
20. Memoirs of Mother M. Mercedes.
21. Ibid.
22. SBS An., 6-170 ff.
23. Local House Annals.
24. Ibid.
25. ASBS.

## FOOTNOTES TO CHAPTER XII

1. Sister Marie Barat Smith, S.B.S., "A History of St. Emma's Military Academy and St. Francis de Sales High School," unpublished Master's Dissertation, Department of Arts and Sciences, Catholic University of America, 1949, p. 5.
2. Ibid., p. 18.
3. Ibid., p. 19.
4. Ibid., p. 20.
5. Ibid., p. 24.
6. St. Emma Military Academy Bulletin, 1965.
7. Smith, op. cit., p. 19.
8. Ibid., p. 20.
9. Sister M. Dolores Letterhouse, S.B.S., *The Francis A. Drexel Family* (Camden, 1939), p. 336.
10. Ibid.
11. Ibid., p. 337.
12. SBS An., 4-199.
13. *Catholic Standard and Times*, Philadelphia, March 26, 1965.
14. ASBS.

15. SBS An., 4-99.
16. Memoirs of Mother M. Mercedes.
17. Ibid.
18. SBS An., 4-277.
19. Ibid., 6-32.
20. Ibid, June 16, 1894.
21. Smith, op. cit., p. 38.
22. Ibid., p. 39.
23. SBS An., 6-75.
24. Ibid., 6-76.
25. Ibid., 6-79.
26. ASBS.

## FOOTNOTES TO CHAPTER XIII

1. Sister Consuela Marie Duffy, S.B.S., Editor, *Navajo Adventure* (Philadelphia, 1952), p. 4.
2. Ibid.
3. Ibid., p. 10.
4. Robert L. Wilken, *Anselm Weber, O.F.M.* (Milwaukee, 1953) , p. 9.
5. Duffy, op. cit., p. 7.
6. Wilken, op. cit., p. 15-16.
7. Edward H. Spicer, Editor, *Perspectives in American Indian Culture Change* (Chicago, 1961) , p. 281.
8. Wilken, op. cit., p. 17.
9. ASBS.
10. Ibid.
11. Ibid.
12. Ibid.
13. SBS An., 5-265.
14. ASBS.
15. AFFC. (Archives, Franciscan Fathers, Cincinnati Province)
16. Ibid.
17. Ibid.
18. ASBS. At the end of this letter after Frank Walker's signature, there is this notation: "This letter was dictated to me by Frank Walker."

--Geo. J. Juillard.

19. Pacificus Kennedy, O.F.M., "Yazzi and the Navajos." *Columbia* (December, 1963), p. 37.
20. Ibid.
21. Ibid.
22. Ibid.
23. SBS An., 6-136.
24. Ibid., 6-10.
25. AFFC
26. Ibid.
27. Ibid.
28. Ibid.
29. Ibid.

30. Ibid
31. Ibid.
32. Ibid.
33. ASBS.
34. SBS An., 7-3.
35. Ibid., 7-13.
36. Ibid., 7-15.
37. Ibid., 7-23.
38. Ibid., 7-42.
39. Ibid., 7-49.
40. Ibid., 7-51.
41. Ibid., 7-53.
42. Ibid., 7-55.
43. Ibid., 7-71.
44. AFFC.
45. Ibid.
46. Ibid.
47. Oral report of Sister Mary of the Annunciation, S.B.S., who was of the first group of Sisters appointed to St. Michael's.
48. ASBS.
49. Sister John Michael O'Rourke, S.B.S., *Student Handbook, St. Michael's High School* (St. Michael's, Arizona, 1963) , p. 7.
50. Elementary day pupils pay $20.00 a year for fees; elementary boarding pupils pay an additional $75.00 a year for board. High School day pupils pay $40.00 a year for fees; high school boarding pupils pay an additional $100.00 for board.
51. *Navajo Times*, January 28, 1965.
52. Ibid., July 16, 1964.
53. SBS An., 7-230

## FOOTNOTES TO CHAPTER XIV

1. Ralph Mcgill, *The South and the Southerner.* (Boston, 1963), p. 276.
2. Rev. Michael V. Gannon, *Rebel Bishop* (Milwaukee, 1964) , p. 121.
3 Ibid., p. 126.
4. Peter Guilday, *A History of the Councils of Baltimore (1791-1884)* (New York, 1932) , p. 213.
5. Gannon, op. cit., p. 125.
6. Second Biennial Report of the U.S. Bishops' Committee for Latin America.
7. John Tracy Ellis, *The Life of James Cardinal Gibbons, I* (Milwaukee, 1952), p. 401.
8. Ibid., p. 402.
9. Ryan-Drexel Correspondence.
10. *History of St. Patrick's* (Philadelphia, 1965), p. 176.
11. Ryan-Drexel Correspondence.
12. ASBS.
13. Ibid.
14. Ibid.
15. Ibid.
16. Ibid.
17. Ibid.

18. Ibid.
19. Ibid.
20. The records of the Chicago Archdiocesan Chancery list him in the Archdiocesan Necrology. He had served as pastor of a newly formed parish for the Colored--St. Monica's. He died at Mercy Hospital July, 1897.
21. ASBS.

## FOOTNOTES TO CHAPTER XV

1. ASBS.
2. NCA. (Nashville Chancery Archives)
3. Ibid.
4. Ibid.
5. SBS An., 8-63.
6. Ibid., 8-77.
7. Ibid., 8-80.
8 NCA.
9. SBS An., 8-111.
10. Ibid.
11. Ibid., 8-113.
12. Ibid., 8-120-124.
13. Ibid., 8-126.
14. Ibid., 8-135.
15. ASBS.
16 Ibid.
17. NCA.
18. SBS An., 8-177.
19. ASBS.
20. Ibid.
21. Local House Annals.

## FOOTNOTES TO CHAPTER XVI

1. May 24, 1942.
2. Paul Gauthier, *Christ, the Church and the Poor* (Westminster, Md.), p. 153.
3. New York Times International Edition, November 24, 1964.
4. ASBS.
5. Memoirs of Mother M. Jerome, S.B.S., to whom Mother M. Mercedes related the discussion of this council meeting.
6. A recent article of Mother M. Katharine's poverty was returned by a Catholic editor as being "Too unusual to be practicable for Sister X . . ." Was he implying her practice of poverty was heroic?
7. Allocution to Religious Superiors, May 23, 1964, in *Review for Religious,* November, 1964.
8. Personal expenses before her entrance into Religion could have been taken care of by her inheritance from her mother.
9. ASBS.
10. Ibid.
11. Ibid.
12. Ibid.
13. Since 1955 the Sisters of the Blessed Sacrament are also engaged in a newly estab-

lished catechetical center in Mallet, Louisiana; and additional schools in Pala and Los Angeles, California; and San Carlos, Arizona (for Apache Indians).
14. ASBS.

## FOOTNOTES TO CHAPTER XVII

1. Ryan Drexel Correspondence.
2. Ibid.
3. SBS An., 5-43.
4. Ibid., 5-32.
5. Ibid., 5-81.
6. Ibid., 5-86.
7. Ibid., 5-76.
8. Ibid., 5-136.
9. ASBS.
10. Ibid.
11. SBS An., 8-49.
12. This incident was recounted to the writer by Mother M. Katharine.
13. Ryan-Drexel Correspondence.
14. ASBS.
15. SBS An., 9-114.
16. Ibid., 9-131.
17. Ryan-Drexel Correspondence.
18. SBS An., 9-189.
19. Ibid., 9-190.
20. Ryan-Drexel Correspondence.
21. ASBS.

## FOOTNOTES TO CHAPTER XVIII

1. SBS An., 12-102.
2. Ibid., 13-1666a.
3. Ibid., 12-238.
4. Ibid., 12-241.
5. Told to the writer by Sister Marian who was stationed at the Philadelphia convent at the time.
6. SBS An., 14-36.
7. Ibid., 14-78
8. Ibid., 14-87.
9. Ibid., 14-82
10. Ibid., 14-89.
11. Ibid., 14-97.
12. Ibid., 14-103
13. Ibid., 14-104.
14. Ibid., 14-215.
15. Ibid., 15-38.
16. Ibid., 15-39.
17. Ibid., 15-91.
18. Ibid., 15-103.

## FOOTNOTES TO CHAPTER XIX

1. Charles B. Rousseve, *The Negro in Louisiana* (New Orleans Xavier University Press, 1937), p. 25.
2. Significant of Archbishop Cody's stand on this question was his statement to a jammed press conference six hours after he arrived in Chicago to be installed as the new Archbishop of Chicago. He stated that the biggest problem facing Chicago was the race issue and added: "I hope to contribute everything I can do to the solving of it." *Catholic Standard and Times*, August 27, 1965.
3. Roger Baudier, *The Catholic Church in Louisiana* (New Orleans, 1939), p. 475, 477.
4. ASBS.
5. Ibid.
6. Ibid.
7. Ibid.
8. Ibid.
9. Ibid.
10. John T. Gillard, S.S.J., *The Catholic Church and the American Negro* (Baltimore: St. Joseph's Society Press, 1929, p. 74.
11. ASBS.

## FOOTNOTES TO CHAPTER XX

1. Minns Sledge Robertson, *Public Education in Louisiana after 1898* (Baton Rouge, 1952), p. 71.
2. Ibid., p. 27.
3. Ibid., p. 16.
4. Paul A. Kunkel, Ph.D., "Modifications in Louisiana Negro Legal Status under Louisiana Constitutions 1812-1957," Journal of Negro History Reprint, January, 1959, p. 15.
5. Ibid., p. 16.
6. Mother M. David Young, S.B.S., "A History of the Development of Catholic Education for the Negro in Louisiana," an unpublished thesis submitted to the Graduate Faculty of Louisiana State University in partial fulfillment of the requirements for the Degree of Master of Arts, 1944, p. 30. 31.
7. ASBS.
8. Ibid.
9. Ibid.
10. Ibid.
11. Ibid.
12. Ibid.
13. Sister M. Josephina Kenny, S.B.S., "Contributions of the Sisters of the Blessed Sacrament for Indians and Colored People to the Catholic Negro Education in the State of Louisiana," an unpublished Dissertation submitted to the Faculty of the Graduate School of Arts and Sciences of the Catholic University of America in Partial Fulfillment of the Requirements for the degree of Masters of Arts, 1942, p. 36.
14. ASBS.
15. ASBS.
16. ASBS.
17. Loretta Butler, "A History of Catholic Elementary Education for Negroes in the

Diocese of Lafayette, Louisiana," submitted to the Faculty of the Graduate School of Arts and Sciences of the Catholic University of America in Partial Fulfillment of the Requirements for the Degree of Doctor of Philosophy, 1963.

## FOOTNOTES TO CHAPTER XXI

1. ASBS.
2. Memoirs, Sr. M. Praxedes.
3. Ibid.
4. All the incidents of this travel are taken from a talk which Mother M. Katharine gave to the community at the Motherhouse on her return.
5. ASBS.
6. Ibid.
7. SBS An., 29-140.
8. Ibid., 29-141.
9. Ibid.
10. Ibid., 29-142.
11. Ibid., 29-175.
12. Ibid., 30-42.
13. Minutes of the Chapter General, 1937.
14. SBS An., (1939).
15. Memoirs, Sr. M. Christopher.
16. The writer was present for this scene.
17. SBS An., 31-162.

## FOOTNOTES TO CHAPTER XXII

1. SBS An. (1941).
2. Mission Fields at Home, May-June, 1941.
3. SBS An. (1941).
4. Mother Katharine Drexel and the Sisters of the Blessed Sacrament Golden Jubilee.
5. Ibid., p 27.
6. Mission Fields at Home, May-June, 1941.
7. Memoirs of Sr. M. Xavier.
8. SBS An., 31-95.
9. Ibid.

## FOOTNOTES TO CHAPTER XXIII

1. SBS An., 33-58.
2. Memoirs, Sister Marie Rosarii.
3. Ibid.
4. SBS An., (1945).
5. Memoirs, Sr. Marie Rosarii.
6. This was said to the writer.
7. Ibid.

## FOOTNOTES TO CHAPTER XXIV

1. ASBS.
2. Ibid.
3. Ibid.

4. Memoirs, Sr. M. Gabriella, S.B.S.
5. ASBS.
6. Ibid.
7. Mother M. Anselm's letter to the Community.
8. ASBS.
9. Ibid. Letter of Mother Mary A. Spallen, R.S.C.J.
10. *Catholic Standard and Times,* March 4, 1955.

## FOOTNOTES TO CHAPTER XXV

1. See pages 151-152.
2. Harry Golden, *Mr. Kennedy and the Negroes* (Cleveland, Ohio, 1964).
3. Ibid., p. 33.
4. ASBS, July 21, 1960.
5. ASBS.

# Index

## A


Academy of Fine Arts, Philadelphia, 26
Acoma, New Mexico, 144
Acomita, New Mexico, 144
Agatha, Mother M., President Emeritus, Xavier University, 167, 238
Alamosa, Navajo settlement, 159
Albuquerque, New Mexico, 192, 210
Allen, Bessie, 40
Allen, E. P., Bishop of Mobile, 178
Allen, Professor, 40
All Saints, New York, 209
American Board of Catholic Missions, The, 194
Amsterdam, Holland, 25
Ancestry of Mother Katharine, 23, 24, 28, 279
Andalusia, Pennsylvania, 123, 127
Anglican Sisterhood of St Mary's, Peekskill, New York, 206
Anselm, Mother M., fourth Superior general of the Sisters of the Blessed Sacrament, 145, 187, 247, 263, 264, 266
Anthony, Sister M., S.B.S., 139
Apostolate, Eucharistic, 249; of the Catholic Church 270; Core of, 107
Apostolic Involvements of the Church, 270
Arapaho Indians, Wyoming, 78, 83, 128
Ardmore, Indian Territory, 165, 193
Arnold, Father, O.F.M. 238
Arthur, Chester A., President, 71
Assisi, 41, 215
Assumption Church, Philadelphia, 23
Atchison, Topeka, and Sante Fe Railroad, 211
Augustine, Sister M., S.B.S., 138
Austrian Tyrol, 24
Auxiliary Society, 252, 253


## B


*Baltimore Sun,* 174
*Banner of Nashville, The,* 183
Barberini Palace, Rome, 213
Bayley, James Roosevelt, Archbishop of Baltimore, 70
Belmead, Virginia, 147, 150, 152
Belmont, North Carolina, 176
Benedictine Fathers, Latrobe, Pennsylvania, 137
Bernadette, Sister M., S.B.S., 215, 240
Bernardine, Sister M., S.B.S., 206
Bethlehem Church, St. John's, North Dakota, 82
Biddle, Nicholas, 27
Birmingham, Alabama, 178
Blackfeet Indians, Montana, 68
Blenk, James H., S.M., Archbishop of New Orleans, 226, 227
Blessed Sacrament Church, New Orleans, 227
Blessed Sacrament Mission, Roxbury, Mass., 212
*Boston Post,* 188
Boucree, Albert, 228
Bourgarde, Peter, Vicar Apostolic, Arizona, 137, 138
Bouvier, Emma, (see Drexel, Emma Bouvier)
Bouvier, Louise C. Vernou, 30, 35
Bouvier, Michael, 30, 35
Bouvier, Mother Louise, R.S.C.J. 30, 35, 36, 40, 267
Brackett, Major, 121
Brendan, Sister M., S.B.S., 216
Brondel, John B., Bishop of Boise City, 114
Brouillet, J., Rev., Vicar General of the Diocese of Nesqually Washington Territory, 71
Brown vs. Board of Education of Topeka, 230
Budenz, Louis, 245
Buerger, Placid, O.F.M., Brother, 157
Bureau of Indian Affairs, 171
Burial Crypt, 267

Burke, John B., Rev., 175
Burke, Maurice F., Bishop of Cheyenne, 129, 134, 130
Burns, James M., Architect, 132
Byrne, Edwin V., Archbishop of Santa Fe, 143, 145
Byrne, Thomas S., Bishop of Nashville, 175, 180, 181, 185, 186, 187

## C

Cabrini, Mother, 199
Caldi, Celestine, S.J., Rev., 238, 239
Canevin, Regis, Bishop of Pittsburgh, 132
Canyon de Chelly, Arizona, 154, 156, 159, 167
Carlisle Indian School, Pennsylvania, 193
Caroli, Monsignor, Rome, 214
Carson, Kit, 155
Carter, C. S., Rev., 23
Cassidy, Mary B., 23, 40, 43, 46, 60, 79, 80, 110
Cataldo, Joseph M., S.J., 239
*Catechism of Christian Doctrine for Navajo Children,* A Navajo-English, 159
Catholic Board for Mission Work among the Colored People, 175
Catholic Bureau for Indian Mission Work, 175
Catholic Charities 1965 Appeal, Archdiocese of Philadelphia, 148
Catholic Church in Action, 270
Catholic Indian Mission, Bureau of, 65, 71, 72, 74, 83, 134, 174
Catholic Interracial Group, New York, 260
*Catholic Standard and Times,* Philadelphia, 265
Catholic Students Mission Crusade Convention, 78
Catholic University of America, Francis A. Drexel Chair of Moral Theology, 65; Conferring of Honorary degree on Mother Katharine, 253; Golden Jubilee Convocation, 253
Cavanaugh, Charles, Monsinor, Secretary to Archbishop Ryan, 195
Cenacle, Rome, 200, 213
Centenary Celebration of Foundation of the American Hierarchy, 111, 271
Centennial Year, 1876, 46, 47
Chapelle, Placide L., Archbishop of Santa Fe, 137, 141, 196
Chapter General of the Congregation, 205, 244, 246
Charity, 272
Charlotte, North Carolina, 176
Chee Dodge, 170
Cherokee Indians, 67, 83, 166, 167
Chesapeake and Ohio Railroad, 148
Cheyenne Indians, Wyoming, 83
Chicago, Illinois, 208
Chickasaw Indians, 165
Child of the Church, Mother Katharine, 105, 195, 248, 270
Childs, George, owner and editor of *Philadelphia Ledger,* 57, 61, 105
Childs, Mrs. George, 57
Chin Lee, Arizona, 168
Chippewa Indians, Odanah, White Earth and Red Lake Reservations, 83
Choctaw Indians, 165
Choka, William, Very Reverend, 115
Christian Brothers, St. Emma's, Virginia; 147; St. Francis de Sales Industrial School, 149
Christian Education of Youth, encyclical Pope Pius XI, 230; An Approach through 233
Cincinnati, Ohio, 157
City Price, Louisiana, 233
Civil Rights Bills 271
Clarke, John, S.S.J., 227
Clave, Justine, 40
Clement, Mother M., Superior General of the Sisters of St. Joseph, Chestnut Hill, 198
Clement, Sister M., S.B.S., 263
Cleveland, Grover, President, 139

Cochiti Pueblo, New Mexico, 143
Cocke, Philip St. George, General, 65, 146, 148
Code Noir, 218
Coeur d'Alene, Idaho, 83
Colaneri, A.M., Rev., 115
Collegio Lombardo, Rome, 214
Collins, George J., C.S.Sp., Very Reverend, Provincial of Holy Ghost Fathers, 254
Columbia, Virginia, 151
Columbus, Ohio, 208
Colyer, Vincent, Secratary of Board of Indian Commissioners, 1870-1872, 69
Comanches, Indian Territory, 67, 83, 165
Commission for Catholic Missions among the Colored People and the Indians, 194
Communion of Saints, 273
Community of the Sisters of the Blessed Sacrament 253, 271
Compassion for the Poor, Katharine Drexel, 260
Compositions of Katharine Drexel, 42
Congress of Vienna, 25
Constanz, Lake, 24
Constitutional Convention of Louisiana of 1878, 224
Contract School System, The, 71, 72, 122
Conwell, Henry, Bishop of Philadelphia, 26
Cornwells Heights, Pennsylvania, changed from Andalusia, 123, 137
Coronado, Francisco Vasquez, 135
Corrigan, Joseph M., Bishop, Rector, Catholic University, 249, 250, 253
Corrigan, Michael Augustine, Archbishop of New York, 196
Council of Baltimore, Second Plenary 174
Cowl, Maurice, Rev., 206
Cox, J. D., Secretary of Interior, 67
Cross, Michael, 40
Crow Indians, Montana, 83
Cushing, Richard J., Cardinal, 212, 250, 272

## D

Da Costa, Doctor, 75
Dahlgren, Lucy, 213, 215
Dahlgren, Lucy Drexel, Mrs., 213
Damrosch, Polly, 213
Damrosch, Walter, 213
Daughter of the Church, 270
Day, Charley, 158
Day, Sammy, 158
Dayton, Ohio, 78
Debut, Elizabeth Drexel, 46; Katharine Drexel, 56
Decree of Definitive Approbation of the Congregation and Experimental of the Constitutions, 204
Decree of Praise on the Community, 1897, 196
Delano, Columbus, Secretary of the Interior, 69
Dever, D., Rev., 199
*Dictionary of the Navajo Language, An Ethnological,* 159
Divine Word Fathers, 270
Dixon, Elizabeth Bouvier, 60
Dodd, Mr. and Mrs., 149
Dodge City, Kansas, 139
Dominican Sisters, Nashville, 180
Dominican Sisters, Speyer, Germany, 216
Dornbirn, Austrian Tyrol, 24, 25
Dougherty, Dennis, Cardinal, 29, 147, 208, 229, 246, 248, 249, 258, 267
Drexel, Anthony J., 27, 61, 105, 106, 123
Drexel, Caroline, 23
Drexel, Elizabeth, (see Smith, Elizabeth Drexel)
Drexel & Co., 27, 29
Drexel, Emma Bouvier, 30, 31, 40, 58; aid to the needy, 31, 32, 35, 37, 59; death, 59
Drexel, Francis Anthony, 23, 26, 27, 30, 37, 38, 41, 57, 58, 59, 60, 61,

65, 188; Will, 60-63, 65, 120
Drexel, Francis Martin 24, 26, 27; autobiography 25
Drexel, Franz Joseph, 24
Drexel, Hannah Langstroth, 23, 28, 29, 105; catechumen, 29
Drexel Harjes & Co., 28, 91
Drexel, Joseph W., 23, 27, 28
Drexel, Josephine, 163, 164, 167
Drexel, Katharine Hookey, (see Drexel, Mrs. Francis, M.)
Drexel, Katharine, Vocation, 85
Drexel, Katharine, vocations from Europe, earliest, 215
Drexel, Louise see Morrell, Louise Drexel
Drexel, Morgan & Co., 28, 188
Drexel, Mrs. Anthony J., 23, 64
Drexel, Mrs. Francis A., (see Hannah Langstroth Drexel and Emma Bouvier Drexel)
Drexel, Sather & Church, 27
Dubois' ranch, New Mexico, 159
Du Conge, Ernest, 228
Dunkards, 29
Duquesne University, 254
E Eden Hall, Torresdale, Pennsylvania, 196, 267
Education, God-centered and God-directed, 272
Education in Louisiana, 224
Eisenmann, Sylvester, O.S.B., 241
Emmanuel College, Boston, 254
Emperor and Empress of Brazil, 49
Encinal, Pueblo Village, New Mexico, 144, 155
Epiphany Apostolic College, 64
European Tours, 43, 60, 75
Evangelist, Mother M., S.B.S., 137, 138, 142, 157, 162, 167
Ewing, Charles, Catholic Commissioner of Indian Affairs, 69, 70
Executive Order Extensions, 156

**F**

Faith, 272
Falconio, Diomede, Cardinal, Apostolic Delegate, 198
Farley, John, Cardinal, 175
Fay Sigourney, Rev., 206
Ferndale, Connecticut, 254
Ferrante, Nicholas B., C. SS. R., 273
Final Profession and motto, Mother Katharine, 141
First Holy Communion, 33; Katharine's longing for, 34
Five Civilized Tribes, A Government report of the, 167
Fort Defiance, 156, 159, 160
Fortitude, 272
Foundress, First Sister of the Blessed Sacrament, 244
Frances, Sister M., S.B.S., 227. 228
Francis A. Drexel Chair of Moral Theology, 65
Franciscan Fathers, Cincinnati Province, 157,159, 160, 161, 168, 171
Franciscan Missionaries of Mary, 214
Free Men of color, 219
"Friend of the Missions," 74
Funchal, Madeira, 35, 213

**G**

Gallup, New Mexico, 158, 159, 161, 170, 238, 240
Garfield, James A., President, 71
Garrity, Father, 248
Gemen, Germany, 28
Gibbons, James, Cardinal, 121, 175, 196, 219
Girault de la Corgnais, Jean Marie, Rev., 233, 234
Glorieux, Alphonse Joseph, Bishop of Helena, 114
Golden Jubilee Celebration, 273
Gold Rush, California, 27
Good Shepherd, Convent of the, Philadelphia, 34
Gotti, Girolamo, Cardinal, 175, 197
*Grammar, A Manual of Navajo,* 159
Grand Canyon, 154
Grant's Peace Policy, 65
Grant, Ulysses, President, 66
Great Society, The, 273

Greenwood Farm, Philadelphia, 28
Guthrie, Oklahoma, 166

## H

Haid, Leo, O.S.B., Bishop of North Carolina, 134, 176
Haile, Bernard, O.F.M., 159
Hall, Sharlot M., 154
Hannon, Philip M., Archbishop of New Orleans, 219
Harlem, 208
Hart, John, 42
Hayes, Rutherford B., President, 71
Head Men, Navajo Reservation, 168
Herrman, Max, Doctor, 241, 242, 258
Heuser, Herman J., Rev., 197, 198, 199, 200
Hildegard, Sister M., S.B.S., 216
Holy Family Mission, Torresdale, 127, 134
Holy Ghost Fathers, 147; Rule, 270, 195
*Holy Gospels for Sundays and Holy Days, Text and Translation,* 160
Holy Providence School, Cornwells Heights, Pennsylvania, 63, 134, 245
Holy Rosary Mission, Pine Bluff Agency, 82, 123
Holy Trinity Church, Philadelphia, 26
Homestead Act, 157, 160
Honorary Degrees conferred on Mother Katharine, 253
Hookey, Katharine, (see Drexel, Mrs. Francis M.)
Hope, 259
Hopi Indians, 156
Horstmann, F., Bishop of Cleveland, 72
Hotel Belle Vue, San Remo, 93
Hotel Danieli, Venice, 92
Hubble Trading Store, 168
Hutchinson, Kansas, 138

## I

Ignatia, Mother M., S.B.S., 215
Ignatius, Mother M., S.B.S., 162, 163, 208
Immaculate Conception, Stephan, South Dakota, 82
Immaculate Mother Academy and Industrial School, Nashville, 186
Incarnata, Sister M., S.B.S., 216
Income, Mother M. Katharine, All given to missions, 191
Indian Agencies, 1870, 67; Letter dividing the Indian Agencies among the Christian Societies, 67
Indian Claims Commission, United States, 171
Indian Territory, Oklahoma, 163, 165
Inez, Mother M., R.S.M., Mistress of Novices, 111, 118, 127
Integration, 167, 271
*Interracial Review,* 254
Ireland, John, Archbishop of St. Paul, 104

## J

Jackson, Helen Hunt, 66
Jackson Specie Circular, 26
James, Mother M.., S.B.S., 176, 200, 203, 208, 210, 212
James River, Virginia, 148, 249
Janssens, Francis, Archbishop of New Orleans, 127, 133, 219, 221, 223;Corrsepondence with Mother M. Katharine Drexel, 221; Death onboard the Steamer *Creole,* 223
Jardin, Alberto, 35, 213
Jardin, Madame, 35; "Cousin Bessie" 213
Jean, Ignatius, O.S.B., Vicar Apostolic of the Indian Territory, 156
Jeanmard, Jules B., Bishop of Lafayette, 234
Jemez, New Mexico, 155
Jesuit Rule, 195
*John of Baltimore,* 26
Johnson, Lyndon B., President, 271
Josephite Fathers, 64, 146, 254
Joy, 273
Juanita, Sister M., S.B.S., 228
*Jubilate,* 251

*Jubilee Book,* 250
Juliana, Sister M. S.B.S., 186, 205
Justice, 273
Jutz, John, S.J., 123 ff., 128

## K

Keams Canyon, Arizona, 160
Kennedy, John F., President, 271
Kennedy, Richard, Bishop, Rome, 199, 201, 203, 208, 209
Kennedy, Robert, 271
Ketcham, William A., Monsignor, Director of Bureau of Catholic Indian Missions, 74, 134, 167
Keyser Family, 28
Kimmage Manor, Dublin, Ireland, 232
Kostka, Mother M., O.S.F., 124
Krol, John J., Archbishop of Philadelphia, 277
Kuppens, Francis X., S.J., 129

## L

Labeau, P. O., S.S.J., 225
La Cebolleta, New Mexico, 155
La Farge, John, S.J., 249, 260
Lafon School, New Orleans, 228
Laguna, New Mexico, 144, 155
La Junta, Colorado, 139
Lake Charles, Louisiana, 232
Lamb, Hugh L., Auxiliary Bishop of Philadelphia, 249
Lamy, John B., Archbishop of Santa Fe 136, 156
Lamy Junction, New Mexico, 140, 163, 240
Langston, Oklahoma, 166
Langstroth, Eliza Lehman, 28, 35, 36
Langstroth, Hannah, (see Drexel, Hannah Langstroth)
Langstroth, Piscator, 28, 36
Lankenau, John, 48, 55, 61,
La Posta, Arizona, 159
Lawler, Jerry, 245
Leavenworth, Kansas, 130, 192
Lehman Family, 28
Leland University, 225
Lercaro, Cardinal, 188
Levering Family, 28
Levering, Rosier, 28
Levering, William, 28
Lewis, William, 228
Lissner, Ignatius, S.M.A., American Provincial of the Society of African Missions, 212, 215
Little Flower, The, 79
Litz, Francis J., C.SS.R., Vice-Postulator of the Cause of Mother Katharine Drexel, 20, 273
London Stock Exchange, 26
Long Branch, New Jersey, 57, 96, 97
Louisiana State Legislature, Act 87, 224
Lourdes, Mother Mary of, S.B.S., 241
Loyola, Mother M., S.B.S., 143, 210, 211

## M

Magdalens, Good Sheperd Convent, 34
Marshall, Burke, 271
Martin, Celine, 79
Martinelli, Sebastian, O.S.A., Archbishop, Papal Legate to U.S., 149
Martin, Mr., father of the Little Flower, 79
Martin, Saint Therese, 79
Marty, Martin, O.S.B., Bishop, Vicar Apostolic of northern Minnesota, 65, 78, 122, 249, Suggests a Motherhouse in South Dakota, 122
Matthews, Washington, Doctor, 158
McAuley, Mother, Foundress of the Sisters of Mercy, 105
McCarthy, Justin, S.S.J., Very Rev., 226
McCarthys, New Mexico, 144
McCloskey, John, Archbishop of New York, 174
McFadden, John F., Doctor, 263, 264
McGarvey, E. I., Rev., 206
McGoldrick, D. J., S.J., 86, 109, 112
McShea, Joseph, Auxiliary Bishop of

Philadelphia, 266
Meerschaert, Theophile, Bishop, Vicar Apostolic of Oklahoma and Indian Territory, 134
Mercedes, Mother M., second superior general of the Sisters of the Blessed Sacrament, 35, 139, 142, 149, 150, 152, 182, 183, 210, 212-216, 226, 227, 237, 242, 243-247, 252, 253; Last Illness and Death, 246 .
Mercy Rule, 195
Merry del Val, Raffelo, Cardinal, 200
Mesita, New Mexico, 144
Mexican War, 155
Minerva, Rome, 201, 215
Missionary Sisters of the Sacred Heart of Jesus, 199
*Mission Fields at Home,* 244
Mission Indians, California, 83
Missions aided by Mother M. Katharine, Lists of, 192, 193
Missions conducted by the Sisters of the Blessed Sacrament, 194
Mitchell Coolidge, 159
Montgomery, Alabama, 178
Morgan House of London, 28
Morgan, J. Pierpont Company, 188
Morgan, Thomas J., Commissioner of Indian Affairs, 122
*Morning Star, The,* New Orleans archdiocesan newspaper, 227
Morrell, Edward, Colonel, 83, 106, 110, 121, 123, 132, 146, 147, 207, 210, 211
Morrell, Louise Drexel, 29, 31, 38, 41, 43, 46, 63, 64, 81, 83, 88, 90, 99, 101, 105, 110, 118, 121, 132, 146, 147, 149, 207, 243, 254, 256, 259, 268; Death of, 260
Morton, Dr., Rev., 58
Mosby, Mr., Rock Castle, 150
Motherhouse of the Sisters of the Blessed Sacrament 28, 85, 197; laying of the cornerstone, 136, 147
Mountain Chant, 168
Mount Pleasant, Virginia, 148
Murphy, Edward F., S.S.J. 249
Murphy, Father, C.S.Sp., 216
Muskogee, Indian Territory, 166
Mystical Body of Christ, 19, 197, 205, 258, 269

## N

Nashville City Council, 182
National Reparation, 270
*Navajo-English Catechism of Christian Doctrine for Navajo Children,* 159
*Navajo Grammar, A Manual of,* 159
Navajo Indians, 137, 156, 170
*Navajo Language, An Ethnological Dictionary of the,* 159
Navajo Text and Translation, *Holy Gospels for Sundays and Holy Days,* 160
*Navajo Times,* 172
New Frontiers, 273
New Iberia, Louisiana, 230
Newman's ranch, New Mexico, 159
New Orleans, Louisiana, 18, 20, 41, 63, 65, 115, 127, 175, 192, 218, 220, 222, 224, 225, 228, 231, 232, 234
New Orleans University, 225
New Religious Congregation Announced, 117
Nez Perce Indians, Idaho, 83
Nicetown, Pennsylvania, 30
Night Adorations, 267
Ninetieth birthday, Mother M. Katharine, 262
Novitiate, Sisters of Mercy, Pittsburgh, 107, 117, 122, 195
Novitiate, temporary, Sisters of the Blessed Sacrament, Torresdale, 127
Nugent, John L., Rt. Rev., 248, 264

## O

Oblate Sisters of the Blessed Sacrament, 241
O'Connell, William, Cardinal, 212
O'Connor, James, Bishop of Omaha,

50, 55, 56, 78, 80, 81, 83, 85, 88, 90, 92, 95, 97, 99, 101, 103, 105, 108, 109, 110, 111, 112, 115, 117, 119, 120, 121, 128, 129, 130, 189, 195, 207, 235, 254, 255, 257, 261; Ordination, 50; Rector of St. Michael's Seminary, Pittsburg, 50; Rector of St. Charles Seminary, Overbrook, PA, 50; Rector of St. Dominick's, Holmesburg, PA, 50, 55; Correspondence with Mother M. Katharine Drexel, 88-105, 109, 111-138, 147-149, 159-160, 176, 265

O'Connor, Michael, Bishop of Pittsburgh, 105

O'Gorman, John, A., C.S.Sp., Bishop, Nairobi, Africa, 197

O'Hara, John F., C.S.C., Cardinal, Archbishop of Philadelphia, 208, 249, 264

O'Hare, Miss, Columbia, Virginia, 152

Osage Indians, Oklahoma, 69, 166

*L'Osservatore Romano,* 190

Our Lady of Lourdes, Atlanta, Georgia, 212

Our Lady of the Blessed Sacrament Convent, Philadelphia, 207, 214

L'Ouverture, Toussaint, 218

Owens, Mr., Building Contractor, 160, 163

## P

Pacelli, Eugenio, Cardinal, (see Pope Pius XII)

Padilla, Joseph, 250

Paguate, New Mexico, 144

Painted Desert, Arizona, 154

Panic of 1837, 26

Panic of 1857, 27

Pantanella, D., S.J., 189, 198

Panziglione, D., S.J., 128

Papago Indians, 138; Reservation, 138

Papal Interview, 78, 79, 80

Paraje, New Mexico, 144

Pardee, Sister Mary Edith, S.B.S., 206

Patrick, Sister M., S.B.S., 133

Patrick, Sister M., Sister of Charity, 211

Pauline, Mother M., S.B.S., 238

Paw-Ne-No-Posh, Joseph, Governor Osages, 70

Pena Blanca, New Mexico, 143

Penn, William, 28, 42

Perpetua, Sister M., S.B.S., 143

Perrot, Emile, 212, 245

Perry, Harold R., S.V.D., Auxiliary Bishop of New Orleans, 219

Petrified Forest, Arizona, 154

Phelan, Richard, Bishop of Pittsburgh, 113, 126

Philip Neri, Mother M., 246, 260

Pino's ranch, New Mexico, 159

Plessy vs. Ferguson, 224

Plunkett, T. J., S.S.J., 182

Pope John XXIII, 188

Pope Leo XIII, Private interview with Katharine Drexel, 78, 81, 100, 197

Pope Paul VI, 190, 219, 274

Pope Pius X, 34, 202

Pope Pius XI, 230, 253

Pope Pius XII, 252, 257, 268

Poquessing Creek, Torresdale, Pennsylvania, 42

Potawatomi Indians, 166

Poverty, Mother M. Katharine, 157

Powhatan, Virginia, 149

Prayer Life, Drexel family, 31, 32, 34

Preparation for Death, Mother M. Katharine Drexel, 263

Prendergast, Edmond F., Archbishop of Philadelphia, 210, 216

Prendergast, Frank, Rev., 216

Prendergast, Mother Peter, Presentation Convent, Lismore, Ireland, 216

Price, Governor of New Mexico, 140

Prince Michael, 57

Profession, Mother M. Katharine Drexel, 123, 126; Final Profession, 141

Propaganda, Rome, 50
Prudence, 272
*Public Ledger,* Philadelphia, 31, 32, 34, 59, 61
Pueblo Indians, New Mexico, 83, 135, 136, 142, 144; Acculturation, 135
Pueblos, Santa Clara, 136; San Indelfanso, 136; San Juan, 136; San Domingo, 136, 142; San Philipe, 136; Santa Ana, 136
Pullman Strike of 1894, 138
Purcell, Oklahoma, 165
Puyallups, Washington, 83

## R

Race Problem, 20, 212, 269, 273
Ramah, New Mexico, 159
Raton, New Mexico, 139
Ready, W. P., 183
Red Cloud, Sioux Chief, 82, 124
Red Lake Reservation, 83, 192
Reidy, Doctor, 211
Religious Reception, Katharine Drexel, 114
Religious Vocation, First thought of, 78
Retreat in Rome, Mother M. Katharine, 215
Reverony, Father, Vicar-General of Bayeux, 79
Ridgefield, Connecticut, 254
Rock Castle, Virginia, 149, 153, 176, 180, 194, 249, 251, 265
Rose Agatha, Sister M. Sister of Charity, 211
Ross, Elliot, C. P., 214
Rule of the Sisters of Mercy, 195
Rule of the Sisters of the Blessed Sacrament, The, 195, 203, 215; Decree of Definitive Approbation of the Congregation and Expiremental of the Constitutions, 204; Final Approbation, 215
Rummel, Joseph Francis, Archbishop of New Orleans, 219
Rural Louisiana, 233
Rural Schools in Louisiana, 235
Ryan, Johanna, 36, 75
Ryan, Patrick John, Archbishop of Philadelphia, 51, 61, 64, 84; Presided at Religious Reception of Katharine Drexel, 114; Address to assembled bishops at Baltimore, 114, 118, 123, 130, 137, 142, 175, 195, 202, 205; Last illness and death, 119, 121, 124, 131, 132, 134, 141, 197, 203, 206, 207, 271

## S

Sabetti, A., S.J., 197
Sacred Congregation of Rites, 203
Sacred Heart, Sister Mary of the, S.B.S., 152
Sacred Heart, Religious of the, 51, 100, 208, 259, 267
Sacred Heart School, Potawatomi Indians, 166
Salpointe, J. B., Archbishop of Sante Fe, 136, 138, 156
San Bernardino Church, 158
San Domingo Pueblo, New Mexico, 142
San Jose Mission, Old Laguna, New Mexico and surrounding Pueblo Villages, 144
San Juan Rio, New Mexico, 159
San Lorenzo, New Mexico, 159
Santa Fe, New Mexico, 136, 141
San Xavier, del Bac, Papago Reservation, 138
Sapir, Edward, Doctor, 159
Satolli, Francesco, Cardinal, 196, 197, 200, 202, 203
Schnorbus, Juvenal, O.F.M., 157
Schrembs, Joseph, Archbishop of Cleveland, 212, 213
Schwartz, Joseph M., C.SS.R., Very Rev., 201, 205, 214
Schwind, Joseph, Canon, Speyer, Germany, 216
Scully, John, S.J., 127, 197
Seama, New Mexico, 144
Sebastian, Mother, R.S.M., superior

general of the Sisters of Mercy, 111, 116, 118, 131
Segregation, 219, 224
Selma, Alabama, 178
Separate Churches, 221
Shakespeare, William, Indian Interpreter, 130
Sharon Springs, New York, 59
Shaw, John W., Archbishop of New Orleans, 229, 233, 234
Sheep Song, the Navajo Maiden, 154
Shoshone Indians, 78, 128
Sioux Falls, South Dakota, 122
Sioux Indians, South Dakota, 83
Sisters of Charity, Leavenworth, Kansas, 130
Sisters of Loretto, Lebanon, Kentucky, 178
Sisters of Loretto, Sante Fe, 137
Sisters of Mercy, Pittsburgh, 100, 114
Sisters of Mount Carmel, Vinita, Cherokee Nation, 166
Sisters of Notre Dame, St. Peter Claver, Philadelphia, 175
Sisters of Perpetual Adoration, New Orleans, 226
Sisters of St. Francis, Philadelphia, 65
Sisters of St. Francis, Stella Niagra, New York, 62, 81
Sisters of St. Joseph, Chestnut Hill, 198
Sisters of St. Joseph, St. John's Orphan Asylum, Philadelphia, Pennsylvania, 147
Sisters of the Blessed Sacrament, Congregation of the, 43; Title decided, 124, 180, 193, 198, 241, 269
Sisters of the Holy Family, New Orleans, 226
Sisters of the Holy Ghost, Steyl, Germany, 216
Smith, Alphonse J., Bishop of Nashville, 187
Smith, Elizabeth Drexel, 23, 31; debut, 46, 57, 64; erects St. Francis de Sales Industrial School, Eddington, Pennsylvania, 64, 75, 81, 88, 106, 110, 115, 118, 121; death, 121, 132, 147, 148
Smith, Walter George, 115, 118, 196, 279
Society for the Preservation of the Faith Among the Indians, 72
*Society for the Propagation of Faith,* US, 194
Society of the Friends, The 71
Society of the Propagation of Faith, Lyons, France, 174
Sorrento, Italy, 239
Southern University, Louisiana, Land grant college, 224, 225
Spalding, Martin J., Archbishop of Baltimore, 174
*S. S. Etruria,* 81
St. Agnes Hospital, Philadelphia, 65
Stanton, John P., C.S.Sp., 248
State Farm, Virginia, 151
St. Augustine's Church, Philadelphia, 26
St. Benedict the Moor's, New York, 175
St. Boniface, Banning, California, 121
St. Catherine of Sienna, 201
St. Catherine's Indian School, Santa Fe, 62, 136, 137, 138, 140, 142, 143, 144, 145, 167, 168, 180, 181; Golden Jubilee, 143
St. Charles, New York, 209
St. Charles Parish, Cornwells Heights, Pennsylvania, 265
St. Charles Seminary, Philadelphia, 50
St. Dominic's, Holmesburg, Pennsylvania 51, 118
St. Dominic's, New Orleans, 225
Stephan, Joseph, Rt. Reverend, Director of the Bureau of Catholic Indian Missions, 65, 72, 74, 78, 81, 82, 83, 122, 124, 130, 137, 156, 157
Stephens, Doctor, Heart Specialist, Philadelphia, 242
St. Edward's Chapel, Belmead, Virginia, 147
St. Emma's Industrial and Agricultural

Institute, 65, 146, 147
Stephens, Doctor, heart specialist, Philadelphia, 242
St. Frances Cabrini, 199
St. Francis de Sales High School, Powhatan, Virginia, 149, 151, 249; (see Chapter 12)
St. Francis de Sales Industrial School, 64, 147, 148, 197, 254
St. Francis of Assisi, 41, 215
St. Januarius Cathedral, Naples, 204
St. John's Church, Manayunk, Pennsylvania, 27
St. John's Mission, Osage Nation, 166
St. John's Orphan Asylum, Philadelphia, 62, 147
St. Joseph's Church, New Orleans, 221
St. Joseph's Church, Philadelphia, 26, 30
St. Joseph's College, Philadelphia, 254
St. Joseph's Hospital, Philadelphia, 62, 242
St. Joseph's Mission, Muskogee, Indian Territory, 166
St. Joseph's, New York, 209
St. Katharine's Church, purchased by the archdiocese of New Orleans, 221; Openingof, 221; Correspondence on, 221
St. Louis Cathedral, New Orleans, 233
St. Mark's, New York, 209, 212
St. Mary's Academy, New Orleans, 226
St. Mary's Church, Philadelphia, 26, 61
St. Mary's Indian Mission, Omak, Washington, 238
St. Michael's School, Arizona, 63, 159, 162, 163, 168; opening of; 169, 170, 171, 173, 181, 192, 240
St. Michael's Seminary, Pittsburgh, 50
St. Michael's, Torresdale, 43, 58, 59, 82, 83, 87, 96, 99, 121, 127; Used as temporary Novitiate, 127
St. Monica's Church, Chicago, 179
St. Monica's Convent, Chicago, 209
St. Patrick's Mission, Comanche Reservation, 165
St. Paulinus Church, City Price, Louisiana, 234
St. Paul's Mission, Marty, South Dakota, 241
St. Peter and the Apostle, Tomb of, 215
St. Peter Claver's Philadelphia, 123, 175
Straight University, New Orleans, 225
Sts. Peter and Paul Cathedral, Philadelphia, 264
St. Stephen's Mission, Wyoming, 128, 130
St. Theresa of Avila, 106, 197
St. Thomas Church, Point-a-la-Hache, Louisiana, 233, 235
St. Thomas, Nashville, 183
St. Thomas, New York, 209
*St. Thomas, The,* 233
St. Vincent's Abbey, Latrobe, Pennsylvania, 147
St. Vincent's Orphan Asylum, Philadelphia, 62
St. Vincent's Sanitarium, St. Louis, 241
Sullivan, John, Legal Advisor, 242
Sumner, Fort, 156
*Sun, Baltimore,* 174
Sunday School, as taught by the Drexel daughters, 43
Super, Maud, R.N., 243, 248

## T

Taney, Secretary of the Treasury, 26
Tekakwitha Mission, Houck, Arizona, 238, 240
Teller, Henry M., Secretary of the Interior, 71
Temperance, 272
Tesuque Pueblo, New Mexico, 143
Textbooks used by Drexel daughters, 40
Thebault, Joseph A., Rev., Chancellor

to Archbishop Janssens, 223
Thomas, Hazel, 252
*Times Picayune,* The, New Orleans, Gwen Bristow interview with Mother M. Katharine, 229
Toledo Pilgrimage, 212
Tolton, John A., Rev., St. Monica's, Chicago, 179
Torreador scene, *Carmen,* Xavier University, New Orleans, 249
Torresdale, Pennsylvania, 29, 42; Poquessing Creek, 42
Travel Diary, Katharine Drexel, 75
Travel of Indian Missions by Drexel Daughers, 1887, 81; 1888, 83
Treaty of 1868, Navajo, 156
Trevi Fountain, Rome, 215
True Cross, Shrine of the, Torresdale, Pennsylvania, 29, 254
Tshohotso, St. Michael's, Arizona, 156
Tucson, Arizona, 138, 192, 193, 199
Turtle Mountain, Belcourt, North Dakota, 82, 192
Tuye, New Mexico, 159
Tyne, Thomas J., 183

## U

"Uncle Zach Kimbro," 152
Ursulines of Brown County, Ohio, 100
Utes, Navajo Country, 155

## V

Van De Vyver, Augustine, Bishop of Richmond, 148, 152
Van Rossen, Cardinal, Prefect of Propaganda, 159
Vatican Council II, Cardinal Larcaro's Declaration on Poverty, and De Ecclesia, 188, 189; *The Constitution on the Church,* 215
Verot, Augustine, Bishop of Savannah, 174
Vieux Carre, New Orleans, 218
Vigil, Martin, 143
Villiger, Father, 126
Vinita, Cherokee Nation, 166
Visitation, Mother Mary of the, third superior general of the Sisters of the Blessed Sacrament, 241, 246; death, 247, 260, 267
Vocation, Mother M. Katharine Drexel, 85; Final solution, 100, 101, 105
Vocations from Europe, Earliest 215; Sister M. Ignatia, 215; Sister M. Bernadette, 215; Sister Hildegard., 216; Sister M. Cecily, 216; Sister Brendan, 216; Sister M. Incarnata, 216
Vorarlberg, Tyrol, 24
Vow of Virginity, 92

## W

Wakem, Mrs. William, 152
Walker, Dominicia, 158
Walker, Frank, 158
Walker, John, 158
Weber, Anselm, O.F.M., 157, 167, 168
Wenatchee, Washington, 238
White Earth Reservation, 83
Wilhelm, Magdalin, 24
Williams, Major, Army Agent, Fort Defiance, 156
Will of Francis A. Drexel, 61
Wilson, Coravigne, 228
Wingate, New Mexico, 159
Wissel, Joseph C.SS.R., 197
Wood, James F., Archbishop of Philadelphia, 34, 55, 120
Wounded Knee Massacre, 123
Wyoming Act, 60

## X

Xavier, Mother M. Francis, S.B.S., 207, 248
Xavier, Sister M., S.B.S., 253
Xavier University, 18, 20, 63, 65, 194, 227, 228, 229, 230, 231, 232, 238, 249; 1917 Normal Course, 228; College of Liberal Arts and Sciences, 229; College of Pharmacy, 229, 231; Graduate School, 230;

Reorganization of Xavier Charter, 230; Alumni, 231; Grand Opera, 232, 249; Fullbright Scholars, 232

## Y

Yakima, Washington, 71
Yankee Stadium, 274
Years of Retirement, Mother M. Katharine, 255
*Yellowstone, The,* 60